The Television Studies
Book

The Television Studies Book

Edited by

Christine Geraghty

Senior Lecturer in Media and Communications,
Goldsmiths College, University of London

and

David Lusted

Head of Media and Film Studies,
King Alfred's University College, Winchester

A member of the Hodder Headline Group
LONDON

First published in Great Britain in 1998
This impression reprinted in 2003 by
Arnold, a member of the Hodder Headline Group,
338 Euston Road, London NW1 3BH
175 Fifth Avenue, New York, NY 10010
http://www.arnoldpublishers.com

Distributed in the United States of America by
Oxford University Press, Inc.,
198 Madison Avenue, New York, NY 10016

British Library Cataloguing in Publication Data
A catalogue entry for this book is available from the British Library

Library of Congress Cataloging-in-Publication Data
The television studies book / edited by Christine Geraghty
    and David Lusted.
        p.   cm.
    Includes bibliographical references and index.
    ISBN 0-340-66232-8 (cl).—ISBN 0-340-66231-X (pb)
    1. Television broadcasting—Social aspects. 2. Television
broadcasting. I. Geraghty, Christine. II. Lusted, David.
PN1992.6.T43 1997   97-15399
302.23'45—dc21   CIP

ISBN 0 340 66231 X (pb)
ISBN 0 340 66232 8 (hb)

6 7 8 9 10

Production Editor: Julie Delf
Production Controller: Sarah Kett
Cover Design: Stefan Brazzo

Typeset by Saxon Graphics Ltd., Derby
Printed and bound in India by Replika Press Pvt. Ltd. Kundli 131 028

Contents

Section III: New Approaches in Television Studies

List of Contributors

Gill Branston lectures on Film and TV Studies in the School of Journalism, Media and Cultural Studies, University of Wales, Cardiff. She is co-author with Roy Stafford of *The Media Student's Book* (Routledge, 1996) and has published widely on TV, Film and Media Studies. She is currently working on the voice in the technologies and discourses of contemporary film and TV.

Charlotte Brunsdon teaches Film and Television Studies at the University of Warwick. She is the author of *Screen Tastes* (Routledge, 1997) and co-editor, with Julie D'Acci and Lynn Spigel, of *Feminist Television Criticism: A Reader* (Oxford University Press, 1997).

Therese Daniels is Senior Lecturer in Media Studies at South Bank University, London. She is co-editor with Jane Gerson of *The Colour Black: Images in British TV* (BFI, 1989) and researched the television documentary *Black and White in Colour* (BBC, 1992) based on her work for the British Film Institute project on the history of black people in British TV.

Uma Dinsmore is a postgraduate research student at Goldsmiths College, University of London, working on a thesis on 'The Domestication of Film: video, cinephilia and the collection and viewing of videotapes in the home'. She has published essays on video diaries and domestic viewing practices in early cinema.

Eric Freedman is Assistant Professor in the Department of Communication at Florida Atlantic University. An independent videomaker and former public access producer, he is working on a book tentatively titled *From Excess to Access: Televising the Subculture*, a national study of public access cable television and subcultural activism in the gay community.

Ivor Gaber is Professor of Broadcast Journalism at Goldsmiths College, University of London. He is also an independent radio and television producer, specialising in political journalism, and was political consultant to the Independent Television News for the 1997 British General Election.

Christine Geraghty is Senior Lecturer in Media and Communication at Goldsmiths College, University of London. She made an early contribution to debates on soap opera in *Coronation Street*, Dyer *et al.* (eds) (BFI, 1981), is the author of *Women and Soap Opera* (Polity Press, 1991) and has written extensively on television, film and cultural studies.

Jostein Gripsrud is Professor in the Department of Media Studies at the University of Bergen, Norway. He is author of *The Dynasty Years: Hollywood, Television and Critical Media Studies* (Routledge, 1995) and has written for journals including *Screen, Cultural Studies* and *Critical Studies in Mass Communication.*

John Hartley is Professor and Head of the School of Journalism, Media and Cultural Studies at the University of Wales, Cardiff, and Adjunct Professor of Media Studies at Edith Cowan University in Western Australia. He is the author of many books and articles on popular media and culture, including *Teleology: Studies in Television* (Routledge, 1992), *The Politics of Pictures: The Creation of the Public in the Age of Popular Media* (Routledge, 1993) and *Popular Reality: Journalism, Modernity, Popular Culture* (Arnold, 1996).

Eric Hirsch is a Lecturer in Social Anthropology at Brunel University. He co-edited *Consuming Technologies* (Routledge, 1992) and *The Anthropology of Landscape* (OUP, 1995) and is the co-author of *Technologies of Procreation* (Manchester University Press, 1993).

Peter Humm is Head of English at the University of Greenwich where he teaches twentieth-century fiction, narrative theory, broadcasting history and video production. He has written on popular fiction, the representation of gender and the teaching of English.

Linda Kintz is Associate Professor of English at the University of Oregon. Her publications include *The Subject's Tragedy: Political Poetics, Feminist Theory and Drama* with The University of Michigan Press and two books forthcoming: *Media, Culture and the Religious Right*, co-edited with Julia Lesage, Minnesota University Press; and *Between Jesus and the Market: The Emotions that Matter in Right-Wing America*, Duke University Press.

Pat Kirkham is Professor of Design History at the Bard Graduate Center for Studies in the Decorative Arts in New York. She has written widely on design, film and gender and is co-editor of *You Tarzan* and *Me Jane* (Lawrence and Wishart, 1993 and 1995) which explore questions of masculinity and film.

David Lusted is Head of Media and Film Studies at King Alfred's University College, Winchester. He has written extensively on film, television and media education, and his publications include *TV and Schooling*, as co-editor with P. Drummond (BFI, 1985); *Raymond Williams: Film, TV, Culture* (BFI, 1989) and *The Media Studies Book* (Routledge, 1992).

Tim O'Sullivan is Reader in Media Education and Cultural Studies at De Montfort University, Leicester. As co-editor, his publications include *Key Concepts in Communication and Cultural Studies*, 2nd edn (Routledge, 1994) *The Media Studies Reader* (Arnold, 1997) and *Liberal Directions: Basil Dearden and Post-War British Film Culture* (Flicks Books, 1997); he is co-author of *Studying the Media: An Introduction* (Arnold, 1994, 2nd edn, 1998).

General Introduction

This is a book not just about television but about the way it has been and is studied. The impetus for it comes from our understanding that this is a key moment not just for television but for Television Studies. The changes predicted for television, for those who work in it and for the audiences who engage with it in various ways, are much debated. Technological possibilities deriving from the digital revolution and global battles over ownership and control are challenging the balance of local, national and international systems which characterised, with different emphases, television as a major media force in countries dominated by commercial factors (e.g. in the USA) or by strong public service traditions (e.g. in Europe). The stress on national systems in which programmes were made to be watched by the family in the home and could be enjoyed, criticised and debated on the assumption that they were available nationally is being challenged, on the one hand, by the fragmentation explicit in the development of multi-channel systems in multi-television homes and, on the other hand, by the concentration of control in international corporations and agencies. Many of the essays in this book are written precisely under the pressure of predicted changes in television production and viewing conditions; they reflect on television as it has been understood and look to learn lessons for the future. Amid the hype of speculation about how television itself is going to be transformed, an opportunity for reflection is called for.

But in Television Studies also we sense a moment when reflection is necessary. Horace Newcomb, introducing his fifth edition of *Television: The Critical View,* commented that 'Television Studies is now an established area of study in many universities' (1994: 4). While the position may not be as secure elsewhere, we would argue that Television Studies is now emerging as an acknowledged area of study with its own constituency of academics, practitioners and students and its own recognised methods. As would be expected in a new discipline, each of these – the area of study, the constituency and the methods – is open to debate and, as Lynn Spigel suggests at the end of her essay for this book, to quite heated disagreement. But, we would argue, Television Studies now has a body of knowledge and a history of how that knowledge developed which can form the basis of debates. It is those debates which this book addresses.

We can best illustrate this perhaps by reflecting on the way in which some key concepts are now being challenged. One such is the concept of 'flow'. In the first section of the book, Jostein Gripsrud argues that the idea of flow has underpinned 'modern critical television theory', which he identifies as beginning with Raymond Williams's description of his first viewing of US television in a hotel in Miami (Williams, 1974). Williams's concept of 'flow' as the central experience of television, an idea reworked by John Ellis in his influential *Visible Fictions* (1982), is looking increasingly problematic. The value of Williams's insight remains but it may no longer be an adequate concept to account for the experience of television in which videos, remote controls, subject-specific channels and interactive web sites have all changed the way in which (some) viewers are addressed. In addition, the use of 'flow', with its connotations of being taken through an evening's viewing, may actually make it difficult for those studying television to talk about the viewers' assessments of their own choices and needs or to contribute to debates about quality. Williams's work is central to this book, as many contributors acknowledge, but not because it is axiomatic; debate over that work will continue to develop Television Studies as a discipline.

Another debate which is at a critical point concerns the role of popular culture and academic attitudes towards it. This is part of a wider debate about how far popular culture offers modes of resistance to groups who are marginalised by dominant cultures, modes of resistance or opposition which can be activated or are called into play by the activity of the audience. Work on music, film and literature has been an integral part of the discussion – indeed, this is an example of the importance of interdisciplinary approaches to the mass media. But the debate has been particularly crucial in Television Studies, where the concept of active audiences seemed necessary to dispute the alleged passivity of television's couch potatoes. Work based on the positive re-evaluation of popular culture can be found in a number of ways in Television Studies in the 1980s. Television – whether it be music videos or soap opera, quiz programmes or chat shows – has been the source of case studies which have tested out key propositions in debates about popular culture; engagement with 'ordinary people' through popular television has been a political motivation for many writers and teachers in the area; and the development of ways of talking about popular aesthetic forms without denigrating or patronising them has been of concern to, for instance, the feminist writers who, as Charlotte Brunsdon and Laura Stempel Mumford point out in Section II, have strongly shaped the formation of Television Studies. More recently, academic concerns about the apparent acceptance of popular forms by those who claimed to be left-wing or progressive have generated a debate which is still unresolved,[1] and one of Television Studies' most urgent questions remains that of how we understand and judge what is popular television. Popular television cannot just be celebrated (though, to be fair, there were few theorists who did that unproblematically); but we need to move forward from this debate, not disregard its insights. A number of essays in this book reflect on this area of work, either directly, as Brunsdon and David Lusted do in Section II, or through case studies in Section III which we hope will provide concrete ways of thinking through the issues involved.

The third area of debate which seems to have reached a critical stage is that of methodology. Television Studies has its roots in a mixture of disciplines and nowhere is this more evident than in the different methods which have been applied to the study of television. Brunsdon's essay offers a clear analysis of the different disciplines from the arts and social sciences which contributed to the formation of Television Studies. What should be noted here is the way in which questions of method have come to the fore, so that a student of television has to consider not only *what* is to be studied but also *how* and, indeed, needs to pay attention to relationships between the two. Attention to methodology has been one of the significant contributions of the social sciences to Television Studies; researchers with a background in sociology or anthropology were, perhaps, more likely to draw attention to the implications of different methods than those with an arts background.[2] An emphasis on method, though, does not mean that Television Studies should confine itself to one approach. The complex nature of television makes it unlikely that one method will be sufficient in itself. Indeed, one of the signs of the new confidence of work in Television Studies has been the way in which the best of it is combining attention to production, text and audience in a challenging and distinctive way. It should not be forgotten that the *Nationwide* project, now famous in the history of television audience studies, included extensive textual analysis of the programmes (Brunsdon and Morley, 1978). Recent textual studies, such as Julie D'Acci on *Cagney and Lacey* (1994) and Gripsrud on *Dynasty* (1995), have also made major contributions to work on production and audiences, while Ann Gray's (1992) audience study of women's relationship with VCRs includes an account of the reading and viewing preferences of her interviewees which could link back to the insights of textual analysis.

Learning about 'methods' in the abstract can be difficult and an excessive reflexivity can mean that more is said about the method (and the researcher) than about what is being studied. But we believe attention to methods is an important feature of contemporary Television Studies and we have signalled the importance of these debates in three ways. Firstly, we have sought a range of writing which itself comes from different traditions and approaches; secondly, Section II includes a number of essays which specifically address particular methods or approaches (Stempel Mumford on feminism, Christine Geraghty on 'ethnography', for example); finally, in our commentary on the case studies in Section III we have specifically drawn attention to questions of method so that it can be seen how, in any particular instance, method and topic interact to inform analysis.

The study of television remains in many eyes a dubious activity. Despite, or perhaps because of, the growth in academic courses which in one way or another take television as their object of study, the notion that 'television' should be studied is in itself enough to provoke arguments about a decline in educational and cultural standards. This knee-jerk reaction can be traced to a number of different sources. Firstly, television, despite its public service history in a number of countries, is most commonly associated with entertainment. The notion that entertainment should not be taken too seriously is a deeply held view. In the pejorative sense, there is a feeling that television is not a culturally worthy object of study and will not repay the effort made; even those more sympathetic sometimes express the view that entertainment, like humour, cannot be analysed without spoiling how it works, that to understand it is to be unable to experience the pleasure of it again. Secondly, and in a somewhat contradictory sense, studying television is a dubious activity because television, far from being just ephemeral entertainment, is deemed to be very effective in destroying the viewer's moral and political standards. Television is thus blamed in a variety of ways for lowering the standards of political debate, for exposing the vulnerable to unacceptable levels of sex and violence and, particularly outside the USA, for imposing foreign values on whole populations as, through satellite provision, foreign television becomes more commonly available. To study television in the dispassionate and rigorous way associated with academic work, therefore, is somehow to collude with its alleged effects. Thirdly, studying television is dubious in a rather different sense because it involves studying the complex creative and business practices in which television practitioners engage. Academics are always vulnerable to the accusation that they study what they cannot do but in Television Studies the accusation is particularly sharp since the students involved often see themselves as preparing for a career in the media, while those working in television can be actively hostile to the methods which have been adopted for the study of television.

Nevertheless, Television Studies has become an important area of study and one with which students are keen to engage. It is one of a number of disciplines – Communications Studies, Media Studies, Cultural Studies, Film Studies – which emerged slowly after the Second World War and which are underpinned by a general aim of understanding the profound changes which the mass media have made. The desire to study television is often linked to a desire to understand the modern world and the way in which television has been not just a product of modern technology but a player in a time of rapid change. The study of television is bound up, as Gripsrud and Eric Hirsch argue in their essays, with questions about the creation of the modern world, with issues of modernity, and, as a number of other contributors suggest, with the perceived fragmentation and even disintegration of that world, and hence with issues of postmodernism. For many, the modern media invoke a sense of helplessness, of technologies, systems and the people who run them being out of control; studying the media may be a way of trying to regain both understanding and some measure of control.

This book is for the reader interested in surveying this new field and is addressed particularly to those engaged in the formal study of television. The first section of the book offers a number of accounts which look at the history (and, indeed, the pre-history) of television and the parallel development of critical accounts of what television is and how it could be studied. The essays here do not offer a standard history but the opportunity to reflect on the development of television as an object of study and to examine the uneasy relationship which academic and other commentators had with a new medium. The second section focuses more directly on approaches which are currently used in the study of television and explores the implications and consequences which are implicit in a choice of method. The essays here map out current developments in the field and provide a critical account of the contributions which different methodological approaches have made to our understanding of television. The third section is devoted to a number of case studies which through detailed accounts of particular aspects of current television point to the new directions in which future work might be developed. Essays in this section offer examples of work on the relationship between theories of television and newly emerging structures, technologies and programme formats. While each essay stands alone as a study of a particular kind of television, we have in our editorial introductions in this section shown how they can be brought together productively through the contributions they make to wider debates. In all sections, we have encouraged contributors to take a creative, polemical and sometimes sceptical stance. We intend this to be a book which provides an overview of Television Studies through a plurality of voices.

We hope that by looking at the development of Television Studies, at the methods with which it works and the areas of interest it has mapped out, we can offer ways of understanding better why the study of television is important and how it might best be developed. John Corner has called for 'steady self-assessment' in Media Studies and its related disciplines (1995: 155). We believe that after a period of remarkable expansion and growth, the same is true for Television Studies, and we hope that the essays in this book contribute to that process. Criticisms of Television Studies are often based on a confusion between what is studied and the act of studying, and so it is assumed that because *some* television is sloppy, badly researched and offensive so too is its study. Essays in this collection demonstrate that Television Studies has produced work which is thoughtful, informed, provocative and conscious of its own history; we hope that this collection helps the reader to reflect on what has been achieved and continues to move the work on.

Notes

1. For an early example of such criticism see Modleski (1986); for later versions, see McGuigan (1992) and the conference papers and discussions collected in Grossberg *et al.* (1992).

2. For a discussion of the way in which different disciplines fed into the establishment of Media Studies, see Corner (1995).

References

BRUNSDON, C. and MORLEY, D., 1978: *Everyday Television: 'Nationwide'*. London: British Film Institute.

CORNER, J., 1995: 'Media Studies and the "knowledge problem"' *Screen*, 36, 2, Summer: 147–55.

D'ACCI, J., 1994: *Defining Women: Television and the Case of Cagney and Lacey*. Chapel Hill: University of North Carolina Press.

ELLIS, J., 1982: *Visible Fictions*. London: Routledge and Kegan Paul.

GRAY, A., 1992: *Video Playtime*. London: Routledge.

GROSSBERG, L., NELSON, C. and TREICHLER, P. (eds), 1992: *Cultural Studies*. New York: Routledge.

GRIPSRUD, J., 1995: *The Dynasty Years: Hollywood, Television and Critical Media Studies*. London: 1995.

MCGUIGAN, J., 1992: *Cultural Populism*. London: Routledge.

MODLESKI, T. 1986: *Studies in Entertainment: Critical Studies in Mass Culture.* Bloomington: Indiana University Press.
NEWCOMB, H., 1994: 'Television and the present climate of criticism'. Introduction to *Television: The Critical View* (5th edn). Oxford: Oxford University Press.
WILLIAMS, R., 1974: *Television: Technology and Cultural Form.* London: Collins.

SECTION I

Television Studies

EDITORS' INTRODUCTION

It is no coincidence that the main focus of Television Studies has been the television of the major Western cultures in the USA and Europe, especially Britain (Blumler, 1992). These national broadcasting systems were the earliest and, as Jostein Gripsrud explores in the opening essay in this section, they contrasted in exemplary institutional and cultural respects. Television in Britain has been a highly regulated, national, public service broadcasting (PSB) system (the standard works are Briggs, 1965–79, 1985; Curran and Seaton, 1991; Scannell and Cardiff, 1991; Smith, 1975), and in the USA, a more lightly regulated, commercial system (Barnouw, 1966–70, 1975; Opotowsky, 1961).

The differences have been plainly discernible too on the screen, in the contrasts between the popular programming forms of the commercial system and the greater mixture of education, information and entertainment composing public service broadcasting. However, since the start of processes behind the global commercialisation of broadcasting in the 1950s, national differences in television genres and forms have become increasingly less distinct. In Britain, for instance, the emergence of dual systems of PSB and commercial broadcasting brought with it greater competition over popular programming (Paulu, 1981; Sendall, 1982–88). Indeed, much public debate over threats to cultural values and national identity targets the very anxieties about increasing similarities between the economies of broadcasting in otherwise very different national cultures.

It is important to observe too that Television Studies developed in the academies of these national cultures precisely as a consequence of the dynamic political and cultural questions that the new medium of broadcasting posed for the study of culture and society in the modern world of communications. The television systems of Britain and the USA were indeed formative for ways of thinking television more generally. Yet the understandable initial bias towards these national systems has acted to overlook the distinctive formations and histories of television in other nation-states.

In more recent scholarship, this Anglocentric bias has been leavened by studies of and from other national systems in Europe, especially Eastern Europe, in Australasia, in the Asias and Latin Americas, and in those global areas coming late to industrialisation and modernisation, loosely but problematically termed 'the Third World'. An initial concern of such studies was simply to correct the bias towards Britain and the USA, to document the distinctive broadcasting arrangements of other nation-states, even where they had adapted the dominant US commercial or European PSB models. One consequence was to de-naturalise the broadcast systems of Britain and the USA, to make them more the examples they are (ones among many possibilities) than the exemplars (the ideal ones) earlier accounts tended by default to construct them as. To see how television was organised in different nation-states demonstrated how it could have developed differently in Britain and the USA under different political and cultural imperatives (for examples, see Boyd Barratt, 1977; Sinclair *et al.*, 1996).

Many of these studies of other broadcast systems developed as a critique of the global dominance of the 'First World' systems, especially often in antipathy to the structural control of the USA, whose powerful technological and servicing organisations have dominated the development of television in other nations. Perhaps even more importantly for scholarship, however, has been the economic power of US television to sell its own products abroad in the international markets and hence to provide images of US culture as the dominant or even hegemonic global culture (see for example Mattelart *et al.*, 1984; Dowmunt *et al.*, 1995). This is the 'cultural imperialism' thesis (Thompson, 1991), of US television fiction and entertainment forms as the dominant model not of what a particular national television is but, because of its global dominance, of what all television ought to be. The image of a subsistence farming family in Sri Lanka, say, using scarce electrical resources to view a diet of old US television products like *I Love Lucy* and *Dallas* speaks its own irony of the massive social, cultural and national inequalities in processes of cultural imperialism.

Against the totalising image of an all-powerful global culture, however, another body of opinion argues a less rigid causal relation between the US media and their cultural imperialism of other nations. Indigenous cultures are seen in struggle with powerful foreign cultures and neither can be viewed as monolithic in their power to control the variety of social and other identities competing for representation on television (Skovmand and Schroder, 1992; Sinclair *et al.*, 1996). Indeed, matters of television and representation have been crucial to the formation of Television Studies, a concern developed in some of the approaches described by contributors in Section II.

But even if the power of American culture is hard to deny, it has also been argued as in some ways more politically democratic and aesthetically spectacular than older national cultures, and not just of Europe, offering important alternative interventions in the cultures of control operating in authoritarian, repressive or conservative nation-states (Tunstall, 1977).

There are important reasons, then, for attending to the complex of national broadcasting systems and their interrelations, especially global ones. Yet, since studies of the broadcast systems of Britain and the USA have historically been at the heart of Television Studies, this first section deals centrally with the concepts, ideas and debates that have arisen from studies of the two European and American models of television. First, Jostein Gripsrud attends to matters arising from an examination of key terms in Television Studies and John Hartley looks at the impact of literary studies* and cultural studies on attitudes to television. Then Gill Branston (on studies of British television) and Lynn Spigel (on studies of television in the USA) combine to conclude this section by attending to how Television Studies has understood the histories of those two national systems as distinctive models of broadcasting.

Television Theory

Jostein Gripsrud looks· to unpick three key terms in Television Studies in order to investigate the place of theory within the discipline. He understands 'television', 'broadcasting' and 'flow' as metaphors, arguing that television refers to technology, broadcasting to its institutional arrangements and flow to the television text. Gripsrud notes that the defining characteristic of television has been its 'capacity for simultaneity', its 'liveness as a key aesthetic value . . . fundamental to television as an ideological apparatus'. What broadcasting did was to organise that technological capacity in a general model of point-to-point communication from a single centre to myriad domestic peripheries. There were alternative, experimental possibilities such as one-to-one exchange (the telephone model) and the earliest public conditions of reception were quickly refused in favour of the now familiar private and domestic ones. Crucially, Gripsrud locates the determinations of this arrangement not only in the commercial demands of 'a modern, politically liberal capitalism' but also in the even wider cultural 'domain fundamental to Modernity'.

Gripsrud then turns his attention to the significant global differences in this general theoretical model, to the differences crucially between the US commercial system, with its arising construction of an audience as consumers, and the European system of PSB that alternatively constituted its audience as citizens. For Gripsrud, the significance of these differences lies not only in their determinations but also in their effects. If the commercial model produced a narrower range of programme forms than PSB, that did not necessarily impact on matters of programme quality. Furthermore, Gripsrud is keen to argue national differences between examples of PSB, contrasting Britain's more socially exclusive paternalist arrangement to Norway's more inclusive social democratic model.

In the first of many references in this book to Raymond Williams's formative concept of 'flow', Gripsrud argues that flow is central to our understanding of the interaction between television production scheduling (what Williams calls 'planned flow') and the everyday experience of watching television as a flow rather than as a series of discrete programmes. Indeed, he argues that flow is culturally widespread, not particular to television but an 'important part of social experience in general'. None the less, he considers that the experience of flow differs according to national systems, specifically that 'watching television [is a] different experience on the two sides of the Atlantic'. He insists on attention to national specificities, even taking into account the similarities imposed by the increasing globalisation of television. He further maintains that flow cannot be the last word; it remains important to theorise audiences as a plurality rather than a singular audience, subject merely of positions offered by television. For Gripsrud, different audiences still make discrete choices, an important perception if we are to understand audiences not as passively swept away by the flow of television but as actively observing and using television as part of their everyday social experience.

It is this perception that leads Gripsrud to conclude with a claim for possibilities of continuing 'democratic developments and global awareness' in television's futures, an important and perhaps surprising assertion to contrast against much criticism in Television Studies which is more suspicious of the powers of television yesterday, today and tomorrow.

Television and Textual Criticism

That history of suspicion is examined in John Hartley's interrogation of the ways in which criticism of television developed historically. In his polemical essay, John Hartley adopts a position against what he calls the 'knowledge class' who have contributed much to the antipathy of elite groups towards television and the study of television that we described in our general introduction.

For most people, television is foremost the programmes we watch. Hartley argues that the same goes for scholars in literary studies and cultural studies whose animus against television has been fought over and is even evident in the programmes themselves. The history of these studies he terms the textual tradition.

Hartley begins with the dominant literary tradition of textual criticism. In an initially familiar critique, he first rehearses its rejection of popular culture and the formation of an education system in opposition to the new entertainment media. For Hartley, that elite struggle against popular culture was waged in particular over the nature of its products; with television, the struggle was over television programmes as cultural texts. He then embarks on a novel thesis: that this voice of disapproval entered into the very structure of those television texts themselves. He analyses the form of a 1935 film documentary, *Housing Problems*, made during the same period as the establishment of broadcasting in Britain, in order to argue the pervasiveness of television's reformist but patrician address to its working-class audiences. Furthermore, Hartley considers that address to have remained dominant throughout a television history in which, regardless of the public service or commercial model of broadcasting, television and the media more generally have popularised 'the hegemony of the modernising knowledge expert . . . in the name of the needs of the ordinary working population'.

Hartley's own textual analysis demonstrates the capacity of textual criticism to reveal what a first glance overlooks. But he wants to consider *Housing Problems* as a symptomatic text, one which in its call to housing modernisation embodies another drive by the television institution to create a 'home' (rather than just a dwelling place) to justify incorporation of the television set into modern family life. (This coincidence of television and modernity was first raised by Gripsrud and is argued more intensely later in Section II by Eric Hirsch.) In common with other commentators on the role of women in modernity, Hartley sees the place of woman as central to this cultural project, not least through an argument he makes about the feminisation of the television text, a theme developed later in this section by Lynn Spigel.

Hartley then moves his analysis on to more recent disciplinary developments in the textual tradition as he plots the transition from (a 'reformist but not oppositional, reflecting but not analysing') literary studies to cultural studies. In the first generations of a developing cultural studies at Birmingham's Centre for Contemporary Cultural Studies, Hartley discerns an attention to working-class material and cultural impoverishment from perspectives politically oppositional to the liberal and social democratic tendencies of literary studies. Yet Hartley argues that the 'anti-democratic left pessimism' of cultural studies echoed the antipathy of the literary tradition towards the popular, arguing that a 'passionate dislike . . . has survived into the textual tradition in Television Studies, not the fun'. In his conclusion, Hartley argues that this dominant rhetoric in the tradition of textual criticism is 'not strictly about television . . . [nor] about politics either' but 'a knowledge-class conspiracy against the audience'.

It is interesting that this conclusion could be shared without affirming Hartley's location of literary criticism as the dominant textual tradition in studies of television. Film Studies has produced sympathetic work on television genres and a substantial body of textual analysis which does not display the same anxiety, perhaps surprisingly given the long-standing conflict of interest between cinema and broadcasting. Later contributors will locate the tradition of television textual analysis in different disciplinary formations or will view aspects of the same tradition as more productive.

Television History and Geography

The remaining two essays in this section are concerned with place and time in television history. Until recently that has dominantly been a history of specific arrangements for television made by different states within their national boundaries. Histories of television are therefore intimately entwined in and specific to different locations for television, what might be termed 'geographies' of television. It is to matters of interconnection between the history and geography of television that Gill Branston and Lynn Spigel attend.

In their two essays on the national specificities of two models of television, Lynn Spigel attends to the model of commercial television in the USA and Gill Branston to the European model of PSB in Britain.

Television in Britain

Gill Branston's account of British television immediately confronts not only its history but also how that history has been understood. The difference is between history and historiography. Branston finds it necessary to immediately assert that there is a history of British television, even if a contested one. At first sight, this may appear unnecessary, for clearly television must have a past. But there is a body of historical scholarship – historiography – which disputes the status of what has conventionally been taken as *evidence of* that past.

Branston's concern is to distance herself from some modernist or postmodernist historiography which argues the theoretical inaccessibility of the past, the implausibility of retrieving 'what really happened' from the overwhelming and partial data that passes as evidence. This is a general problem of historiography, by no means confined to the study of television, but no less of a problem for all that. It is bound up with a general crisis of confidence among some contemporary scholars over the very status of knowledge itself and a critique of the positivist beliefs of earlier generations of scholars in an unmediated access to a past that can be made knowable through study.

In contrast, Branston wants to assert that, despite the difficulties of establishing what can pass as evidence, empirical study – that is, the study of observable phenomena such as television's past programmes, documentation and ephemera – remains valuable in the context of those debates in which history is always embroiled. She relates empirical study to the procedures of archaeology and critically interrogates the useful metaphor of 'archaeological imagery' in the process of historical enquiry. For Branston, empirical evidence is what is 'for the time being . . . true enough for particular purposes'.

By taking the national cultural case of the British Broadcasting Corporation (BBC) and reviewing dominant histories of the BBC in the light of more recent revisionist studies, she seeks to demonstrate the continuing importance of historical evidence to arguments about how the history of television can be understood. This, in turn, is a necessary prerequisite for adjudging what television means. Branston does not view 'evidence' simply but uses the metaphor of archaeological imagery to demonstrate that what constitutes evidence is precisely subject to interpretation and argument.

The place of the BBC as a national institution has historically been bound up with prevailing assumptions about British culture. By scrutinising those assumptions in

Britain and to some extent in the USA, Branston seeks to demonstrate how debate over the status of empirical historical evidence is crucial to challenging long-standing, taken-for-granted orthodoxies about the BBC and its history of public service broadcasting. Importantly, those challenges are not just in the service of a general oppositional historiography. Her own position as a woman living in a national culture marginalised by the dominant English culture – here, Wales – moves her to argue both the partiality of orthodox histories and the need for their revision from specific national and gender points of view.

Hence can be understood her concern to interrogate the role established for and by the BBC on its formation in the first days of broadcasting in Britain in the light of subsequent historical developments. She argues for the periodisation of television history – through the idea of historical moments – in this light and explores what she terms a triangulated relation between moments of the formation of the BBC, its competition with a new commercial channel in the 1950s and the contemporary moment when its future is under political threat.

The crucial figure in the early history of the BBC was doubtless its first Director General, John Reith, and his promulgation that the BBC's public service remit enabled it to make 'the nation as one man' was ideologically crucial to the role both the BBC and its political paymasters saw it playing in Britain's cultural life. Branston deconstructs the phrase and explores its range of meanings in ways she sees as potentially both negative and positive for a range of historical and contemporary national, social and gendered identities.

Television in the USA

While Gill Branston takes up a position within debates about historiography, defending a view of history as in important senses recoverable and therefore knowable, Lynn Spigel challenges a view of television history as independent of Television Studies. To do this, she goes back to the 1950s. While Branston raises issues about the making of television history in general, Spigel's essay demonstrates the importance of attending to national differences, both in their individual histories of television and of Television Studies.

Spigel's argument is distinguished from John Hartley's earlier characterisation in that she, like Brunsden later in Section II, locates the crucial genesis of television scholarship among television reviewers of the 1950s. Their initial hopes for the new medium soon gave way to suspicions among social scientists about its likely effects and a related concern with 'quality' television among literary elites in the 1960s. Ruminating on the treatment of television by scholars in the humanities since that time, Spigel demonstrates the extent to which television scholarship in the USA has been historically inseparable from the television institution. Her argument is that Television Studies from this period demonstrates 'strange alliances' between the television industry and the academy, among which vested interests on both sides found grounds 'to legitimate their practice'. Television Studies in the USA, she claims, was 'invented by the broadcast industry'. A longer quotation makes the complexity and subtlety of her point:

> emerging critical discourses . . . found their genealogies in and through . . . commercial discourses. If not always directly causal, the relation between intellectuals and [television] industrialists are nevertheless contextual and conjunctural, as each came together in mutual relations of support, antagonism and even indifference in a social world where knowledge . . . is produced according to the logic of the commodity form.

Nor do contemporary scholars escape this characterisation. Even a new generation of scholars currently concerned less with earlier definitions of art than with cultures of 'everyday life' are none the less 'fully implicated in and even constituted by the commodity form'.

In her history, Spigel takes key book publications as historically founding texts, charting symptomatically the many struggles over connection and independence. These include works emerging from the activity of networks, as in the attempt by CBS's *Eyewitness* series to promote a cultural pluralist view of television consumption; struggles between various archive and production interest groups 'rooted in an effort to do away with . . . discursive indeterminacy between public service and public relations'; the role of the Academy Foundation which she sees as responsible for a structural divide between history (West Coast archives, political economy) and criticism (East Coast journals, textual studies); and the new editorial line of *Television Quarterly* in 1971, stimulated by 'shifts in cultural sensibilities' associated with post-1968 new social movements and anti-establishment black, feminist and youth campaigns. Spigel concludes by exploring the current 'legitimation crisis' for television criticism in this history of interconnection between the television industry and television scholarship. Her work raises important issues about television and independent scholarship, especially for the funding of research, and not only in the USA.

Television Studies

Collectively, these four essays reflect in different ways on the establishment of Television Studies as a discipline. The purpose has been to look in general ways at how television has been understood as an object of study, to explore what we understand by 'television' as the product of the attention it has received in the history of thinking and writing on the subject. Yet in their differences, more than emphases or nuances are clearly at stake. If much of Jostein Gripsrud's account serves an idea of television's emancipatory possibilities, Lynn Spigel's concern is more with a manipulatory relationship between the television institution and television scholarship.

Nor can the difference in national broadcasting systems fully explain differences implied in Spigel's analysis between Television Studies in Britain and the USA. John Hartley's construction of a reductive tradition of textual analysis in Television Studies differs from Gill Branston's account of a wider economy of studies even though both write from within the same national context of Britain.

What emerges from this first section, then, is a need to understand better how differences over debates are related to distinct and sometimes competing or at least contrary approaches in Television Studies. That is the work of the next section.

References

BARNOUW, E., 1966–70: *A History of Broadcasting in the USA,* 3 vols. New York: Oxford University Press.
—— 1975: *Tube of Plenty.* New York: Oxford University Press.

BLUMLER, J., 1992: *TV and the Public Interest*. London: Sage.

BOYD BARRATT, O., 1977: 'Media imperialism: towards an international framework for the analysis of media systems'. In James Curran, Michael Gurevitch and Janet Woollacott (eds), *Mass Communication and Society*. London: Edward Arnold.

BRIGGS, A., 1965–79: *The History of Broadcasting in the UK*, 4 vols. Oxford: Oxford University Press.

___, 1985: *The BBC: The First 50 Years*. Oxford: Oxford University Press.

CURRAN, J. and SEATON, J., 1991: *Power Without Responsibility: The Press and Broadcasting in Britain*. London: Routledge.

DOWMUNT, T., *et al.* (eds), 1995: *Channels of Resistance*. London: Routledge.

MATTELART, A. *et al.*, 1984: *International Image Markets*. London: Routledge/ Comedia.

OPOTOWSKY, S., 1961: *TV: The Big Picture*. New York: Dutton.

PAULU, B., 1981: *TV and Radio in the UK*. London: Macmillan.

SCANNELL, P. and CARDIFF, D.D, 1991: *A Social History of Broadcasting, Volume 1 1922–39*. London: Basil Blackwell.

SENDALL, B., 1982–88: *Independent Television in Britain*, 2 vols. London: Macmillan.

SINCLAIR, J., *et al.* (eds), 1996: *New Patterns in Global Television*. Oxford: Oxford University Press.

SKOVMAND, M. and SCHRODER, K., 1992: *Media Cultures: Reappraising Transnational Media*. London: Routledge.

SMITH, A., 1974: *British Broadcasting*. London: David & Charles.

——1975: *The Shadow in the Cave*. London: Quartet.

THOMPSON, J., 1991: *Cultural Imperialism*. London: Pinter.

TUNSTALL, J., 1977: *The Media Are American*. London: Constable.

1

Television, Broadcasting, Flow: Key Metaphors in TV Theory

Jostein Gripsrud

Metaphors in Theory

The word 'television' literally means 'distant sight'. But, as we all know, when watching television we are actually just seeing something a few feet away – an image on the glass front of the box we call a TV set. 'Television' is in other words a metaphor, intended to describe what this box, this experience, this form of communication, is all about.

There is nothing wrong with metaphors in themselves. All kinds of human language are necessarily full of metaphors – as illustrated by this very expression, which compares language to some kind of container that can be 'filled'. While a metaphor is rarely entirely false, it does give prominence to some features of the phenomenon in question and leaves others in the shade. This is why all metaphors should be regarded with a degree of suspicion. The 'television' metaphor, for instance, leaves out the very important fact that the medium normally only lets us see things happening far away via a huge, complex combination of people and technology in a broadcasting institution of some sort. Moreover, as an all-encompassing concept, it makes us think of all kinds of television as being basically the same thing, thus possibly obscuring important differences.

Metaphors refer to things by way of *comparison*. The tensions between the meanings of the elements compared are productive; they may give rise to imaginative explorations of various implications of the comparison made. This aspect of metaphor is not only central to its use in poetry and other arts, it is also of fundamental importance to its functions in all kinds of scientific and scholarly work. Certain metaphors are successful in kindling the imagination of whole communities or generations of scholars, thus providing (part of) a basis for great numbers of books, papers, lectures and conversations over many years. They are, in other words, central to the establishment of what Thomas S. Kuhn, with reference to the natural sciences, once called *paradigms*; 'universally recognized scientific achievements that for a time provide model problems and solutions to a community of practitioners' (Kuhn, 1971: viii).

The aim of this essay, then, is to present and discuss three of the central metaphors in television studies, relating them, on the one hand, to the historical and geographical circumstances under which they were conceived, and, on the other, to the medium as it currently appears. *Television, broadcasting,* and *flow* refer to three different levels on which the medium can be theorized: its fundamental technological features, its social organization as a medium and its construction as text.

Television: Seeing at a Distance

Those who want a relatively simple definition of television can check out a dictionary such as 'America's #1 Paperback Dictionary' i.e. *The New Merriam-Webster Dictionary* (1989 edition). It says that television is the 'transmission and reproduction of images by a device that converts light waves into radio waves and then converts these back into visible light rays'. A dictionary will in other words define the medium by way of its fundamental *technical* features.

The technical capacity remains the core of a whole bundle of ideas about the medium. Whether the pictures transmitted and reproduced show what is going on somewhere as it happens, have been stored for a while, or have been created by computers is irrelevant to the dictionary's definition. Still, the capacity for simultaneity between a 'real' event and its transmission and reception as audio-visual representation is central among television's *differentia specifica*, its specificity as a medium. It shares a form of distribution (broadcasting) with radio, it shares subject matter also with newspapers, magazines and books, it shares the audio-visual form of representation with film. The capacity for simultaneity is also the basis for the use of the technology for video surveillance, an idea explored already in the medium's infancy (Allen, 1983). The limits to the technological definition are already obvious here: we do not think of video surveillance as 'television'. The latter refers to a particular social *use* of the technology.

It is, however, important to have a closer look at the notion of simultaneity in broadcast television. Historically, the medium was early on envisaged as an extension of already existing two-way communication technologies, such as the telegraph and the telephone. The fact that a 53-year-old Norwegian dictionary I checked (*Gyldendals Fremmedordbok*, 1943) translates 'television' as 'picture-telegraph' (*billedtelegraf*) is a relatively late indication of this. The idea of a 'picture-telegraph' was proposed as early as the 1840s, and successful demonstrations over considerable distance occurred in the 1860s (Williams, 1975: 17). The British journal *Punch* in 1879 featured a cartoon showing a mother and father watching, on their living-room wall in England, a tennis match in Ceylon where their daughter was playing. At the same time, they could speak to her over a long-distance telephone (Wheen, 1985: 11).

Two-way communication of these kinds is *direct*, in the sense that transmission and reception take place simultaneously (the delay being so minimal it is of no importance). But the telegraphed message might have been written by hand hours or days before its transmission. And as soon as recording techniques for sound were developed, the voices or musical instruments heard at a distance might have been recorded even years before they were transmitted. Radio was soon filled with pre-recorded material, and the same eventually happened to television. Early television was all 'live', but the development first of machinery for transmitting film and later, from the late 1950s onwards, the development of video machines, entailed a fundamental shift in the balance between 'live' and pre-recorded material. Nearly all television programming is now pre-recorded, hours, days or years before transmission takes place. What we 'see at a distance' is most of the time what at that moment is being played on the broadcaster's VCR. There is still simultaneity in that sense – technical problems with the video machinery can immediately be perceived by viewers. But such problems also disrupt the illusion that the events we have been watching were taking place as we watched them.

This illusion is actively sought by television producers and broadcasters. Immediacy or 'liveness' is a key aesthetic value in television, it seems. It is quite interesting to note the contrast to theatre and most movies here. Bertolt Brecht thought that revealing the technical machinery 'behind' a theatrical play would break the illusion of 'reality' and produce the effect of 'estrangement' (*Verfremdungseffekt*) which would make the audience reflect on the *constructedness* of what they had experienced as 'real'. But since most television is 'non-fiction', the showing of cameras, cables and microphones has quite the opposite effect: it underlines the 'reality' of what goes on, saying 'this is exactly how it happens/happened: we have not added or removed anything'. This is related to what, after Roland Barthes (1981), is known as the 'photograph effect': when we see a photograph we (used to) know that what is in the picture has actually once been in front of a camera. In film, reminding the audience of the presence of a camera at the scene where something is filmed, as when instable or badly focused images demonstrate that a hand-held camera is being used, has the effect of assuring us that what we see actually took place. It gives the film a 'documentary feel', explored by many film-makers at least since Jean-Luc Godard's *A bout de souffle* (1959). Television wants this, and more: not just 'this really happened', but 'this really happens, right now!'. In other words, not just the documentary's 'photo effect', but also television's own effect of *immediacy*, simultaneity, 'liveness'.

The importance of liveness as an aesthetic value for both producers and audiences can be gathered from all the efforts that go into the production of liveness precisely as an *effect*, not necessarily as a *fact*. The everyday presence of television, the regularity of its schedule, helps to produce a feeling of general contemporaneity, and this is consciously exploited in a drama genre like soap opera (cf. Geraghty, 1991: 12). Studio debates, interviews and variety shows will either be live – or try to appear to be. And even with obviously pre-taped shows like sit-coms, we are frequently told that they are 'taped in front of a live studio audience'. Liveness is particularly important to newscasts, since 'news' as a genre is based on getting as close to immediacy as possible. US television in particular often takes this idea *ad absurdum* when reporters talk to the camera – 'live', 'on the spot' – at a dark place where nothing is happening (any more). The reason for this is an equation of 'live' with 'real': liveness means reality. Live is taken to mean 'not staged'. The capacity for transmission of 'reality in the raw' is what separates television from other media, and it thrives on what seems to be an almost insatiable demand for *reality* in modern societies.

Television's technological capacity for liveness is, then, not just the basis for a certain aesthetic, it is also fundamental to television as an *ideological* apparatus.

A medium which can give us 'reality in the raw', unfolding as it happens, cannot lie, it would seem. The possibility for direct transmission of events tends to lend a particular quality of immediacy, realism or truth to much more than live programming (cf. Heath and Skirrow, 1977). It is in order to preserve television's position as the medium most trustworthy because it is 'closest to the real' that 'liveness' as an aesthetic value becomes more important than ever as the development of technologies and styles of presentation progressively make the medium *less* 'live' (cf. Feuer, 1983). Take sports events, for instance, where instant replays in slow motion have become central to all television coverage. The coverage of any major public event will often include pre-taped background materials, various uses of computer graphics, etc.

Graphics and other elements deciding the 'look' of television have on the whole gained a qualitatively new importance over the last 15 years or so. John Caldwell (1995) has recently argued that television is more and more becoming a medium not about outside 'events' but about *style*: 'In short, style, long seen as a mere signifier and vessel for content, issues, and ideas, has now itself become one of television's most privileged and showcased signifieds' (5). Caldwell warns that television theory which 'continues to overestimate the centrality of liveness in television – even as it critiques liveness – ... will also underestimate or ignore other modes of practice or production: the performance of the visual and stylistic exhibitionism' (30).

Television's own technological and stylistic developments have, then, in a sense left a question mark over the very name of the medium – if it is to mean that it provides direct perception of events outside of television itself. The metaphor lives on, though, both since there is still much live programming, and since liveness is a key element in the medium's social role as provider of 'reality'. Caldwell's diagnosis of current US television may be seen as an invitation to very interesting comparative studies of the space and role of 'live' television in different television systems around the world. Such studies might, for instance, indicate whether the photographic or video image retains a privileged status as documentation, as Truth, in otherwise quite different cultures, and how television is used rhetorically in struggles over the definition of social reality.

Such variations between different forms of television in different countries is related to the different meanings of the metaphor of *broadcasting*.

Broadcasting: The Social Shaping of a Technology

'Broadcasting' originally meant sowing (spreading seeds) broadly, by hand. It is in other words not only an agricultural metaphor, it is also .one of optimistic modernism. It is about planned growth in the widest possible circles, the production, if the conditions are right, of a rich harvest.

The metaphor presupposes a bucket of seeds at the centre of the activity, i.e. the existence of centralized resources intended and suited for spreading – and reproduction. In other words, it designates a system which is basically centralized, i.e. defined by a difference between centre and periphery. The question to be looked into first, here, is why the technology which electronically transmits words and pictures was organized in a way which made this agricultural metaphor seem adequate.

Visions of Television

As noted above, since television as a technology is related to various two-way forms of communication, it is all the more striking how early ideas about it as a centralized 'mass' medium actually appeared. A French artist by the name of Robida produced a series of drawings in 1882 showing moving pictures transmitted to people's living rooms. On one screen a teacher was giving a lesson in mathematics, on another a dressmaker was showing his products, on a third screen there was a ballet performance and on a fourth the people could see a desert war: in other words, the distribution of education, advertising, art/entertainment and news to private homes (Wheen, 1985: 11). It is an interesting indication of how widespread such ideas were, that the Norwegian writer Arne Garborg in 1891 published a novel in which a character representing positivist belief in the future said he could foresee a time when people had screens in their homes which allowed them to watch and listen to opera, ballet, circus, religious services, parliamentary debates or concerts. That same year, Thomas Alva Edison proclaimed 'he was within a few months of achieving direct transmission of live events into the home' (Sklar, 1976: 11), and stories about the advent of television circulated widely in books and magazines.

These examples may indicate that it is time to revise Raymond Williams's classic formulation that 'it is not only that the supply of broadcasting facilities preceded the demand; it is also that the means of communication preceded their content' (Williams, 1975: 25). The demand for the specific forms of broadcasting that developed in the Western world from the late 1920s onwards was not strong and explicit, but latent, potential. As the above examples from the 1880s and 1890s demonstrate, transmission to private homes from some centralized unit was simply in keeping with both socio-economic structures and the dominant ways of life, in modern and modernizing societies. Attempts or experiments with other forms of organization in the long run remained just that – attempts and experiments. Two little-known, distinct alternatives deserve mentioning since they highlight what television might have been – that is, if the social system had not been a modern, politically liberal capitalism.

Total Decentralization: Grass-roots Opportunities?

Jeanne Allen has written about 'the possibilities of two-way television and the constraints on its development' in the USA in the 1930s. She considered that 'two-way or interactive television represented perhaps one of the most explicit challenges or oppositions to the centralized and centralizing structures of commerce, government and the military which Raymond Williams has cited as basic to broadcasting's development' (Allen, 1983: 110). Late 1920s' AT&T experiments with two-way television as a possible replacement for the ordinary telephone were, so to speak, picked up by radio amateurs in the early 1930s. Various popular science journals (such as *Radio News* and the British *Practical Radio*) had detailed articles about how to construct television transmitters and receivers. In 1931 a complete receiver kit, minus tubes and cabinet, was advertised in *Radio News* at a price of $56.25 (114). In 1940 complete receiving and transmitting equipment providing 120-line pictures could be purchased and assembled for less than $300 (115). Throughout the 1930s, experimenting amateurs were active in many parts of the country, communicating much in the way radio amateurs do. But Big Business, represented by the Radio Manufacturers Association, in 1938 agreed upon standards for television equipment and channel regulations which drove the grass-roots activists out. So there went the historical 'moment' for a 'countercultural development of television as a widely diffused grass-roots egalitarian form of communication rather than as a concentrated professionalized and generally restricted means of diffusing economic and governmental information using entertainment as a means of gaining audience attention' (116). Broadcasting in some form was, however, tied not only to strong economic interests, but also to the deep-structures of modern societies.

Television as Theatre: Public Viewing

In spite of the activities of TV amateurs, television was, also according to Allen, primarily a medium for theatrical exhibition in the USA in the early 1930s, and as such often thought to be a potential competitor of the film industry (1983: 110). In fact, television was throughout the 1930s predominantly watched in public settings also outside of the USA.

The BBC televised on an experimental basis from its own studios from as early as 1931 on, but the first 'fully public broadcast' is normally said to have taken place on 2 November 1936. At that time, there were about 300 sets in private homes, sold at an average price of £100 – quite close to the average working-class annual wage (Corrigan, 1990: 137). In 1939 the number of receivers was an estimated 20 000 – but this estimate did not specify how many of these sets were in private homes (149). This is important, since Philip Corrigan has discovered through archival research that *public* viewing of television seems to have been the way in which most of the early BBC audiences actually experienced the medium. In 1937 as many as 109 public viewing rooms were known in London. The television supplement to the BBC's *Radio Times* would list these rooms if the quality of the equipment was guaranteed. Sets could be found in big stores like Harrods, in restaurants, with audiences varying between 10 and 100 – but also for instance at Waterloo Railway Station, where up to 20 000 ticket holders had seen television in the course of 10 weeks in 1937 (146). At least in terms of audience numbers, then, British television in the 1930s was largely a medium for public exhibition.

This was even more the case in Germany, where the Nazi government (and the democratic governments before it) in a very determined way supported the development of television. Regular television broadcasts began as early as 22 March 1935, and direct transmissions from the 1936 Olympic Games in Berlin became a showcase for the advances made in German television technology (in cooperation with large American corporations). While the BBC ended television services as the war broke out in September 1939, the Germans continued transmitting, also for instance via the Eiffel tower, until the military collapse. When their transmission towers were bombed in 1943, they switched to a cable system which had been developed since 1936. Television was throughout watched almost exclusively in public viewing halls all over the country, seating between 40 and 400 people. This was a political choice, related to the idea that propaganda worked most efficiently when people were exposed to it in larger groups. The electronics industry was, however, all the time more interested in the sales of sets for domestic use, and production of such sets was just about to start when plans were cancelled because of the war. (For all of the above: Uricchio, 1989.)

The End Result: Broadcast TV for Domestic Viewing

While the vision of a 'grass-roots' or amateur, two-way television was quite obviously doomed to a very marginal position at the very best, television systems largely based on collective, public reception were in fact operating in several countries in the 1930s and may thus seem to have been more of a real alternative to the domestication of the medium. But they were not.

Manufacturers saw the possibilities for mass sales of domestic sets as soon as the price could be reduced, and this interest would only be effectively opposed for reasons of (soon outmoded) propaganda theory in totalitarian regimes. Given the division and relation between the public and the private/domestic domains fundamental to modernity, centralized broadcasting to a dispersed domestic audience was clearly the most adequate organization of the medium. The ideological equation Leisure = Home = (individual) Freedom was the basis already of the visions of television in the 1880s and 1890s. As working-class people achieved improved standards of living and entered 'consumer society' from about 1920 onwards, the dreams of the home as a fully equipped centre for entertainment and diverse cultural experiences became realizable for the majority of inhabitants of Western nation-states. And this is now also happening on a global scale.

Raymond Williams (1975) was probably the first to point out very clearly the relations between basic processes of social modernization and the dominant structures of broadcasting. While social and economic modernization meant increasing centralization and concentration of capital and political power, the break-up of traditional communities produced new ways of life, aptly summed up in Williams's term 'mobile privatization'. Mobility was both social and geographical, and both forms implied that individuals and households were both literally and metaphorically 'on the move' in ways that left them relatively isolated compared to people in much more stable pre- and early modern communities. Centralized broadcasting was both an answer to the need felt by central powers to reach all citizens with important information efficiently, and a highly useful instrument in the production of the harmonizing, stabilizing 'imagined community' (Anderson, 1991) of the nation-state. The pervasiveness of these structured processes and interests rendered broadcasting the 'naturally' victorious organization of both radio and television.

There is, however, one more factor to be mentioned. The above arguments are all about economic interests (those of the electronics industry), a political interest in controlling and dominating mobile, privatized populations, or an 'ideological' interest in making the home a somehow self-sufficient unit in terms of entertainment and cultural experiences. What is left out here is the more positive view of broadcasting as a social form suitable also for *democracy*. In the formulation of broadcasting policies between the World Wars, the interest in broadcasting as a means of securing equal access to resources necessary for conscious, informed and autonomous participation in political, social and cultural life played a very important role in many countries. In fact, the relative strength of such interests in different social formations was quite decisive in terms of making television, in spite of a shared broadcasting structure, a quite different phenomenon in different national and regional contexts. In the following section, basic principles of two different main types of broadcasting will be briefly described and discussed.

Two Kinds of Broadcasting: US Commercialism vs. European Public Service

In the USA, television was modelled on the system of commercial radio, with advertisers originally sponsoring whole programmes and in part also organizing programme production tailored to their commercial interests. This is for instance the basis for the development, first in radio, of the 'daytime serial drama', a genre which already in the 1930s became known as 'soap opera'. These serials were made to sell household products, primarily detergents, and a major manufacturer of such products such as Procter & Gamble would own its own radio and, later, television shows. The rationale behind broadcasting was in other words the industrial interest in marketing commodities. Audiences were addressed primarily as *consumers*, as individuals interested in improving their everyday lives by purchasing certain things with whatever money they had. Broadcasting institutions were – and are – in the business of selling audiences to advertisers. This was of course also the case after spot advertising replaced the old sponsorship system in the 1950s. It was during this decade that the oligopolistic structure in national US television was established, with three (now four) networks owning a handful but controlling the programming of hundreds of local stations from coast to coast.

European television was differently constructed, also following the development of radio. Even if radio in many countries started out as a commercial operation, governments intervened in the late 1920s and early 1930s, creating monopoly broadcasting corporations that were obliged to perform according to certain general principles formulated by parliaments or governments in the various countries. These principles were not least intended to secure a certain profile in programming. An emphasis on raising the general level of education or 'culture' in the population was particularly important, but, related to this, so were ideas about solid professional standards, impartiality in news coverage, etc. An important underlying idea was that broadcasting should serve 'the nation' as a whole, and hence provide both a common focus for everyone and a programming menu catering to a variety of tastes and interests – within certain limits more or less loosely determined by standards of 'quality' and 'relevance'. The idea that broadcasting was to serve the nation as a whole, the whole population, meant that equal access to broadcasting services became an important goal in many places – rich or poor, city folk or country folk, all should be able to participate in the resources provided by public service broadcasting. Public service radio and, later, television basically addressed their audiences as *citizens*, as members of politically liberal democracies, with a right and an obligation to be well informed about all matters of common interest. Broadcasting services were to be financed by quite low, politically defined licence fees, even if some countries also allowed public service corporations to carry some advertising for additional income. But the form of finance was not necessarily decisive. When advertising-supported television was introduced in the UK in the mid-1950s, it was quite strictly regulated and in principle supposed to operate according to public service ideals.

A basic problem with the public service model was its inherent degree of pater-nalism, i.e. the tendency towards a 'father-knows-best' prescription of what social and cultural elites decided was a sound programming menu. In terms of the 'broadcasting' metaphor, one could say that the 'cultural father' was the farmer spreading the seeds. This was all the more problematic in a monopoly situation, probably less so with the UK duopoly. But the attitudes to, for instance, popular culture within public service institutions would also vary from country to country, in line with differences in socio-cultural structures and political power relations. For instance, the Norwegian parallel to the BBC, the NRK, was more inclusive than exclusive in its cultural forms and modes of address, reflecting the strong position of the social-democratic labour movement and various regional and rural-based organizations. In other words, the functioning of broadcasting sys-tems is not only decided by the abstract centre–periphery dichotomy – one must also ask what *kind* of centre we are dealing with, and what are the more precise relations between the centre and the periphery? In the Norwegian case, the lead-ing circles of the 'popular' social forces were, however, united with influential political conservatives in a critical and partly outright hostile attitude to transna-tional, commercial popular culture. Transnational commercial culture was in consequence denied a share of programming in some proportion to its broad popularity with audiences. The most striking example of this exclusion of certain popular cultural forms is the exclusion of continuing serial drama, i.e. soap opera, until the US prime-time soap *Dynasty* finally made its way into the sched-ule in 1983 (cf. Gripsrud, 1995. ch. 2).

On the whole, though, public service television has been marked by a greater diversity in terms of programme forms and styles than that of purely commercial systems such as that of the USA. A relatively early documentation of this was presented by Raymond Williams in his classic *Television: Technology and Cultural Form* (1975). He compared the programming of three British (BBC1, BBC2, IBA Anglia) and two American channels (KQED) (public television, San Francisco) and Channel 7 (ABC, San Francisco)). A very simple table, list-ing 'comparative percentages of types of programming' on the five channels between 3 and 9 March 1973, pretty much sums up his findings (*see* Table 1.1). Here Williams grouped programmes in two categories, type A and type B. Type A included news and public affairs, features and documentaries, education, arts and music, children's programmes, and plays. Type B included drama series and serials, movies, and general entertainment.

Table 1.1 Types of programming on five selected channels (%)

	BBC1	BBC2	Anglia	KQED	Channel 7
Type A	71	75	42.9	86	20.5
Type B	21	22.5	38.1	10.5	59.5

Source: Williams, 1975: 84

As Williams pointed out, there are two kinds of comparisons that are interesting here. First, between commercially financed channels (Anglia, Channel 7) and the public channels in each country: type B programming is clearly much more prominent in commercial channels. But second, one may also look at the differences between the UK and the USA, and then 'it is clear that the situation in American television is more sharply polarised'. What this means is that certain kinds of programming are simply missing in each of the American channels, while both types of channels in the UK have a more broadly composed schedule, simply richer in terms of variety. During the sample week ABC's Channel 7 had just 0.6 hours of features and documentaries, no educational programming, 5.2 hours of children's programmes (as compared to 11.4 at BBC1 and 8.3 at Anglia), and no single plays – meaning that most of its 'type A' programming was newscasts (11.6 hours out of a total 19.0 devoted to news and public affairs). On the other hand, KQED had only 4.7 hours of drama (BBC1 had 11.5, Anglia 20.3, Channel 7 22.4) and no 'general entertainment' at all (BBC1 had 7.4 hours, Anglia 9.8 and Channel 7 32.4).

Such quantitative measurements of programme categories may tell us important but relatively simple things about programming profiles. They do not say anything about the 'quality' of programmes as such. It is also clear that a drama series episode can treat, for instance, social issues in ways that may be more relevant and interesting than an abstract and more or less boringly 'serious' discussion or documentary. These are important points to remember, especially for those who are eager to condemn US commercial, network television for being without social relevance, as mere 'eye candy'. The problem with the US system is rather that only a small, well-educated and rather affluent part of the total television audience will be watching public television in addition to the commercial services and thus get a broader variety of information, knowledge and perspectives. In fact, as late as 1980, and probably to some extent even today, those well-educated and socially and politically most active in the USA on the whole would tend to watch quite little television (cf. Winston, 1985, quoted in Gripsrud, 1995: 41). The majority sticks to network and local commercial television which presents a programming menu almost totally lacking certain important genres and contents. Such a television system is likely to reinforce or even increase rather than reduce socially produced differences in terms of resources for active citizenship, i.e. participation in a variety of political, social and cultural processes and events.

But what about the experience of watching television within these different systems? To what extent is the experience similar, and to what extent is the formal organization of the televisual text the same? In attempts to formulate a general, textual and reception-oriented theory of television over the last 20 years, one metaphor has been particularly important: that of television as *flow*.

Flow: A Transatlantic Trope

Modern, critical television theory can be said to have begun one night in Miami, Florida, as the British literary scholar Raymond Williams sat down to watch US TV for the first time. His own description of his experience has become a classic:

still dazed from a week on an Atlantic liner, I began watching a film and at first had some difficulty in adjusting to a much greater frequency of commercial 'breaks'. Yet this was a minor problem compared to what eventually happened. Two other films, which were due to be shown on the same channel on other nights, began to be inserted as trailers. A crime in San Francisco (the subject of the original film) began to operate in extraordinary counterpoint not only with the deodorant and cereal commercials but with a romance in Paris and the eruption of a prehistoric monster who laid waste New York. ... I can still not be sure what I took from that whole flow. I believe I registered some incidents as happening in the wrong film, and some characters in the commercials as involved in the film episodes, in what came to seem – for all the occasional bizarre disparities – a single irresponsible flow of images and feelings. (Williams, 1975: 91–2)

Williams's problems here may well have been connected to his still being dazed after the sea voyage. But his physical condition only accentuated the experience of what were (and are) intersubjectively observable features of the kind of audio-visual sequence presented to him: there were no markers of 'interval' between the scheduled film and the inserted commercials and trailers for other films, and it was possible to construct meaningful relations between the disparate elements. This produced what he elsewhere, in a piece of criticism published in the BBC's *The Listener*, called 'some surrealist effects' (Williams, 1989: 25). Back in Britain, the notion of surrealism seems to have appeared less adequate as a term for describing the typical television experience. But Williams did find the metaphor *flow* applicable also to the sequential organization of British public service television:

Even when, as on the BBC, there are no interruptions of specific 'programme units', there is a quality of flow which our received vocabulary of discrete response and description cannot easily acknowledge. It is evident that what is now called 'an evening's viewing' is in some ways planned, by providers and then by viewers, *as a whole*; that is in any event planned in discernible sequences which in this sense override particular programme units. Whenever there is competition between television channels, this becomes a matter of conscious concern: to get viewers in at the beginning of flow. Thus in Britain there is intense competition between BBC and IBA in the early evening programmes, in the belief – which some statistics support – that viewers will stay with whatever channel they begin watching. (1989: 93)

'The Central Television Experience'?

The notion of 'flow' is in other words tied to the development of programming in a situation of competition between broadcasting channels. But, on the other hand, Williams claims that 'the fact of flow' is also *'the central television experience'* (1989: 95, emphasis added). And that experience is almost beyond words:

It is indeed very difficult to say anything about this. It would be like trying to describe having read two plays, three newspapers, three or four magazines, on the same day that one has been to a variety show and a lecture and a football match. And yet in another way it is not like that at all, for though the items may be various, the television experience has in some important ways unified them. (1989: 95)

This is a claim which there are very good reasons to doubt. Williams's only attempt at empirical support for the idea, outside of his Miami experience, is that (a) 'most of us say, in describing the experience, that we have been "watching television", rather than that we have watched "the news" or "a play" or "the football" "on television" ', and that (b) 'many of us find television very hard to switch off' (94). While both of these statements are partially true, they are contradicted in various ways by Williams himself, directly and indirectly. He keeps saying that of course people still watch specific programmes, and his abundance of specific comments about specific programmes indicates the extent to which he himself finds individual programmes interesting. The 'flow' perspective on the TV experience is also contradicted by the fact that viewers both then and now actively prefer certain programmes over others and also speak of watching particular programmes. Day-to-day talk about television among people tends to be about specific series, discussions, documentaries or whatever. And this becomes even more obvious in a multi-channel situation: the question at work or wherever else people meet is not 'did you watch TV last night?' but 'did you see *Coronation Street*/*The X-files*/the soccer match?'.

Furthermore, flow, according to Williams himself, is primarily a quality of *broadcasting*. Hence it is also a quality of radio, and thus not something peculiar to television. It could also be tied to the textual organization of more or less serious newspapers and the act of reading them. As the reader goes through news items, political commentaries, gossip about celebrities, advertising, sports coverage, book reviews and comics, the experience is quite clearly analogous to that of flow. As pointed out by Williams, flow is, moreover, a form of experience which may be said to characterize not just the media but important parts of modern social experience in general:

> This trend, towards an increasing variability and miscellaneity of public communications, is evidently part of a whole social experience. It has profound connections with the growth and development of greater physical and social mobility, in conditions both of cultural expansion and of consumer rather than community cultural organisation. Yet until the coming of broadcasting the normal expectation was still of a discrete event or a succession of discrete events. People took a book or a pamphlet or a newspaper, went out to a play or a concert or a meeting or a match, with a single predominant expectation or attitude. (1989: 88)

One may ask which single predominant expectation or attitude people used to take to the local music hall or vaudeville theatre or any other place with variety shows. These shows also included items with quite different aesthetic, affective and cognitive characteristics. But the main point here is that the notion of flow covers so wide an area, embraces so many different phenomena, that it is hardly apt as a description of 'the central *television* experience'.

'Flow' and Images of the Audience

When applied to television, the 'flow' metaphor does not only point to the fact that quite unrelated things happen in unbroken sequence on TV. It also adds to this sequence a sense of *power*, an energy, a relentlessness in the stream which viewers can be overwhelmed by, *dragged into and along with*. Williams's notion of 'flow' can thus easily be tied to a particular image of what TV viewers and their relationship to the box is like: basically passive and non-discriminating. This passive and non-discriminating viewer is clearly related to the image of the mass audience in classical mass culture theory, where, in some versions, the ability of the mass media to 'inject' opinions and attitudes directly into people's heads was assumed. In other versions, like that of the Frankfurt School, the long-term 'effect' was presumed to be more an ever-increasing passivity and conformity, a wiping out of critical consciousness. In my opinion, there are reasons to suspect that Adorno and Horkheimer were on to something important here, but even Adorno himself realized (in the 1960s) that the culture industry would never completely succeed in subsuming the heads of its customers (cf. Gripsrud, 1995: 7–8). The main point in connection with Williams's 'flow' metaphor, anyway, is that it carries some of the fear typical of his generation of critical intellectuals in relation to modern mass media.

But the audience is only going to be swept away by the flow if they fall into it, so to speak. There is also another option when relating to a stream, flow or river – which is precisely to watch it from a distance, not really get into it, regard it somehow as a whole, without significantly differentiated parts. This perspective obviously informs the theory that television is normally watched at a *glance*, as opposed to the *gaze* of film audiences (cf. Ellis, 1982). The 'flow' metaphor in other words carries what seem to be two diametrically opposed images of the television experience: that of being swept away by an external force, and that of coolly and calmly regarding a river at a distance, possibly now and again distracted by what goes on in the immediate surroundings.

These images of two ways of relating to TV form the basis for quite different approaches to television as an object of research and criticism. What they share, however, is a theoretical and hence fundamental disrespect for *the programme text* in television, i.e. for the individual units around which TV production is organized, on which the television *schedule* is based, and which still tend to regulate much of most people's viewing, in a daily, weekly and seasonal rhythm. Television theory based on or closely related to the 'flow' metaphor thus tends to be at odds with both the practices of production *and* the most widespread practices of reception. Most TV viewers are – in spite of the zapping possibilities of the remote control – still drawn towards specific programmes: the news, a favourite soap, a particular talk show. Both the intense competition between channels over successful programmes and the actual zapping patterns revealed by people-meter technology demonstrate this.

The Systems, Theories and Politics of Television

It was of course no coincidence that it was while visiting the USA that Raymond Williams created the *flow* metaphor. His own description of the syntactic organization of US network television, and anyone else's experience of the same thing, explains why he at that time had to leave Britain in order to think of such a term. Even if television elsewhere has been moving towards more similar forms of organization, with commercials within and/or between programmes, increasing use of channel promos, etc., US network television still has a more pronounced flow quality than that of many other countries.

It is not surprising, then, that so much television theory in the USA has been particularly preoccupied with understanding television's flow and its implications. Three contributions could be mentioned as central examples of this type of discourse. Beverle Houston's essay 'Viewing television: the metapsychology of endless consumption' (1984) launched a psychoanalytical perspective on the typical form and function of TV watching in America. The 24-hour flow of television programming is claimed to be unconsciously linked to a baby's dream of an eternal flow of milk from the mother's breast. But the imaginary promise of complete satisfaction is again and again shattered by interruptions – ads informing viewers that the only real satisfaction is to be found in the nearest supermarket or mall. Lawrence Grossberg presented a postmodernist view in his article 'The in-difference of television' (1987), where he says specific TV programmes are not 'texts to be interpreted' but rather 'billboards to be driven past' (31). Margaret Morse's 'An ontology of everyday distraction: the freeway, the mall, and television' (1990) explores the analogy between watching television, driving and shopping, activities that are characterized by a 'semifiction effect', a 'partial loss of touch with the here and now', a feeling of being both 'here' and 'elsewhere' at the same time.

In spite of their theoretical differences, all three articles are marked by the particular flow quality of American television and its commercial basis. To a foreign observer, it is striking how such theorizing tends to ignore specific types of programming. 'Television' is treated as a stream of audio-visual signs with the promotion of consumption and consumerism as common denominator; differences in terms of genres, themes, forms of address, etc. are of little or no significance in the analysis.

While such very abstract theorizing is hardly a uniquely American tendency, European contributions to a general theory of television (such as Ellis, 1982) seem to devote more attention to the differences between programming categories. This is likely to have something to do with the differences in television systems and programming traditions between the USA and (Western) Europe, as indicated by Williams's early findings (see above). 'Watching television' has simply been a quite different experience on the two sides of the Atlantic. It is also worth noting that the harshest critiques of the television medium have come from critics who have little or no experience with it outside the USA. Book-length, wholesale condemnations of TV – the 'plug-in drug' – have come from US writers who do not bother to specify what *version* of television they talk about (for example, titles such as *Four Arguments for the Elimination of Television*, Mander, 1978). Whatever else this may be taken to mean, it indicates that the ways in which television is thought and spoken about are related not so much to its technology as such, but to the specific organization and uses of this technology. Theories of television ought to specify to which television system(s), with which kinds of relations to their audiences, and with which kinds of programming they refer.

This is not to say that there are no similarities worth thinking about. On the contrary, the radical changes that have taken place in television around the world over the last 15 years or so have made the experience of the medium anywhere much more similar to that formerly just characteristic of the USA. The centralized, broadcasting form has always been roughly the same, and so have considerable elements of programming. Now advertising and tough competition for ratings between several channels have also become well known elsewhere, and via satellites and cables we can even watch the same programmes at the same time. Satellite television represented the end to the exclusively national television of the decades before 1980. Norwegian rules banning advertising in television were in the mid-1980s ridiculed and overrun by satellite television, beamed in Norwegian from London. The direct transmission from abroad comes in addition to the use of imported programmes, in most smaller countries making up 50 per cent or more of total programme hours. Programme 'concepts' are bought and sold too, and ideas travel from country to country. Most of the traffic in programming, concepts, ideas, styles, etc. is one-way, though: from the USA, and to some extent the UK, to the rest of the world. But even this picture is getting more complex – there are important exceptions to the rule, such as the rise of Mexico and Brazil as major exporters of drama serials (*telenovelas*, a form of soap opera). However, US dominance is still overwhelming, and US formats, styles and ideas count as worth learning from in TV production milieux all over the globe. This is why theories and concepts originally developed with a reference to US television are increasingly relevant to television studies everywhere.

All three key metaphors of television theory which have been presented and discussed in this essay risk being outmoded or at least less adequate as we approach the next century. If 'television' increasingly becomes a video machine, a medium in which 'style' is the primary signified and 'liveness' is a purely ideological hoax, then it should perhaps be given another name. If 'broadcasting' is transformed not only into 'narrowcasting' but into a totally 'personalized', privatized viewing of 'videos on demand', then this metaphor will soon be seen only as referring to a particular organization of audio-visual technology during a certain centralized phase of social modernization. 'Flow' may survive as a name for the endless stream of sounds and images from 500 channels from which each of us (at least those who can afford to pay the admission fees) can compose our individual sub-flows.

With these potential prospects in mind, it seems to me that the central meanings of tele-vision and broad-casting (in its public service form) are both worthy of defence, theoretically and politically. A possible key to such a defence is to insist that the 'flow' is (or should be) made up of a great variety of programmes, made by people with a purpose and a responsibility, for audiences that share a number of interests and concerns. However the specific legal, financial and technological means for its continued existence may be developed, public service broadcast television can provide a counter-force to widening information gaps and the erosion of a democratic public sphere.

At the time of writing, 'live' coverage of the Olympic Games in Atlanta is the focus for up to three billion people. Such 'live broadcasting of history' is an important ritual on a global scale (cf. Dayan and Katz, 1992). Every night, national newscasts, with 'live' segments, get the attention of large numbers of viewers, interested in finding out what goes on in the(ir) world. Broadcast television constitutes and supports communities, a sense of shared conditions, concerns and interests which may be essential for democratic developments and global awareness.

References

ALLEN, J., 1983: 'The social matrix of television: invention in the United States'. In E. A. Kaplan (ed.), *Regarding Television: Critical Approaches – An Anthology*. American Film Institute, Los Angeles: University Publications of America, 109–19.

ANDERSON, B., 1991: *Imagined Communities: Reflections on the Origins and Spread of Nationalism*. London and New York: Verso.

BARTHES, R., 1981: *Camera Lucida: Reflections on Photography*. New York: Hill and Wang.

CALDWELL, J., 1995: *Televisuality: Style, Crisis and Authority in American Television*. New Brunswick, NJ: Rutgers University Press.

CORRIGAN, P., 1990: 'On the difficulty of being sociological (historical materialist) in the study of television: the "moment" of English television, 1936–1939'. In T. Syvertsen (ed.), *1992 and After: Nordic Television in Transition*. Report no. 10, Department of Media Studies, Bergen: University of Bergen, 130–60.

DAYAN, D. and KATZ, E., 1992: *Media Events: The Live Broadcasting of History*. Cambridge, Mass. and London: Harvard University Press.

ELLIS, J., 1982: *Visible Fictions: Cinema, Television, Video*. London: Routledge and Kegan Paul.

FEUER, J., 1983: 'The concept of live television: ontology as ideology'. In E. A. Kaplan (ed.), *Regarding Television: Critical Approaches – An Anthology*. American Film Institute, Los Angeles: University Publications of America, 12–22.

GERAGHTY, C., 1991: *Women and Soap Opera: A Study of Prime Time Soaps*. Cambridge: Polity Press.

GRIPSRUD, J., 1995: *The Dynasty Years: Hollywood, Television and Critical Media Studies*. London and New York: Routledge.

GROSSBERG, L., 1987: 'The in-difference of television'. *Screen*, 28, 2, Spring: 28–45.

HEATH, S. and SKIRROW, G., 1977: 'Television: a world in action'. *Screen*, 18, 2, Summer: 7–59.

HOUSTON, B., 1984: 'Viewing television: the meta-psychology of endless consumption'. *Quarterly Review of Film Studies*, 9, 3, Summer: 183–95.

KUHN, T., 1971: *The Structure of Scientific Revolutions*. Chicago: University of Chicago Press.

MANDER, J., 1978: *Four Arguments for the Elimination of Television*, New York: William Morrow & Co.

MORSE, M., 1990: 'An ontology of everyday distraction: the freeway, the mall, and television'. In P. Mellencamp (ed.), *Logics of Television: Essays in Cultural Criticism*. Bloomington, Indianapolis, London: Indiana University Press and BFI Publishing.

SKLAR, R., 1976: *Movie-Made America: A Cultural History of American Movies*. New York: Vintage Books.

URICCHIO, W., 1989: 'Rituals of reception, patterns of neglect: Nazi television and its postwar representation'. *Wide Angle*, 11, 1: 48–66.

WHEEN, F., 1985: *Television*. London: Century Publishing.

WILLIAMS, R., 1975: *Television: Technology and Cultural Form*. New York: Schocken Books.

——, 1989: *Raymond Williams On Television: Selected Writings*, ed. A. O'Connor. London and New York: Routledge.

WINSTON, B., 1985: 'Showdown at culture gulch'. In R. E. Hiebert and C. Reuss (eds), *Impact of Mass Media: Current Issues*. New York and London: Longman.

2

Housing Television: Textual Traditions in TV and Cultural Studies

John Hartley

Textual Traditions

The textual tradition in British TV studies began when people trained in literary theory and 'practical criticism' turned their attention to popular culture. Unfortunately for the cause of television analysis, such training tended to emphasize strong hostility to popular cultural aesthetics, and fear of the cultural impact of new entertainment media. So whereas many traditions of study in the general area of the arts have presumed some pleasurable investment by the student in the object of study, the textual tradition in television studies set out with the avowed intention of denouncing television and all its works. People who specialize in the textual study of forms like literature, the visual arts, photography or even cinema are presumed either to *like* their chosen form, or to have some talent in its textual *creation*. But the opposite was true of TV studies when it entered the academy; the successful student was the one who could catalogue most extensively the supposed evils associated with television, although of course these evils only affected *other* people, possibly because the students were not encouraged to watch TV themselves, only to opine haughtily about it. This powerful rhetoric of denunciation was in place, complete with a full repertoire of concepts, theories, even phrases, ready to be applied to television before it was invented, since the small screen was simply assumed to be an extension (perhaps even more pernicious) of previously despised popular media from newspapers to Hollywood – a threat to the traditions of culture. I. A. Richards, 'inventor' of the influential literary analytical method of 'practical criticism', explicitly linked these fears about a threat to cultural 'standards' with an equal fear of democratization:

> With the increase in population, the problem presented by the gulf between what is preferred by the majority and what is accepted as excellent by the most qualified opinion has become infinitely more serious, and appears likely to become threatening in the near future. For many reasons, standards are much more in need of defence now, than they used to be. (Richards, 1924: 36)

Television was not even on the public horizon when Richards expressed this need to defend 'qualified opinion' from 'what is preferred by the majority' in 1924. It follows that the critical onslaught which television has faced throughout its existence has its roots not in the medium itself, but in a pre-existing discourse of anxiety about popularization and modernity: a quite straightforward fear of and hostility to the democratization of taste. In this context 'what is accepted as excellent by the most qualified opinion' *is* 'the textual tradition' of literary culture and criticism, which Richards believed to be 'much more in need of defence' than in a period before 'the increase in population' associated with the Industrial Revolution.

Richards was not a lone voice, but part of a class action, as it were. Perhaps the best-known advocates of the 'textual tradition' were T. S. Eliot and F. R. Leavis, who elaborated, during the period when television was being invented, institutionalized and popularized (principally the 1930s to 1950s), a 'way of understanding' literature which was to prove enormously influential in the thinking of educators, policy-makers and commentators in schools, government departments and in the middlebrow press, from those days to these. Their idea of 'tradition' was to say that Literature (with a capital L; the received literary canon) was not something an author, much less a reader, could add or respond to on a case-by-case basis, but was an 'organic' whole, a 'tradition' which must be grasped imaginatively *as* an organic whole by those who would seek to understand or to contribute to it. Leavis took the previously descriptive notion of 'the great tradition' – a succession of named 'texts' by 'great' authors – and upgraded it into a full-blown ideology of 'culture'. This ideology caught on among educators through the remarkable success of Leavis's journal *Scrutiny*, which spread its judgemental, finger-wagging certainties through the school staffrooms of middle England. It held that 'the great tradition' provided the *antidote* to modern life, industrialization, and what Leavis called 'machine-applied power'. In a famous passage, Leavis and his collaborator Denys Thompson set out what they were *against:*

> The great agent of change, and from our point of view, destruction, has of course been machine-applied power. The machine has brought us many advantages, but it has destroyed the old ways of life, the old forms, and by reason of the continual rapid change it involves, prevented the growth of the new. Moreover, the advantage it brings us in mass production has turned out to involve standardization, and levelling-down outside the realm of mere material goods. Those who in schools are offered (perhaps) the beginnings of education in taste are exposed, out of school, to the competing exploitation of the cheapest emotional responses; films, newspapers, publicity in all its forms, commercially-catered fiction – all offer satisfaction at the lowest level, and inculcate the choosing of the most immediate pleasures, got with the least effort. (Leavis and Thompson, 1933: 3)

This pessimistic snobbishness so wants to sneer at cultural forms which are 'cheap' (at point of sale only of course; popular entertainment is far from cheap to produce and distribute) that it cannot entertain for a moment the idea that standardization might produce *good* products, or that 'choosing immediate pleasures' might be OK (it is what art-lovers do), or that 'rapid change' *is* (rather than '*prevents*') the growth of new forms, or that the 'old ways of life' were abandoned, by those whose lives they were, just as soon as modernity allowed, or that 'education in taste' suffered from 'competition' outside school because it was not really what Leavis thought it was – an absolute standard of objective quality – but actually a prejudicial ideology of supremacism based not on the 'perfection' of the 'great tradition' but on the fact that the 'taste' in question was a projection of a rather narrow, sectional cultural hierarchy on to the entire 'semiosphere' (see Lotman, 1990).

For those born of industrialization and urbanization, the growth of 'mass' society was not experienced as a cultural calamity but as life, and mass communication, whether physical (transport and tourism) or virtual (popular media and entertainment), was not a 'competing exploitation' to which innocent victims were 'exposed', but an intrinsic component of a socialized mode of living.

Leavisite textualism took hold for two rather prosaic reasons – it was suited to classes and classrooms. First, it was suited to the class position, life-outlook and professional skills of a particular group – middle-class, college-educated school-teachers, bureaucrats and administrative workers, products of neither of the 'fundamental' classes of 'capital' and 'labour', whose only means to take power in the world was to textualize it, and thence to manipulate the texts into orders which *could* be controlled and managed (see Frow, 1995). Second, Leavisism offered a coherent and principled stance which was radical without being political (i.e. it was militant, but not Marxist), and which seemed to be able to make sense of modernity without being part of it. In other words, it offered its adherents a sense of personal exemption from the rigours of historical change ('decline'), and put in place a system of what it claimed were timeless values – ideology posing as objective truth. It was thus perfectly suited to adoption in the classroom as the moral successor to religious faith in a secular, modern world; it quickly became what it most wanted to be – the moral centre of the school curriculum:

> The school-training of literary taste does indeed look a forlorn enterprise. Yet if one is to believe in education at all, one must believe that something worth doing can be done. And if one is to believe in anything, one must believe in education. We cannot, as we might in a healthy state of culture, leave the citizen to be formed unconsciously by his environment; if anything like a worthy idea of satisfactory living is to be saved, he must be trained to discriminate and resist. (Leavis and Thompson, 1933: 3–4)

And so literary contempt for modernity in its commercial and popular aspects did not remain confined to professors of English who did not like mass culture, but infiltrated the schools as part of an agenda for *resistance* by the radical Right, an agenda which is still evident within the National Curriculum.

While officially 'political' propaganda was forbidden in schools, Leavisite 'training in resistance' was officially encouraged. Here is a government-sponsored report of 1938 on secondary schooling:

> Teachers are ... not to be envied their struggle against the natural conservatism of childhood, allied to the popularization of the infectious accents of Hollywood. The pervading influence of the hoarding, the cinema, and a large section of the public press, are (in this respect as in others) subtly corrupting the taste and habits of the rising generation. (The Spens Report, quoted in Goulden and Hartley, 1982: 14)

This 'struggle' against childhood and Hollywood was conducted with *texts* – 'culture' – and it was waged against industrialization. Here is another government report, this time the Symonds Report on *The Education of the Adolescent*, of

1926, the year of the General Strike, itself the most public and theatrical manifestation of the 'dangers' of industrialization in the period leading up to television:

> Industrialization has its grave effects on national life. It demands, only too often, a narrow specialization of faculty: it produces, only too readily, a patterned uniformity of work and behaviour; it may, unless it is corrected, infect the minds of men with the genius of its own life. Education can correct industrialization by giving to the mind the breadth and the fresh vitality of new interests, as it can also make industry more effective. (Quoted in Goulden and Hartley, 1982: 14)

It transpires, what luck, that 'culture' is the antidote to the 'infections' of industry, the genius of whose own life included not only standardization and uniformity, but also class antagonism and, in 1926, political resistance. Ever since Matthew Arnold had first come up with the idea of 'culture' as the antonym of 'anarchy' (Arnold, 1869), educators were taught that culture could tame 'the Englishman's' propensity to use his freedom merely to riot. The 'textual tradition', then, is *for* the textualization of cultural value (and its 'inculcation' in schools); it is *against* the 'infections' of popular culture, but its underlying agenda is the control and management not of the culture so much as the population. It is a species of counter-revolutionary ideology in a period of 'mass' politics, 'mass' production, 'mass media'.

In this context, television did not stand a chance to develop its own reputation on it own merits. It was prejudged: 'cheap emotional responses', 'satisfaction at the lowest level', 'immediate pleasures got with the least effort' – Leavis had written the script of what has since become the standard line of criticism before television was even on the air. Its 'pervading influence' would be the same as the rest of popular culture, apt to 'corrupt the taste and habits of the rising generation' before that generation was even born. It was into this intellectual environment that television itself was launched on 2 November 1936.

Housing Problems

In 1935, one year before the official 'first' television broadcast in Britain, a short film called *Housing Problems* was released. It has since become very famous, being a staple on courses in film and cinema studies (at least in Britain), where it is used as an example of documentary film-making in the tradition established by John Grierson.[1] *Housing Problems* is a very good starting-place for television studies too, because it is an influential surviving example of screen semiosis (i.e. sense-making practices) from the very outset of the new medium. *Housing Problems* brings together themes of public spectacle and domestic life; showing urban modernism mixed with the private lives of working people, public policy applied to family circumstances, and for the audience, the sensation of being *away* from home (at the cinema) to *think* about home (as a 'problem').

The film is very short at 15 minutes, and comprises two main sequences. The first sets up the 'problems' of the title, showing slum housing in London's East End, with a commentary by a local councillor and a succession of working-class tenants speaking for themselves, telling the viewer about the lack of light, water, clean air and cooking facilities, and illustrating with vivid unscripted anecdotes the dilapidation, vermin and noxiousness, the want of privacy, sound-proofing and amenity, of their tiny flats and rooms. The second section produces what are clearly meant to be seen as ideal solutions to these problems, introduced by an unseen and unidentified 'expert' voice-over, with a professional, male authoritativeness. We see a series of models of steel-framed and concrete housing blocks, and although the point is not pressed, it transpires that the room-heaters, hot water systems and cookers are all powered by gas. The film's sponsors, the British Commercial Gas Association, are buying PR rather than advertising. They are not attempting to sell gas installations or contracts to cinema-goers (the film is not an advertisement); rather, they are trying to associate themselves with positive values, which are seen in the film as modernization, urban renewal, planning, hygiene, mass production using modern materials and scientific methods – a clean break with the unhealthy, unplanned, exploitative and inhumane conditions of the past.

Housing Problems was regarded from the moment of its first release as a radical film, and its enduring reputation rests upon its importance in the history of semiosis. Its most radical innovations are the very aspects that are now most easily overlooked, for the simple reason that what was surprising and never-before-tried in 1935 has since impressed enough producers and directors to have become the bedrock of standard practice. *Housing Problems* uses real people, not actors. They are named in the film, which lets them speak in their own words in their own houses, not to a verbally tidied-up, editorially vetted and visually prettified script. It treats a mundane subject seriously, ordinary life with respect, and working-class people without patronization. Even the voice of 'authority' – a municipal councillor – speaks in tolerant tones of 'taking people as you find them'. In today's television parlance, the film is an 'actuality segment' in a 'current affairs' slot using 'vox pops' together with the viewpoints of authoritative and expert figures. The compelling quality of the film comes from the use of real people in natural locations, its 'show and tell' simplicity. It has a televisual, eye-witness logic, rather than the logic of formal argument; viewers can tell at a glance not only that this is obviously a 'problem', but also that *this* is clearly what must be done about it.

On reflection, such logic is far from compelling, especially in the harsh light of hindsight, for the cure proposed was in some places to prove worse than the disease. With sincere conviction and militant self-confidence, the film shows how uncomfortable and intolerable life is for slum-dwellers, using shots of women sweeping and beating the dust out of rugs in the back alleys, while the children muck around. But these are the very scenes which the next generation would claim as illustrations of the solidarity, community and supportive mutuality of working-class life. They show the unself-conscious communality that Richard Hoggart is famously elegaic about, just as it was passing out of history, in his epoch-making book *The Uses of Literacy* (Hoggart, 1957: 20–6; 41–52). Hoggart describes the working-class neighbourhoods of his own youth in the 1930s – the very kind to which *Housing Problems* is so opposed – and contrasts this culture with the rootless 'candy-floss' world of mass housing, mass education and mass entertainment. *The Uses of Literacy* established itself as one of the two or three founding texts of contemporary cultural studies; the first academic book in Britain to be taken seriously for taking popular media and culture seriously, reading each in terms of the other, and both in terms of class:

> The more we look at working-class life, the more we try to reach the core of work-ing-class attitudes, the more surely does it appear that the core is a sense of the per-sonal, the concrete, the local: it is embodied in the idea of, first, the family and, second, the neighbourhood. This remains, though much works against it, and partly because so much works against it. (Hoggart, 1957: 20)

In fact, the slum clearances which began in the early 1930s and which were con-tinued after the war into the 1950s and 1960s, stuck at the physical heart of 'fam-ily' and 'neighbourhood'. It was only later that commentators started blaming 'the media' – television especially – for the dislocated culture, 'broken' families, and hostile neighbourhoods of some working-class life. Meanwhile, *Housing Problems* is passionate for working families to live in high-rise concrete blocks of flats, and in giant housing developments like Quarry Hill in Leeds (Hoggart's home town). These were the 'solutions' that in turn became major social, archi-tectural and political problems after the Second World War. An architect's model of Quarry Hill is presented in *Housing Problems* as the last word in light, airy, healthy, clean, convenient and pleasant living, It was indeed built, but it was eventually demolished as an eyesore unfit for human habitation, taking a good deal of blame as the cause of individual isolation, family breakdown, juven-ile disaffection, petty crime and social disintegration: a form of mass housing so brutal that it managed to produce the same human desolation it was designed by the experts to replace.

But in *Housing Problems*, the *semiotic* imperative is oblivious to such – or indeed any – consequences. The film is driven not by the needs of the people so memorably interviewed, but by its own need for narrative closure. *Housing Problems* has the political intention of improving conditions for working fam-ilies, but it has the semiotic effect of producing not *solutions* to *problems*, but *vic-tims* for *experts*. It is this move which has become traditional in television reporting ever since: 'Given that the victim was to become a staple of the realist documentary, especially on television, the significance of *Housing Problems* can-not be overstated' (Winston, 1995: 45). News and actuality stories routinely adopt the same 'grammar' as *Housing Problems*:

Subject: visualizing the 'problem moment' (Winston, 1995: 42), together with vox pops of victims;
Verb: action by experts who also represent corporations, whether commercial or governmental;
Predicate: happy consumers commenting enthusiastically on the measurable improvements they have experienced.

In these narrative terms, then, *Housing Problems* is a founding text of televisual-ity, establishing the conventions by which reality was to be recognized, before the medium itself was invented, and in that sense it looks very contemporary. But some elements of it now seem peculiar or even slightly ludicrous, as one would expect from a 60-year-old film. For instance, the interview shots *look* very odd to a TV-literate eye. The subjects are mostly posed very formally, look-ing directly into the eye of the viewer. The framing is too wide, the lighting too perfect, the composition very formal, the camera too static, the take too long. The whole thing is too cinematic, classic, in its composition, causing the action to occur in front of the coolly observant camera, rather than taking the camera into the action. Paradoxically, the film-maker Edgar Anstey, thought it was precisely this detached, disciplined immobility which gave the film over to its subjects. He later explained the effect he and Arthur Elton were looking for:

Nobody had thought of the idea which we had of letting slum dwellers simply talk for themselves, make their own film . . . we felt that the camera must remain sort of four feet above the ground and dead on, because it wasn't our film. (Quoted in Sussex, 1975: 62)

Housing Problems glimpses television's intimacy and involvement by going into the homes of ordinary people, but it retains a cinematically trained vision of what such intimacy ought to *look like*.

Similarly, the interviews, which are its main claim to fame, *sound* very peculiar to the TV-tuned ear. It is perhaps quite hard to recover a sense of how innovative they were at the time. In 1935 ordinary people did not participate in public culture without a script. Interviewees on BBC radio, for example, had to follow a script, even if they were engaged in what was intended to sound like an impromptu or improvised conversation. Working people, speaking for themselves, were almost unknown in mainstream cinema, which was in its spectacular, fictional, commercial, American heyday at this time. The idea of seeing real people tell the truth of their own circumstances in their own words, without the aid of an on-screen interviewer, was indeed an innovation, but of course it has since become standard practice. What is odd about the interviews to the post-television viewer is exactly that part which did not take hold as a routine semiotic practice. The people are speaking directly to 'us' with eye-contact (the interviewer is never seen). Their stories are constructed out of the anecdotal traditions of working-class speech, which makes them sound rambling and repetitive to the ear trained in the sound-bite.

Housing Problems prefigures *institutional* as well as semiotic attributes of television. As a socially campaigning film which was none the less sponsored by a commercial interest, it provides an exact model of the *commercial* form of 'public service broadcasting' that is still in place today. It managed to show, seemingly quite naturally, out of the realities of the situation, that the commercial interest of the gas industry (increased supply) was also the national or public interest (better housing). The film's public service agenda is still central to the editorial doctrines of TV journalism: investigating problems in the organization of modern society; focusing on improving the everyday; prioritizing the needs of ordinary people in central government planning; showing an almost mystical belief in the ability of (capital-intensive) technological inventions to solve social problems. *Housing Problems* is in many ways a straightforwardly commercial film, being funded by commercial investment, made by a production team which charged commercially for its services, and shown in commercial cinemas as part of a visual experience which consumers paid for. But all this was seen as quite compatible with innovative semiotic and social ideas that promoted non-commercial, even radical interests. In short, the 'mixed economy' of public semiosis and private enterprise which has been a feature of television ever since was fully in place before TV was born.

Housing Problems was revolutionary in the same way that Bolshevism was revolutionary – it favoured centralized planning and the imposition of expert knowledge to implement modernizations whose form was governed by experts, not by the people whose problems they were expected to solve. This revolutionary modernism extended to the use of film itself as the most advanced and the most popular information medium of the day to propagandize these changes in people's lives. *Housing Problems* proposes the destruction of entire neighbourhoods and their replacement with hitherto untried schemes whose novelty is only matched by their breathtaking scale. The housing projects are promoted on the basis of values like hygiene, convenience, privacy and afford-ability, but none of the experts who designed them is ever seen on screen, nor asked to defend their schemes to the viewer, or discuss them face-to-face with the 'victims' of the slums who will be moved into them. Here, then, is the begin-ning of the use of the visual media (and television is still the most important site for this) for the *hegemony* of the modernizing knowledge-class expert (see Frow, 1995) to be established over the needs of the ordinary working population. This process capitalizes on the one productive force that knowledge-class profes-sionals can command (information), by turning it from merely instrumental power ('know-how') into real social power (the management of populations and of social change).

Meanwhile, of course, the eyewitness-victim, who plays no part in the decision-making process that results in a nice new tower block to live in, is wheeled back in at the end to comment, invariably favourably, on the improve-ments they have been 'given' by the experts. So it is in *Housing Problems*. The gratitude of the woman in her bright and breezy flat is palpable and touching (and achieved by *good lighting*), as is the urgent need of the man who has already 'lost' two of his children to the lethal conditions of the slums. But the truth of their emotion is no guarantee of the thing it most powerfully underpins, namely the ideology of expertise, which semiotically preys upon the condition of the working class in England to take power over the means of material and social reproduction in their name. This is the power of *Housing Problems*, and of tele-vision after it – a power to cause change as well as to record it, by naturalizing *as* public opinion the passions of the knowledge class, and thence, in due course, swaying government policies and public resources towards its own mediated image of the desire of publics.

Housing Television

Notwithstanding its semiotic difficulties, *Housing Problems* certainly illustrates a real 'problem' for television. Only a year before its inaugural regular broadcasts, many people were short of decent housing in which to put a TV set. Many pre-TV dwellings are not very promising sites for domesticity, leisure and con-sumption. The 'slum-dwellers' of *Housing Problems* had to cook on a gas-ring in the same room they slept in, and could not store food overnight because it would either go off with the combined bad breath of five or more people sleep-ing, or it would be subject to vermin attack (both of these points are made by interviewees in *Housing Problems*). Cooking, washing and keeping the place clean were difficult with communal water taps out in the yard or landing, and doing heavy laundry was impossible. So there was a strong incentive to spend as much time as possible out of the home: sending the children outside for their health, eating in cafés, and taking the washing to laundries. Talk and play were available in the back alleys; entertainment in the pubs and other urban attractions.

Television was invented not as a 'mass' medium, but a *domestic* one. Its economic platform and cultural form were developed in the USA in the 1940s to provide programming as entertainment, rather than as individualized two-way communication like the telephone. Programming was supplied by central-ized agencies (networks) to private consumers. In New Deal America, and throughout the 1940s and 1950s, 'mass' private housing was perfected, in sub-urbs and high-rises, as the necessary precondition for television, which in turn became the advertising medium for promoting the values of domesticity and the products and services by means of which that ideology could most visibly be espoused (see Spigel, 1992; Attallah, 1991). For TV to succeed, consumers had to be at home. To be at home, they needed two things:

1. *capital investment* in the home to *sustain* their activities there;
2. an *'ideology of domesticity'* which would *maintain* their pleasures there – rather than in the street, pub, cinema, music-hall – or even in brothels or communism.

'The home' – as opposed to mere dwelling – was initially a fantasy in the minds of social planners and engineers, Victorian philanthropists who were motiv-ated equally by the 'plight' and the threat of the uncontrolled urban working poor. It was thus a solution to the problems of urbanization, industrialization and population-explosion in modernizing societies in the nineteenth century (see Donzelot, 1980). The 'problem' was an uncontrolled and ever-increasing urban working class, but instead of controlling such a beast from the outside, with repressive state apparatuses like the law, government, armed forces, prisons, police, and eventually psychologists, it was thought better by some to create the conditions for self-control and self-administration by the populace, producing a regime in which their wilder tendencies would be governed by themselves. In this campaign, the principal recruits were women. If women could get men off the streets, cause them to govern their unbridled lusts for alcohol, night-life and seditious assembly, then there would be no need for direct coercion. Women became the focus for a number of campaigns to achieve social docility, chief among which were temperance, hygiene and domesticity. A mother and wife offers alternative attractions to those of the city street; the home is a technology invented to amplify, secure and separate this alternative attraction. Comfort, cleanliness, cooking, security and regu-lated monogamous sex were on offer.

The home was invented as a single family unit, cut off from the neighbours by physical boundaries – walls at least, but ideally defensible space in the form of a front garden, however tiny. The interior was designed to accommodate a married couple and their children, with some minor variations like grannies (or lodgers, in declining numbers) in the back bedroom. The internal topography 'produced' family functions, with special emphasis on separating sex, hygiene and living – heterosexually conjugal parents in one bedroom, out of sight of their asexual children, who were ideally in single rooms each, or at least sorted by gender into pink and blue areas. Cleaning (surfaces, clothes and bodies) was separated from social living, wet areas from dry, as was cooking and food preparation, although many families contradicted planners by living in the kitchen. Capital investment in 'mass housing' was dedicated to this model of the family/home.

The ideology of domesticity needed to 'people' such an environment was promoted via campaigns, both political and commercial, that were grounded in existing aspects of respectable life like religion, femininity, thrift, shame, privacy, self-help and property (see Spigel, 1992). These now centred on the home rather than on their earlier sites – the soul, as in Bunyan, or the workshop, as in traditional artisanship. The home became more than a dwelling, more than a refuge. It became a lifestyle in itself and in the activities it was expected to sustain. Individual dwellings were *proletarianized* in the first half of the twentieth century, extending both upwards, with high-rise and high-density social housing in urban centres, and outwards, as suburbia went from the bourgeois exclusiveness of the Victorian period to mass-housing developments on uniform, speculatively built housing estates. Housing was *democratized* after the Second World War, and television made its domestic appearance as an essential part of that process.

Thenceforth television was associated with the company it kept – personal experience, private life, suburbia, consumption, ordinariness, heterosexual family-building, hygiene, the 'feminization' of family governance; in short, the ideology of domesticity. Indeed, these things have become so ineradicably a part of the general description of TV's 'textuality' that by looking at the historical conditions of its earliest context-of-use, we have arrived at a recognizable description of the 'textual tradition' *within* TV without looking at a single programme. TV is one of those many arts where form follows function, and thus 'textual analysis' is required of the semiotic environment surrounding the medium, not simply of individual shows or segments.

Housing Problems – Take Two

The semiotic environment of *Housing Problems'* day included something of a craze for slum-clearance stories in the media, on the radio, literary documentary and journalism. An intriguing example, published in the year before *Housing Problems* was released, is a double-page story in the *Weekly Illustrated* of 17 November 1934, under the headline 'Pull Down the Slums!' (see *Creative Camera*, 1982: 586). Pictures by Kurt Hutton show overcrowded tenements in East London, and compare them with the light and airy pleasantness of new developments and new suburbs or a 'big block of modern flats': exactly the strategy used in the later film. The news-copy reports on a 'great National scheme of slum clearance' that had been launched in March 1933, pointing out that *media publicity* has made it into everyone's business, not just that of the slum-dwellers themselves: 'Now, at last, pictures, films, books and articles – above all the statistics and opinions of health-workers and scientists – have brought home to every one of us the need for complete, immediate clearance of the slums.' The photographs are juxtaposed as a photo-essay, and captioned to present a stark, binary choice:

How human beings live.
A row of old houses in a slum quarter of London. Life here is one long
struggle to keep the home clean and tolerable . . .
. . . AND HOW THEY OUGHT TO LIVE.
A big block of modern flats for workers in St. Pancras.

A CONTRAST IN HOMES – THE GRATING 'FRONT WINDOW' OF A BASEMENT,
AND THE FRESH AIR OF A GARDEN SUBURB.

'Down below that grating is a window. Behind that window is a single room.
Inside that single room there live five people – three of them children.' The contrasting suburb gives the bright hope: 'What does it mean to boys and girls to be
removed from the filth of the slums and set down where there is sunshine, air,
trees, rabbits, [*rabbits?*], and green fields?' Naturally, the caption-writer (almost
certainly Tom Hopkinson) cannot wait long enough to answer his own question,
but the answer does not matter, for all the ideological work is done by the pictures – they make it seem *self-evident* that 'removal' to a green-field site in the
middle of nowhere is better than a grating in the middle of Town.

Weekly Illustrated's treatment of 'housing problems' pre-dates the film, but
uses exactly the same 'arguments' as *Housing Problems,* and even hints at a bit of
a media 'feeding frenzy' on the issue during 1933–35. But there is more. 'Pull
Down the Slums!' belongs to another visual tradition which is just as important
as that represented by *Housing Problems.* The creative force behind *Weekly
Illustrated* was Stefan Lorant, who went on to found *Picture Post*, and *Picture
Post*'s editor during its legendary, wartime years was Tom Hopkinson, associate
editor and caption-writer for *Weekly Illustrated.* The photographer responsible
for the slum story, Kurt Hutton, also went on to become a staff photographer on
Picture Post. Just as *Housing Problems* occupies a pioneering place in the history
of screen semiosis and in film studies, so the much less well-known *Weekly
Illustrated* story marks a pioneering moment in British photojournalism, for it is
the vision – the punchy radicalism of the *photo that shows* and the *caption that
tells* – that is carried through to fruition in the great days of *Picture Post* (see
Hopkinson, 1982: 580–95).

The link between 'Pull Down the Slums!' and *Picture Post* goes beyond the
biographies of the creative personnel. Their interests in popular visual media, in
the material conditions of working-class people, and in radical politics, were in
turn carried right through to the beginning of another, much more recent tradition, this time an intellectual one, namely *cultural studies.* Kurt Hutton's 1934
Weekly Illustrated picture of 'a slum quarter of London' was retaken by *Picture
Post* (possibly by Hutton himself), in April 1939, to illustrate 'the conditions
which have led up to the rent-strike'. After another 30-odd years, the same picture was republished as the frontispiece for some of cultural studies' own founding texts in *Working Papers in Cultural Studies* (*WPCS* No. 2, 1972) – in this issue,
Stuart Hall analysed 'the social eye of *Picture Post*' while Phil Cohen located
'subcultural conflict and working class community' in the very housing estates in
London that *Housing Problems* had wished upon the population:

> The pattern of social integration that had traditionally characterised the East End
> began, dramatically, to break down. . . . This breakdown coincided with the whole-
> sale redevelopment of the area, and the process of chain reactions which this

triggered. . . . No-one is denying that redevelopment brought an improvement in material conditions for those fortunate enough to be rehoused. . . . But while this removed the tangible evidence of poverty, it did nothing to improve the real economic situation of many families . . . But to this was added a new poverty – the impoverishment of working class culture. (Cohen, 1972: 14–16)

Among other cultural effects, Cohen suggests that the physical redevelopment of East End slums produced a new reliance on consumerism, on media-defined needs, arising from a new form of social organization which isolated people into families, and families into homes: the neighbourhood and extended kinship networks were no longer accessible to young mothers in high-rises, and while 'only market research and advertising executives imagine that the housebound mother sublimates everything in her G-Plan furniture, her washing machine or non-stick frying pans', the alternative is pathologized – 'feeling herself cooped up with the kids, cut off from the outside world, it wouldn't be surprising if she occasionally took out her frustration on those nearest and dearest!' (1972: 17). The result, suggests Cohen, was the development of subcultures like Mods and skinheads, whose dress (*see*), music (*hear*), speech (*say*) and ritual (*do*) formed the original *subject* of cultural studies itself: a three-level strategy of analysis:

1. *'historical analysis'* (meaning class analysis);
2. *'structural or semiotic analysis'* of the subsystems and the way they are articulated and change;
3. *'phenomenological analysis'* (which became better known as ethnography). (1972: 22–3)

This is a new beginning for the 'textual tradition' in cultural and therefore in television studies; a recognition, on the one hand, that 'semiotic' (textual) analysis of meaning systems (seeing, hearing, saying, doing) is required in order to understand socio-structural change and, on the other, that such analysis must be set in the context of history and life.

Textual Traditions – Take Two

It is significant that the Birmingham Centre for Contemporary Cultural Studies (CCCS), founded by Richard Hoggart as the most influential recent British powerhouse of theorizing about 'culture' and thence television, should have taken its cues from *Picture Post*, from the condition of the working class in England, and from mid-century radicalism. Under the directorship of Stuart Hall, and with a collective 'speaking position' which was Marxist, the CCCS began to work systematically towards an analysis of culture which was class-based, theorized from (Marxist) first principles, and intended not to describe culture but to change it (and a lot more about Britain besides). In short, the CCCS became a radical think-tank, and as a result it was interested not in tradition at all, but in radical ruptures – 'conjunctures' in history in which intellectual movements may coincide with popular discontents to produce new challenges to 'traditional' power structures.

The effect of this agenda on Stuart Hall's reading of *Picture Post* (in the same issue of *WPCS* as Cohen's article) is instructive. He obviously *likes* it, and in a long article where he analyses it from several points of view – historically, semiotically and politically – he is both astute and complimentary about its achievements. But *Picture Post* was a commercial undertaking, not a political one, and its success beyond its own covers was *democratic*; it did not represent a 'sharp break with the past', and its politics was based on reform, not resistance:

> *Picture Post*, in photographs and text, registered with remarkable veracity the substance and quality of ordinary life. Its mode of 'telling' was direct. It was strongest in capturing the native strengths of English life 'under pressure'. Its 'social eye' was a clear lens. But its 'political' eye was far less decisive. It pinpointed exploitation, misery and social abuse, but always in a language which defined these as 'problems' to be tackled and remedied with energy and goodwill: it was instinctively *reformist* – in both a good (humanist) and bad sense. It never found a way ... of relating the surface images of these problems to their structural foundations. In this dimension, we can see a clear continuity between *Picture Post* and the 'social problem' area of television documentary in a later period. (Hall, 1972: 109)

In short, *Picture Post* was 'strongest' in capturing the 'native strengths of English life',[2] as well as its 'problems'. Hall makes a forward link between *Picture Post* and television, and he also makes an explicit link back to *Housing Problems*: 'The British documentary impulse was rooted in the Thirties: without it, *Picture Post* could never have happened' (1972: 96).

But what were Hall's *political* objections to *Picture Post*?

> The brisk, activist, resiliently *cheerful* note in the magazine, inscribed everywhere in its pages, paralleled the stubborn cheerfulness, the underplayed heroism, the wartime quips and repartee, the shelter-humour and the Blitz folk-lore which were authentic manifestations of a collective popular spirit; in essence, a 'culture' of the Home Front. (1972: 103)

So far, so good; but in Hall's analysis, cheerfulness, authenticity and 'perfect equivalence' with the 'collective popular spirit' are by no means good enough:

> There is a highlighting in a *Picture Post* photograph – of the Blitz, of unemployment, of people's everyday pursuits: an accenting of the essentially *human* and the essentially *ordinary* qualities of experience. There is a rhetoric of change and improvement there, of people capable of resilience and courage: but there isn't anywhere a language of dissent, opposition or revolt. ... *Picture Post*, as Orwell saw, could retain its authenticity only because it was constantly and resolutely in touch with a movement for change which had surpassed 'party labels' and 'the old distinction between Right and Left', and because it spoke straight to 'multitudes of unlabelled people who have grasped ... that something is wrong'. But *what* was wrong *Picture Post* had no language for. (1972: 109)

The effort to create the 'language' for 'what was wrong' was in fact the project of CCCS in the disputatious 1970s; in such a context, the *textual tradition* of *Picture Post* – cheerfulness, ordinariness, talking straight and voting Labour – was a *defeat*. As far as Hall is concerned, and Orwell is his key witness (indeed, his only one), the chances for an 'English Revolution' had come and gone somewhere between 1941 and 1944. In the early part of the war, Orwell wrote, in what Hall signals as a 'crucial' passage:

> If one wishes to name a particular moment, one can say that the old distinctions between Right and Left broke down when *Picture Post* was first published. ... [Such media as *Picture Post*] ... merely point to the existence of multitudes of unlabelled people who have grasped within the last year or two that something is wrong. But

since a classless, ownerless society is generally spoken of as Socialism, we can give that name to the society towards which we are now moving. The war and the revolution are inseparable. (George Orwell, quoted in Hall, 1972: 105)

Later, Orwell recanted – he called the passage above a 'very great error', for 'after all we have not lost the war . . . and we have not introduced socialism' (Orwell, in Hall, 1972: 107). Hall comments that the war drew the classes together, rather than polarizing them, but this democratizing tide was an impediment to 'structural change':

Orwell was right, then, to remark that the conditions were there for an 'English Revolution' of a quite new and remarkable kind, and that such conjunctures would be few and far between: what he did not see ... was how quickly a popular movement, without benefit of conscious radical leadership and articulation, would crest and find its limits. ... The radical version of social democracy, which attained its peak in the early days of the 1945 Labour Government, was as much as that popular drift to the Left could manage unaided. And *Picture Post* represented the high water-mark of the tide of social democracy as a legitimated 'structure of feeling'. (1972: 108)

The analytical rhetoric which makes *democracy* a *defeat* is highly characteristic of the British Left, Old and New, and it has entered contemporary television studies in interesting ways, not least through the work of one of the New Left's most important writers, Raymond Williams, whose phrase 'structure of feeling' (which is sometimes revived as a kind of 'definition' of culture) Hall borrows here to signify the moment when all was lost, from the revolutionary point of view. There is a characteristic trace of this *anti-democratic* leftism in the textual tradition in TV studies to this day: a pessimism about the political potential of the popular media, and a habit of reducing 'popularity' to 'populism,' democracy to defeat.

But in fact the new popular media were taken up at the time as being the very place where the old distinctions between Left and Right, working class and capitalist class were least relevant, least sustainable. Rather than insisting upon them, popular media ignored them, gathering their audiences and topics from both sides of the class and political divides. Before television was invented, radio broadcasting was attracting attention as the place where cultural change could be heard and felt by everyone, as Philip Gibbs observed when he met Sir John Reith, founding Director General of the BBC:

There is a never-ending conflict between the high-brows and the low-brows, who try to tear him down, because the first accuse him of pandering to the lowest tastes and the others accuse him of intellectual snobbery. The Die-Hard mind charges him with using the air as an instrument of subversive propaganda. The Left Wing mind asserts that he is the paid agent of Toryism. . . . It is all very difficult for Sir John Reith. But the B.B.C. has entered the life of England with immense and irresistible influence. (Gibbs, 1935: 129)

Since 1935 the idea that if it is upsetting 'both sides' it must be getting things about right has become a self-serving cliché of the BBC, but the point remains, that broadcasting *gathers* different populations, politics and tastes, rather than choosing between them, and it is precisely this – the fact that everyone is exposed to points of view they do not hold and cultural material they do not like – that critics of both Left and Right have disliked about television's textuality.

Similar descriptions of – and doubts about – the new England of broadcasting, suburbia and democracy were expressed by literary writers from Priestley and Gibbs, via Orwell, to Williams, Hoggart and Hall, all the way to contemporary cultural studies. But it is worth stressing that something was lost along the way. The radicals of the Left disliked 'social' democracy, suburbia and the 'unaided' political consciousness of the ordinary suburban population as much as did the radicals of the Right. They did not like popular visual culture's ordinariness and authenticity, but this rhetoric can also be used against democracy itself, for stupidly remaining cheerful and having fun, when there is *structural change* to be done. Raymond Williams has this mood too, as the book of his TV criticism makes clear. The editor, Alan O'Connor, explains at one stage:

> The radical May Day Manifesto movement, in which Williams played a key role, wished to break the Labour–Conservative hegemony over national politics but itself collapsed over the issue of whether or not to run its own candidates in the election. Williams later developed a sharp criticism of representative democracy and electoral politics, arguing for the more radical demands of a system of direct rather than representative democracy. (O'Connor, in Williams, 1989: 106)

This is the textual tradition in TV studies: 'radical demands' which neither television nor democracy seem able to meet, resulting in a passionate dislike for representative – democratic – fun (see Attallah, 1991). Here is Williams himself, from a column written in 1969:

> There have been things so bad recently, yet so characteristic, that the struggle over whether to mention them is acute. But what sort of life can we be living if we are prepared to sit down and watch a quiz show between 'the William Rushton trio' and 'the team of the Rt. Hon. Quintin Hogg MP? . . . It is necessary to say, flatly, that one doesn't like the look of it. (Williams, 1989: 67–8)

'What sort of life can we be living?' One where it was not self-evidently a disaster for figures from popular culture and politics to sit down and have fun together;[3] one where television, like *Picture Post*, suburbia and the Labour Party, was taking the path of social democracy, rather than radical restructuring and resistance (settling for 'old orders and young pseudo-freedoms', in Williams's view). Williams's passionate dislike of its results – having fun in an early version of *Have I Got News for You?* – has its roots in the period before television was around, and interestingly enough it is the passionate dislike that has survived into the textual tradition in TV studies, not the fun.

Enough!

I want to close by pointing to the damage done, not by social-democratic television, but by the 'textual tradition' of denunciation TV has suffered. I have argued all along that since this rhetoric pre-dates television it is not strictly about television, and since it seems to be held equally by critics of the Right and the Left it is not strictly about politics either. It is more like the home-talk of the knowledge class; the class which wants to take power over information media and cultural technologies like television, not only by running the culture business on behalf of the shareholders and stakeholders, but by regulating it, and controlling the literacies and discourses by means of which it is understood. The 'default setting' of this knowledge-class chit-chat about television is as pernicious as it is hypocritical.The television critic Chris Dunkley points out why this is so dangerous:

> Although in terms of numbers television is the most popular mass medium the world has ever seen, in Britain it appears to have virtually no friends, or none with much influence. Politicians, press, lawyers, police, academics, clergy, the solid centre of the middle-class intelligentsia, all seem more or less inimical to television. (Dunkley, 1985: 119)[4]

Dunkley quotes a teacher who thinks reading the *Beano* comic would benefit her 10-year-old students more than watching David Attenborough's *Life on Earth*, on the grounds that anything is better than 'bloody television'. He makes an important general point:

> Worst of all for the future of the medium is the antagonism not of any particular professional group but of a seemingly large proportion of that band of people known as 'opinion formers': authors, journalists, critics, designers, playwrights, publishers, theatre and cinema producers, and so on. It is depressing to find that the very people who should be leading the way in bringing discrimination to the use of this new mass medium are still dismissing it lock, stock, and barrel. (1985: 125–6).

This 'deeply dispiriting array of virulent reactionism, folk mythology and Luddism' persists, though Dunkley does not put it this way, as a knowledge-class conspiracy against the audience – a conspiracy by 'opinion leaders' against the led. As Dunkley suggests, new digital, satellite, cable and multimedia technologies are forcing change, and it is the control of these changes that is sought by the knowledge class (or loss of it feared, more accurately). In this context, the textual tradition in TV studies turns out to be part of the conspiracy, training audiences to discount their own encounters with television, and to speak *about* it as if they are cultural or social critics still locked into the fears and passions of the 1930s. Certainly much of that we currently 'know' about television's textuality has been taught not by television itself, but by opinions that pre-date it. Perhaps by now, when the 'new mass medium' is 60 years old, the time is ripe for the textual tradition to look to its own past and its own processes, rather than trying to govern television's future, and everybody else's with it. Meanwhile, the residents of the real East End, where *Housing Problems* was filmed, are re-immortalized in the gritty authenticity of their own TV soap opera, *EastEnders*. But despite more than 60 years of semiotic investment, they still live in the poorest borough in England.[5]

Notes

1. *Housing Problems* (1935, 15 minutes) was made by Arthur Elton and Edgar Anstey for the Gas Council of the British Commercial Gas Association. It is available for hire from the British Film Institute.
2. 'Native', even though it was the creation of an *émigré* Hungarian Jew, Stefan Lorant, and used *émigré* German photographers, Kurt Hutton, Felix Man and Tim Gidal, among others. See Tim Gidal (1982), 'Modern photojournalism – the first years', *Creative*

Camera, No. 211, 572–9. He says: 'It should be stated here that *Picture Post*'s photojournalism, and this means to a very great extent British photojournalism, was imported into London by three reporters ("three bloody foreigners") who were emigrants from Germany and immigrants to England.' Bill Brandt, another legendary *Picture Post* photographer, was brought up in Germany.

3.   It is fascinating to find that Willie Rushton (cartoonist, comedian) and Quintin Hogg (politician) as quiz-show guests so irritated Williams, for Rushton was a co-founder of the magazine *Private Eye*, scourge of Fleet Street and the establishment in the 1960s, but never allied with a Left faction, and Hogg – better known as Lord Hailsham – was one of the last of the 'One Nation' Tories, noted for coming out strongly in favour of the Welfare State, in the pages of *Picture Post* no less, against his own parliamentary colleagues, when the Beveridge Report was being debated in 1943. In other words, both Rushton and Hailsham were cultural and political *radicals*, and both were also 'popular' celebrities, but they occupied the very space of social-democratic optimism that Williams dismissed as 'degutted and personality-mongering'.

4.   Chris Dunkley was 'Fleet Street's first mass media correspondent and also television critic' while working for *The Times* from 1968, before becoming television critic of the *Financial Times* from 1973.

5.   The London borough of Tower Hamlets. Official statistics, released in February 1997.

References

ARNOLD, M., 1869: *Culture and Anarchy*. [ed. John Dover Wilson, 1932], London: Cambridge University Press.

ATTALLAH, P., 1991: 'Of homes and machines: television, technology and fun in America 1944–1984.' *Continuum: The Australian Journal of Media and Culture*, 4, 2: 58–97.

COHEN, P., 1972: 'Subcultural conflict and working class community.' *Working Papers in Cultural Studies*, 2: 4–51.

CREATIVE CAMERA, 1982: 'Fifty Years of Picture Magazines', No. 211, July/August.

DONZELOT, J., 1980: *The Policing of Families*. London: Hutchinson.

DUNKLEY, C. 1985: *Television Today and Tomorrow: Wall-to-Wall Dallas?* Harmondsworth: Penguin Special.

FROW, J., 1995: *Cultural Studies and Cultural Value*. Oxford: Oxford University Press.

GIBBS, P., 1935: *England Speaks: Being Talks with road-sweepers, barbers, statesmen, lords and ladies, beggars, farming folk, actors, artists, literary gentlemen, tramps, down-and-outs, miners, steel-workers, blacksmiths, the-man-in-the-street, high-brows, low-brows, and all manner of folk of humble and exalted rank, with a panorama of the English scene in this year of grace 1935*. London: William Heinemann.

GOULDEN, H. and HARTLEY, J., 1982: '"Nor should such topics as homosexuality, masturbation, frigidity, premature ejaculation or the menopause be regarded as unmentionable." English Literature, schools examinations and official discourses'. *LTP: Journal of Literature Teaching Politics*: 1, 4–20.

HALL, S., 1972: 'The social eye of *Picture Post*'. *Working Papers in Cultural Studies*, 2:70–120.

HOGGART, R., 1957: *The Uses of Literacy: Aspects of Working-Class Life with Special Reference to Publications and Entertainments*. London: Chatto & Windus.

HOPKINSON, T., 1982: '*Weekly Illustrated*: photojournalism's forgotten pioneer'. *Creative Camera*, No. 211: 580–95.

LEAVIS, F. R., and THOMPSON, D., 1933: *Culture and Environment: The Training of Critical Awareness*. London, Chatto & Windus.

LOTMAN, Y., 1990: *The Universe of the Mind: A Semiotic Theory of Culture*. Bloomington and Indianapolis: Indiana University Press.

RICHARDS, I. A., 1924: *Principles of Literary Criticism*. London: Routledge & Kegan Paul.

SPIGEL, L., 1992: *Make Room for TV: Television and the Family Ideal in Postwar America*. Chicago: Chicago University Press.

SUSSEX, E., 1975: *The Rise and Fall of British Documentary*. Berkeley: University of California Press.

WILLIAMS, R., 1989: *Raymond Williams on Television*, ed. Alan O'Connor. London and New York: Routledge.

WINSTON, B., 1995: *Claiming the Real: The Documentary Film Revisited*. London: BFI Publishing.

3

Histories of British Television

Gill Branston

As soon as a powerful institution is founded, its practices imply a history. That history is implied through the slightest of signifiers: the choice of a coat of arms or memos which invoke traditions while they may still only be bad habits. Institutions of television are no different and in the practices of Britain's oldest and most traditional broadcaster, the British Broadcasting Corporation, such history-making is no less evident.

Then come the historians, official and unofficial. In the case of the BBC, its unofficial history-making can be discerned in its publicity and in the televised repeats and compilations of programmes through which it celebrates its anniversaries. Clearly, in this process, the BBC is constructing its history in partisan ways. But more formal histories – those constructed by historians – are also always implicitly positioned. They may support the BBC's public service obligations or revise them from another perspective – for instance, feminist or free marketeering. They may be a product of Television Studies of the 1960s or 1990s, with their very different moments and interests. Whatever their positions, material has to be selected from which to make a version of history and to claim authority (to justify public/ation) for it, however much claims of authority may be more or less conscious of their partiality.

Increasingly even the decisions involved in choosing for study one period or emphasis over another are now rightly scrutinised as an undeclared part of 'history', as a discourse which makes the past a comfortingly boundaried and narrated place. Over time, the most powerful versions of history are reconfirmed, they become sedimented down, pressed into new narratives and accounts. These always involve taken-for-granted assumptions which in turn shape the relationship of television's legislators, trainees, practitioners and historians in an imaginary past and an even more speculative future.

This essay explores the BBC in the changing histories of British television and the different places, discourses and debates where those histories are found and made. Through this, I want to question some of the imagery through which it is currently most academically acceptable to argue and construct television histories.

TV Archaeologists

Imagery of archaeological excavation can be eloquent in evoking the fragility and difficulty, as well as the pleasure, of making argument and proof in historical enquiry. The language of glimpsing absences as well as evidence, of the settling down of data so it comes to seem the natural dark loam of context itself, has inspired much recent writing (see Thumim, 1995). Oddly, though, such imagery often seems to use and re-image archaeology – a very material method of historical enquiry – in order to reinforce the 'over-correction of empiricism' (Corner, 1995a: 152) in recent theory. When archaeological imagery is used in accounts which are radically sceptical of the possibility of *any* kind of proof or evidence, some reminder of the material structuring of archaeological research may be useful.

Archaeologists are as materially positioned as any other type of historian. They are funded, with research grant expectations and hypotheses; some sites are available for excavation and others are not; they look to piece the scattered shards of history together according to pre-existing theories. But this need not mean that certain objects cannot be – *for the time being and for particular purposes* – convincingly assembled as evidence.

The problem is a familiar dichotomy, one side of which is the way empirical data can sometimes take on a life (and an interest for the audience) of its own. It is hard simply to note that research in the television archives shows that visibly bad teeth were much more taken-for-granted in 1950s' television celebrities than they are now, without stopping your audience in its tracks for a moment. But the theory needed to configure such empirical evidence towards more than anecdotal status often works in an over-abstract and totalising gear change, and indeed can have the effect of rendering the evidence invisible again.

Archaeological imagery, emphasising the fragility of data, is only one of several ways to display an awareness that the past is both partially retrievable or 'in evidence' and at the same time can no longer be viewed as unarguable historical fact. Historical (including archaeological) evidence continues to be, has been and always will be embroiled in attempts to appropriate it in debates which are political, in Stanley Fish's sense of 'the attempts to implement some partisan vision' (Fish, 1994: 116). Accounts of television's past need to invoke more openly images of struggle, and to make 'good enough' conclusions for working political purposes. Again, in Fish's words:

> When the present shape of truth is compelling beyond a reasonable doubt, it is our moral obligation to act on it and not defer action in the name of an interpretive future that may never arrive. (1994: 116)

For instance, William Boddy offers convincing evidence that it was not at all certain that television in the USA of the 1940s had any commercial potential; manufacturers expressed doubts that people would devote time and concentration to it. Later, in the 1950s, under intense pressure from advertising lobbies, there were huge struggles – involving blacklisting and intimidation – over the issue of how to define and extend 'quality' television (Boddy, 1990a: 63–89). Because of such historical work, these struggles can be deployed in academic and journalistic debates on broadcasting where the model of American television is often simply asserted as an effortlessly acclaimed, popular media environment suited to marketing commodities.

Relatedly, US and British broadcasting in the 1930s has been recently shown to be as often a public medium – viewed in cinemas and laundrettes in Britain as late as the 1950s – as much as the private, domestic medium commonly assumed. Early histories of broadcasting, too, are often told as compelling stories, oddly combining a technological teleology with imagery of biological birth, growth and maturity. The assumptions here can be tested against evidence of the 1930s' relationship between CBS radio network and Paramount Film Studio in the USA, and between radio and the military in both the USA and in Britain. In all these cases, such evidence deserves retrieval for political debate as well as for the making of rigorous, sophisticatedly empirical histories.

Writers in this book, like all television scholars, are positioned by our place and moment in the history of Television Studies. Trying to judge, argue the nature of our moment as well as of the past is of course part of what is at stake in such debates. The contemporary, late 1990s' moment seems to be one when the area is no longer dominated by interest in factual television forms. The 'bite' of insisting on the place of fantasy, pleasure and audiences has become something of an orthodoxy of study. It is certainly a moment when the continued existence of public service broadcasting (PSB) in Britain is at risk and needs re-thinking and re-remembering. In terms of what can be most easily written, it has to be said that for academics the moment is one when the conditions of higher education make shorter, especially conceptual pieces of writing more feasible and rewarded than long-term, especially empirical work (Gray, 1995: 166).

All this is to say that this essay, like any attempt at television history, has to be cautious about the nature of evidence, and the discourses and interpretations to which evidence is subject. Yet to deny that anything can be stated as true (or, at least as 'true enough for working purposes') shades into a crippling theoretical relativism, devastating for the vitality and momentum of intellectual or political argument. The case for evidence, for a theoretically aware empirical dimension to argument, needs maintaining, especially in the area of political debate, which now includes tabloid journalism. Walter Benjamin's imagery of a flashing historical recognition being grasped for the purposes of polemic deserves repeating:

> The past can be seized only as an image which flashes up at the instant when it can be recognised ... To articulate the past historically does not mean to recognise it 'the way it was' (Ranke). It means to seize hold of a memory as it flashes up at a moment of danger. (Benjamin, 1973: 257)

The Nature of the Evidence

In the case of television, debates over what is to count as evidence are troubled by the ephemerality of its raw material, even at the relatively tangible level of programmes made. Of course, there are archives like those of the UK's National Film and Television Archive and the BBC's Written Document Archive where scripts, publicity, production documents and videos can be studied. But more early television programmes are simply not available for study than is even the case with early film, which at least has continuous if incomplete material from the 1890s onwards. Though some television was recorded on film from the earliest years of television in the 1930s, video recordings by television professionals, which really make study based on programmes possible, only began to be used in 1958 for the pre-recording of programmes (Bryant, 1989: 13).

The more widespread use of video by television audiences begins much later in the early 1980s with the introduction of affordable VHS and Betamax systems and, with them, millions of individual, amateur archives of favourite programmes and cinema films screened on television (see Gray, 1987 for gender aspects of this process).

Oddly enough, all this makes evident the opposite problem – the impossibility of imagining even the output of one television channel as a physical object of study because of the sheer amount of what ought to count as textual evidence, let alone the problem for all archives of assessing the perishability of the records on the still unknown quantity of video tape.

Yet such archival problems are never simply matters of space or when video recording becomes possible, affordable or reliable. They are inextricably bound up with value judgements and struggles over choices and preferences for limited space, whether in the archive or in versions of history. The assumption that, compared to cinema and emerging from radio, television's defining characteristic was its 'liveness' meant that video recording was not adopted as early as it might have been. Relatedly, the low status of television as pastime in its early years (in Britain, from 1936 to 1939 and again from 1946 onwards) produced the attitude that television's output was simply not worth preserving (Bryant, 1989: 19).

Hence, the predominant early use of video was in making programmes rather than in preserving them. Later, when preservation was perceived as a financial and then commercial possibility, news and documentary programmes were largely alone the ones deemed important enough to preserve and therefore now constitute the most readily available early 'historical evidence'. Other types of programme have disappeared, especially entertainment forms, because of historically powerful assumptions about their lack of seriousness and worth, and the significance accorded to male and more middle-class audience preferences.

Of course, this is not a direct result of elite power groups reproducing 'great and good' programmes. As Steve Bryant points out about the early days of television:

> From the broadcasting organisation's point of view, the main reasons for preserving parts of its output are for its own re-use or for sale to other broadcasters; both as complete programmes or sections thereof . . . the problem then arises of how to predict which items will be most sought after. (Bryant, 1989: 2)

Then there is the nature of the archive itself and the way it often reproduces the practices of its parent institution: how information is selected, catalogued, displayed, retrieved or easily overlooked. Finally, for some groups the process may work in reverse, as seasons of archive material produce new histories like the ones on gay and lesbian television beginning in 1992 at the National Film Theatre in London.

Moments and their Reconstruction

For the purposes of this essay, historical study of British television can be organised around several themes and debates. It is worth noting that the choices are governed by a contemporary agenda. In 10 years time, it is likely that these themes and debates will change; perhaps via the growing popularity of the Internet and its ways of constructing news and debate differently from the press and television, or its potential for cheap screen-editing, for example.

First, there is the debate about changing attitudes towards the BBC as a *public service*, beginning with its founding moments. Key words here are *entertainment, quality* and (in forms designated 'non-entertainment') *impartiality*. This has so far corresponded broadly to the preoccupation of early Television Studies with factual and news programming, and its emergence from a male-dominated Sociology rather than Film Studies/Literature, its other parent.

Second, these key words can now be seen as deeply bound up with perceptions of and anxieties about *American-ness*. This was often identified with commercialism, and then – a key move – conflated with free-market positions. It was often also conflated with the hegemony and spectacular success of American entertainment forms across the media, and the different degrees of seriousness attributed to *the viewing practices of men and women,* given that women were often assumed to be the ones enjoying these suspect American forms. Feminist histories and excavations into generic status, viewing pleasures and domestic reception have partly stemmed from challenges to these perceptions, as well as from desires to explore and validate women's experience and achievements both within and outside television. The spirit has often been that of the feminist slogan 'the personal is political' and has tended not to be interested in issues of *public* service.

Finally, emphases first made by Raymond Williams (1974) on production *technologies* have developed to include histories of the technologies of consumption: television sets and other screen forms in the home rather than the transmitter's production of colour signals (Silverstone, 1994; Moores, 1993; O'Sullivan, 1991). These are part of the opening up for historical study of television's domestic context and the gendering of its *audiences* which is distinct from the preoccupations with the political economy and production of television in earlier, often male-dominated research such as the Glasgow Media Group's work on news or Asa Briggs's history of broadcasting. Williams's formulation against technological determinism is still a key one, now for production, reception and also audience measurement technologies, emphasising as he does the need to 'restore *intention* to the process of research and development. The technology would be seen ... as being looked for and developed with certain purposes and practices already in mind' (Williams, 1974: 14).

Moments and Excavations of 'Public Service'

The useful image of the historical moment can easily slip into the over-tentative way of historicising which I have argued *can* be part of archaeological imagery. Nevertheless I want to offer an account of an important 'moment' in the history of British Television, which includes what some would say is its pre-history: radio. The moment is the emergence of PSB which, borrowing navigational imagery, I will try to position in a triangulated relation to the place of PSB in more recent years, and to television in the 1950s.

The furore in the summer of 1996 over proposals to merge BBC Radio's World Service with domestic radio news services flashed up yet again the rhetorical and political possibilities of discourses about public service via various appeals to history. These appeals were often submerged in quite different discourses involving ambassadorial reminiscences, drenched in nostalgia for the rituals of the British Empire and in celebrations of its imperial and commercial global media power (and silences about the vetting role of MI5, the Foreign and Commonwealth Office etc.). For instance:

> In 1964 I married my Persian bride ... in the cool of the garden, under the trees, lunch would be served. At precisely 2pm each day a short wave radio would be brought to the table and everyone would go silent to listen to the BBC World Service news' ... (Temple Morris, Letter, *Guardian*, 20 July 1996)

and, again:

> successive governments have thought it worth while to fund the World Service ... [it] is an invaluable asset for British business too. It is one institution which does make Britons abroad proud to be British. (Mark Tully, *Guardian* 21 July 1996)

Ideas of public service in this case are clearly bound up in the service of residual ideologies of imperial power. At the same time, however, the concept of public service allowed campaigners to mobilise discourses of impartiality which, though subject to important critiques over the last 30 years, have been a strategic resource for defending investigative and critical broadcasting in Britain. The notion of PSB itself, then, is by no means self-evident.

It appears as a concept in Britain around 1922, based on ideas of public service among the Victorian ruling order (Curran and Seaton, 1991; Scannell and Cardiff, 1991), service done by the great and the good to the not-great and ungood. Public service has long been posed against commercial interests. Yet two commercial drives in the formation of broadcasting are now clearly visible, partly because of the strength of free-market emphases in the 1990s, and a growing awareness that these need not be synonymous with commercial, let alone materialist, ones.

The public corporation of the Post Office was made responsible in 1922 for licensing pre-VHF airwaves. The purpose was to avoid the chaos argued to have arisen from unregulated broadcasting in the USA. But, like the radio manufacturers who wanted to sell as many sets as possible, the Post Office also wished to profit from the service it licensed. These two bodies therefore collaborated to establish the British Broadcasting *Company* to create a market for radio receivers. Advertising, so often fingered as the motor of the later rival commercial system, was rejected as a funding basis not out of any principled objection but because of the resistance of the powerful popular press which risked losing advertising revenue. Indeed, newspaper opposition ensured that not until much later was the BBC allowed its own news-gathering staff or to broadcast daily news before 7 p.m. (after the sale of evening newspapers), even though all news derived from the same sources – press agencies like Reuters.

Nevertheless this founding moment is also one of *public* commercial corporations. One of the early enquiries into British television, by the Sykes Committee of 1923, defined broadcasting as 'a public utility' like water or clean air. It was famously stipulated that broadcasting should be neither a commercial monopoly nor subject to direct state control. A series of further committees thereafter enacted the dialogue between the state's definition of public interest and the broadcasters' claims to defend it. Of these latter, the most spectacular agent was of course John Reith, Managing Director of the BBC in 1923–26 and then first Director General of the replacement British Broadcasting Corporation.

The key points of Reith's manifesto to the 1923 Crawford Committee were: PSB should be a universal service with right to access for all; PSB depends on 'unity of control' or what Reith later called 'the brute force of monopoly'; it should not be used for entertainment purposes alone; it should lead rather than pander to public taste; it has an educative role; it can help create an enlightened and informed democracy; it has the capacity for 'making the nation as one man', often through the broadcast of national ceremonies.

As with all positions, these need to be read in their historical context. To take one instance, Reith's emphasis on the democratic, educative potential of PSB needs to be read as a response to the restriction of the Post Office and the press on the BBC's ability to deal with *any* matter of public controversy at the time.

Public: 'The Nation as One Man'

In recent histories, there has been a slight but significant revision of Reith's reputation at the centre of broadcasting history (see, for instance, Scannell and Cardiff, 1991: 6–8). Such shifts of course make up the ways that urgent contemporary debates – such as, here and currently, the future of the BBC – shape the contours of historical perception. Yet, digging down into the loam of Reith's historical presence, the words 'making the nation as one man' still constitute particularly vivid evidence for contemporary readers, many of whom could pose very pointed questions of them.

For instance, whose national identity is presumed here? England, or rather a very select/ed part of the Home Counties is implicit in the accents, assumptions and even the sporting events covered by early broadcasting. If the UK is 'the nation', how are the nationalities of Ireland, North and South, to be treated? If it is Britain, how do Wales and Scotland feature? John Davies's account of the history of broadcasting in Wales makes it clear that from the beginning one of the key *national* difficulties for Wales was that some Welsh communities could more easily be reached by radio from England than from the Welsh capital of Cardiff.

Relatedly, to which social class is this man assumed to belong? As late as 1955, the following parliamentary statement was possible. It relates to the 'fortnight rule', an agreement between Prime Minister Churchill and the BBC towards the end of the Second World War which forbade BBC comment on matters tabled up to two weeks before and during debate in Parliament, a rule that remained in force until 10 years after the war:

> [The fortnight rule] is going to be settled by the people who broadcast, and among these is commercial television. This alters the situation. If it were only the BBC I could understand some argument for a gentleman's agreement, but with commercial television we are, by definition, not dealing with gentlemen. (Patrick Gordon Walker, *Hansard*, quoted in Sendall, 1982: 239)

Walker's evident aristocratic animus against the commercial class relates to the social exclusions that resonate in Reith's defining ideas of public service broadcasting: the exclusion from decision-making processes of social classes other than his own. The fortnight rule also elicited expressions of anxiety by members of the main political parties that the BBC could ultimately appropriate for itself the status of a forum for public debate to match that of Parliament (Allan, 1997).

It is worth asking after the connection between notions of public service, Reith's nation-binding 'ceremonies' and their apparent historical polar opposite, 1990s' tabloid journalism's preoccupation with the Royal Family. Consider that the BBC's 1930 Yearbook proudly boasts that 'Broadcasting's *greatest opportunity of service* in the past year lay in keeping the nation informed of the King's health' (53: *my emphasis*).

Is it a 'nation' or really a state which is so taken-for-granted? And who is making this nation? Again, the following from the moment of the General Strike in Wales (rather than the more familiar English example) focuses technological and national histories untypically:

> [Reith] was particularly anxious that broadcasts should be available in the coalfield, for they could, he believed, 'do much to combat the doctrines of Communism and Bolshevism so sedulously preached there'. For this reason Cardiff was among the first of the provincial stations to operate on the highest power of kilowatts. (Davies, 1994: 15–16)

Finally, questions of gender. 'One man': what about the nation's women? Feminist studies of television's man-made history have focused, although unequally, on women as workers within television industries and on women as audiences, approaches which have valuably developed a more optimistic empirical model of the female audience (Geraghty, 1996: 320). Furthermore, just how 'manly' is Reith's 'man'? Would camp comedian Julian Clary count as a national role model? Andy Medhurst's (1991) account of the painful homosexual repressions of 1950s' television celebrity Gilbert Harding is a rare sketch of how television patrolled heterosexual identities.

The final part in the triangulation concerns the moment of the 1950s as focused by threats to Channel 4 in the 1990s. It is now easier to make the case that the 1954 Broadcasting Act which introduced commercial television to Britain was an extension rather than an erosion of PSB. Indeed, the contradictions of a commercial, profit-orientated network founded with PSB requirements without the benefit of funding from license-fee have recently surfaced quite sharply in arguments about Channel 4. Though funded by advertising, Channel 4 had arguably the most exciting public service remit of all channels in its 1980 terms of reference: 'as a particular charge the service of special interests and concerns for which television has until now lacked adequate time ... a favoured place for the untried to foster the new and experimental in television' (Lambert, 1982: 170).

Channel 4 was set up as a statutory corporation able to plough back profits into the programmes it commissioned. Michael Grade, Head of Channel 4, saw that state of affairs threatened by rumoured government plans to privatise Channel 4. As the *Guardian* newspaper reported, 'Ironically, it is precisely because many Tory MPs and media analysts believe [Grade] has successfully stretched his [PSB] remit to commercially successful limits that the station is in their sights ...' (Culf and White, 1996).

Related developments in the 1950s can illuminate debates not only over PSB in the 1990s but also its relation to gender, ethnic and national identities. Take a very specific national example from 1957. The commercial English regional company, Granada, began to broadcast a series of hour-long Welsh language programmes twice weekly. This astonished BBC Wales, whose PSB remit extended to only 30 minutes' broadcasting weekly in the Welsh language. There were urgent commercial imperatives for Granada to augment its income by adding advertising time while the BBC could not afford to expand its hours of broadcasting. Again, in 1957, Independent Television (ITV), the network commercial channel, was determined to undermine the notion of 'prescribed hours' allocated by regulation to specific audiences such as children. ITV won a scheduling victory when it abandoned the 'toddler's truce', enabling it to provide general programming in the coveted 6–7 p.m. empty slot provided by a break in transmission between children's programmes and the rest of the evening's provision. The result impacted on regional broadcasting as well as on discourses of the family, the female audience and television (Davies, 1994: 212–16). In both cases, commercial imperatives drove advertising-led channels to embody a fuller sense of 'public service' than the official 'public service' BBC.

Such instances of an increase in cultural democracy effected by directly commercial broadcasting imperatives are also evident in histories of the representation and prospects of media employment of black British people, now available for recognition partly as a result of more recent struggles around the same areas of representation and employment. Jim Pines's collection of interviews with media workers is a rich source of evidence (Pines, 1992). Two examples: 1956 saw the establishment of the first agency to represent and promote black acting talent in Britain. It also saw black actor Cy Grant, one-time RAF pilot, prisoner of war and barrister 'singing the news' in calypso on *Tonight*, a BBC current affairs programme which was itself a response to the fresher style of ITV information programmes. For matters of archiving, there were several appearances in the early 1960s by two black actors on the long-running soap opera *Coronation Street*, though this was overlooked when the series celebrated its 30th anniversary in 1990.

Recent and current research by feminist scholars such as Pat Holland, Joy Leman and Janet Thumim into 1950s' British television production will make more visible this period when cinema audiences were in decline, when television's perceived importance was increasing and when key areas of audience research methods, programming and scheduling were consolidated.

Conclusion

There is much to make of current television developments. There will soon be multi-channel provision with increased audience choices dissolving into new patterns of consumption like surfing and netting, with new viewing experiences and challenges to the quality of attention given to the television screen. Nevertheless, it is likely that some sense of 'the public' will persist and therefore, alongside it, traditional political and socio-economic levels of argument (Corner, 1995b). Indeed, it sometimes seems that the polarisation of 'postmodern' and 'fundamentalist' structures of feeling which characterises both contemporary theory and political rhetoric is also constructed in the frequent contrast made between a multi-channel-surfing-future and tabloid/political fears about the disastrous effects of something called TV. All this suggests that, whatever changes are to come, notions of PSB will remain at the centre of British television and therefore of debates about its future and the nature of its past.

The imagery for debates over television histories, and the crucial estimate of PSB within those, needs to be continually struggled over, and there is recognisable energy and purpose in metaphors such as archaeological method and the 'flashing' recognition of historical moments and evidence. But an *over*-corrective emphasis on the provisional and always-discursive will not allow a sufficient appeal to empirical enquiry which, though always-mediated, has value, not least for connections with the experiences of others. It also risks losing the possibility of appeal to a less defensive, more future-oriented sense of the always-partisan, always-constructed nature of seeing and making history and futures called politics.

There are also possibilities within this perspective for feminist enquiry: to identify and pursue particular areas of research which lie around and beyond textual and audience work, now well established, and which would redefine where 'public' and 'private' are to be found. As Christine Geraghty points out, there has been a gender split between historians and theorists of, on the one hand, media production, regulation and control, and on the other, media texts, audience consumption and pleasures. Males have dominated the former area and female research has taken place centrally in the latter area. In her partisan slogan of 'taking the toys from the boys', Geraghty encourages important new directions for female scholarship in television history and Television Studies.

Dedication

I would like to thank David Lusted, Christine Geraghty, Janet Thumim and Kevin Williams for encouragement and advice during the writing of this essay.

References and Further Reading

ALLAN, S., 1997: 'News and the public sphere: towards a history of objectivity and impartiality'. In M. Bromley and T. O'Malley *The Journalism Reader*. London: Routledge.

BBC Yearbook, 1930.
BENJAMIN, W., 1973: *Illuminations*, London: Collins.
BODDY, W., 1990a: *Fifties Television: The Industry and its Critics*. Urbana and Chicago: University of Illinois Press.
———, 1990b: 'Building the world's largest advertising medium: CBS and television 1940–60'. In Tino Balio, (ed.), *Hollywood in the Age of Television*. London: Unwin Hyman.
———, 1991: 'Spread like a monster blanket over the country: CBS and television 1929–33' in *Screen*, 32, 2.
BRIGGS, A., 1985: *The BBC: The First Fifty Years*. Oxford: University Press.
BRYANT, S., 1989: *The Television Heritage: Television Archiving Now and in an Uncertain Future*. London: British Film Institute.
CORNER, J., (ed.) 1991: *Popular Television in Britain: Studies in Cultural History*. London: British Film Institute.
———, 1995a, 'Media Studies and the "knowledge problem"', *Screen*, 36, 2.
———, 1995b: *Television Form and Public Address*. London: Edward Arnold.
CULF, A. and WHITE, M. 1996: 'Fight over Tory plan to sell off Channel 4'. *Guardian*, 27 August.
CURRAN, J. and SEATON, J., 1991: *Power Without Responsibility: The Press and Broadcasting in Britain*. London: Routledge.
DAVIES, J., 1994: *Broadcasting and the BBC in Wales*. University of Wales Press/BBC Press.
FISH, S., 1994: *There's No Such Thing as Free Speech and It's a Good Thing Too*. New York and Oxford: Oxford University Press.
GERAGHTY, C., 1996: 'Feminism and media consumption'. In J. Curran, D. Morley and V. Walkerdine, *Cultural Studies and Communications*. London: Edward Arnold.
GLASGOW UNIVERSITY MEDIA GROUP, 1976: *Bad News*. London: Routledge.
———, 1980: *More Bad News*. London: Routledge.
———, 1986: *War and Peace News*. London: Routledge.
GRAY, A., 1987: 'Behind closed doors: video recorders in the home'. In Helen Baehr and Gillian Dyer (eds), *Boxed In: Women on and in Television*. London: Pandora.
———, 1995: 'I want to tell you a story: the narratives of *Video Playtime*'. In Beverley Skeggs (ed.), *Feminist Cultural Theory*. Manchester: Manchester University Press.
LAMBERT, S., 1982: *Channel Four: Television with a Difference*. London: British Film Institute.
MEDHURST, A., 1991: 'Every wart and pustule: Gilbert Harding and Television Stardom'. In John Corner (ed.), *Popular Television in Britain: Studies in Cultural History* London: British Film Institute.
MOORES, S., 1993: *Interpreting Audiences: The Ethnography of Media Consumption*. London: Sage.
O'SULLIVAN, T., 1991: 'Television, memories and cultures of viewing 1950–65'. In John Corner (ed.), *Popular Television in Britain: Studies in Cultural History*. London: British Film Institute.
PINES, J., 1992: *Black and White in Colour: Black People in British Television Since 1936*. London: British Film Institute.
SCANNELL, P., and CARDIFF, D., 1991: *A Social History of Broadcasting Vol. 1 1922–39*. London: Basil Blackwell.
SENDALL, B., 1982: *Independent Television in Britain, Vol. I Origin and Foundation 1946–62*. London: Macmillan.
SILVERSTONE, R., 1994: *Television in Everyday Life*. London: Routledge.
THUMIM, J., 1995a: 'Common knowledge: the nature of historical evidence'. In Beverley Skeggs (ed.), *Feminist Cultural Theory*. Manchester: Manchester University Press.
———, 1995b: 'A live commercial for icing sugar – researching the historical audience:

gender and broadcast television in the 1950s'. *Screen*, 36, 1.
————, forthcoming: 'Mrs Knight *must* be balanced: methodological problems in researching early television'. In C. Carter, G. Branston and S. Allan (eds), *News Gender and Power*. London: Routledge.
WILLIAMS, R., 1974: *Television: Technology and Cultural Form*. London: Collins.

4

The Making of a TV Literate Elite

Lynn Spigel

> We are looking for the electronic medium's version of Izaak Walton's Compleat Angler, a man who combined a poet's passion with an encyclopedic technical knowledge ...
>
> Lawrence Laurent, 'Wanted: The Complete Television Critic', 1962.[1]

On 20 January, 1961, on the occasion of John F. Kennedy's inaugural address, Robert Frost recited a poem before the television cameras. As legend has it, during his appearance on live TV, the sun was so blinding that Frost had to discard his manuscript and recite from memory. Commenting on this, one TV critic claimed that Frost 'humanized and ennobled the merely formal ceremonies. Everyone at such a moment is in the position of "seeing Shelley plain".'[2]

At the end of the decade in 1969, a lesser-known poet, Professor Robert Baram, published a piece in the Television Academy's journal, *Television Quarterly*. Entitled 'Television – The Fifth Dimension – a poem', its sensibility was somewhere between the premier Beat poet Alan Ginsberg (who had earlier written a poem about TV) and TV comedian Henry Gibson (who played the buffoonish 'poet laureate' on *Rowan and Martin's Laugh-In*). In two columns of verse running down the page, Baram spoke of television's vapid commercialism ('Bah Bah Black Sheep/have you any bull/yessir, yessir, three networks' full'), of TV intellectuals ('There's David Frost/from across the sea/to bring us electronic/intellectuality'), and of momentous national events made possible through the merger of space science with telecommunications ('That's the way it is/Walter Cronkite/with one small mankind/for stepping on evil men/our enemies/Moon, June, Spoon/bring back some rocks/from the Detroit riots').[3]

Although many people at the time would have said that Robert Baram was no Robert Frost, historians might view this tale of two poets as a particularly significant parable for the way America imagined television in the 1960s. While Frost's TV appearance at the beginning of the decade was largely done in the 'New Frontier's' utopian spirit of national uplift through the arts and sciences, Baram's verse expressed the disappointments of a TV nation where commerce reigned, where the arts were represented by pseudo-intellectuals with British accents, and where science served only to expose the country's misconceived technological agenda.

Despite the differences between these two examples, the fact that poetry was being used not only on TV, but also to talk about TV, was itself symptomatic of transformations in the ways in which people conceptualized the medium in the 1960s. In the previous decade, aesthetic criticism of television was primarily conducted under the auspices of the newspaper review, where it was mainly delegated to arts and entertainment critics (the most influential of whom were New York theatre critics). Meanwhile, in the universities, television scholarship was largely the purview of social scientists and administrative researchers who extended their interest in radio broadcasting toward questions of TV's effects, especially its effects on family life. The 1960s, however, saw the inauguration of a new kind of television criticism. Now television became an object of debate among a more 'literate' culture of intellectuals, including English professors, poets and visual artists. So widespread was this ethos at the turn of the decade that even Newton Minow, Chairman of the Federal Communications Commission (FCC), drew on the renewed popularity of American poets when he delivered his famous T. S. Eliot-inspired 'Vast Wasteland' speech to the National Association of Broadcasters in May 1961. In that speech, Minow not only criticized the networks for their 'steady diet' of formulaic commercial pap to the exclusion of quality (meaning arts and educational) TV. He also gave official government standing to a new form of 'quality' TV criticism that was laced with allusions to a literate culture and written with a scholar's penchant for poetry and rhetorical flourish rather than the newspaper columnist's breezy jingoism or the crack reporter's fetish for facts.

How did this figure of the erudite TV scholar emerge? How did he or she develop a critical protocol through which to define what exactly constituted 'knowledge' about television as well as the form through which this knowledge should be communicated?[4] How have TV scholars defined their reading publics? Why have they, and the knowledge they have produced about the medium, been so divorced from newspaper criticism? And why have they been relatively detached from policy decisions such as the recent budget cuts for PBS (Public Broadcasting System) or the decisions leading to Congress's 1996 Telecommunications Act?

As a way to understand the history of Television Studies in the humanities, I want to trace the institutional sites and discursive fields through which it was generated. Above all, I want to show that academic Television Studies emerged through the set of shifting relations between high and low, business and art, fun and ethics, the arts and sciences, the academy and press that generally characterize the cultural tensions of postwar America. In fact, one of the central paradoxes running through my own attempts to define this field (if we can call it that) is the refusal of Television Studies to organize itself according to the typical binaries which assert that culture exists apart from the material spaces of commerce and everyday life.

The emergence of Television Studies in the 1960s is a paradigmatic case history of the intimate relationships between industrial and intellectual production. Indeed, despite its attempts to retain some degree of critical distance from the broadcast industry, academic television scholarship was – in part – invented by it. In the following pages, I especially focus on the role that the Columbia Broadcasting System (CBS) and the National Academy of Television Arts and Sciences (NATAS) both played in the organization of this academic field. Along the way, I demonstrate that the role of the critic in contemporary Television Studies is constituted by the unlikely merger of two seemingly antagonistic ideals: the classical ideal of criticism as a 'public service' in a democratic public sphere and the modern industrial ideal of criticism as a form of promotion and public relations.

Of Hacks and Highbrows

By the end of the 1950s, the television industry was in the midst of a serious public relations crisis. Generally seen as the end of a 'Golden Age,' this crisis entailed the move from New York 'live' production (especially the prestige anthology dramas like *Goodyear Playhouse*) to series production in Hollywood. It was capped off by the infamous Quiz Show Scandals in which producers and sponsors were accused of rigging the games by feeding answers to contestants before the shows. The Scandals precipitated a set of ongoing tensions among networks, affiliates, sponsors, syndicators, packagers, regulators, producers, agents, actors, policy-makers, audiences, and – most importantly for my purposes – TV critics. Golden Age press critics such as Robert Lewis Shayon, Jack Gould and Gilbert Seldes spoke in increasingly antagonistic ways about Hollywood commercialism, blaming networks as well as regulators for their irresponsible management of the public trust.

The networks responded in kind. As William Boddy has shown, network executives publicly denounced the critics as 'egghead' intellectuals who wanted to impose their 'marginal' tastes on the population.[5] Characterizing them as undemocratic snobs, casting doubt on their credentials, and claiming that they had no influence on anyone anyway, industry executives effectively cut the critics off at the pass.

Despite such battles, however, the structural relation between the television industry and the press was not founded on competition *per se*; instead it was characterized by the tensions inherent in the vested interests between them. At the press, television was a lucrative source of 'news' in its own right. By 1958, almost 80 per cent of US daily newspapers with a circulation rate over 50 000 had television editors, a percentage higher than that for business-finance, real estate, garden, education, and art editors.[6] What made the job of the TV critic so important to the press was his or her close liaison with television stations and networks, which needed to publish and promote their schedules (and numerous newspaper chains themselves owned and operated TV stations). Even while television industry executives attacked newspaper critics, they still had to find ways to court and flatter them.

An illuminating example here is NBC public relations czar Sydney Eiges, whose files contain his correspondences with people at the press. In his letters, Eiges addressed newspaper columnists with the gift-giving language of courtship, sending them flowers, steuban glass vases, champagne, RCA TV sets, air conditioners, and even such personal items as hankies and dresses. Moreover, if we can judge by the letters that Eiges saved in his files, most of the recipients for these gifts were women; and even if the recipient was male, Eiges addressed him as if he were in the 'feminine' role of romantic 'conquest'. The journalists usually responded in handwritten script on personal stationary, even flowery note cards, engaging in the flirtatious game that Eiges set in motion.[7]

Given their close ties with public relations departments – as well as their 'feminized' status – it comes as no surprise that TV critics were often attacked as hacks and hypocrites. Their feminized role as 'love' object of the Don Juans of public relations made television critics the 'whores' of the newspaper trade.

In this regard, TV critics were caught in the structural contradictions of a fully commodified public sphere. On the one hand, they were ideally supposed to operate in and through the utopian ideals of a 'free press' – a place where democratic speech and reason prevailed. On the other, they were expected to answer to market forces – readership statistics, advertising revenue, promotional activities. While all other labour at the press operated in and through the same ambivalences and contradictions, the peculiar nature of a journalist who provided 'information' about 'entertainment', who spoke of private industry as if it were imbued with public purpose, who evaluated mass culture through a classical tradition of criticism, all of this made the TV critic especially vulnerable to charges of hypocrisy, and particularly in need of defence.

TV critics at the time wrote voluminously about the need to define what it meant to be a critic and the need to legitimate themselves as respectable sources of knowledge. This 'role of the critic' genre regularly spoke to the impossibility of writing about mass culture from within its own institutional spaces – especially within and through the popular press. Newspaper columnists often discussed the conflicts inherent in their double task as TV promotions staff and proper critics, complaining that they had to work in noisy news rooms; address a largely uneducated, even disinterested public; write meaningfully at overnight speeds. Moreover, unlike theatre or movie critics, TV critics wrote 'after-the-fact' about fly-by-night programmes that would probably never be seen by anyone ever again. For such reasons, TV critics wondered about their overall function *vis à vis* the more accepted role of the popular critic – i.e. edification through evaluations that would (supposedly) raise the tastes of the 'masses'.

At its extreme, these labour conditions led to tales of desperation, depression, wasted lives. Jack Mabley of the *Chicago Daily News* found the job so debilitating that in his farewell column he explained, 'It would have been ten solid years if I had held out a few more months, but I won't, I quit'. Mabley was so exasperated with the job that he characterized TV viewers (also presumably, his readership base) as 'gunks who sit in front of that screen'. 'As for the professional critics who have been at it for five or eight or ten years', he claimed, 'I don't see how they can stand it.'[8] Mabley's disdain for his working conditions – a disdain he displaced onto his readers – was widespread. One form of relief came through the change in workplace and labour relations as the space of TV criticism moved from the newspaper to the college campus. The re-situating of knowledge about TV would (at least ideally) counteract some of the major concerns critics had about their labour. They would no longer be forced to write for deadlines, they would not have to work in noisy rooms and they would not be demonized as PR men. Even if all this meant that their audiences would narrow to the point where they were speaking to people who never even watched TV, critics might (ideally) escape the vagaries of self-loathing that led Mabley to throw in the towel. Given these idealized divisions between commerce and education, it is particularly ironic that, in large part, it was the television industry itself which offered critics this 'academic' defence against reality. As they moved from the newsroom to the classroom, TV critics invariably found themselves metaphorically walking in and out of the revolving doors of a third space – the industry boardroom.

Quality Criticism at CBS

The dismay that newspaper critics like Mabley felt about their jobs in the late 1950s dovetailed in the 1960s with the needs of other cultural institutions which saw ways to usurp the role of the critic and use it for their own purposes. Foremost among these institutions were television networks, museums, non-profit organizations, universities, publishing houses, and by the end of the 1960s, the Corporation for Public Broadcasting and the underground press. Often working cooperatively with one another, these institutions created strange liaisons between commerce and education that makes it difficult at best to distinguish the substantive difference between 'public service' and 'public relations'. In order to make that theoretical point – which is the major point I wish to make in this essay – I want to provide a genealogy of television criticism as it passed in and between these leading cultural institutions in the 1960s.

One of the first major attempts to overtake the role of the critic came from the television network, CBS – the only network to be directly indicted for its role in the rigging of quiz shows. Like the other networks, CBS alternately demonized TV critics as unschooled hacks and elitist highbrows. However, it also tried other tactics. Rather than simply mocking and repressing critics, CBS actually tried to create more criticism. CBS attempted to institute a new critical movement that quite literally would 'move' TV criticism out of the auspices of the popular press (where presumably it was read widely)[9] and into the ivory tower (where presumably it wasn't). Indeed, academic television scholarship was – like programming, audiences, advertising, and all other elements of the system – imagined and, in part, generated by the networks. We are, in that regard, the wish-fulfilment of the industry.

If this revelation seems hyperbolic, it is nevertheless the case that CBS was among the first initiators of a 'properly' academic brand of television criticism, a discursive form we can now recognize as something practised in Anglophone countries (especially the USA and Britain). In 1960 the network began commissioning articles for a quarterly magazine of television criticism.[10] Although the CBS journal never came to fruition, it did materialize in book form as *The Eighth Art*, edited by Robert Lewis Shayon and published by Holt, Rinehardt and Winston in 1962. As Shayon explained in the introduction, 'Some twenty-three articles were prepared and presented to the publisher with the understanding that the network would buy and distribute a portion of the first edition.'[11]

Given that Shayon was himself one of the Golden Age critics whom the networks had previously attacked (if not personally, then by implication), it is no surprise that he spent some time in this introduction reconciling himself and his readers to the fact that a network had helped to pay for the book. First, he reminds readers that 'this was not the first time that the Columbia Broadcasting

System has played patron to a book' (he was referring to CBS's sponsorship of Joseph T. Klapper's *The Effects of Mass Communications*). However, while Klapper's study fits into the long tradition of social scientific inquiry and/or market research supported by the broadcast industry, *The Eighth Art* was the first foray into qualitative television criticism that explored TV as a social and aesthetic practice.

For Shayon, the CBS logo did obviously pose ethical problems. He spent a good deal of time in the introduction expressing his ambivalences about the fate of criticism in the age of television. Noting that the interest in TV criticism was thin, he asked:

> Would this book have been published without a patron? Would a publisher, in a normal manner and upon its own initiative and investment have issued a comparable miscellany of critical essays on television which were all originals and not reprints? [12]

In response to his rhetorical question, Shayon seems to have reconciled himself to the company plan by engaging tropes of democracy so fundamental to the critic's discourse (at least since the Greeks). In this vein, he boasted that his book contained a gamut of views – not just corporate boosterism, but also negative critique.

Why, then, did CBS decide to initiate such a project? It seems likely that in 1960 the network had a lot to gain from becoming a patron of the TV arts. At a time when it was under heated attack, CBS attempted to control the climate of criticism by funding the critics – a true testimony to the power of corporate hegemony and its ability to incorporate dissenting views. I do not mean to suggest that all the people involved in the CBS project were by nature conspiring to stave off controversy. Instead, it seems more probable that they worked at cross-purposes with divided interests and ambivalent sentiments.

Whatever the case, it is clear that Shayon and CBS generated a book that looks more like contemporary Television Studies in the humanities than any other before it. It includes critical essays by professors of literature and qualitative communications, as well as the established newspaper critics and trade reporters. *The Eighth Art* contains ruminations on the social impact and meaning of television; essays on the industry, overcommercialism, and the future of educational/public television; early stabs at genre criticism as well as narrative analysis and interpretation. It even includes Laurant's self-reflexive essay on the state of TV criticism, as well as another article about the paucity of scholarly 'literature' about the medium.

Importantly too, *The Eighth Art* showcases British scholars and film-makers, thereby establishing what would become an ongoing, if somewhat 'never-quite-clear' relationship, between US and British Television Studies. But *The Eighth Art* presents British critics in a tokenistic fashion, offering no insight into the different national contexts and intellectual traditions in which British and US critics work. Instead, the inclusion of British scholars was probably more symptomatic of the book's overall concerns to distinguish itself as a form of legitimate scholarly criticism. In so far as 'Britishness' had always been associated with intellectuals and the 'arts', the British critics lent the CBS project a sense of higher learning and higher purpose. So too, the biographical notes on authors typically made reference to the university backgrounds – from Cambridge to

Harvard – from which this new breed of TV critics came. Thus, as opposed to simply mocking the eggheads, CBS flattered and showcased them. In effect, this book authenticated a new kind of critical elite which was singularly endowed with the 'purposeful' mission of knowing what constituted quality TV and knowing what constituted quality writing about it.

In this sense, the institutionalization of 'quality' TV was intertwined with the parallel construction of 'quality' TV criticism. Quality TV criticism was, according to the logic of the CBS paradigm, essentially different from the critical apparatus at the popular press, even if it drew on its major writers. It formulated a new range of enunciative rules. Its authors imagined themselves as learned thinkers slow to make conclusions rather than impressionistic hacks writing under deadlines. Its implied space of enunciation (that is, the place from which its statements seemed to be produced) was the cloistered campus rather than the bustling hubbub of newspaper rooms. Its implied reader was 'bookish' (someone who wanted to read about TV) rather than 'fanish' (someone who wanted to watch it). Its production practices and resources were also different. Rather than essentially an arm of the network public relations department, the TV critic was now 'funded' by network grants. That is to say, while CBS retained its economic stronghold over critics, it redefined the way it represented labour relations between them. Now critics were less explicitly part of the PR apparatus as the network became a patron of the TV 'arts'.

This patronage system gave CBS a more 'democratic' public image – especially since the book projected itself in the classical sense of criticism as a forum for debate. But, because democratic debate in late capitalism is always (or at least usually) already mediated through such commodified public spheres as television, its utopian aspirations are typically underachieved. Instead, like patrons for the arts more generally, CBS imagined an extremely cynical form of alienated intellectual labour. The intellectual would write for a few other intellectuals, which also means the corporation can stop the cash flow on the basis that the project they funded was 'irrelevant' to the general public and democratic debates at large. In this way, patrons can use the rhetoric of democracy to fund 'minority' intellectual interests when it suits them, or else stop funding these interests when it does not.

In this case, even while many people involved with the CBS exploits were probably working with good intentions, it seems likely that the network's executive offices were not simply in this for the pursuit of knowledge. Instead, these forays into TV criticism were also a form of public relations, a way that CBS could control its corporate image. And while the generation of critics to follow might never have perceived themselves as company men – and were in fact attempting to distance themselves from the criticism levelled at them in this regard – the critical project nevertheless developed in relation to, or at least on a parallel track with, the corporate discourse of PR.

While education and the arts continued to be an interest at all the networks, the development of Television Studies took place in other realms. As CBS withdrew its plan to publish a journal on the TV arts,[13] the discursive merger between television scholarship and corporate PR was cultivated by that most oxymoronic outlet of the culture industry – the 'non-profit' corporation.

Public Relations and Public Service at NATAS

One of the first institutional spaces where the transformation from journalist to 'scholar' took place was in and through the National Academy of Television Arts and Sciences (NATAS). During the late 1950s and throughout the 1960s, NATAS was a confused and often embattled organization, fraught with political infighting over purpose, power and prestige. These conflicts often hinged on the relationship between education and entertainment.

Founded in 1946, and first known simply as ATAS, the Academy was a paradigmatic example of the tensions inherent in American mass communications. On the one hand, it was dedicated to models of culture based on classical notions of democracy, edification and public service. On the other hand, in order to sustain itself, it had to make itself a commercially profitable organization that was not simply incidental to, but rather necessary for, the maintenance of the entertainment industry from which it sprang. Founded by TV reporter Syd Cassyd, along with a UCLA professor, an engineer at Paramount, and ATAS's first president, ventriloquist Edgar Bergen, the Academy's original board succinctly suggests the coupling of education and commerce at the heart of this endeavour.

Given its numerous constituencies, it is not surprising that ATAS was vulnerable to political divisiveness. Almost from the start, there were internal conflicts over the way this Los Angeles-based organization was representing itself as the official site for the production of 'national' standards for the television arts and sciences. Its Hollywood locale angered the New York newspaper critics, especially Ed Sullivan, host of the popular Sunday night show, *Toast of the Town*, and an influential theatre columnist in his own right. Sullivan fought to get control of the organization away from Hollywood, and he garnered support from local chapters across the country, which were equally bitter about what they perceived to be the Hollywood bias of the Emmy awards. By 1957, the original Academy of Television Arts and Sciences was transformed into the National Academy of Television Arts and Sciences, and Sullivan was elected as its first president. During the 1960s, then, NATAS served as the national organization that oversaw local chapters. Despite its local constituencies, however, NATAS was often caught up in political battles between the New York and Los Angeles chapters, which domineered over all other chapters.

These coastal wars were often represented as a split between education (high culture) and entertainment (popular culture). For example, when commenting on Sullivan's initial take-over, Dick Adler of the *LA Times* wrote:

> There have always been rumblings of discontent inside the television academy since it began as a Hollywood-based organization ... New York appears to have always looked upon Hollywood as the sausage factory, the place where canned comedy and cop shows came from. Hollywood's attitude toward its eastern colleagues was equally derisive: They were elite snobs who thought that their involvement in news and live drama gave them special status.[14]

This logic of coastal divide is, in hindsight, a vast oversimplification of the tensions between education and entertainment. Even while Syd Cassyd developed the pomp and pageantry of the Emmy awards and solicited stars to preside over his organization, he was committed to educational pursuits and held out against hiring public relations companies to promote the Academy and TV industry. Meanwhile, Sullivan was the quintessential cheesy showman, hawking Lincoln sedans and featuring the most historic of popular performances (Elvis, the Beatles), even as he imagined his stage to be a space of cultural enrichment, adorned with the Russian ballet and Italian opera. The Hollywood–New York split, then, was less based on science than it was on fiction. It came to represent a pleasing explanation for the very messy and chaotic indeterminacy surrounding critical judgements of television and its national purpose.

This indeterminate relationship between education and entertainment, symbolized by the geographical split, resurfaced symptomatically in the Academy's major educational pursuits of the early 1960s, which were conducted under the auspices of the Academy Foundation which was formed in 1959. At the start of the 1960s, and through the decade, the Foundation's major initiatives included: the formation of a television library and museum; the establishment of international links between NATAS and television industries around the world; educational television and lecture series (which it called the 'Forum'); sponsorship of university courses and fellowships; and the publication of its journal, *Television Quarterly*.

While it seems probable that many of the individuals involved in these Foundation activities were sincerely concerned with education and the arts, the Foundation was structurally conceptualized as a NATAS vehicle for public relations. It is significant in this regard that virtually all Foundation board leaders had ties to the television industry and virtually all were NATAS members. Educators were not generally on the various trustee boards and committees, and they did not attend meetings. At best, they sometimes served as liaisons or consultants. Most typically, however, educators were positioned in NATAS rhetoric as the grateful recipients of the public services that the Foundation performed.

The fact that the Foundation did not include educators on its governing board is symptomatic of its larger role as a public relations arm for NATAS. Although NATAS occasionally supported educators with seminars and a few scholarships, the Foundation more typically functioned as a spin doctor for both the industry and for NATAS itself. This PR function was so central to this 'non-profit' organization that NATAS and its New York and Los Angeles chapters all hired public relations companies to promote their concerns throughout the 1960s. In fact, the head of public relations for the New York chapter, Peter Cott, also helped direct the Foundation and oversaw many of its educational pursuits.

At the April 1966 meeting, the Academy recommended that PR campaigns be 'mounted with three publics in mind', including the National Academy membership (who needed a 'sense of pride' in the organization), the television industry and the public at large. Under the category of 'industry', the following suggestion was entered into the minutes:

> Through its public relations, the Academy should establish itself as the industry organization speaking for its highest ideals through such activities as the publication of *Television Quarterly*, its many forums and seminars, its fellowship and scholarship program, the National Library of Television and such services as the ETV Committee, the programs to inform users of public service time, etc.[15]

As the minutes suggest, the Foundation's educational efforts were conceptualized as a mode of public relations. Throughout the 1960s, NATAS used its educational programmes as a way to bolster the image of a television industry. In addition, NATAS launched these programmes in order to alleviate some of its own embarrassments about the Emmy awards, which by the early 1960s were considered something of a 'glitz and glamour' joke by industry insiders, rather than a mark of scientific or artistic excellence. A standard mode of operation, public relations was thus the very means by which the pursuit of public service could exist in the first place.

My argument, in this regard, is significantly different from a historiographical perspective that examines educators as a kind of 'heroic' group which exists – *a priori* – apart from and in conflict with the industry and its cynical, commercial goals. Instead, I am concerned with the way educators and industrialists often wind up as strange bedfellows, speaking the same language of 'public interest' even when their intentions and their interpretations of this term might be radically different because of what I have been calling a fundamental indeterminacy between the meanings of public service and the meanings of public relations.[16]

There have been numerous historical struggles to differentiate these terms, and scholars have been part of these. However, the problem is that clear-cut distinctions between public service and public relations, between education and commercialism, do not hold up. For as the cases of CBS or NATAS show, the institutions that govern broadcasting are always doing both at once, and are always reinterpreting the lines between them. The formation of Television Studies was very much rooted in an effort to do away with this discursive indeterminacy between public service and public relations. Indeed, the growth of Television Studies at the dawn of the 1960s can be seen as an attempt to create a semantic order, a binary opposition between public service and public relations and between the opposing terms these two fields of discourse generate (binary oppositions like education vs. commercialism, information vs. entertainment, art vs. kitsch, interactive vs. passive, etc.).

This attempt to create a field of 'semantic order' was registered in the first book-length studies of the medium. In his 1961 *TV: The Big Picture*, for example, journalist Stan Opotowsky tells his readers, 'The assignment was for an outsider, a man trained as a reporter but otherwise as naive as any other casual TV viewer, to invade the industry and find out the whos, hows, and whys'.[17] Opotowsky's assumption of the role of crack reporter immediately distances him from the degraded plight of PR-man for the TV industry. In many ways a transitional text, written by a journalist and yet academic in nature, *TV: The Big Picture* began with the historical development of the industry and ended with considerations of educational television and the 'future'. Opotowsky envisioned educational TV as a bold alternative to the present-day commercial system, implying that educators and the 'public' could and should exist outside of market forces. This basic logic continued with Yale Roe's 1962 book *The Television Dilemma*, Newton Minow's 1964 book *Equal Time,* as well as Erik Barnouw's seminal three volume history of broadcasting.[18]

The emergence of these books can therefore be seen as a symptomatic response to the discursive indeterminacy between education and commercialism. This scholarship is a reaction to the anxiety produced by the fact that people working in modern broadcasting institutions, including TV critics, are unable to separate PR from public service. Although scholars often shudder to think of themselves as part of the system, educational pursuits are typically generated by the self-interested discourse and practice of PR. From this point of view, the rise of Television Studies is not a simple matter of a few wise men at universities fighting against the cynical money grubbers at the networks, even if their books romantically propose this. (In fact, we might recall, as he does in his recent memoir, that Barnouw had worked in the industry for years before he emerged as its central historian.) The discursive practice we call Television Studies has a complex genealogy that crisscrosses through a hard-to-untangle web of cultural institutions and commercial industries – through production houses, networks, stations, advertising agencies, newspaper offices, non-profit corporations, industry unions, Congressional committees, publishing houses, cultural centres, museums, and universities.[19]

NATAS was part of this complex web, and it therefore seems useful to explore how the discourse of public service that NATAS used to relate to its publics dovetailed with the discursive rules that educators used to relate to theirs. These links were forged in the Foundation's major activities that set a stage for Television Studies and carved out a place for the emergence of TV scholars.

Of all the Foundation's activities, the museum and journal were the most rigorously pursued and successful. Moreover,while not directly intended to do so, they both have an important place in the genealogy of discourses that comprise contemporary Television Studies. They represent the formation of a critical canon by which programmes and related materials have been selected and preserved. They also represent the construction of discursive rules that generated objects, questions, topics, and ways to speak about television that were recognizably 'scholarly' and thereby differentiated from the standard 'review' format of the newspaper critic.

The efforts to build what was alternatively referred to as a library or museum were central to the Foundation from the start. In part, these efforts were propelled by competition among other museums and universities which also wanted to create a canon of TV art and an exhibition venue for it. As I have detailed elsewhere, the nation's leading museums took an interest in television from the start, seeing it as a possible venue for the exhibition of their collections.[20] In the early 1960s, NATAS considered partnerships for an archival site with museums in three major urban centres: the Museum of Modern Art in New York (which spoke of the 'obvious need for a central television archive analogous to [its] Film Library' as early as 1955, and which featured a 'Television Retrospective' in 1962[21]); the Hollywood Museum of Film and Television in Los Angeles (which, after numerous planning sessions and building starts, never came to fruition); and the Cultural Center in Washington (which was typically more interested in the fine arts than in mass media). But these partnerships never crystallized.

Instead, the Academy Foundation more aggressively sought liaisons with universities, of which the University of California in Los Angeles emerged as the most important. Although attempts were made in 1963 to nationalize the library efforts through what the Foundation called a 'National Literary Subcommittee' that operated out of New York, UCLA had typically served as the university liaison to the Academy. Throughout the 1950s, Cassyd spoke of his plans to create a television library at UCLA; in 1960 when UCLA began holding materials for the Academy, Cassyd was appointed Acting Curator by the Chancellor; by 1968, UCLA had established itself as the central university television archive in the nation.[22]

The holdings at the UCLA archive reflect NATAS's wider business and self-promotional concerns. As early as 1959, when the Academy Foundation first incorporated, public relations executive Peter Cott outlined a plan that served as the basic architecture for the library.[23] Cott's plan was also the basis of a set of discursive rules – that is to say, a 'canon' – for generating notions of what was 'collectable' from an educator's standpoint. He told Academy members of the need to 'establish criteria' for selecting programmes to preserve. He also spoke of the need to court 'networks, agencies, producers, etc.' for programme sources and to 'develop [the] relationship of [the] Library with unions and other organizations whose cooperation in terms of clearance and use of Library collection will be vital'. Thus, the canon was not established in some 'ivory tower' of critical distance; rather, it was established in relation to wider industry practices of copyright, ownership and tax exemptions, as well as the need to bolster the public image of NATAS, the television industry and the university itself. Indeed, anyone interested in the way television history has been conducted in the USA should start with the basic knowledge that terms like 'Golden Age' are never indicators of 'quality' in a non-commercial, 'art-for-art's sake' sense, but rather exist because of the marriage of public service and public relations. In fact, it is in the connection between public service and public relations that we discover the foundation upon which television came to have a history even before it had a certain future.

While Los Angeles thus became the home for television's historical preservation, New York emerged as the residence for television criticism. In 1959 Syracuse University approached NATAS with the possibility of starting a publication with a subscription base built into Academy membership dues. *Television Quarterly*'s first volume appeared in 1961, with a founding board appointed by NATAS and composed mostly of industry insiders including PR and advertising executives, television producers, broadcast journalists, network executives and Guild directors. PR man Sydney Eiges served as chairman of the original editorial board. *Television Quarterly*'s industry-heavy orientation was symptomatic of its more general attempt to produce critical scholarship of the medium while also serving the interests of commercial broadcasters. Its contributors ranged from educators to lawyers to literary professors to journalists to creative artists to station managers.

Over the course of the 1960s, NATAS used the journal as a vehicle for legitimation, promoting it as a source of detached and objective commentary, something entirely different from the newspaper hack. A 1961 report states, 'The journal will not be a "trade" magazine, or an industry news magazine – it will be a high-level, profound reflection of the world's greatest medium of mass communications through commissioned articles, transcripts of meetings and speeches, and features which will stimulate reader participation'.[24] At a 1966 national meeting of the board of trustees, Academy members linked *Television Quarterly* to a more general public relations campaign that it launched in part to counteract the print media's dislike for television. The minutes reflect that *Television Quarterly* was considered to be a central part of a NATAS public relations campaign through which the 'Academy should establish itself as the industry organization speaking for its highest ideals'.[25] In this respect, *Television Quarterly* was reminiscent of the 'quality criticism' generated by CBS; it rechannelled the critical project so that TV criticism (whether negative or positive) bolstered the television industry's image.

These educational efforts at the Academy Foundation played a structural role in the field of Television Studies. Their greatest legacy was the establishment of a structural divide between history and criticism that has been generative of the discursive rules for Television Studies generally. This structural divide was quite literally a coastal divide between the archive/library and the journal. The fact that historical research and access to programming were initially held regionally distant and institutionally distinct from critical writing on the medium has meant that much of the writing about TV is conducted by people who do not actually have access to research materials and programmes in the nation's major collections. The critical analysis of television programmes, in this regard, has tended to be impressionistic rather than contextually grounded in the history of a series' run and the 'supertext' of advertisements, promos and surrounding programmes in which it appeared. Meanwhile, television history was conceptualized within the framework of political economy which emphasized institutional analysis over narrative analysis. This writing emerged through the historiographical tradition of 'proper history' found in broadcast journalism with its penchant for the objective description of observable 'data' and its relative dismissal of subjective experiences (like aesthetics or pleasure). Most historians did not really make use of the archival holdings in the sense a critic – or critical historiographer interested in textuality – might.[26]

The kinds of essays published in *Television Quarterly* seem almost schizophrenic from this point of view. On the one hand, there are essays about the politics and structure of regulation, censorship, internationalism, educational television – essays informed by the rhetoric of objectivity and science inherited from broadcast journalism. The only programmes these scholars tended to discuss were news, documentaries and educational formats. On the other hand, the textual criticism published in the journal tended to be written either by English professors (who were mostly interested in the thematics of entertainment programmes and their relation to wider social issues), or else by industry people (who spoke about the techniques entailed in, for example, set design). Finally, as with the CBS project, British criticism was sometimes represented; but again, as with CBS, this seems to have been a way for the editorial board to pronounce its cultivated taste for 'quality' and 'public service' rather than a serious engagement with the British tradition of television criticism and practice.

The eclectic nature of this first scholarly journal was matched by its implicit view of its readership. From the start *Television Quarterly* was constituted in a triangulated purpose: it was a 'public service'/research institute for educators; a training ground and 'publicity' machine for the industry; and a public relations vehicle for NATAS itself. While these three functions did sometimes harmonize, they more typically produced conflicts and tensions between entertainment and education. At best, the journal had something for everyone. At worst, it was too commercial for professors, too academic for general readers and industry people, and a money drain in any case.

The confused editorial direction of *Television Quarterly* defeated the 'PR' purpose it was meant to serve. Over the course of the 1960s, NATAS and Foundation board members spoke of problems the journal had supporting itself. Because NATAS assumed the journal would eventually be self-supporting, it sought advertising dollars in addition to a subscriber base. But advertising funds did not materialize in sufficient quantities. In the early 1970s, *Television Quarterly* changed its editorial direction. By October 1973, NATAS President Thomas S. Sarnoff moved the journal from New York to California where, he stated, 'the cost would be less', and he aggressively sought support from advertisers and a distribution deal from NBC Entertainment. In his yearly report, he proudly took credit for the more commercial character of the journal. Reminding NATAS members that it is 'one of the Academy's best public relations efforts', Sarnoff reported that *Television Quarterly*:

> has now completed its first full year as a new magazine inside and out ... Its paid subscription list already exceeds the highest number reached in its previous nine years of publication; it carried four times the number of advertisements it ever had and it appproaches being self-supporting ... most importantly, however, TVQ's academic tone was successfully replaced with a more contemporary, relevant, lighter and readable format.[27]

As this statement suggests, the revamping of *Television Quarterly* was precipitated not only by the journal's financial distress, but also by NATAS's perception that academic criticism no longer served the purpose of PR. In fact, by 1978 the discursive protocols of academia and those of public relations had become so estranged that NATAS decided to split its publications in two. While retaining *Television Quarterly* in a quasi-academic format, in the winter of 1979 it introduced a new slick magazine known as *EMMY*. In that first issue, the editorial claimed *EMMY* was 'written for and about the TV industry' and would 'stimulate', 'entertain' and even make its readers 'laugh'.[28]

NATAS's rejection of the 'academic tone' should be seen in the context of more general shifts within academic culture and its relationship to the various social movements (civil rights, feminism, the youth movement) that gained momentum in the 1960s. Although the NATAS minutes never discuss it, the pages of the journal suggest that by the end of the 1960s *Television Quarterly* could no longer sustain the tensions inherent in its divided purpose to be both a PR vehicle for the television industry and a forum for the 'high ideals' of quality criticism as practised in the changing climate of 1960s' university life.

Indeed, by the end of the 1960s it was no longer possible to have the same degree of consensus about what constituted quality TV criticism in the first place. No longer necessarily an embrace of 'highbrow' Golden Age formats or even a literary-minded 'thematic' examination of Hollywood series, quality TV criticism – at least at the university and at some factions of the press – was now often put to the service of a more trenchant, even radically leftist critique of television. Whereas the 1960s were ushered in by Newton Minow's reform agenda, by the end of the decade television critics were increasingly engaged with the anti-establishment ethos on campus.

Notes on the Underground

While Television Studies was very much generated by the 'system', this market-driven critical climate gave way to a more Marxist-driven critical practice as the decade progressed. Quite paradoxically, the spaces for criticism that the public relations/commercial industry and non-profit corporate arena opened up in the early 1960s were actually instrumentalized in the second half of the decade by leftist intellectuals identified with the various social movements.

The reasons for this are complex, and deserve much more analysis than possible here. Primarily, it seems to me that the more 'movement' identified generation of critics were the product of a particular historical conjuncture in which the critical practices encouraged by the industry, by non-profits, and by the Federal Communications Commission were met by a series of larger cultural shifts taking place in the arena of 'fine' arts and fine art criticism. The primary shift in cultural sensibilities, of course, was the increasing problematization of high and low culture through such movements as Popism, Opism, Minimalism and Psychedelic art, as well as the increasing legitimation of popular culture in university curricula.

In this general climate of critical inquiry, it is not surprising that the whole institution of criticism was itself called into question. In the art scene, toward the end of the 1960s, various critics associated with the avant-garde distanced themselves from the elitism of museum art. These critics engaged the spirit of earlier avant-garde movements (such as Dada), often embracing art that they perceived to be more fully integrated into everyday life (which in the late 1960s especially meant new electronic media like video). While television critics did not share the same critical practice as people writing for the likes of *Art News*, they did at times travel in the same circles, and they were engaged in the general issue of their own 'value' as critics of a commercial medium. One could even find articles in *Television Quarterly* that investigated TV commercials as an avant-garde form or compared *My Three Sons* to *Last Day at Marienbad*.[29]

The links between television criticism and a more avant-garde/art historical critical practice were no doubt propelled by the field of communications studies, and its notable spokesperson, literary scholar Marshall McLuhan. Most importantly, here, McLuhan – or at least the popularization of McLuhanism – made television criticism a kind of hip, cutting edge practice replete with easy to repeat slogans like 'cool media' and 'global village'. The popular representations of McLuhan, moreover, dovetailed with developments in the visual arts as numerous depictions of him used op-art backgrounds and psychedelic colours to register the 'radical' nature of his vision. McLuhan's critical style, however, did not really inspire the direction of Television Studies at the university, especially in so far as leftist politics were concerned. Instead, Television Studies was much more influenced by the work of British scholar Raymond Williams and his book *Television: Technology and Cultural Form*, which sharply criticized McLuhan for his technological determinism and his related refusal to conceptualize the ways people might use media to create positive social change.[30]

Even before the heyday of McLuhanism – and certainly throughout the years of McLuhan's popular fame – the project for a media revolution was instead initiated by activists who came from a series of postwar social movements. The

African-American community was in this respect foundational. The history of African-American broadcast criticism goes back to radio, and in the earliest days of television it merged with civil rights discourses and practices. In local papers like the *Harlem Amsterdam* and the *Chicago Defender*, black critics moved in a kind of parallel critical universe, almost entirely segregated from the white newspaper and trade journal critics. In the mid-1950s, the most notable African-American voices were heard in the criticism generated through the protests against networks and stations (the agitation campaigns against the racist practices of station WLBT in Jackson, Mississippi, and the 14-year federal suit that followed is key here).[31] In addition, civil rights leaders and black critics devised ways to use the PR departments at networks and stations to their bene- fit. At NBC, the dialogue between black critics and the network was handled by Sydney Eiges's department, so that race relations were quite literally the aus- pices of public relations.[32] By the end of the 1960s, the NATAS minutes reflect numerous considerations of how the organization would position itself in rela- tion to charges of industry-wide racism in the employment of minorities. Despite these discussions, venues for 'quality' television criticism – such as *Television Quarterly* and, more recently, academic journals – did not typically feature black voices. Instead, those voices were (and still are) primarily heard in the black press. Here, the separation between newspaper criticism and aca- demic criticism that took place over the 1960s can also be seen as a means of 'critical apartheid' – that is to say, it is a form of structural racism that perpetu- ates the segregation of black from white critical projects.

The feminist movement also found ways to use the system as a means by which to forge a negative critique of television. In 1964, one year after the pub- lication of her groundbreaking book *The Feminine Mystique*, Betty Friedan wrote a two-part article for *TV Guide*. Entitled 'Television and the feminine mystique', the article announced, 'Television's image of the American Woman, 1964, is a stupid, unattractive, insecure little household drudge who spends her martyred, mindless, boring days dreaming of love'.[33] That Friedan should find a place in the pages of the industry's major PR vehicle, *TV Guide*, is testimony to the fact that commercial media industries can and do incorporate the terms of oppositional critical practices. This is not to say that big industry is a 'market place of ideas' or a true democratic forum; rather Betty Friedan was published by *TV Guide* because she had herself become a form of popular cultural capital – a best-selling author who would obviously appeal to *TV's Guide's* heavily female readership (and feminine-oriented advertising) base. Indeed, the great- est paradox here – given Friedan's notorious critique of advertising's demeaning image of women – is that her article shares lay-out space with a series of what (from her point of view) were classically 'sexist' ads. These include an ad for 'Angel Face' make-up (with a huge close-up of a woman's 'utterly heavenly' face), followed by another for 'D-Con Mouse-Prufe' (which shows a terror- struck woman jumping on a chair while screaming, 'EEK! A Mouse').

As this case demonstrates, media industries can at times find ideological cri- tiques of their own operations to be a lucrative source of income. Moreover, this case shows that Television Studies in the academy was in part generated by this strange liaison between big business and the social movements. Although in indirect ways, this early example of feminist television criticism brought to us by *TV Guide* provided a discursive context out of which a more academic branch of feminist Television Studies could develop in the 1970s with critics such as Carol Lopate writing about daytime TV for the *Feminist Review* or Tania Modleski writing about soaps for *Film Quarterly*.

Finally, the emergence of Television Studies in the university was also related to the youth culture movements of the 1960s. A new generation of television scholars grew up at a time when leftist intellectuals – eager to strip the academy and art world of its old guard elitism – defended the study of popular culture. Motivated by such 1960s' luminaries as Leslie Fielder and Susan Sontag, the academic study of popular culture was embraced by the young generation at such classically unpopular universities as Yale (which in 1966 featured a student-run exhibit of comic books). This elevation of popular culture as a form of intellectual currency was met by a more radical critique of the popular arts, especially television. Intellectuals such as Herbert Marcuse and Angela Davis provided a general critique of media that was inspired by Marxist and separatist politics, as opposed to the liberal/reformist/assimilationist politics of a Newton Minow or a Betty Friedan.

Meanwhile, underground papers, largely read by college students identified with the youth movement, began publishing diatribes against media. Harlan Ellison's column in the *Los Angeles Free Press* (which he called 'The Glass Teat') regularly attacked the television industry and its programming for everything from banality to political misinformation. In 1970 Ace Press published Ellison's 'Glass Teat' columns in a book of the same title. According to Ellison, he received 'hundreds of letters from college students and teachers who were using the book in their classes', and 'several colleges ordered large quantities and adopted the book for their "media" classes'.[34] Ellison's book adhered to the strict binary oppositions of the 'free press' vs. the commercial media, to the point where he developed a conspiratorial view of the industry, which he envisioned as the money-grubbing enemy. The cover of the book drew a vivid picture of the 'anti-establishment' TV critic. A cartoon depicted a young TV critic with shades on, long hair, no shirt, and the legs of an animal. This hippie critic was seated on a stool that was drawn with a pig head and American flag integrated into its contours.

In this context, the pages of *Television Quarterly* also began to show signs of the youth movement's effects on TV criticism. Most vividly here, in 1969 the journal published an attack on network censors entitled 'Will bureaucracy finally kill art?'. Written by Smothers Brothers manager John R. Barrett, the article blasted television's 'value system', which Barrett claimed was 'white, Anglo-Saxon middle class, suburban dwelling ... hardly reflective of the values of a changing and troubled nation'.[35] Even while *Television Quarterly* had always provided space for negative criticism of television (especially around the 'wasteland' metaphor), these contributions, written from the spirit of the radical left college campus, were of an entirely different order. It seems likely, then, that the emerging 'movement'-based criticial practices made it impossible for NATAS to sustain its appeal to its biggest supporters – the industry. The 'lightening' up of *Television Quarterly* and the publication of *EMMY* might be seen in part as a response to the changing nature of 'quality criticism' practised among 1960s' leftist intellectuals and college students.

Certainly, the various movements' generative impact on Television Studies has become a central way in which the history of this field is written by its premier post-1968 critics. In an article on the development of Television Studies in the 1970s, Horace Newcomb (certainly one of its inaugural figures) attests to the influence of the 1960s' political movements on the field.[36] Newspaper critics, for their part, also identify the college-based movements and the university's growing tolerance for media courses with a change in the nature of critical practice at the press. Looking back on the period, Rena Pederson, the TV editor at the *Dallas Morning News*, speaks of the impact of college courses and even refers to the new TV criticism as 'the movement', thereby collapsing the social revolutions of the 1960s with the discursive shifts in her field.[37]

In short, by the end of the 1960s a 'counter-criticism' had emerged with a critical practice that found its way into more sober university-based Television Studies in the 1970s as a new generation of scholars began to write criticism, theory and histories of commercial television. While clearly not identified with the offices of CBS or NATAS, these emerging critical discourses, I want to suggest, found their genealogies in and through those commercial institutions. If not always directly causal, the relations between intellectuals and industrialists are nevertheless contextual and conjunctural, as each has come together in mutual relations of support, antagonism and even indifference in a social world where knowledge – like other types of labour – is produced according to the logic of the commodity form.

Critical Conditions

Television Studies in the humanities was built on the unlikely alliances between people in profit and non-profit corporations, at the press, at universities, and to a lesser degree in broadcast law and policy, who wanted – for different reasons – to legitimate their practice. For CBS, television scholarship and the possibility of a TV journal seem to have represented a way to control the climate of criticism. For the Television Academy, scholarship was related to its primary role as a public relations arm of the industry and to infighting over the establishment of a national standard for 'quality' that suited a network system. For the individual critic, academic Television Studies provided a defence against perceived disrespect and disenfranchisement from the system as well as the related desire to speak outside of the corporate discourse of PR.

While its respectability and academic 'status' continue to be a major concern among scholars, Television Studies is now practised on numerous campuses in the USA. Perhaps even more than in the 1960s, at the postmodern, post-public university, one of the central functions of Television Studies is PR. Ironically, because it has the potential to generate capital from the industry, the public relations aspect of Television Studies is one of the central ways to convince deans and provosts of the need for serious research on the medium. Indeed, public relations and public service are even more intertwined and mutually interdependent than they were in the pro-education days of the 1960s.

That said, most academics do not really make it as media pundits, and educational pursuits are often frustrated by the meagre amounts of grant money, university facilities and teaching positions doled out to television scholars. In fact, even while Television Studies has carved out a niche for itself, the legitimation crisis for the TV critic has not really ended. Television Studies is still filled with self-flagellating stories, and its classrooms are often rife with faculty contention that surfaces among the student population in very honest questions like 'Why are we studying TV anyway?' or 'Are you really a professor, Mrs Spigel?'.

The students' scepticism about Television Studies is not just, or even primarily, propelled by the same ivory tower snobbism of some of our most trenchant colleagues. Rather, their doubts probably have more to do with the fact that Television Studies has also become a branch of the culture industries. Now we have cable networks like Nick at Nite preserving 'our television heritage' and offering Dr Television's psychoanalytic readings of *Bewitched*. Fan activities through zines, underground video stores and the Internet also present people with educations about television history and criticism.

So too, we have seen the burgeoning of new cultural institutions such as the privately funded Museum of Television and Radio (MTR), which was established in New York in 1976 by CBS's President William Paley, and which just opened a new site in Beverly Hills. Just down the block from the celebrity eatery, Planet Hollywood, and sporting a *Star Trek* costume exhibit and souvenir store that are reminiscent of the costume/memorabilia displays at the restaurant, the MTR is the logical outcome of a postmodern sensibility where the old semantic order between public and private, education and entertainment, art and commercialism, no longer apply. The MTR also views education in rather entrepreneurial ways. Recently, one of the curators for its satellite seminar series phoned to ask me if I could send him students to act as an audience for the lectures. The idea of students as 'filler on the set' seems to me the logical outcome of the discursive indeterminancy between public relations and public service that have characterized the public sphere and modern media institutions since industrialization. Less cynical than systemic, there is finally no distinction between a classroom for students and a studio audience.

These alternative venues for TV education mean that students often come to our classes with a certain kind and degree of TV literacy that implicitly challenges what we do and why a university should employ us to do it. This 'no respect' problem is also related to the self-defeating scapegoatism to be found among television scholars themselves who still complain about the shoddy state of scholarship in US Television Studies. Because such conversations typically take place in 'off stage' spaces (hallways at conferences, at dinner tables, on telephones – but more significantly behind the closed doors of tenure review meetings and publications boards), what I am describing is not entirely documentable. The written forms of this 'shoddy scholarship' reproach can be found in the more general essays that question the value of Cultural Studies.

Such attacks on Television Studies tend to propose a binary logic – either you do shoddy trendy Cultural Studies that comes from the Centre for Contemporary Cultural Studies at Birmingham (or its Americanized friends) or else you do 'proper' unpopular history of broadcasting that grew up in the field of broadcast journalism and mass communications. One is 'trivial' (i.e. ahistorical, anecdotal, and wishy-washy), the other is 'rigorous,' (i.e. filled with hard to find facts, indicative of trips to the archive, and conclusive). Most explicitly here, in a recent essay, broadcast historian Robert W. McChesney has specifically blamed Cultural Studies for what he perceives to be trivial topics and lack of rigour in television scholarship.[38] Symptomatically, such arguments never consider new historicism and the anthropological turn in history, nor do they consider the impact these academic movements have had on challenging the empiricist assumptions and the sorry state of interpretive method in so-called 'rigorous' broadcast history.

It does seem useful to think about how these attacks on Television Studies wind up being a version of a much older strain of disciplinary scapegoating and self-flagellation that gave rise to Television Studies in the first place. As we have seen in the past, this self-flagellation has to do with a defence against perceived disrespect. Moreover, this 'bad scholarship' battle cry can easily work on behalf of the very culture industry that the critic is supposedly criticizing. On the one hand, the industry can use this kind of academic infighting as a way to prove that all critical statements about the medium are the pointless babble of nutty professors who fight over the damnedest things. On the other hand, and more complexly, the kind of anxiety this sets in motion gives way to the psychoanalytic condition of transference. That is to say, the 'shoddy scholarship' battle cry forged by critics such as McChesney promotes a dynamic among scholars in which we project our own anxieties about our purpose and stature onto others, claiming that this or that kind of scholarship or this or that object of study is *a priori* 'bad'. While such transference can work as a defence against our own beleaguered egos in a field that gives us 'no respect', it is easily exploited by institutions – such as CBS in the 1960s – that are willing to flatter the critic's ego, to feed his or her narcissistic projections, for their own purposes. In other words, if your peers tell you that you are worthless, you might be more willing to work as a critic or consultant for corporations, which at least give you some money and bolster your ego.

My point here is not that it is bad to 'sell out'. Rather, my point is that the kind of scapegoatism these attacks set in motion breaks up the power of the critical project. This leads towards a legitimation of disciplinary boundaries which is ultimately (and ironically) in synch with the corporate logic of alienated labour – in this case through alienation of the critic/historian from their practice, publics, and community of colleagues on campus. Most ironically, despite the fact that Television Studies grew up in dialogue with 1960s' social movements and drew on Marxist/feminist traditions, this call for academic rigour rarefies criticism to such a degree that it places Television Studies back in the sanctuary of the ivory tower where scholars work mostly in the confines of the dusty archive with little, and usually no, relation to a broader community of thought. This is undialectical materialism in the extreme.

I say this, actually, as someone who loves to sit in archives all day, and with full knowledge of the different forms of pleasure and achievement one gets by doing that as opposed to other kinds of critical labour. But, it does seem important to resist making these calls for tried-and-true 'factory-tested' academic standards, if for no other reason than the fact that the whole idea of academic standards has so much in common with the corporate logic of quality control. As with the case of CBS in the early 1960s, this logic of 'quality criticism' performed by people with credentials in their field was instrumental in taking critics out of the broader sphere of critical thinking. It worked (although, not perfectly) to produce the unfortunate divide between popular newspaper criticism and 'proper' academic Television Studies in which US television scholars find themselves today.

Despite my disenchanted tone, I do not think that the field of Television Studies is contaminated – *a priori* – by its difficult relations (both past and present) with corporate America. Nor am I suggesting that corporate America is engaged in some kind of conspiracy to shut us up. Instead, the 'making of a TV literate elite' should remind us that terms like 'rigour' and 'trivial' are part of a longer historical struggle between intellectuals and industrialists working in and on TV. Although it would be ludicrous to say that all forms of criticism are equally insightful and significant, it is important to understand that the urge to discipline and publish in the university can and does often dovetail with the interests of the culture industries. The movement of television criticism from the newspaper to academia – and the ongoing disaffection between the two – is in many ways a worst case scenario of the rarefaction of knowledge produced through the rise of Television Studies.

Rather than debating the legitimacy of Television Studies solely in the context of (disputed) academic criteria, it seems more useful to consider why journalists, professors, archivists, curators, television programmers, members of non-profit organizations, and TV fan cultures have been so effectively divided in their pursuit to generate a critical understanding of television. It seems more crucial to consider why the making of a TV elite has been so efficiently executed that most television scholars with PhDs would not even think about writing for the press (and, of course, the same could be said for the newspaper editor who would never think of publishing a TV scholar).

This situation cannot be repaired in any simple 'just get out there and do it' way. The divide between journalism and academia is, as I have been suggesting, historically achieved. Its future does not lie primarily with individual triumphs which, for the most part, produce celebrity professors like McLuhan but do not encourage collective re-evaluations of television or television criticism. In this regard, the 'making of a TV literate elite' is a deeply ironic trope that I use to underscore – and ideally to break – the silence we have achieved as people with credentials to speak.

Notes

1. Lawrence Laurent, 'Wanted: the complete television critic', in Robert Lewis Shayon (ed.) *The Eighth Art* (Holt, Rinehart and Winston, 1962), p. 155.
2. Richard J. Stonesifer, 'A new style for TV criticism', *Television Quarterly*, 6, 2 (Spring 1967): 50.
3. Robert Baram, 'Television – The Fifth Dimension, – a poem', *Television Quarterly*, 8, 4 (Fall 1969): 73–5.
4. Four notable histories of television criticism include John Caughie, 'Television criticism', *Screen* 25, 4–5 (July–October 1984):109–121; David Littlejohn, 'Thoughts on television criticism', in *Television as a Cultural Force*, ed. Douglass Cater and Richard Adler (New York: Praeger, 1976), pp. 147–73; Horace Newcomb, 'American television criticism, 1970–1985', *Critical Studies in Mass Communications*, 3, 2 (June 1986): 217–28; and Hal Himmelstein, *On the Small Screen: New Approaches in Television and Video Criticism* (New York: Praeger, 1981). All authors consider the relationship between newspaper and academic criticism, although in ways different from my interests here. Caughie's concerns are most germane to my own in so far as he calls for increased dialogues between newspaper critics and university scholars.

5.   William Boddy, *Fifties Television: The Industry and Its Critics* (Chicago: University of Illinois Press, 1990) , pp. 187–255.

6.   Himmelstein, *On the Small Screen*, p. 29.

7.   For the letters see Sydney Eiges, Booster Files, Box 165: Folder 15, 1950–February 1954. National Broadcasting Company Records, State Historical Society, Madison, WI. Hereinafter referred to NBC Records.

8.   Mabley cited in Stan Opotowsky, *TV: The Big Picture* (New York: E. P. Dutton, 1961), pp. 255–6.

9.   By the early 1980s, Himmelstein reported that the 'television page is the second most avidly read section in newspapers'. See *On the Small Screen*, p. 29.

10.   The *Journal of Broadcasting*, which began publication in the winter of 1956–57, had already included some qualitative criticism of television. As opposed to the CBS project, however, it featured essays on radio as well as television, and it typically included more social scientific and legalistic approaches than qualitative criticism of television *per se*.

11.   Shayon, *The 'Eighth Art*, p. vii.

12.   Shayon, *The Eighth Art*, p. ix.

13.   In his introduction, Shayon claims a major reason why CBS did not continue with the journal was NATAS's publication of *Television Quarterly*.

14.   Dick Adler cited in Thomas O'Neil, *The Emmys: Star Wars, Showdowns, and the Supreme Test of TV's Best* (New York: Penguin, 1992), p. 9.

15.   National Minutes, 15, 16, 17 April 1966, p. 14, Box 1: Folder 1963–67, Academy Archives.

16.   My argument concerning the indeterminate meanings of the term 'public interest' and policy discourse more generally is indebted to the work of Thomas Streeter. See his *Selling the Air: A Critique of the Policy of Commercial Broadcasting in the United States* (Chicago: University of Chicago Press, 1996).

17   Opotowsky, *TV: The Big Picture*, p. 9.

18   Yale Roe, *The Television Dilemma: Search for a Solution* (New York: Hastings House, 1962); Newton N. Minow, *Equal Time: The Private Broadcaster and The Public Interest*, ed. Lawrence Laurent (New York: Atheneum, 1964); Erik Barnouw's three-volume history of broadcasting includes *A Tower in Babel: A History of Broadcasting in the United States to 1933* (New York: Oxford University Press, 1966), *The Golden Web: A History of Broadcasting in the United States 1933–1953* (New York: Oxford University Press, 1968, and *The Image Empire: A History of Broadcasting in United States from 1953* (New York: Oxford University Press, 1970).

19.   The murky boundaries between education and public relations were evident in the first television curricula available at universities, even before Television Studies *per se* instituted itself as a sub-discipline.

20.   Lynn Spigel, 'High culture in low places: television and modern art, 1950–1970', in *Disciplinarity and Dissent in Cultural Studies*, ed. Cary Nelson and Dilip Parameshwar Gaonkar (New York: Routledge, 1996), pp. 314–46.

21.   Douglas Macagy, *The Museum Looks in on TV* (New York: Museum of Modern Art, 1955), p. 291.

22.   Minutes: National Board of Trustees Meeting, 13, 14, 15 September 1963, p. 36, Box 1: Folder 1963–67, Academy Archives.

23.   Even in the 1950s, Cassyd had considered liaisons with UCLA; in 1960 he placed the first NATAS holdings with that university.

24.   'The Journal of the Academy of Television Arts and Sciences', 1961, Ed Sullivan Files, Box 1, State Historical Society, Madison, WI.

25.   Minutes: National Board of Trustees Meeting, 15, 16, 17 April, p. 14, Box 1: Folder 1963–1967, Academy Archives.

26.   While I do not intend to recount the problems with this view of history and objectivity, I should note that I am sceptical of any broadcast history which attempts to reduce television to observable data. This objective reporter ethos is not commensurate with the

task of understanding the subjective states and belief systems which entertainment industries tap into and encourage among audiences.

27.   Thomas W. Sarnoff, 'President's Annual Report, 1972–1973', pp. 13–14, presented 19 October 1973, Box 1: Folder 'Los Angeles 1968', Academy Archives. (Note that the report is misfiled in a folder for a previous year.)

28.   *EMMY*, 1, 1 (Winter 1979): editorial. Note that the division of publication efforts followed upon the division of NATAS itself. Between 1975 and 1977, the Los Angeles chapter split off from NATAS, which retained headquarters in New York.

29.   For more on the links between fine art, the avant garde, and television see my essay, 'High culture in low places: television and modern art, 1950–1970'.

30.   Raymond Williams, *Television: Technology and Cultural Form* (New York: Schocken, 1975).

31.   For an excellent discussion of local African American agitation against WLBT see Steven Classen, 'Southern discomforts: the racial politics of popular entertainment', in *The Revolution Wasn't Televised: Sixties Television and Social Conflict*, ed. Lynn Spigel and Michael Curtin (New York: Routledge, 1997).

32.   See 'The Proposed Offering of the Opera: "Emperor Jones",' Eiges, '1953 Negro Public Relations', Box 164; Folder 25, NBC Records.

33.   Betty Friedan, 'Television and the feminine mystique', *TV Guide*, 24 January 1964, p. 6.

34.   Harlan Ellison, *The Glass Teat* (1969; Manchester: Savoy Books, 1978). This citation comes from the reprinted 1975 supplementary introduction to the Pyramid edition, which is reprinted in this collection.

35.   John R. Barrett, 'Will bureaucracy finally kill art?', *Television Quarterly* 8, 3 (Summer 1969): 20.

36.   Newcomb, 'American television criticism', p. 218.

37.   Pederson cited in Himmelstein, *On the Small Screen*, p. 34.

38.   See his 'Communication for the hell of it: the triviality of U.S. broadcasting history', and a reply by Thomas Streeter in *Journal of Broadcasting and Electronic Media*: 40, 1996, pp. 540–57.

SECTION II

Approaches in Television Studies

The first section of this book examined the central constitutive areas of television theory and history. Section II begins with a connecting essay by Charlotte Brunsdon on the history of Television Studies and goes on to offer several essays which explore some of the key methodological approaches and debates associated with the current study of television. As the first section demonstrated in practice and Brunsdon makes explicit, Television Studies has developed as an interdisciplinary field, each discipline bringing with it its own conventions and procedures which have, in turn, merged and developed distinct approaches of their own. There are, therefore, a complex of approaches to separate for analysis.

This is also a time of considerable change in the economy of television and in scholarship more generally. As they explore a range of the most central approaches to television, then, contributors in this section are mindful not only of the multivarious disciplinary interconnections but also the new challenges to conventional methods currently affecting Television Studies.

The import of this new moment is evident in Charlotte Brunsdon's concluding words: 'Whatever we thought the television of television studies was when it was being invented in the 1970s, what is becoming increasingly clear is that what it is now is history.' This refers in part to the defining changes facing television in the future, brought about paramountly by the substantial technological developments in satellite, cable and digital technology, and also by changing economic and political policies which are re-regulating and fragmenting the traditional broadcast model (Hollins, 1984; Hood, 1994). More than the significance of these new developments in the history of television, however, Brunsdon's phrase also alerts us to the import of this historical moment for the histories and the imagined future of Television Studies itself.

A History of Television Studies

Brunsdon opens with questions about what Television Studies is, what it studies and where it comes from. For her, television is 'a production of a complex interplay of different histories'. This immediately establishes that what we might otherwise take for granted as the object of study we call television is itself contested by the many different 'bodies of commentary' which have sought to define it.

The history of Television Studies she thereby constructs is a history of the object 'television' that emerged, and how it emerged, from those various disciplines. She locates the emergence of Television Studies historically in the 1970s and 1980s and characterises three contributing formations. The first, echoing Lynn Spigel, is journalism, which produced 'a television watched and judged'. The second, inflecting John Hartley's contribution to Section I somewhat differently, is literary and dramatic criticism, with its focus on an authored broadcast drama, valued in terms of art and high culture. If the first two areas produced a legacy of approaches to television as texts, the third, social science, produced a very different object of study. Social science focused more on television as an institution, 'more often an instance or site than a text'.

Through the novel device of comparing the contents pages of key books in the period, Brunsdon demonstrates the significance of certain scholarly disciplines in constructing what we now know as Television Studies. She offers a chronology of symptomatic works: starting with books of mass communications and critical sociology, with their 'international vision' of television; cultural studies and 'second wave' feminist research, which shifted focus from a public notion of television to its role in the private sphere; Film Studies, which increased the range of television genres studied; and, instrumental in that process, feminism, which attended to popular cultural genres like soap opera rather than the respected forms of earlier approaches, like news and drama.

For Brunsdon, Television Studies in the 1980s is characterised by greater 'definition of the television text and investigation of the television audience': not only the programmes but how they are watched. In a further reference to Raymond Williams's formative concept of 'flow', Brunsdon sees other key concepts like 'segmentation' and the 'viewing strip' emerging from it. Looking forward to Christine Geraghty's later essay, Brunsdon sees this work combining with media ethnographies of viewing in the contemporary moment of international television scholarship.

Brunsdon concludes by relating this interdisciplinary history to the contemporary position in Television Studies. She discerns the concerns of the social sciences in empirical investigations into television audiences, converging with textual approaches to the ways television programmes formally construct meaning for their audiences and with Cultural Studies' approaches which stress the ways audiences resist and negotiate the domination of contemporary culture. The remaining essays in this section tease out and explore further some of the approaches Brunsdon explores.

Television, Representation and Identity

Perhaps no approaches to the study of television have crossed disciplinary boundaries so much as academic feminism and black studies. What they share is a founding concept of representation and its relation to and impact on the formation of personal identity. As Lynn Spigel described in Section I, the concept of representation grew out of the post-1968 struggles by interest groups on the political and social margins. Groups such as women, black peoples and youth were activated by feelings of inadequate political representation, that their voices were not being properly heard. Struggles over political representation were matched by arising academic concerns, especially in Cultural Studies, to understand the complex psychology of group and individual identities. In Media Studies, the communications media in general were understood as re-presenting or constructing rather than merely relaying their own or external events; in particular, as Charlotte Brunsdon described above, there was a concern with representations of gender, race and age. Studies of representation thereby entered Television Studies around concerns over production (who was representing), textual form (what was being represented and how) and reception (how representations were understood).

The concept of representation was found particularly valuable in debates about realism, especially in Film Studies. But television was dominated by realist forms with high status too, like news, documentary and naturalist drama. The concept of representation enabled arguments to be made about the limitations of television representations and to undermine an earlier confidence in the authenticity or objectivity of news and documentary. The concept of representation also made wider genres and forms – like soap opera and situation comedy – more visible for study. To ask how television represented, rather than a more neutral term like 'treated' was to make clear the active, constructive nature of television and its signification, including its ideological role in making meaning about social groups and their relations.

Feminism and Television Studies

In her essay, Laura Stempel Mumford asserts the shared interdisciplinary interest of feminism and Television Studies in enquiry into such questions of representation and cultural identity. If feminism was interested in the cultural production of gender identities, television was located as a prime medium for cultural representation, and not only for women as female audiences. Stempel Mumford considers the range of issues feminism has contributed to Television Studies, from identifying previously ignored or denigrated genres like soap opera to focusing on the private, domestic female sphere of television reception. In this way, she locates Television Studies' revival of textual analysis and extension into audience ethnography in the stimulus of feminism.

Stempel Mumford draws on a case study of soap opera to demonstrate how feminist-inspired approaches have been fundamentally constitutive in the mainstream of Television Studies; that work on soap opera, for instance, has influenced the range and nature of analyses of other television genres and has come to be seen as 'paradigmatic of television in general'. Yet she is keen to emphasise the plurality of approaches within feminist academic studies, to see them as productive in Television Studies precisely because they proffered debate rather than a unitary position. She traces some history within that continuing debate beginning with an early concern to locate on television what were discerned as 'negative' and 'positive' images of women, especially in terms of stereotyping. Then, drawing on Film Studies' interest in psychoanalytic models, an interest in gendered spectatorship: television's address to and formal construction of a particular gendered audience, which made more complex an understanding of what and how representation might come to signify. Then, in a turn against cine-psychoanalysis, feminism inspired a shift from the text to the audience, from the spectator as a subject of the text to viewers as primarily a social category.

In a final move, Stempel Mumford looks forward to Christine Geraghty's argument that audience reception studies were responsible for reconstituting the television audience not as a singular entity but as a collection of distinct and yet shifting positions and identities.

Television and Race

A companion essay is Therese Daniels's study of research into television's representations of race. Daniels characterises inadequacies in the amount and conceptual sophistication of research in this area, drawing attention to a need for greater academic attention to and institutional funding of race research in general. She charts a history of studies beginning with the marginal interest in the representation of race on British television among disciplines associated with the early days of Television Studies. In mass communications, for instance, the emphasis in the 1970s was on social class. Under the impact of academic feminism, gender-based studies emerged, which in turn stimulated some race studies. The first studies of television's representation of black people on screen focused on their negative imagery. Research here, perhaps unsurprisingly, drew attention to the employment of black peoples in production, as well as to their under-representation and mis-representation on and off-screen.

Daniels points up a research tradition of 'quantitative analysis of black images and their qualitative evaluation' and, drawing on the arguments of Stuart Hall, she calls for more race research which is both more interventionist and yet sensitive to the complex and conflicting ideological role of the television institution and its programmes. The disparity in the quantity and quality that emerges from her essay between the related representational areas of gender and race is startling and disturbing. Daniels's essay and its contrasts with the formative work described by Stempel Mumford make transparent the need for better funding of and an increase in scholarship and research in the area of television and race.

Audience Reception Studies

Christine Geraghty's essay then marks an important shift from concerns about textual analysis in much of the earlier essays to television audiences during the 1980s. She begins by noting how audience studies emerged in the interface between Cultural Studies, Anthropology and Sociology at the time, before charting the significance of a turn from 'work *on* audiences to work *with* audiences' in the problematic relation of audience studies to the concept of ethnography.

Exploring methodological and theoretical issues raised by audience reception theory, Geraghty notes the strong pragmatic and empirical base to the new approach. She argues that, none the less, audience reception theory 'retained close relationships with more abstract and general theoretical accounts', even as it was in part a counter to their tendency to extrapolate audience understandings or readings from forms of textual or institutional analyses.

Geraghty charts a typology of audience reception studies, attending to what they study, types of approach (with special attention to the new relationship between researcher and researched), and the problems of generalising from their often specific findings. In the process, she notes the importance of a shift towards treating viewers not as an abstract singular audience but as particular social groupings who may identify themselves as, say, fans of or a gendered audience for a particular programme or series.

Importantly for research methods, Geraghty describes ways in which a research pool is constituted, how and why research tends towards the qualitative, and why it tends to be based on semi-structured interview. She sees certain problems for research conclusions arising from these methods but demonstrates that what emerges from the research is less the experience of television in general than ways in which particular groups of viewers articulate that experience. From this, she argues that there is no more one way of viewing television than there is one audience for it, and that what determines ways of viewing is not television itself but 'a variety of contexts' which may be linked to the social arrangements of domestic reception.

Geraghty concludes by connecting to issues of representation in earlier essays. She calls for the views of audiences in this research to be heard in ways other than through its conventional research report, for its research pool to become subjects and 'given a public voice within discussions of television itself'.

Eric Hirsch's following essay offers in its second part a case study of the ethnographic approach analysed by Geraghty. The case study is of a family and its relation to the television screen but also to the computer screen. The study follows a critical history of the place of new communications technology in and around television.

New Technologies

It is commonplace now to point out the impact of the new communications technologies on the imminent shape of television globally. So it was important in this book to find space for analysis of the debate about television and the new communications technologies. Hirsch is keen to explore the ways in which such technological change is part of a longer historical process in which 'new' technologies are simultaneously 'old'. He situates technological innovation in a socio-cultural history of increasing domestic self-sufficiency and separation from the wider economy and society. In this broader perspective, technical developments are seen as part of wider organisational developments fuelled – over 200 years, in stages carefully examined by Hirsch – by commercial imperatives and middle-class ideals of domestic living.

For Hirsch, these developments also brought with them risks to the stability of social power-relations, so he argues that this technological history was simultaneously bound into mechanisms of systems control. These are mechanisms which not only enter into institutional arrangements for television and related new technologies like the telegraph, telephone, consumer electronics and, most recently, micro electronics, but also into the domestic sphere. Here, 'the consumer was soon perceived as linked to ... regulated technological systems ... just as the individual/family was linked to the social whole through ... separate public institutions'.

Since the 1970s, Hirsch argues, the political promotion of 'privatised choice' has connected in particular ways to domestic consumption around the 'older screen of broadcast television ... [and the] new ... screen of the personal computer'. What has been produced in this configuration is both 'new technologies and new uses'. Crucially though for Hirsch, such 'convergence does not depend on technological innovation alone', but on 'a mutually constitutive relationship between "new" forms of domesticity and the connections such self-sufficiency renders visible for "new" technologies'.

It is in this spirit that Hirsch reads the domestic use of new technology by one family in his research case study. What emerges is a family adapting waves of new technology according to their own changing work patterns and as the children grow older. The physical sites in the home for new technology are determined by each member's leisure preferences and by the adults' desire to maintain separation between work and home. Hirsch relates this historical analysis to the ethnographic study when he concludes that the 'relations that constitute the domestic context' inform choices of technology and the extent and nature of its uses.

The Popular Culture Debate

In the final essay in this section, David Lusted turns attention to a wider debate about popular culture which, as indicated in our introduction, has had a strong impact on Television Studies. Like John Hartley, Lusted discerns a long tradition of suspicion of popular culture which he locates in a particular national cultural resentment in Britain of its discerned American-ness. He reconstructs notions of populism, a term with particularly negative associations in common and critical debate, in order to review connections between popular culture and the particular audiences who make their cultural choices from within it.

Taking the case of light entertainment on television, Lusted seeks to demonstrate how this programme form includes many television genres which share modes of address and political and cultural associations of populism. The important populist features he identifies include: the construction of what Richard Dyer has called a utopian sensibility, where feelings of inclusion emerge from qualities of sentiment and spectacle; struggles over the definition and role of populist hero and community among and between television professionals and on-screen audiences and contestants; the social class division between those who are constructed by light entertainment forms as members of the populist audience and those who are considered to exclude themselves from it; and the interactive relations between light entertainment forms and the family audience in the social context of their domestic viewing conditions.

Lusted's argument is that light entertainment, like popular culture more generally, shares certain formal and interactive features which connect in pleasurable but also challenging ways to the social conditions of reception and the cultures of, in particular, the problematic grouping of the urban working-class family. He also argues that these very features of inclusion are what exclude elite groupings, among whom he includes television scholars, from its potential populist pleasures and significations. Lusted's concluding anecdote about what he calls 'his own family melodrama' connects his essay briefly and symptomatically to the audience reception studies above of Geraghty and Hirsch.

What emerges from this section is how distinctive disciplines combine in new relations in response to changing cultural, political and technological conditions. New scholarly approaches to and debates over television have developed over time into the new inter-disciplinary field of Television Studies. Yet almost immediately this returns us to Charlotte Brunsdon's caution, mentioned earlier, about this Television Studies being bound up with history as television itself is subject to the most radical and dramatic changes.

References

HOLLINS, T., 1984: *Beyond Broadcasting: Into the Cable Age.* London: BRU/BFI.
HOOD, S. (ed.), 1994: *Behind the Screen: The Structure of British TV in the 1990s.* London: Lawrence & Wishart.

5

What is the 'Television' of Television Studies?

Charlotte Brunsdon

The existence of this book, published for the first time in 1997, in the company of other recent readers and introductory texts such as Corner and Harvey's *Television Times* (1996) or Selby and Cowdery's *How to Study Television* (1995) testifies to the existence – at least in the minds of some authors, teachers and publishers – of something called television studies. Indeed, it is possible, in the 1990s, in Britain, to take degree courses in television studies in a way which was inconceivable in as recent a past as the 1970s. In this essay I want to unpick the obviousness of television studies – *question:* what is television studies? *answer:* it's the study of television, of course – to show how the television of the discipline, like the flow of talk now thought of as normal for the medium, is particular and historical. My main concern will be the tracing of the hybrid origins of television studies in answer to the question 'where does television studies come from?'. In this endeavour, I will sketch one outline of the ways and sites in which television has been attended to seriously. My underlying argument, however, is that there is nothing obvious about the television of television studies. This television, the television studied in television studies, is a production of the complex interplay of different histories – disciplinary, national, economic, technological, legislative – which not only did not exist until recently, but is currently, contestedly, being produced even as, simultaneously, the nationally regulated terrestrial broadcasting systems which are its primary referent move into convulsion. Where does television studies come from and what does it study?

Television studies is the relatively recent, aspirationally disciplinary name given to the academic study of television. Modelled by analogy on longer established fields of study, the name suggests that there is an object, 'television', which, in courses named, for example, 'Introduction to Television Studies', is the self-evident object of study using accepted methodologies. This may be increasingly the case, but historically, most of the formative academic research on television was inaugurated in other fields and contexts. The 'television' of television studies is a relatively new phenomenon, just as many of the key television scholars are employed in departments of sociology, politics, communication arts, speech, theatre, media and film studies. If it is now possible, in

1996, to speak of a field of study, 'television studies' in the Anglophone academy, in a way in which it was not in 1970, the distinctive characteristics of this field of study include its disciplinary hybridity and continuing debate about how to conceptualise the object of study 'television'. These debates, which are and have been both political and methodological, are further complicated in an international frame by the historical peculiarities of national broadcasting systems. Thus, for example, the television studies that developed in Britain or Scandinavia, while often addressing US television programmes, did so within the taken-for-granted dominance of public service models. This television, and this television studies, was one in which, at a deep level, there was an assumed address to a viewer as citizen. John Corner's recent book, *Television Form and Public Address* (1995), provides a fine example of this tradition. In contrast, the US system is one organised on commercial principles, textually distinguished by the normality of advertising spots and breaks. The viewer is primarily a consumer. In the first instance, then, television studies signifies the contested, nationally inflected, academic address to television as primary object of study – rather than, as I discuss below, television as part of international media economies or television as site of drama in performance.

Television Studies: A Story Told in Six Anthologies

There have been two prerequisites for development of the primarily Anglophone discipline of television studies. The first was that television as such be regarded as worthy of study. This apparently obvious point is significant in relation to a medium which has historically attracted distrust, fear and contempt. These responses, which often involve the invocation of television as both origin and symptom of social ills, have, as many scholars have pointed out, homologies with responses to earlier popular genres and forms such as the novel and the cinema. Debate about the significance and value of television persists, and much academic and popular writing about the medium is haunted by anxiety about the cultural legitimacy of watching television. The second prerequisite was that television be granted, conceptually, some autonomy and specificity as a medium. Thus television had to be regarded as more than simply a transmitter of world, civic or artistic events and as distinguishable from other of the 'mass media'. Indeed, much of the literature of television studies could be characterised as attempting to formulate accounts of the specificity of television, often using comparison with, on the one hand, radio (broadcast, liveness, civic address), and on the other, cinema (moving pictures, fantasy), with particular attention, as discussed below, to debate about the nature of the television text and the television audience.[1] Increasingly significant also are the emergent histories of television – whether it be the autobiographical accounts of insiders, such as Grace Wyndham Goldie's history of her years at the BBC, *Facing the Nation* (1978), or the painstaking archival research of historians such as William Boddy with his history of the Quiz scandals in 1950s' US television (1990), or Lynn Spigel with her pioneering study of the way in which television was 'installed' in the US living room in the 1950s (*Make Room for TV*, 1993).

Television studies emerged in the 1970s and 1980s from three major bodies of commentary on television: journalism, literary/dramatic criticism and the social sciences. These are the main bodies of work in which attention was paid to television, although the attention, and the television, of each was different, as I will show. Each, in the 1970s and 1980s, was also affected by the changing ideas about gender provoked by second wave feminism, a movement which turned out to have its own interests in television. Of the founding bodies of commentary, the first, and most familiar, was daily and weekly journalism. This has generally taken the form of guides to viewing and reviews of recent programmes. Television reviewing has, historically, been strongly personally voiced, with this authorial voice rendering continuity to the diverse topics and programmes addressed.[2] The repeated production of a discriminating 'I who view' could also be seen as a compensatory symptom of the anxiety about viewing in the first place, most marked in the instances when the review seems insistently about critic rather than programme. None the less, some of this writing has offered formulations of great insight in its address to broadcast form – for example the work of James Thurber (1948), Raymond Williams (1968, 1974), Philip Purser (1992) or Nancy Banks-Smith (in the *Guardian*) – which is only now being recognised as one of the origins of the discipline of television studies. This television is a television watched and judged for a range of reasons: as entertainment, for information, as a national event, although rare is the critic who comments on the news or those elements of broadcast output thought of as unexceptional and normal, such as continuity announcing or long-running chat shows.

The second body of commentary is also organised through ideas of authorship, but here it is the writer or dramatist who forms the legitimation for the attention to television. Critical method here is extrapolated from traditional literary and dramatic criticism, and the television attracts serious critical attention as a 'home theatre'. Indicative texts here would be the early collection edited by Howard Thomas, *Armchair Theatre* (1959) or the later, more academic volume edited by George Brandt, *British Television Drama* (1981). Television here is broadcast drama, interesting both because a new medium makes new demands on creative personae and because new technologies make available new audiences. Until the 1980s, the address of this type of work was almost exclusively to 'high culture': plays and occasionally series by known playwrights, often featuring theatrical actors. This emphasis can be clearly seen by contrasting the contents pages of Brandt's 1981 collection and his 1993 collection, *British Television Drama in the 1980s* (*see* Fig. 5.1). The 1981 volume is organised into chapters named after writers. This points to the significance of the writer as author within this understanding of television, and to the privileging of a notion of authorial *œuvre* over individual work. Only with an understanding of this traditional approach to television drama is it possible to see how exceptional Raymond Williams's defence of television soap opera is in *Drama in Performance* (1968), or Horace Newcomb's validation of popular genres in *TV: The Most Popular Art* (1974). Brandt's 1993 volume reveals a considerable shift of emphasis. While there is still a residual, formative structure of the writer, chapters here are named by programme, and lower forms, such as the soap opera and the situation comedy, make an appearance. Not all authors and artists are men. Most indicative, perhaps, of the emergence of television as an object of study on new terms is a contrast of Appendix 1 of each book. In 1981 the appendix is of 'Plays

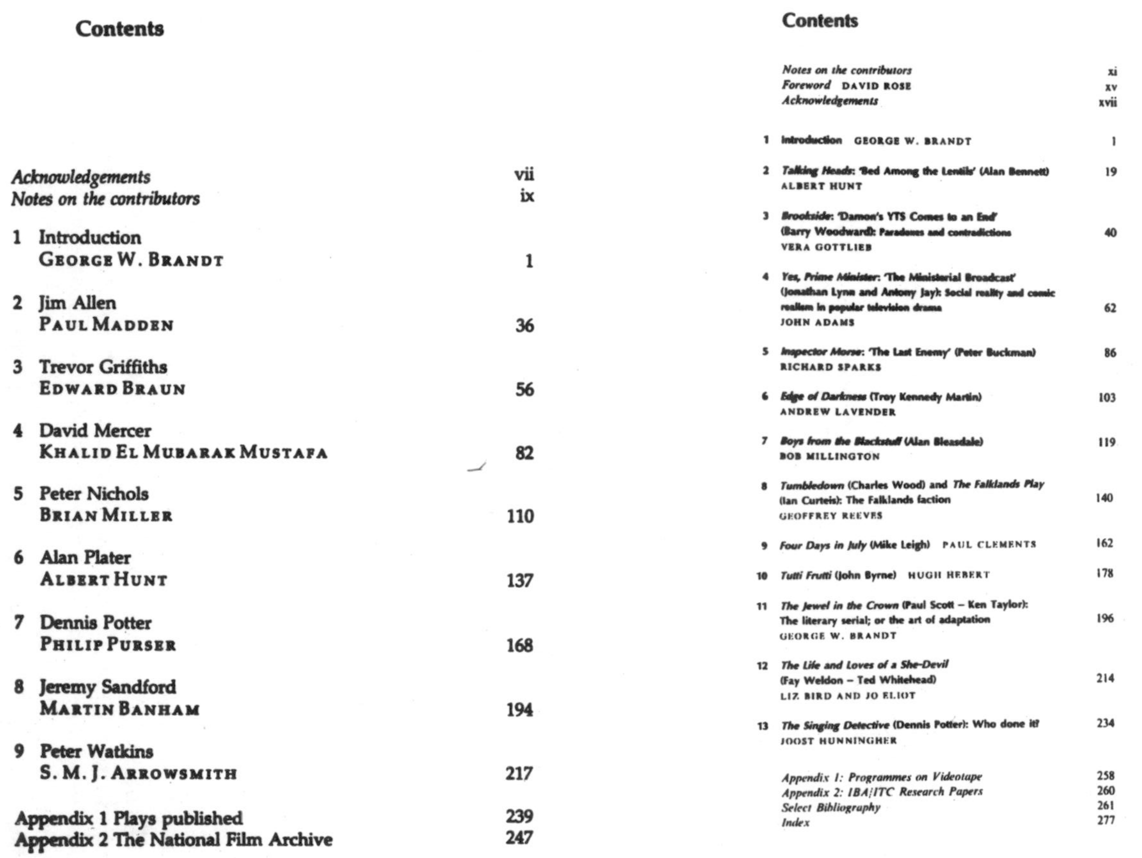

Contents

Contents

Fig. 5.1 Contents pages of George Brandt (ed.) *British Television Drama* (Cambridge: Cambridge University Press, 1981) and George Brandt (ed.), *British Television Drama in the 1980s* (Cambridge: Cambridge University Press).

published'. In 1993 it is 'Programmes on videotape'. Although his 1993 introduction expresses considerable hostility to television studies, I would argue that
by 1993 Brandt's notion of television drama has been 'television studied'. To
understand how this has come about requires a return to my sketch of the origins of the discipline.

Both of these bodies of commentary, the journalistic and the literary/
dramatic, are mainly concerned to address what was shown on the screen, and
thus conceive of television mainly as a text within the arts/humanities academic
traditions. The privileged object is generally a self-bounded work of fiction.[3]
Other early attention to television draws, in different ways, on the social sciences to address the production, circulation and function of television in contemporary society. Here, research has tended not to address the television text
as such, but instead to conceptualise television either through notions of its
social *function* and *effects*, or within a governing question of *cui bono?* (whose
good is served?). Thus television, along with other of the mass media, is conceptualised within frameworks principally concerned with the maintenance of
social order; the reproduction of the *status quo*, the relationship between the
state, media ownership and citizenship; the constitution of the public sphere.
With these concerns, privileged areas of inquiry have tended to be non-textual:
patterns of international cross-media ownership; national and international regulation of media production and distribution; professional ideologies; public
opinion; media audiences. Television, here, is more often an *instance* or *site*
than a text. Methodologies here have been greatly contested, particularly in the
extent to which Marxist frameworks or those associated with the critical sociology of the Frankfurt School have been employed. For scholars differ as to
whether the mass media should be studied as one element in the smooth functioning of society, or as contributing to the reproduction of particular patterns
of dominance – for example, the blonde 'Anglo' idea of feminine beauty as a
world-wide ideal for all women. *Mass Communication and Society*, a collection
edited by James Curran, Michael Gurevitch and Janet Woollacott in 1977, as a
course textbook for the Open University, provides an indicative text here (*see*
Fig. 5.2).

While television is addressed in this volume – for example, Chapters 9 and 10
offer specific case studies, while Chapter 2 is primarily concerned with the
establishment of the BBC – it is television conceived of within the field of mass
communications. Television is conceived of as part of a web of communications
media which mediate, reproduce and are reproduced by cultures structured
through patterns of class dominance. What is particularly interesting about this
reader is the way in which it also seeks to problematise the field of mass communication, repeatedly preferring the work of scholars working within the traditions of critical sociology and the emergent cultural studies to the US traditions
of 'mass comm'. The editors' introduction makes this point trenchantly, with its
clearly articulated project of a *theoretical* rather than 'empiricist' or 'instrumen-
talist' comunication studies. How else to explain the presence of Walter
Benjamin, who wrote, in the 1930s, not about television, but about how the status of art was transformed in the age of mechanical reproduction?

But if the inclusion of James Carey, Stuart Hall, Dick Hebdige and Walter
Benjamin in this volume points to the increasing relevance of the emerging discipline of cultural studies to the understanding of culture and communication –

Contents

Except where otherwise indicated, all the articles in this volume are original and have not been previously published.

Fig. 5.2 Contents page of James Curran, Michael Gurevitch and Janet Woollacott (eds), *Mass Communication and Society* (London: Edward Arnold, 1977)

and television (these are terms here understood in a *public* sense). The conceptualisation of the field is a conceptualisation of a global economy – this *is* an international vision – and overlapping public spheres. It is the contrasting emphasis on the private, the intimate and the domestic which has distinguished feminist approaches to the media in general, and television in particular. Much early feminist research on television in the mass communications field was concerned with questions of women's employment and their lack of visibility on the television screen. But very quickly feminists also began to investigate the idea of television as a despised domestic medium with programming aimed at housewives. The key genre here was the soap opera, a genre which exists in many different forms all over the world. And although different national serials do have different types of format, they share the contempt with which they are often regarded, the way in which they are seen as feminine and much less important than the world of politics and the public sphere. An indicative collection here is *Regarding Television* published by the American Film Institute in 1983. This book, which was edited by E. Ann Kaplan from a conference she organised at Rutgers University in 1981, begins to show the impact of feminist research on television in a more sustained way than the individual articles that were being published (*see* Fig. 5.3). Here there are four articles on soap opera, while others, such as Margaret Morse's work on sport, also address questions raised by feminist theory.

The way in which the essays on soap opera address their object is also significant. For while some of the essays, such as Sandy Flitterman's, are concerned with the television text, others, such as Tania Modleski's, are concerned with the distracted ways of watching that the genre allows. The influence of feminist scholars on television studies, then, on the one hand, directed attention to the despised genre of soap opera, and on the other, drew attention to the ways in which television was watched in the home.

The impact of this research can be seen if we compare the 1977 Curran, Gurevitch and Woollacott reader (*see* Fig. 5.2) with a 1991 Curran and Gurevitch reader, *Mass Media and Society* (*see* Fig. 5.4). While there are a range of differences between the first and second readers, with the second generally tending towards survey articles rather than case studies and reprinted material, what is noticeable in this context is what is surveyed. As with the Brandt, there is a noticeable feminisation of the object of study. Lower forms appear: here, 'romantic drama', there, soap opera. There are two articles which make a direct address to feminist media research, those by Ang and Hermes, and van Zoonen. While the field is still conceived in ways familiar from the 1977 collection, there have also been some shifts in the recognition of the gender agenda. Here we see that television is still conceptualised within the broader international frameworks of mass communications, but in fact the feminist essays are strongly dependent on television research to make their arguments. The definition of television has shifted between this anthology and the earlier 1977 one.

One further contents list from the 'early' period (1981) is illuminating here, showing the way in which television studies also emerged from a cluster of work best understood as film and cultural studies. This contents page comes from a reader for another Open University course, *Popular Television and Film*, edited by Tony Bennett, Susan Boyd-Bowman, Colin Mercer and Janet Woollacott (*see* Fig. 5.5). Like the Kaplan collection, this collection has articles by film

Table of Contents

Fig. 5.3 Contents page of E. Ann Kaplan (ed.), *Regarding Television* (Los Angeles: American Film Institute, 1983)

Contents

Fig. 5.4 Contents page of James Curran and Michael Gurevitch (eds), *Mass Media and Society* (London: Edward Arnold, 1991)

Contents

Acknowlědgments viii
Preface ix

PART I: GENRE
Introduction 3
1/STEPHEN NEALE
Genre and Cinema 6
2/MICK EATON
Television Situation Comedy 26
3/GEOFFREY HURD
The Television Presentation of the Police 53
4/Parodying Genre: The Case of *Gangsters* 71
5/PAUL KERR
Gangsters: Conventions and Contraventions 73
6/RICHARD PATERSON
Gangsters: The Pleasure and the Pain in the Text 79

PART II: THE DISCOURSES OF TELEVISION
Introduction 85
1/STUART HALL, IAN CONNELL, LIDIA CURTI
The 'Unity' of Current Affairs Television 88
2/CHARLOTTE BRUNSDON AND DAVID MORLEY
Everyday Television: *Nationwide* 118
3/Introduction: Television and the World Cup 142
4/COLIN MCARTHUR
Setting the Scene: *Radio Times* and *TV Times* 144
5/ANDREW TUDOR
The Panels 150
6/GEOFFREY NOWELL-SMITH
Television—Football—The World 159
7/CARL GARDNER AND ROBERT YOUNG
Science on TV: A Critique 171

PART III: POPULAR FILM AND PLEASURE
Introduction 197
1/STEPHEN HEATH
Jaws, Ideology and Film Theory 200
2/LAURA MULVEY
Visual Pleasure and Narrative Cinema 206
3/COLIN MACCABE
Realism and the Cinema: Notes on some Brechtian Theses 216
4/RICHARD DYER
Stars as Signs 236
5/THOMAS ELSAESSER
Narrative Cinema and Audience-Oriented Aesthetics 270

PART IV: HISTORY, POLITICS AND CLASSICAL NARRATIVE
Introduction 285
1/COLIN MCARTHUR
Historical Drama 288
2/The *Days of Hope* Debate: Introduction 302
3/COLIN MCARTHUR
Days of Hope 305
4/COLIN MACCABE
Days of Hope: A Response to Colin McArthur 310
5/COLIN MACCABE
Memory, Phantasy, Identity: *Days of Hope* and the Politics of the Past 314
6/KEITH TRIBE
History and the Production of Memories 319
7/JOHN CAUGHIE
Progressive Television and Documentary Drama 327

Film and Television Availability Note 353
Index 355

Fig. 5.5 Contents page of Tony Bennett, Susan Boyd-Bowman, Colin Mercer and Janet Woollacott (eds), *Popular Television and Film* (London: British Film Institute in association with the Open University, 1981)

scholars writing about television, but here the book is clearly seen to be about both film and television. The television is British television, although the cinema is Hollywood.

This collection offers much more attention to television as text, and marks a significant move away from conceiving that text solely as serious drama. Thus there are articles on football and sitcoms although the last part of the book does concentrate on *Days of Hope,* a four-part series directed by Ken Loach and produced by Tony Garnett about the British General Strike in 1926. Whilst the collection does include Laura Mulvey's famous article on visual pleasure, feminist work is not much in evidence. The move away from high art is a move to football, science and crime series. However, it is also clear that approaches from film studies, particularly through notions of genre, produce yet another understanding of television, which is here also informed by work in cultural studies. This collection was published in the same year as the first George Brandt collection, but has very different emphases. However, when we examine them together, as I have here, the 1993 Brandt collection is much easier to place. We see how *Television Drama in the 1980s* is the result of much broader definitions of what in television is worth paying attention to, just as we can see that the 1991 Curran and Gurevitch collection has responded to some of the same debates.

What Does Television Studies Study? Text, Audience and Representation

From these diverse origins developed the 'television' of television studies. In contrast to the television of the social sciences, this television was very 'textualised'. The concentration was on programmes and genres rather than industry and economy. This was not, in general, a television discussed in relation to issues of working practices, labour relations, exports and national and international legislation. In contrast to the emphases of literary and dramatic criticism, it was a television of low and popular culture. A television of sitcoms, soaps and crime series, rather than a television of playwrights, a television of ideology rather than aesthetics. And there have proved to be three particular areas of interest in the literature of this television studies: the definition of the television text, the textual analysis of the representations of the social world offered therein, and the investigation of the television audience. I will discuss each of these areas briefly, concentrating on debate about the television text partly because it is here that we find debate specific to the medium and partly because other chapters in this book offer extended discussion and examples of research into audiences and the textual analysis of programmes and genres.

Much innovatory work in television studies has been focused on the definition of the television text and this debate could be seen as one of the constituting frameworks of the field. The common-sense view points to the individual programme as a unit, and this view has firm grounding in the way television is produced. Television is, for the most part, made as programmes or runs of programmes: series, serials and mini-series. However, this is not necessarily how television is watched, despite the considerable currency of the view that it is somehow better for the viewer to choose to watch particular programmes rather than just having the television on. Indeed, BBC television in the 1950s featured 'interludes' between programmes, most famously *The Potter's Wheel*, a short film showing a pair of hands making a clay pot on a wheel, to ensure that viewers did not just drift from one programme to another. It is precisely this possible 'drifting' through an evening's viewing that has come to seem, to many commentators, one of the unique features of television watching, and hence something that must be attended to in any account of the television text.

The inaugural formulation is Raymond Williams's argument, in his 1974 book, *Television: Technology and Cultural Form*, that 'the defining feature of broadcasting' is 'planned flow' (1974: 86). Williams developed these ideas through reflecting on four years of reviewing television for the weekly periodical *The Listener*, when he suggests that the separating of the television text into recognisable generic programme units, which makes the reviewer's job much easier, somehow misses 'the central television experience: the fact of flow' (1974: 95). Williams's own discussion of flow draws on analysis of both British and US television and he is careful to insist on the natural variation of broadcasting systems and types and management of flow, but his attempt to describe what is specific to the watching of television has been internationally generative, particularly in combination with some of the more recent empirical studies of how people do (or don't) watch television.

If Williams's idea of flow has been principally understood to focus attention on television viewing as involving more viewing and less choosing than a critical focus on individual programmes would suggest, other critics have picked up the micro-narratives of which so much television is composed. Thus John Ellis approached the television text using a model ultimately derived from film studies, although he is precisely concerned, in his book *Visible Fictions* (1982), to differentiate cinema and television. Ellis suggests that the key unit of the television text is the 'segment', which he defines as 'small, sequential unities of images and sounds whose maximum duration seems to be about five minutes' (1982: 112). Broadcast television, Ellis argues, is composed of different types of combination of segment: sometimes sequential, as in drama series, sometimes cumulative, as in news broadcasts and commercials. As with Williams's 'flow', the radical element in Ellis's 'segment' is the way in which it transgresses common-sense boundaries like 'programme' or 'documentary' and 'fiction' to bring to the analyst's attention common and defining features of broadcast television as a medium.

However, it has also been argued that the television text cannot be conceptualised without attention to the structure of national broadcasting institutions and the financing of programme production. In this context, Nick Browne (1984) has argued that the US television system is best approached through a notion of the 'super-text'. Browne is concerned to address the specificities of the US commercial television system in contrast to the public service models – particularly the British one – which have been so generative a context for formative and influential thinking on television such as that of Raymond Williams and Stuart Hall. Browne defines the 'super-text' as, initially, a television programme and all introductory and interstitial material in that programme's place in a schedule. He is thus insisting on an 'impure' idea of the text, arguing that the programme as broadcast at a particular time in the working week, interrupted by ads and announcements, condenses the political economy of television.

Advertising, in Browne's schema, is the central mediating institution in US television, linking programme schedules to the wider world of production and consumption.

The final concept to be considered in the discussion about the television text is Newcomb and Hirsch's idea of the 'viewing strip' (1983). This concept suggests a mediation between broadcast provision and individual choice, attempting to grasp the way in which each individual negotiates their way through the 'flow' on offer, putting together a sequence of viewing of their own selection. Thus different individuals might produce very different 'texts' – viewing strips – from the same night's viewing. Implicit within the notion of the viewing strip – although not a prerequisite – is the remote control device, allowing channel change and channel-surfing. And it is this tool of audience agency which points us to the second substantial area of innovatory scholarship in television studies, the address to the audience.

The hybrid disciplinary origins of television studies are particularly evident in the approach to the television audience. Here, particularly in the 1980s, we find the convergence of potentially antagonistic paradigms, represented most vividly in an interdisciplinary conference on the television audience held in 1990 at the University of Illinois, where scholars from a range of disciplines met to debate and contest their versions of the audience, and how it can be appropriately investigated (Schroder, 1987; Hay, Grossberg and Wartella, 1996). Very simply, on the one hand, research traditions in the social sciences focus on the empirical investigation of the already existing audience. Research design here tends to seek representative samples of particular populations and/or viewers of a particular type of programming (adolescent boys and violence; women and soap opera). Research on the television audience has historically been dominated, particularly in the USA, by large-scale quantitative surveys, often designed using a model of the 'effects' of the media, of which television is not necessarily a differentiated element. Within the social sciences, this 'effects' model has been challenged by what is known as the 'uses and gratifications' model. In James Halloran's famous formulation, 'we should ask not what the media does to people, but what people do to the media' (1970). Herta Herzog's 1944 research on the listeners to radio daytime serials was an inaugural project within this 'uses and gratifications' tradition, which has recently produced the international project on the international decoding of the US prime-time serial, *Dallas* (Liebes and Katz, 1990).

This social science history of empirical audience investigation has been confronted, on the other hand, by ideas of a textually constituted 'reader' with their origins in literary and film studies. This is a very different conceptualisation of the audience, drawing on literary, semiotic and psychoanalytic theory to suggest – in different and disputed ways – that the text constructs a 'subject position' from which it is intelligible. In this body of work, the context of consumption and the social origins of audience members are irrelevant to the making of meaning which originates in the text. However – and it is thus that we see the potential convergence with social science 'uses and gratifications' models – literary theorists such as Umberto Eco (1994) have posed the extent to which the reader should be seen as active in meaning-making. It is, in this context, difficult to separate the development of television studies from that of cultural studies, for it is within cultural studies that we begin to find, in the 1980s, sophisticated theorisations and empirical investigations of the complex, contextual interplay of text and 'reader' in the making of meaning, as in, for example, the work of Janice Radway (1984) on the readers of romance fiction.

The inaugural formulations on television in the field of cultural studies are those of Stuart Hall in essays such as 'Encoding and decoding in television discourse' (1974) and David Morley's audience research (*The Nationwide Audience*, 1980). However, this television-specific work cannot theoretically be completely separated from other cultural studies research which stressed the often oppositional agency of individuals in response to contemporary culture. British cultural studies has proved a successful export, the theoretical paradigms there employed meeting and sometimes clashing with those used, internationally, in more generalised academic re-orientation towards the study of popular culture and entertainment in the 1970s and 1980s. Examples of influential television scholars working within cultural studies paradigms would be Ien Ang and John Fiske. Ang's work on the television audience (1985, 1991, 1995) ranges from a study of *Dallas* fans in the Netherlands to the interrogation of existing ideas of audience in a postmodern, global context. John Fiske's work has been particularly successful in introducing British cultural studies to a US audience, and his 1987 book *Television Culture* was one of the first books about television to take seriously the feminist agenda that has been so important to the recent development of the field. For if television studies is understood as a barely established institutional space, carved out by scholars of television from, on the one hand, mass communications and traditional Marxist political economy, and on the other, cinema, drama and literary studies, the significance of feminist research to the establishment of this connotationally feminised field cannot be underestimated, even if it is not always recognised.

The interest of new social movements in issues of representation, which has been generative for film and literary studies as well as for television studies, has produced sustained interventions by a range of scholars, approaching texts with questions about the representation of particular social groups and the interpretation of programmes such as, for example, *thirtysomething, Pee Wee's Playhouse, Cagney and Lacey* and *The Cosby Show*. Feminist scholars have, since the mid-1970s, tended to focus particularly on programmes for women and those which have key female protagonists. Key work here would include Julie D'Acci's study of *Cagney and Lacey* (1994), which is unusual in its attention to the conditions of production, and the now substantial literature on soap opera. In the USA, the televised proceedings of the Anita Hill/ Clarence Thomas hearings prompted much analysis, which, while almost never about television alone, did reveal the ways in which cultural studies approaches to television generated complex and sophisticated analyses of media events (Lubiano, 1993). Research by Sut Jhally and Justin Lewis (1992) has addressed the complex meanings about class and 'race' produced by viewers of *The Cosby Show*, but most audience research in this 'representational' paradigm has been with white audiences. Jacqueline Bobo and Ellen Seiter (1991) argue that this is partly a consequence of the 'whiteness' of the academy which makes research about viewing in the domestic environment potentially a further extension of surveillance for those ethnicised by the dominant culture. Herman Gray (1993) has suggested that there is a repeated 'avoidance and deferral of racial difference' in critical television analysis, a deferral achieved partly through the separation of the analysis of the formal operations of the television apparatus from attention to issues of race. This argument has resonance here, for we could suggest that the television of television studies, to a considerable degree echoing the address of Anglophone broadcast television, in the post-war period, has been constructed 'whitely'. This would be a matter, not so much of who is writing, but what they write about and to whom it is addressed. There is a growing body of work which suggests the beginning of change – for example, Darnell Hunt's 1997 analysis of the televising and viewing of the Rodney King beating, which analyses what Hunt nominates as a process of 'race-ing' for spectators, or Lynn Spigel's work on the white flight of the space race as figured in 1950s' US sci-fi sitcoms (1997). However, in the context of a discussion of the television of television studies, these are minority and relatively recent works.[4] So it becomes not only a question of what is the television of television studies, but, as indeed with the question of the address of the medium, who is assumed to be the student?

Conclusion: History

The television of television studies, then, is a relatively recent phenomenon. It has been produced in the last period in which television broadcasting will be dominated by nationally regulated terrestrial broadcasters, the last three decades of the twentieth century. Its origins lie in more established fields of study, principally literature and the social sciences, with a strong contribution from the theoretical models used in film and cultural studies. Feminist scholarship has been particularly significant in pointing to the private and domestic aspects of a medium which, in the social sciences, has been mainly conceptualised in terms of the public sphere. Generally, the television of television studies is a contemporary, politicised television analysed because it is understood to be a powerful medium. However, these politics are generally understood at a textual, rather than an institutional level, with much research undertaken to investigate the way in which the social world and particular social groups are – or are not – represented, rather than the more traditional political economy approaches, which see patterns of ownership and regulation as politically determining.

I started this essay by posing the idea that it is not obvious what the television of television studies is. Television, as an object of study, has been produced differently by different scholars and interest groups, and I have offered only a brief sketch. I have, for example, given little attention here to the television studied by those primarily concerned with its effects on children, or to research conducted by advertisers and broadcasting institutions.[5] But I hope I have established the significant contours in the development, particularly in Britain, of the infant discipline, television studies. Throughout the essay, I have suggested the ways in which this television is different to the television studied in other contexts. I am not trying to draw lines of disciplinary purity – this study *is* television studies, that isn't – although the disciplinary provenance of particular research is always illuminating. Instead, I have tried to show the way in which books such as Williams's *Television: Technology and Cultural Form* (1974) and John Fiske and John Hartley's *Reading Television* (1978) inaugurated and represent new ways of thinking about television. What seems exciting about this hybrid

discipline is its hybridity. The field of television studies is only enriched by returning to some of the questions and emphases of its originary disciplines. For example, the internationalism of studies of the political economy of the media
sometimes seems lacking in television studies, as does an understanding of the
production of texts, as opposed to their productivity. The significance of qualitative audience research in television studies should not prevent the recognition of
the importance of working with larger samples. Deconstructing the assumption
that the only television of aesthetic interest is the single play should not lead to the
abandonment of the critical analysis of the role of the writer on television. If 'television studies' now has some recognition, its dynamic potential is best realised not
in policing its boundaries, but in providing a context in which scholars working on
what is often considered a trivial medium can meet rigorous assessment by colleagues and the benefits of inter- and multidisciplinary approaches.

   This can perhaps be most interestingly exemplified in relation to the different
histories we can find in television studies. For if, on the one hand, the archives
of the broadcasting institutions and production companies offer relatively conventional sources for the historian, the absence of much television history *as
television* is rather more demanding. Similarly, the increasing tide of ephemera
generated by the medium raises historiographical questions also posed by the
use of sources of contested evidentiary status such as women's magazines. In the
1990s, explicitly historical projects which use this range of material, such as
Janet Thumim's (1995) research on British television for women in the 1950s,
meet older, contemporary production studies which trace the complex interplay
of factors involved in getting programmes on screen. Examples here might
include Tom Burns's study of the professional culture of the BBC (1977), *Movie*
magazine's study of *Upstairs, Downstairs* (Barr, Hillier and Perkins, 1975) or
Philip Schlesinger's study of 'The News', *Putting 'Reality' Together* (1978). That
is, as television studies enters the text-book stage of its existence, it is possible to
look back and see a very wide range of texts as contributing to its development.
This broad view, I would argue, is necessary if the television of television studies is not to be a limited and impoverished object of study. But also, this broad
view begins to give us a much richer understanding of the history of television
and how it has been understood historically. This history of television is a
rapidly expanding field, creating a retrospective history for the discipline, but
also documenting the period of nationally regulated terrestrial broadcasting
which is now coming to an end. Whatever we thought the television of television
studies was when it was being invented in the 1970s, what is becoming increasingly clear is that what it is now is history.

Notes

An earlier version of part of this essay has been published as the entry on 'Television
Studies' in Horace Newcomb (ed.), *Encyclopedia of Television* (Chicago: Fitzroy
Dearborn, 1997). Thanks to Laura Mulvey's BFI MA group (1996–7), the Midlands
Television Research group, Jason Jacobs and David Morley for comments.

   1.   Scannell and Cardiff's *Social History of British Broadcasting* (1991), while concerned
with the history of radio, establishes the framework for the consideration of British
television as a broadcast medium, something developed in Scannell's edited collection,

Broadcast Talk (1991). John Ellis's *Visible Fictions* (1982) provides an interesting counterpoint in its discussion of television in relation to cinema.

2. Detailed discussion of the reviewing and criticism of television can be found in McArthur (1980), Caughie (1984) and Poole (1984).

3. David Edgar (1982) makes a strong argument for the significance of drama documentary within the output of television, but this was relatively unusual at the time.

4. Other work relevant here would be George Lipsitz's (1988) account of the mobilisation of immigrant identities into early US network shows; Jim Pines's edited collection of interviews with black contributors to British television (1992); John Fiske's *Media Matters* (1995); Karen Ross's history of the intertwined origins of black film-making and television (1996); and Richard Dyer's discussion of 'whiteness' in the British television serial, *The Jewel in the Crown.* (1996).

5. See Buckingham (1996) and Seiter (1993).

References and Further Reading

ANG, I., 1985: *Watching Dallas*. London: Methuen.

———, 1991: *Desperately Seeking the Audience*. London: Routledge.

———, 1995: *Living Room Wars*. London: Routledge.

BARR, C., HILLIER, J. and PERKINS, V., 1975: 'The making of a television series: *Upstairs Downstairs' Movie* 21: 46–63.

BENNETT, T., BOYD-BOWMAN, S., MERCER, C. and WOOLLACOTT, J. (eds), 1981: *Popular Television and Film*. London: British Film Institute in association with the Open University.

BOBO, J., and SEITER, E., 1991: 'Black feminism and media criticism'. *Screen*, 32.3, reprinted in C. Brunsdon, J. D'Acci and L. Spigel (eds), 1997, *Feminist Television Criticism: A Reader*. Oxford: Oxford University Press.

BODDY, W., 1990: *Fifties Television: The Industry and its Critics*. Urbana and Chicago: University of Illinois Press.

BRANDT, G., 1981: *British Television Drama*. Cambridge: Cambridge University Press.

———, 1993: *British Television Drama in the 1980s*. Cambridge: Cambridge University Press.

BROWNE, N., 1984: 'The political economy of the television (super) text'. *Quarterly Review of Film Studies*, 9, 3, reprinted in Horace Newcomb (ed), 1994, *Television: The Critical View*. New York: Oxford University Press.

BUCKINGHAM, D., 1996: *Moving Images. Understanding Children's Emotional Responses to Television*. Manchester: Manchester University Press.

BURNS, T., 1977: *The BBC: Public Institution, Private World*. London: Macmillan.

CAUGHIE, J., 1984: 'Television criticism: a discourse in search of an object'. *Screen*, 25, 4–5, 109–20.

CORNER, J., 1995: *Television Form and Public Address*. London: Edward Arnold.

CORNER, J., and HARVEY, S. (eds), 1996: *Television Times: A Reader*. London: Arnold.

CURRAN, J. and GUREVITCH, M., 1991: *Mass Media and Society*. London: Edward Arnold.

CURRAN, J., GUREVITCH, M. AND WOOLLACOTT, J., 1977: *Mass Communication and Society*. London: Edward Arnold.

D'ACCI, J., 1994: *Defining Women: Television and the Case of Cagney and Lacey*. Chapel Hill: University of North Carolina Press.

DYER, R., 1996: '"There's nothing I can do! Nothing!": femininity, seriality and whiteness in *The Jewel in the Crown*'. *Screen*, 37, 3 : 225–39.

ECO, U., 1994: 'Does the audience have bad effects on television?' (first published 1977). In R. Lumley (ed.), *Umberto Eco: Apocalypse Postponed*. London: British Film Institute.

EDGAR, D., 1982: 'On drama documentary'. In F. Pike (ed) *Ah! Mischief*. London: Faber and Faber.

ELLIS, J., 1982: *Visible Fictions*. London: Routledge and Kegan Paul.

FISKE, J., 1987: *Television Culture*. London: Methuen.

————, 1995: *Media Matters*. Minneapolis: University of Minnesota Press.

FISKE, J. and HARTLEY, J., 1978: *Reading Television*. London: Methuen.

GOLDIE, G. W., 1978: *Facing the Nation: Television and Politics 1936–1976*. London: The Bodley Head.

GRAY, H., 1993: 'The endless slide of difference: critical television studies, television and the question of race'. *Critical Studies in Mass Communication*, June : 190–7.

HALL, S., 1980 'Encoding/decoding' (first published 1974). In Hall *et al.* (eds), *Culture, Media, Language*. London and Birmingham: Hutchinson and the Centre for Contemporary Cultural Studies.

HALL, S, HOBSON, D., LOWE, A., and WILLIS, P. (eds) 1980:*Culture, Media, Language*. London and Birmingham: Hutchinson and Centre for Contemporary Cultural Studies

HALLORAN, J., 1970: *The Effects of Television*. London: Panther.

HAY, J., GROSSBERG, L. and WARTELLA, E. (eds) 1996: *The Audience and its Landscape*. Boulder, CO: Westview.

HEIDE, M., 1995: *Television Culture and Women's Lives*. Philadelphia: University of Pennsylvania Press.

HERZOG, H., 1944: 'What do we really know about daytime serial listeners?'. In Paul Lazarsfeld and Frank Stanton (eds), *Radio Research 1942–43*. New York: Duell, Sloan and Pearce.

HUNT, D. M., 1997: *Screening the Los Angeles 'Riots': Race, Seeing and Resistance*. Cambridge: Cambridge University Press.

JHALLY, S. and LEWIS, J., 1992: *Enlightened Racism: The Cosby Show, Audiences and the Myth of the American Dream*. Boulder, CO: Westview Press.

KAPLAN, E. A., 1983: *Regarding Television*. Los Angeles: American Film Institute.

LIEBES, T. and KATZ, E., 1990: *The Export of Meaning*. Oxford: Oxford University Press.

LIPSITZ, G., 1988: 'The meaning of memory: family, class and ethnicity in early network television programs', *Camera Obscura*, 16: 79–116.

LUBIANO, W., 1993: 'Black ladies, welfare queens and state minstrels: ideological war by narrative means'. In Toni Morrison (ed.) *Race-ing Justice, En-gendering Power*. London: Chatto and Windus.

MCARTHUR, C., 1980: 'Points of review: television criticism in the press'. *Screen Education*, 35: 59–61.

MORLEY, D., 1980: *The Nationwide Audience*. London: British Film Institute.

————, 1992: *Television, Audiences and Cultural Studies*. London: Routledge.

NEWCOMB, H., 1974: *TV: The Most Popular Art*. New York: Anchor.

NEWCOMB, H. and HIRSCH, P., 1983: 'Television as a cultural forum'. Reprinted in Newcombe (ed.) (1994) *Television: The Critical View*. New York: Oxford University Press.

PINES, J., 1992: *Black and White in Colour*. London: British Film Institute.

POOLE, M., 1984: 'The cult of the generalist. British TV criticism, 1936–83' *Screen*, 25, 4–5: 41–61.

PURSER, P., 1992: *Done Viewing*. London: Quartet.

RADWAY, J., 1984: *Reading the Romance: Women, Patriarchy and Popular Literature*. Chapel Hill: University of North Carolina Press.

ROSS, K., 1996: *Black and White Media*. Cambridge: Polity.

SCANNELL, P. (ed.), 1991: *Broadcast Talk*. London: Sage.

SCANNELL, P. and CARDIFF, D., 1991: *The Social History of Broadcasting, Vol.1 1922–1939*. London: Basil Blackwell.

SCHLESINGER, P., 1978: *Putting 'Reality' Together*. London: Constable.

SCHRODER, K. C., 1987: 'Convergence of antagonistic traditions? The case of audience research'. *European Journal of Communication*, 2, 7–31.

SELBY. K. and COWDERY, R., 1995: *How to Study Television*. Houndmills: Macmillan.

SEITER, E., 1993: *Sold Separately: Parents and Children in Consumer Culture*. New Jersey: Rutgers University Press.

SPIGEL, L., 1993: *Make Room for TV*. Chicago: University of Chicago Press.

———, 1997: 'White flight'. In L. Spigel and M. Curtin (eds), *The Revolution Wasn't Televised*. New York: Routledge.

THOMAS, H. (ed.), 1959: *The Armchair Theatre*. London: Weidenfeld and Nicolson.

THUMIM, J., 1995: '"A live commercial for icing sugar". Researching the historical audience: gender and broadcast television in the 1950s'. *Screen* 36, 1: 48–55.

THURBER, J., 1948: *The Beast in Me and Other Animals*. New York: Harcourt Brace.

WILLIAMS, R., 1968: *Drama in Performance* (extended edition). London: C.A. Watts.

———, 1974 : *Television, Technology and Cultural Form*. London: Collins.

———, 1989: *Raymond Williams on Television*, ed. Alan O'Connor. London: Routledge.

6

Feminist Theory and Television Studies

Laura Stempel Mumford

The field we presently know as Television Studies has had the mixed fortune to experience some of its most important growth in an era of enormous change for both television and academic study. The expansion of cable and satellite use, the spread of VCR technology, the increasing impact of US programming in other countries, and vast alterations in programme content have utterly transformed the television landscape. Shifts in broadcast standards, greater first-run syndication opportunities, and the rise of so-called 'narrowcasting' and 'boutique programming'[1] have helped to destabilize some of TV scholars' most basic assumptions about our object of study. At the same time, widespread challenges to long-standing academic and theoretical premises, such as the possibility of scholarly objectivity, have fundamentally altered the way scholars look at cultural phenomena in general, and television in particular.

Most well-established fields of study, such as literature or history, are defined in terms of traditional disciplinarity, in which scholars apply their methods of analysis to a closely related body of work. TV Studies, on the other hand, has been actively shaped from its beginnings by the concept of *interdisciplinarity*, with scholars drawing on a variety of related academic areas and methodologies in order to construct an approach that crosses those traditional boundaries. This concept of academic boundary-crossing has been crucial in the development of fields like Afro-American and Women's Studies, whose founders discovered that existing analytical models could not fully explain the social meanings and consequences of widespread cultural phenomena such as racial or gender differences. Similarly, no single discipline or methodology can really be adequate in a field like TV Studies, whose interests range from content to demographics, from industry histories to sign systems.

As other essays in this volume make clear, both the British and US incarnations of TV Studies have complex histories, due in part to this very attempt to merge several separate but related disciplines, such as film, literature and mass communications, not to mention a variety of theoretical schools. Perhaps no theoretical perspectives have been as influential in the recent analysis of television as Women's Studies and the feminist theory that underlies it. A body of scholarly work on television existed before the 1970s, largely within mass communications departments, and the legacy is evident today in the continuing interest in 'effects', quanititative research and ethnography, all of which derive at least in part from earlier social science paradigms. But the mainstream of contemporary TV Studies tends to be somewhat more humanities-oriented, and to draw on insights originally developed in both film and literary theory, the areas in which many of the first generations of TV Studies practitioners – those writing in the late 1970s and early 1980s – were trained. Not coincidentally, these were fields that had also already begun to be significantly transformed by feminist theory and scholarship, and it was inevitable that those perspectives would also have a powerful influence on TV Studies (Allen, 1985; Kaplan, 1992).

Still, feminism's impact is not simply a convenient historical accident, or merely the result of certain prominent scholars' training or biases. Feminist theory is a congenial companion to TV Studies because the basic concerns of these two areas of inquiry overlap significantly. The fundamental questions of feminism focus on issues of cultural identity and position: What does it mean to live as a woman or a man? How do we learn to do it in the first place? To what extent does gender – our own identities as male or female, our ideas about what that might mean – shape our experience of the culture around us? These questions neatly inflect the fundamental question of TV Studies – what are we doing when we watch television? – and prompt us to ask how television works to establish or promote not just specific gender identities, but existing cultural relations generally.

The convergence of feminist theory and TV Studies has had a number of consequences that go beyond the specific area of feminist TV scholarship, which the bulk of this essay will explore. Feminist theory's high profile has helped to ensure that even scholars who are not explicitly committed to that area nevertheless pay at least lip-service, and in some cases serious attention, to gender, as well as to other crucial relationships of difference, such as those involving sexuality and (albeit somewhat less successfully) race. The prominence of feminist analysis has also guaranteed TV Studies' interest in a specific array of genres, such as soap opera and family melodrama, which past research had frequently ignored or denigrated. And feminist theory has pushed scholars to take seriously such aspects of the medium as its domesticity (which is typified by the TV set's placement in the home and the intensely personal uses viewers make of the programmes they watch), along with the ways in which even non-academic public debates about television are themselves inflected by gender.[2]

In addition to these valuable positive results, of course, feminist theory's dominance has undoubtedly imposed some limitations on the scope and direction of TV Studies as well, and has perhaps foreclosed, if only temporarily, some potentially useful avenues of investigation. But long before we consider how feminist theory may have limited our scholarly horizons, we need to be clear about exactly how it has enhanced and enlarged the possibilities for understanding television and its audiences. And before we can understand that, it is crucial to recognize that 'feminist theory' itself is a complicated and contested term. Although the popular media, including television, tend to define it as monolithic, there are many different incarnations of feminism (and thus of feminist criticism and theory), incorporating a wide variety of attitudes and assumptions. However, both popular and academic writers often divide feminism into general categories that represent a fairly narrow range of political perspectives and cultural analyses. For instance, radical feminism may be identified as a category that traditionally assumes that the oppression of women is the root of or the model for all other forms of oppression, such as racism; while in socialist, Marxist or materialist feminisms, women's position is linked directly to capitalist relations of production; liberal feminism seeks to alter current gender relations by working through or within the current economic and political system; and psychoanalytic feminism uses the central principles of psychoanalysis to explain how we learn to be gendered beings.

These descriptions represent only a narrow sampling of the various 'types' of feminisms, but it should be apparent that such differences in definition lead to differences in emphasis as well. (For instance, psychoanalytically oriented feminism is particularly interested in the unconscious processes by which we acquire our identities, while Marxist feminism tends to look more closely at how gender is connected to the reproduction of the labour force, and radical feminism often concentrates on issues related directly to sexuality.) Equally important, while these and other categories are often discussed as if they are mutually exclusive and stagnant, they have never really been so. In fact, critiques by women of colour, lesbians, and others have demonstrated that these and other familiar versions of feminism share not only a set of common interests, but certain common flaws as well, including a tendency to extrapolate from white, Western, middle-class, heterosexual women's experiences on the assumption that all women share the same problems or perspectives – or even that there is some inherent social or cultural perspective rooted in biological femininity ('essentialism'). These urgent critiques have inspired many women who feel excluded from mainstream feminist theory to develop new analyses that take more seriously the experiences of marginalized and non-dominant groups. (Grossberg *et al.*, 1991 provide a collection of conference papers that suggests the range of such engagements beyond the field of TV Studies.)

Other frameworks have also reshaped feminist approaches to popular culture. After a substantial critique of its biases towards male experience, for example, many feminist scholars have also found Cultural Studies' investigation of the production and circulation of meaning extremely congenial (Fiske, 1992; Franklin *et al.*, 1991; McRobbie, 1991; van Zoonen, 1994). In recent years, other innovative forms of criticism and theory have also developed, such as poststructuralist and postmodernist feminisms, which base their analyses of gender on new understandings of the operations of language, sign systems and discourse, while still other theorists have extended the principles of interdisciplinarity to methodology itself, employing an eclectic mix of approaches rather than identifying themselves with a single school or position.

No matter how loosely defined, however, these categories are imprecise and even potentially misleading, especially when they are used to subdivide an area of scholarship like feminist TV Studies, which already crosses so many disciplinary boundaries. There are many other fruitful ways of distinguishing among feminist approaches (Brunsdon, 1993; van Zoonen, 1994), yet all forms of feminist theory share the basic idea that gender is a socially constructed phenomenon, a set of learned behaviours and attitudes, rather than some natural and therefore immutable condition. All feminisms have in common an interest in how gender is learned and experienced, a critique of current gender relations, and an insistence that these relations can be changed through political action, premises that are especially important in the application of feminist theory to scholarship. Although all academic analysis carries an implicit set of political assumptions, feminist studies was one of the first approaches to take as part of its rationale an open acknowledgement of this fact, and all forms of feminist scholarship have always been directly linked to the idea of political change. The connection between academic study and the 'real' world of politics and social relations has been particularly crucial to feminist TV Studies, where much attention has been paid to questions about how the medium's representations of women and femininity may reflect or refract viewers' ideas about how their lives are to be lived.

Feminist critics and theorists agree that television, like other forms of mass or popular culture, plays a significant role in teaching and maintaining the political and social *status quo*. There is substantial disagreement about just how powerful that role is, and exactly how free viewers are to reject or resist TV's ideas about gender, sexuality identity and other issues. While most writers see television (and, indeed, all cultural products) as contested terrain, in which meaning is created by both producers and consumers, competing theoretical approaches place different weight on the role *negotiation* plays in that process. For some, the ideological content of the programme itself is often stronger than the viewer's resistance (Mumford, 1995); some put a greater emphasis on resistance (Brown, 1994); and still others understand the entire process as a struggle in which power shifts back and forth among various sites of meaning-making (D'Acci, 1994). But despite these rather profound disagreements about how exactly viewers accept and/or refuse what TV offers, there is no dispute among feminists about one central fact: that the medium functions ideologically, working with other social and cultural institutions to reflect, reinforce and mediate existing power-relations and ideas about how gender is and should be lived.

The process by which television's meanings are generated is usually defined in terms of three main elements, each associated with a particular aspect of the TV apparatus: production (the TV industry), reception (audience members), and text (the programmes, ads, promos, and so on). Few individual scholars attempt to examine all of these elements at once (D'Acci, 1994 is one of the few exceptions), but they provide a useful frame for understanding feminist TV Studies' various obsessions. Charlotte Brunsdon (1995) follows this general structure, for example, when she identifies the four main objects of feminist attention as women working in the television industry (e.g. as writers and producers), the presence of women on the TV screen (e.g. as newsreaders), the programmes themselves (specific content and images connected to women or gender), and the television audience. I would add to this the discourse that surrounds television, the ways in which critics, theorists, viewers, politicians and others talk about and position the medium and its programming, which is often explicitly or implicitly done in terms of gender (Joyrich, 1991–92; Petro, 1986).

While content and audience have tended to dominate recent feminist work, it is clear that analysis in all five of these areas shares the basic assumption that informs feminist TV Studies: that there is some relationship between the representations of gender that occur on television and the way that gender operates in viewers' lives. This means, among other things, that the work of feminist TV critics and theorists takes political and social events seriously, and considers both television and its viewers and producers as implicated in and shaped by the political world beyond TV. The fact that the feminist slogan 'the personal is political' has become a cliché does not erase its essential insight, that political mechanisms and relations of power can be understood and illuminated through our personal experiences – and vice versa – because politics do not operate simply in the public realm, but in the personal as well. This applies directly to the study of television: when we watch, we are not simply being entertained in some neutral way; we are having a political and ideological experience as well, and both our viewing practices and our ways of making sense of what we watch are articulated within a particular political and social context.

The attention to this bond between the social and televisual worlds has also led feminist TV scholars to take a special interest in the programming that women consume – genres such as the soap opera and the family melodrama – and those in which questions of gender play a prominent role, such as the domestic sitcom. This has been a way of taking women viewers seriously, by respecting their viewing choices, and it is also an obvious route to dissecting the interactions between certain cultural products (TV programmes) and the surrounding society (viewers). Although we now tend to take for granted that forms like soap opera deserve scholarly interest, before the rise of feminist studies dominant analyses of television tended to dismiss these very forms as trivial and not worthy of serious critical attention (Allen, 1985). Indeed, one of feminist and other politicized scholarships' central contributions to the study of culture has been the idea that genres and forms previously seen as 'minor' because they were produced and/or consumed by non-dominant groups may have even more to teach us about how culture operates and how ideology is enforced than the traditional canon. (It remains somewhat ironic that this challenge was necessary within TV Studies, since its scholars have struggled for decades to persuade other academics and the culture at large that television itself is a worthy object of study.)

Because genres such as soap operas, family melodramas and domestic sitcoms tend to emphasize aspects of life in which gender plays an obvious role, they have tended to serve as feminist TV Studies' primary examples. The fact that much basic work in feminist TV Studies derived from certain key insights of the feminist literary and film theory of the 1970s helps to explain the directions the field has taken, as well as some of its ongoing internal conflicts. The extremely influential work of the film theorist Laura Mulvey (1975) drew heavily on psychoanalysis to enter the ongoing debate about cinema spectatorship – namely, how is the film viewer constructed and positioned by the text and by the experience of movie-going? In examining certain classic Hollywood productions, Mulvey asked specifically whether film even creates an authentic viewing position for women, and this question of the woman as spectator was brought to bear on the study of television as well. In contrast, much feminist literary criticism of the same period was concerned with constructing an alternative canon of women writers and with examining the ways in which women, men and gender relations are represented within works of literature. These two theoretical threads were by no means mutually exclusive, either in film or literature, and from its earliest days, feminist TV Studies has tried to deal with both on-screen representation and audience response (the latter buoyed by the increasing popularity of Cultural Studies' focus on audience). However, because feminist litcrary criticism's attention to images dovetailed with the women's movement's interest in the impact of media in women's daily lives, much of the initial feminist work on television emphasized the discovery and analysis of 'positive' and 'negative' representations of women. And just as Cultural Studies' interest in audience was easily articulated with feminist approaches, the fact that much existing mass-communications theory relied on a so-called 'hypodermic' model, in which mass media exerts a direct (and often negative) influence on its consumers,[3] provided an additional framework for work on the TV portrayal of women's experience.

In some ways, the two threads of representation and audience can be seen as complementary ways of dealing with the field's key themes of *pleasure* and *identity*. One of the fundamental tensions within and among feminist theories is between the notions of women as victims and as agents, objects and subjects. In TV Studies, this tension expresses itself in work on television characters, where analyses of TV's objectification of women may contrast with discussions of heroic women figures (D'Acci, 1994), as well as in studies of viewers, which may see TV as a powerful reinforcer of traditional ideas about gender and women as also capable of resisting those ideas (Seiter *et al.*, 1989). Feminists of all perspectives, however, begin with the premise that women viewers obtain some degree of pleasure from watching TV, whether that means the direct enjoyment of individual television programmes, of resisting dominant media messages or constructing alternative meanings from those media, or of sharing the viewing or the interpretive experience with friends and family. (By 'pleasure' I mean something more than simple enjoyment, a complex kind of satisfaction that occurs at both the conscious and unconscious levels, but that is not necessarily sexualized in the conventional Freudian sense.) Where critics and theorists differ, however, is in identifying the exact sources of that pleasure and in drawing conclusions about its significance. Put crudely, there is considerable disagreement about whether it is a good or a bad thing that viewers – and women in particular – should enjoy mass-media products such as soap opera, precisely because of these products' power to articulate and reinforce the *status quo* and women's position within it. Is there any such thing as 'innocent' pleasure in a sitcom or a soap, or does enjoyment inevitably work to keep things as they are – at great cost to women and other non-dominant viewers?

This is a more complicated question than it might at first seem, and it is all too easy to focus exclusively on *either* viewers' enjoyment or the damaging influence of traditional ideology (White, 1992b: 166), to choose between an understanding of TV as 'just entertainment' and one that sees the medium as an all-powerful manipulator of mass opinion. Instead, both pleasure and ideology are constantly at work when we consume TV or any other cultural artifact, and the dilemma of how to understand the tension between them is necessarily at the centre of all progressive cultural theory. It is especially important to feminist TV Studies, which takes the possible relationships between the medium and gender inequality as one of its primary subjects.

Similarly, identity is widely acknowledged as fundamental to the process of viewing and making meaning of television. People are presumed to watch from their particular, socially situated identities, although no one argues that every single component of identity (race, gender, sexual preference, class position, age, job, family membership, etc.) is necessarily triggered by every TV programme. The very possibility of talking about *women* watching television assumes that at least some of the time, the viewing experience is inflected by a certain aspect of identity – in this case, membership in the social category 'women'. Other differences may stand in the way of watching primarily 'as women' – for instance, women of colour may not make the same meaning of a particular *Cosby* episode as the one made by white women (Jhally and Lewis, 1992; Press, 1991); or such differences may inflect the viewing experience without creating completely different meanings, as when women of different generations attempt to make sense of a programme in which age or cultural history plays a significant part. It is crucial to recognize, however, that there is no intrinsic connection between biological femininity and any particular viewing sensibility, or any direct and automatic relationship between gender and response. Instead, feminist TV scholars point to women's socially constructed social position(s) and the ways in which particular cultural artifacts – e.g. television programmes – inscribe a position for women viewers that evokes the cultural skills associated with femininity. Interventions by and about women of colour (Bobo and Seiter, 1991) and postcolonial audiences continue the critique of feminism's historical tendency to generalize from heterosexual women's experience by reminding us just how culturally specific these skills are, while recent work by writers who identify themselves with queer theory has both built on and interrogated feminist approaches to mainstream media, emphasizing the importance of gender while also insisting on the necessity of a specific theory of ' "queerness" as a mass culture reception practice' (Doty, 1993: 2).

Feminist TV theorists have also increasingly complicated the ideas of spectatorship and audience, identifying the former as primarily a textual and the latter as primarily a social category. According to Annette Kuhn (1984), social audience members – real women sitting in front of their TV sets – become spectators 'in the moment they engage in the processes and pleasures of meaning-making' (343). Women viewers are *interpellated* – addressed and positioned – by the television text in terms of their cultural expertise, and to the extent that they respond to this hail, they are positioned as female (rather than male, ungendered, multiply gendered, etc.) spectators (Gledhill, 1988; Ang and Hermes, 1991). Postmodern theory further questions the entire existence of unitary identity, whether gendered or otherwise, insisting instead that what we think of as identity is actually a constantly shifting set of positions created through various social and cultural practices (Ang and Hermes, 1991), and this way of thinking about identity has had considerable influence on recent feminist TV Studies as well.

Although feminists have always looked at both 'positive' and 'negative' images of women, early work tended to emphasize the latter, pointing out that, for instance, the traditional domestic sitcom's portrayal of family life actively promoted an acceptance of women as primarily concerned with personal or familial issues, happily subordinated to men's interests, and incapable of autonomous action (Bathrick, 1984). This attention reflected a broad feminist concern with the impact of cultural stereotypes. Later studies have often dismissed these early forays as theoretically unsophisticated, because they seem to discount viewers' complex relationship to the TV shows they watch (Ang and Hermes, 1991), yet such preliminary work was absolutely necessary for two major reasons. First, it provided forceful evidence about the ways in which dominant representations reinforce existing gender roles and institutions. While this notion has been substantially retheorized, the idea that narrow, conventional depictions of experience exert some influence on viewers remains key to feminist and other critical approaches to culture. The early emphasis on stereotypes also raised, although it did not adequately answer, one of the most important questions for feminist TV Studies: how do women reconcile the apparent gaps between what they see on television and what they experience in their lives?

Along with these analyses of 'negative' images, however, came a search for more encouraging interpretations of women's experience, and that search took several different forms. Many critics expressed straightforward enthusiasm for TV roles in which women characters were presented as strong, independent, smart, economically powerful, or socially involved, rather than identified primarily in terms of their relationships to men. Programmes such as *The Mary Tyler Moore Show* and *Cagney and Lacey* were praised for their recognition of women's work outside the home, their emphasis on the bonds between women characters, and for the crucial off-screen roles played by women producers and creators (Bathrick, 1984). At the same time, shifts in television – some of them wrought by feminism itself – not only helped to shift the agenda and direction of feminist TV Studies, but made the importance of its project even more evident. For instance, the traditional crime drama seemed to provide little space for a consideration of domestic life, but the success of the series *Cagney and Lacey* brought conventionally feminine interests such as romance and family into the police station, as well as pushing analysts to recognize the exact degree to which 'masculine' police dramas had always dealt, albeit indirectly, with questions related to gender. As both the portrayals of women characters and the relationships between so-called 'women's' programming became more complex, detailed studies by scholars such as Julie D'Acci (1994) made clear the necessity of examining not simply what we see on the screen, but the processes by which the programmes themselves come to exist.

More sophisticated theoretical tools, a wider spectrum of interests, and the influence of Cultural Studies have gradually led feminist TV scholars to consider 'images of women' in a new way. Rather than identifying these representations as self-evidently *either* 'negative' or 'positive', and assuming that viewers take them up in some simple and obvious way, critics and theorists began to suspect that the process was more complicated, contradictory and ambiguous than previous work seemed to have assumed, and to look instead at what viewers actually describe themselves as doing with the programmes they watch. Feminist scholars began to recognize, for instance, that women viewers could experience apparently 'negative' figures as 'positive', turning the representations produced by television to their own purposes. (Tania Modleski [1979] helped to begin this trend in her work on women viewers' potential identification with soap opera villainesses, but Seiter *et al.* [1989] demonstrate the more recent range of such approaches, including work that focuses on the specific genre of soap opera, and audience studies that consider viewers according to their age, gender, or sexual orientation.)

In a similar vein, theorists such as Patricia Mellencamp (1992) used classic sitcom figures like Lucy (*I Love Lucy*) and Gracie (*The Burns and Allen Show*) to illuminate the densely entangled processes by which women experience the 'double whammy' of ideological containment: 'identification *and* (by or with) annexation' (314). More recently, Kathleen Rowe (1995) has explored the cultural terms within which stars like Roseanne are positioned, not only by the programmes in which they appear, but by the (often openly misogynist) media discourse that surrounds them, in a sense reviving the issue of stereotypes and demonstrating once again that watching television is no simple, ideologically neutral act.

At the same time, critical theory of all sorts has increasingly come to question the whole idea of representation. In particular, many theorists say that it is impossible to identify or define a specific 'TV text' – to claim, for instance, that a particular television programme exists outside of the experience of viewing it, which makes it as much a product of its viewers' practices as of its industrial producers. This position has featured prominently in feminist work on audiences, especially in ethnographic studies that focus on the sense that soap opera or *Star Trek* fans make of their favourite programmes (Brown, 1994; Jenkins, 1992). Finally, work by feminist historians of television such as Lynn Spigel (1992) places both TV programming and audience members' viewing practices in far more precise context by examining both the social situation and the discourses surrounding important early developments, such as the television set's physical location within the home.

It would be a mistake to suggest that feminist TV Studies has moved on a straightforward path from naïve content analysis to some super-sophisticated understanding of discourse that utterly rejects the idea of media images' independent meanings or impact on those who consume them. Work continues on all aspects of television, using a wide range of interpretive models, and feminist theorists and critics continue to produce textual analyses that insist on the importance of the programmes' manifest content and narrative form alongside studies that use extratextual materials such as interviews and archival documents to demonstrate viewers' power to construct their own meanings out of whatever producers offer them. And when we turn to feminist work on individual genres, we find not only that a number of quite different theoretical approaches co-exist simultaneously, but that even those writers who seem most focused on audience are also concerned with content and structure, and vice versa. In fact, it is the interplay between those two that forms the crux of feminist TV Studies.

My outline of feminist TV Studies' trajectory identifies some of the major mileposts, but in order to understand it more fully, it helps to look at the field in terms of a genre that has been uniquely important to feminist critics and theorists: soap opera. Cultural and critical attitudes toward soap operas provide a convenient paradigm for the attitudes toward so-called 'women's' programming in general, and while the study of soap operas has its own particular history, it provides an excellent example of how the larger field has developed and some insight into the questions that have been most important to feminist analysis of television as a whole. As Charlotte Brunsdon (1993, 1995) has argued, soap opera's prominence within feminist TV Studies is also closely tied to the gradual movement of feminist work on television from outside to inside the formal institutions of academic study.

Historically, soaps were denigrated for their blatantly commercial origins (because they were explicitly designed as radio programmes to attract women consumers), their fixation on the details of personal life, their melodramatic performance style and relatively low production values, and their primarily female audience. Although many early feminist critics also saw soap operas as simply demeaning to women as both viewers and characters (Embree, 1970: 182), this attitude soon changed, as feminist analysis began to focus more empathetically on the popular culture forms that women enjoy, and to explore more carefully the pleasure women viewers have traditionally derived from their favourite shows. Work by theorists like Christine Geraghty (1981) helped to demonstrate the genre's complexity by carefully examining the programmes' most basic structures, while others (Seiter, 1982a, 1982b) investigated the genre in terms of new theories about the relative openness of particular kinds of texts, and the freedom they allow for viewers to make their own meanings.

Feminists have long identified soaps' narrative structure as a key component of women's fondness for the genre. One of the most influential formulations of this idea came from Tania Modleski (1979, 1984), who pointed out that the programmes' patterns of repetition and interruption mirror the daily experience of their target audience, women working within the home. Unlike the traditional linear, closure-oriented sitcom or prime-time drama, soaps' multiple, fragmented storylines and their open-ended serial format not only resonate with the rhythms of women's overlapping, never-completed chores, but actually make it possible for these viewers to follow their favourite programmes despite their distracting domestic responsibilities. Modleski also argued that the large ensemble casts deny viewers drama's usual opportunity to identify with a single protagonist, forcing them instead into multiple identifications that resemble those of the 'ideal mother' (1984: 92).

The insight that certain forms set up a unique resonance with their viewers' personal experience at the very level of structure provided an important premise for much feminist work on soaps, encouraging scholars to look closely at serial structure, the feature that distinguishes soap opera from most other TV genres. For example, Sandy Flitterman-Lewis (1983, 1988) considered some ways in which soap viewers attempt to deal with the form's open-endedness, suggesting that the tidily resolved commercials might compensate for soaps' frustration of the desire for closure, and outlining the ways in which the programmes turn conventional dramatic resolutions on their heads.

Although these theorists emphasized narrative structure, they also acknowledged the role that soaps' specific content plays in viewers' interest. For instance, Modleski (1984) argued that soap opera villainesses are uniquely powerful representations of female autonomy, while male characters' obsession with personal life allows women viewers to imagine that such men might really exist. Charlotte Brunsdon (1982) went even further, identifying this focus on the personal sphere as one of the genre's most powerful sources of pleasure for women viewers. She called personal life the genre's 'ideological problematic' (78), although it is really *cultural competence* – in this case, 'the culturally constructed skills of femininity' (81) – that soaps engage and within which they make sense.

Because of the differences in telecast practices, the US distinction between daytime and prime-time does not really apply to the programmes that British and other European scholars categorize as soap operas, and their attention has from the beginning been on evening serials like *Coronation Street* and

Crossroads (Brunsdon, 1982) and on re-broadcasts of US prime-time serials (Geraghty, 1991). By drawing directly on women viewers' descriptions of their own experience, Ien Ang (1985) and Dorothy Hobson (1989) have been able to examine the uses women actually make of soaps, both in their individual lives and as a means of bonding with friends in the workplace. Even among US scholars, prime-time serials have provided the basis for important insights into viewer response. Jane Feuer's work on gay viewers of *Dynasty* (1984), for instance, elaborates on the ways in which specific audience fractions make meaning through their own gendered and sexual identities.

The long-standing feminist interest in audience has also been enhanced by Cultural Studies' adaptation of ethnographic study. Thus, a number of feminist and feminist-influenced scholars have inquired into soap fans' own understandings of their viewing practices, often emphasizing the ways in which gender shapes both the meanings they construct and viewers' sense of their relationship to the programmes (Seiter, 1990; Ang and Hermes, 1991; Press, 1991; Brown, 1994). This approach has been particularly important in enriching our understanding of the role that ethnic, racial or national identities may play in audience response, as researchers have examined the specific viewing practices of Korean soap fans (Lee and Cho, 1990), or Israeli viewers of *Dallas* (Liebes and Katz, 1990), and such studies also exemplify the give-and-take between feminist analysis and the new cultural critiques arising out of postcolonial theory. Robert C. Allen's anthology of essays on 'soap operas around the world' (1995) also demonstrates the way in which feminist insights are increasingly being brought to bear on an international range of TV texts and audience.

Finally, Allen's own work is also an excellent example of how deeply feminist theories can inform soap opera studies that are not strictly speaking feminist. His *Speaking of Soap Operas* (1985) was one of the first major books to treat soaps as important scholarly terrain, and while its analysis of soap opera's narrative structure, discourse and history derives primarily from reader-response theory, Allen incorporates not only specific feminist insights, but the commitment to taking women viewers seriously that is a cornerstone of feminist criticism.

In addition to the shifts that have occurred in feminist approaches, which are reflected in the literature on soap operas, certain changes in television itself have made the study of soaps even more illuminating. For example, the migration into prime-time US television of narrative structures associated with daytime soap operas has greatly altered almost every major TV genre in some way. Along with the immense popularity of 'prime-time soaps', including *Dallas* and *Dynasty*, series such as *Hill Street Blues*, *St. Elsewhere*, and *L.A. Law* have used the open-ended serial format and overlapping multiple storylines of soaps to depict subjects – crime, medicine, law – usually dealt with in linear, closure-driven dramas. The use of soap-style irresolution has grown so popular that season-ending cliffhangers and multi-part story arcs have become common even on programmes that do not usually make use of other soap opera features. In fact, these developments, which began in the late 1970s, were in some ways anticipated by an earlier change in sitcoms such as *The Mary Tyler Moore Show* and *M*A*S*H*, the shift from discrete episodes, in which characters seemed to suffer from a kind of week-to-week amnesia, to a sense that characters learned from their experiences and evolved over the course of a series' life (Feuer *et al.*,

1984; Mumford, 1994–95). This move toward series-long character develop-ment mirrors soap operas' own emphasis on gradual and long-term growth, and might be seen as the real beginning of the genre's colonization of prime time.

One result of these changes has been that soaps no longer seem isolated day-time islands of interest only to the women who watch them. Instead, theories developed to explain the narrative and social functions of soap opera have come to be seen as increasingly relevant to the examination of other kinds of fictional, and even non-fictional, television programming. The formal and theoretical connections between soap opera and other TV forms has been especially import-ant for scholars committed to feminist TV Studies. As Brunsdon (1995) points out, the investigation of soap operas points us toward all of the key issues in the field of feminist TV Studies. As a genre designed for and watched primarily by women, concerned mainly with questions about domestic and personal life, and as a form that has come to be cultural shorthand for both the trivial and the fem-inine, soaps have effectively been impossible for feminists to ignore. The pro-grammes have always exhibited the central tension between TV's progressive and regressive tendencies, a fact that is demonstrated by theorists' conflicts over exactly what role they play in the production and preservation of ideology; as a result, soaps have proved rich ground for exploring some of the medium's most revealing complexities. Finally, I would argue that feminist work on soaps offers forceful evidence of the way in which the study of content and audience inter-sect around the question of pleasure, in this case women viewers' pleasure. When we look at soap opera, we necessarily raise one of the most basic issues that feminist TV Studies – indeed, feminist theory of all sorts – must confront: how and why do women so deeply enjoy what seems to oppress them?

Soaps have become such a familiar core for feminist work on television that even analyses of seemingly unrelated genres are often at least partially framed by them. For example, Lynne Joyrich momentarily couches her consideration of genre and gender representation on *Star Trek: The Next Generation* in terms of soap opera form, calling the series not 'a space western' but 'a space soap' (1996: 74), while discussions of industry practices such as off-network stripping (Mumford, 1994–95) take soap-opera viewing practices as a model for the con-sumption of other forms and genres. One noteworthy effect of the emphasis on the television genres women enjoy – and on soap opera in particular – has been to promote a specific understanding of the television text as fragmented, un-authored, domestic, governed by 'flow', and amenable to a kind of viewing that takes the form of the glance instead of the gaze. Because soaps actually do appear to be structured in this way, the focus on them may have created a circu-lar theoretical stance, in which soaps are understood as paradigmatic of TV in general. Many feminist TV theorists (including myself) have taken this very position, using soap operas to demonstrate the operations of the entire medium of television. Charlotte Brunsdon, for example, describes them as 'in some ways the paradigmatic television genre (domestic, continuous, contemporary, episodic, repetitive, fragmented, and aural)' (1989: 123).

Critiques of this conception of the television apparatus suggest one direction in which feminist TV Studies might proceed if soaps were not the main theoret-ical touchstone. Rather than understanding TV viewing practice as ruled by the casual glance, for example, John Thornton Caldwell (1995) places visual style at the centre, claiming that the attentive gaze is at least as valid a model. This shift from distraction to concentration also has the potential to shift our theoretical attention from genres like soaps, which accommodate the viewer who is performing other tasks while watching, to others – such as spectaculars, specials, certain kinds of TV movies, and even visually excessive tabloid and talk shows – which require and reward a greater degree of attentive focus.

In tandem with the Cultural Studies paradigm, feminism's emphasis on questions of agency and on culture's role in ideology, as well as its generally progressive political agenda, have also pulled us toward a concentration on the relationship between the TV text and its audience. This focus on agency, discourse and culture has encouraged scholars to understand the TV text as a complex product created by both viewer and producer, and to recognize that viewers are socially and culturally situated, but that move has possibly occurred at the cost of closer attention to the industry itself. Finally, the very same attention to supposedly 'feminine' genres like soaps and melodramas that has so deeply enriched TV Studies may also have led, inevitably, to the neglect of certain traditionally 'masculine' programming forms like sports and news, and of other stylistic and structural aspects of television (including specific types of visual and stylistic excess) that are not clearly exhibited in 'feminine' forms. It is possible that this neglect has reinforced the tendency to theorize the television apparatus through forms like soap opera (rather than, say, sitcoms).

Even within explicitly feminist work, it is clear that the traditional concentration on women and woman-oriented programming has had theoretical consequences. While the analysis of TV's representations of femininity and of women's experience, and the study of women as viewers and producers, have been absolutely crucial, they necessarily tell only part of the story. Gender is not, after all, constructed only through cultural products or ideological practices that address women, and yet, as Ang and Hermes (1991) point out, it is possible to see even feminists' focus on women's media consumption as the result of 'a more general bias in society, in which women are defined as the problematic sex' (308). For some postmodernist and poststructuralist theorists, the very project of focusing on women viewers' practices rests on a set of questionable assumptions, including the idea that TV viewing is always either exclusively or primarily a gendered experience, and that 'women' exist as some objective, unified whole, rather than being a fragmented and polysemous category under constant construction by and through social and cultural practices.

These are extremely valuable interventions which must be taken seriously as feminist TV theory continues to evolve. It is particularly important that we recognize the ways in which the conventional focus on women – as viewers, as target audiences, as performers or characters or producers or textual positions'– controls feminist TV Studies' most basic ideas about how television operates. But I want to conclude this essay by cautioning as well against erasing real women from the TV picture in our eagerness to move beyond the confining notions of masculinity and femininity that are such prominent features of dominant ideology's regulatory strategies (Modleski, 1991). As long as binary systems of gender that disadvantage real women remain fundamental to the cultures in which television is produced and consumed, and in which viewers are constructed and positioned, women must remain at the centre of the feminist project.

Notes

An earlier version of this essay was presented at the Telecommunications Colloquium, Department of Communication Arts, University of Wisconsin-Madison, where I benefited from the participants' generous and interesting suggestions for filling in all the spots where I had only written 'blahblahblah'. And thanks as always to Julie D'Acci, for her collegial enthusiasm and many entertaining snacks, and to Nancy St Clair, for things that have nothing to do with television.

1.   'Narrowcasting' refers to cable networks' practice of selecting or producing programming designed to appeal to a specific target audience, such as viewers of a particular age, gender or ethnic identity. In the USA, cable services such as Lifetime (which targets women), Black Entertainment Television, Nickelodeon (children), and various Christian networks are among the most successful at using this approach to develop a loyal core audience. 'Boutique programming' refers to the practice, used most often by US commercial broadcasters, of selecting or producing programmes that target demographic fragments that, while often relatively small, are economically desirable to advertisers.

2.   To cite one of the most blatant examples of the role that gender plays in public debates about television's cultural value or influence, consider the practice of denigrating certain kinds of dramas or made-for-TV movies by calling them 'soap operas,' a commercial genre created explicitly for women radio and then television consumers. This link, along with the identification of certain kinds of male-targeted programming (e.g. major sports events) as worthy of more serious attention, rests on a long-standing association between women and 'trash', the assumption that the forms of popular culture women most enjoy are less valuable – or in some cases perhaps more actively dangerous – than those enjoyed by men. Joyrich (1991–92) offers more subtle examples of this tendency, while Rowe (1995) demonstrates the role that the discourses around gender play in the construction of star personae.

3.   As the word suggests, the 'hypodermic' model assumes that the mass media 'inject' relatively passive consumers with specific messages or ideas. Although the position is usually associated with mass-communications studies (Allen, 1992: 13–16), it also bears an obvious resemblance to early Marxist approaches to mass culture, which see consumers as 'dupes'. Morley (1989) offers an excellent review of the 'changing paradigms in audience studies', including the tensions between notions of the audience as passive and active.

References and Further Reading

ALLEN, R.C., 1985: *Speaking of Soap Operas*. Chapel Hill: University of North Carolina Press.
——, 1989: 'Bursting bubbles: "soap opera", audiences, and the limits of genre'. In Ellen Seiter, *et al.* (eds), *Remote Control: Television, Audiences and Cultural Power*. London: Routledge, 44–55.
——, 1992: 'Introduction to the second edition, More talk about TV' In Robert C. Allen (ed.), *Channels of Discourse, Reassembled: Television and Contemporary Criticism*, 2nd edn. Chapel Hill: University of North Carolina Press, 1–30.
——, (ed.) 1995: *To Be Continued...: Soap Operas around the World*. London: Routledge.
ANG, I., 1985: *Watching Dallas: Soap Opera and the Melodramatic Imagination*, trans. Della Couling. London: Methuen.
——, and HERMES, J., 1991: 'Gender and/in media consumption'. In James Curran, and Michael Gurevitch (eds), *Mass Media and Society*. London: Edward Arnold, 307–28.

BATHRICK, S., 1984: '*The Mary Tyler Moore Show*: women at home and at work'. In Jane Feuer, Paul Kerr and Tise Vahimagi (eds), *MTM: 'Quality Television'*. London: British Film Institute, 99–131.

BOBO, J., and SEITER, E., 1991: 'Black feminism and media criticism: *The Women of Brewster Place*', *Screen*, 32, 3: 286–302.

BROWN, M. E., (ed.), 1990: *Television and Women's Culture: The Politics of the Popular*. London: Sage.

———, 1994: *Soap Opera and Women's Talk: The Pleasure of Resistance*. Thousand Oaks, CA: Sage Publications.

BRUNSDON, C. E., 1982: '*Crossroads*: notes on soap opera', *Screen*, 22, 4: 32–7.

———, 1989: 'Text and audience'. In Ellen Seiter *et al.* (eds), *Remote Control: Television, Audiences and Cultural Power*. London: Routledge, 116–29.

———, 1993: 'Identity in feminist television criticism'. *Media, Culture and Society*, 15: 309–20.

———, 1995: 'The role of soap operas in the development of feminist television scholarship'. In Robert C. Allen (ed.), *To Be Continued...* . London: Routledge, 49–65.

BYARS, J., 1987: Reading feminine discourse: prime-time television in the U.S.', *Communication*, 9, 3–4: 289–303.

———, 1988: 'Gazes/voices/power: expanding psychoanalysis for feminism film and television theory'. In Deidre Pribram (ed.), *Female Spectators: Looking at Film and Television*. London: Verso, 110–31.

CALDWELL, J. T., 1995: *Televisuality: Style, Crisis, and Authority in American Television*. New Brunswick: Rutgers University Press.

D'ACCI, J., 1994: *Defining Women: Television and the Case of Cagney and Lacey*. Chapel Hill: University of North Carolina Press.

DEMING, C. J., 1990: 'For television-centred television criticism: lessons from feminism'. In Mary Ellen Brown (ed.), *Television and Women's Culture: The Politics of the Popular*. London: Sage, 37–60.

DEMING R., 1992: 'The return of the unrepressed: male desire, gender and genre'. *Quarterly Review of Film and Video*, 14, 1–2: 125–47.

DOTY, A., 1993: *Making Things Perfectly Queer: Interpreting Mass Culture*. Minneapolis: University of Minnesota Press.

DYER, R., GERAGHTY, C., JORDAN, M., LOVELL, T., PATERSON, R. and STEWART, J., 1981: *Coronation Street*. London: British Film Institute.

EMBREE, A., 1970: 'Media Images 1: Madison Avenue brainwashing – the facts'. In Robin Morgan (ed.), *Sisterhood Is Powerful: An Anthology of Writings from the Women's Liberation Movement*. New York: Vintage, 175–91.

FEUER, J., 1984: 'Melodrama, serial form and television today'. *Screen*, 25, 1: 4–16.

———, 1989: 'Reading *Dynasty*: television and reception theory' *SAQ*, 88, 2: 443–60.

FEUER, J., KERR, P. and VAHIMAGI, T. (eds), 1984: *MTM: 'Quality Television'*. London: British Film Institute.

FISKE, J., 1987: *Television Culture*. London: Methuen.

———, 1992: 'British cultural studies and television'. In Robert C. Allen (ed.), *Channels of Discourse, Reassembled: Television and Contemporary Criticism*, 2nd edn. Chapel Hill: University of North Carolina Press, 284–326.

FLITTERMAN-LEWIS, S., 1983: 'The *real* soap operas: TV commercials'. In E. Ann Kaplan (ed.), *Regarding Television: Critical Approaches – An Anthology*. Los Angeles: American Film Institute, 84–96.

———, 1988: 'All's well that doesn't end: soap operas and the marriage motif'. *Camera Obscura*, 16: 119–27.

FRANKLIN, S., LURY, C. and STACEY, J., 1991: 'Feminism and cultural studies: pasts, presents, futures'. *Media, Culture and Society*, 13: 171–92.

FUQUA, JOY V., 1995: 'There's a queer in my soap!: the AIDS/homophobia storyline of *One Life to Live*'. In Robert C Allen (ed.), *To Be Continued...* . London: Routledge, 199–212.

GERAGHTY, C., 1981: 'The continuous serial – a definition'. In Richard Dyer *et al.*, *Coronation Street*. London: British Film Institute, 9–26.

———, 1991: *Women and Soap Opera: A Study of Prime Time Soaps*. Cambridge: Polity Press.

GLEDHILL, C., 1988: 'Pleasurable negotiations'. In Deidre Pribram (ed.), *Female Spectators*. London: Verso, 64–89.

———, 1992: 'Speculations on the relationship between soap opera and melodrama'. *Quarterly Review of Film and Video*, 14, 1–2: 103–24.

GROSSBERG, L., NELSON, C. and TREICHLER, P., 1991: *Cultural Studies*. New York: Routledge.

HOBSON, D., 1982: *Crossroads: The Drama of a Soap Opera*. London: Methuen.

———, 1989: 'Soap operas at work'. In Ellen Seiter *et al.* (eds), *Remote Control: Television, Audiences and Cultural Power*. London: Routledge, 150–67.

JENKINS, H., 1992: *Textual Poachers: Television Fans and Participatory Culture*. New York: Routledge.

JHALLY, S. and LEWIS, J., 1992: *Enlightened Racism: The Cosby Show, Audiences, and the Myth of the American Dream*. Boulder, CO: Westview.

JOYRICH, L., 1988: 'All that television allows: TV melodrama, postmodernism and consumer culture', *Camera Obscura*, 16: 129–53.

———, 1991–92: 'Going through the e/motions: gender, postmodernism, and affect in television studies'. *Discourse*, 14, 1: 23–40.

———, 1996: 'Feminist enterprise? *Star Trek: The Next Generation* and the occupation of femininity'. *Cinema Journal*, 35, 2: 61–84.

KAPLAN, E. A., 1992: 'Feminist criticism and television'. In Robert C. Allen (ed.), *Channels of Discourse, Reassembled: Television and Contemporary Criticism*, 2nd edn. Chapel Hill: University of North Carolina Press, 247–83.

KUHN, A., 1984: 'Women's genres: melodrama, soap opera and theory'. *Screen*, 25, 1: 18–28.

LEE, M., and CHO, H. C., 1990: 'Women watching together: an ethnographic study of Korean soap opera fans in the U.S.', *Cultural Studies*, 4, 1: 30–44.

LEWIS, I. A., 1990: *Gender Politics and MTV: Voicing the Difference*. Philadelphia: Temple University Press.

LIEBES, T. and KATZ, E., 1990: *The Export of Meaning: Dallas*. Oxford: Oxford University Press.

LOPATE, C., 1976: 'Daytime television: you'll never want to leave home', *Feminist Studies*, 3, 3–4: 69–82.

MCROBBIE, A., 1991: 'Settling accounts with subcultures: a feminist critique'. In Angela McRobbie (ed.), *Feminism — and Youth Culture: From Jackie to Just Seventeen*. London: Macmillan, 16–35.

MELLENCAMP, P. (ed.), 1990: *The Logics of Television: Essays in Cultural Criticism*. Bloomington: Indiana University Press.

———, 1992: *High Anxiety: Catastrophe, Scandal, Age, and Comedy*. Bloomington: Indiana University Press.

MODLESKI, T., 1979: 'The search for tomorrow in today's soap operas'. *Film Quarterly*, 37, 1: 12–21.

———, 1984: *Loving with a Vengeance: Mass-Produced Fantasies for Women*. New York: Methuen.

———, 1991: *Feminism without Women: Culture and Criticism in a 'Postfeminist' Age*. New York: Routledge.

MORLEY, D., 1989: 'Changing paradigms in audience studies'. In Ellen Seiter *et al.* (eds), *Remote Control: Television, Audiences and Cultural Power*. London: Routledge, 16–43.

MULVEY, L., 1975: 'Visual pleasure and narrative cinema'. *Screen*, 16, 3: 6–18.

———, 1981: 'Afterthoughts on "Visual pleasure and narrative cinema", inspired by

Duel in the Sun'. In Constance Penley (ed.), *Feminism and Film Theory*. New York: Routledge, 69–79.

MUMFORD, L. S., 1994–95: 'Stripping on the girl channel: lifetime, *thirtysomething*, and television form'. *Camera Obscura*, 33–34, 167–90.

——, 1995: *Love and Ideology in the Afternoon: Soap Opera, Women, and Television Genre*. Bloomington: Indiana University Press.

PETRO, P., 1986: 'Mass culture and the feminine: the "place" of television in film studies', *Cinema Journal*, 25, 3: 5–21.

PRESS, A. L., 1991: *Women Watching Television: Gender, Class, and Generation in the American Television Experience*. Philadelphia: University of Pennsylvania Press.

PROBYN, E., 1990: 'New traditionalism and post-feminism: TV does the home'. *Screen*, 32, 2: 147–59.

RADWAY, J. A. 1984: *Reading the Romance: Women, Patriarchy, and Popular Literature*. Chapel Hill: University of North Carolina Press.

ROWE, K., 1995: *The Unruly Woman: Gender and the Genres of Laughter*. Austin: University of Texas Press.

SEITER, E., 1982a: 'TV Guide – the soaps'. *Tabloid*, 5: 36–43.

——, 1982b: 'Promise and contradiction: the daytime television serials'. *Film Reader*, 5: 150–63.

——, 1990: 'Making distinctions in TV audience research: case study of a troubling interview'. *Cultural Studies*, 4, 1: 61–84.

SEITER, E., BORCHERS, H., KREUTZNER, G. and WARTH, E.-M. (eds), 1989: *Remote Control: Television, Audiences and Cultural Power*. London: Routledge.

SPIGEL, L., 1992: *Make Room for TV: Television and the Family Ideal in Postwar America*. Chicago: University of Chicago Press.

TORRES, S., 1989: 'Melodrama, masculinity and the family: *thirtysomething* as therapy'. *Camera Obscura*, 19: 86–106.

WHITE, M., 1992a: *Tele-Advising: Therapeutic Discourse in American Television*. Chapel Hill: University of North Carolina Press.

——, 1992b: 'Ideological analysis'. In Robert C. Allen (ed.), *Channels of Discourse, Reassembled: Television and Contemporary Criticism*, 2nd edn. Chapel Hill: University of North Carolina Press, 161–202.

VAN ZOONEN, L., 1994: *Feminist Media Studies*. London: Sage Publications.

7

Television Studies and Race

Therese Daniels

This essay provides a critical overview of the small volume of published research into the representation of race on British television. It explains that most academic studies have been concerned with analysing the representation of people of African and Asian descent and with theorising the effect of representations on society. In its analysis of the research, this chapter highlights the need for an increase in the output of publicly accessible, recent and reliable data. It also suggests that public service television offers the potential for protecting minority interests in all their diversity, and that this should be acknowledged by researchers.

Social Divisions and Television Studies

'Race' is a concept that, while carrying residual notions of genetics and bio-logical lineage, varies in its scope and meaning in different societies and at different periods. Currently in Britain the term is often used to mean culture or ethnicity, and sometimes religion. Some groups, distinguished by their ethnicity or religion, are seen by themselves and by the wider society as discrete and identifiable entities, internally unified and with self-preservation and regeneration as core interests.

From amongst the numerous ethnic groups that exist in Britain, a few are at any time accorded significance; for most of the post-1945 era people of African-Caribbean and Asian descent have been of primary importance in public debates about race. In the field of academic media studies these two groups have been the subjects of attempts to theorise the relationship between the media and race. While conflation of the two groups under the political defini-tion 'black' is now becoming problematic and perhaps even unacceptable in present social theories of the present day (Solomos and Back, 1994; Modood, 1994), the two groups have been the subject of the bulk of recent race-related media research. As there is special programme provision for the two groups on

BBC and Channel 4 television, the broadcasting institutions recognise them as being groups to which television bears a particular responsibility.

The study of the mass media emerged in Britain as a sub-discipline of sociology during the 1960s (Hall, 1985). However, until relatively recently the subject of race was either ignored or marginalised within mass communications research. During its first decade or more, much of the theoretical work of media studies was devoted to discovering the relationship between the media, conceptualised as being tools of capitalist ideology, and social classes, in particular the working class. Deriving their theoretical frameworks from the dominant critical paradigm within the parent discipline of sociology, many studies of the media explored what was held to be the essential division created by capitalism, that of social class. By studying media treatment of, for example, working-class struggles such as industrial disputes, or the state's role in international conflict, they showed the media's roles in privileging the interests of the British state and dominant economic groups against the state's detractors and subordinate groups. (For example, the Glasgow University Media Group's series of studies, 1976, 1980, 1982, 1985.)

As class was held to be the primary social division in capitalist societies, other forms of subordination, such as those based on race, gender or sexuality, were in consequence marginalised by both sociology and media studies. However, within sociology, from the 1970s onwards, there was an increasing number of challenges to the dominance of class theory. For some theorists, the 'base and superstructure' model could be adapted to account for gender and race-based social divisions. These divisions were held to be a product of capitalism, and the conflicts produced by them were as corrosive as those manifested as class struggles (Mitchell, 1966, Miles, 1982; Sivanandan, 1982).

Within media studies, gender-based issues gained at first a fragile, and gradually a more secure hold as areas of research. There is still, however, comparatively very little published research on race, and not much of that focuses on television. Race is still today a very minor area of academic media research. This is despite the great increase in interest in race taken by other areas of social research, such as sociology and social policy. In those disciplines, there has been a marked response to the racialisation of social issues that has taken place since the 1980s in Britain. Money and expertise have been devoted to examining issues such as housing, education, health and minority rights, and there are competing and conflicting arguments being raised, all of which enrich the field of study. This is far from being the case in media studies. There are relatively few individuals or institutions carrying out research on race and few British publications to which one can refer for discussion of recent issues and developments. Teachers and students within the field are forced to rely on a small amount of published research material, much of it badly dated, that focuses on a narrow range of themes.

One of the main lines of enquiry taken in British studies of television and race has been the survey of black representation. A small number of published surveys have undertaken a quantitative analysis of black images and their qualitative evaluation. In the main these have been small-scale and there is little access to wide-ranging research carried out within the last decade.

Another line of enquiry has been the discussions of issues related to working within the television industry. These include the experiences of black people employed by the institutions and the way in which contracts are awarded by commissioning editors. Most of these describe a series of frustrations and disappointments, although some suggest that there are opportunities afforded by the structure of public service institutions (Saakana, 1982; Wadsworth, 1986; Pines, 1992; Hussein, 1994; Givanni, 1995). Again, the number of such studies is small, which is in part a reflection of the fragile relationships that black workers have to the broadcasting institutions, but also reflects the marginalisation of black experiences within academic media studies.

Surveys of Black Images on Television

The major problem when attempting to discuss television's output from a contemporary perspective is the absence of reliable data. There is no published database containing recent, comprehensive information on television output that can be drawn on when discussing the medium as it currently operates. Of the handful of published surveys of black images on television, two have dealt with programmes transmitted during the 1970s (Hartmann and Husband, 1974; Commission for Racial Equality, 1982). The Commission for Racial Equality (CRE) has also surveyed the early 1980s. Two surveys so far published include programmes from the 1930s to the 1990s (Barry, 1988; Ross, 1996).

Surveys of television images of black people have drawn upon two variables in order to assess the treatment of black images. The first is quantitative, measuring the number of times black people have appeared on television over a given period of time. The second is qualitative, assessing the context in which these appearances are made. Data has usually been collected using a sample of television output over the chosen period. From the data gathered in the sample, generalisations have been made about the whole field of television output.

Quantitative Findings

Most television surveys have looked at the representation of black people in drama and light entertainment. There is very little information available on the coverage of black people in news, current affairs and documentaries. Cottle's study is one recent example of a survey that includes in its scope black images in television actuality programmes. However, this is a study of television's reporting of the urban riots of the 1980s, and not of race *per se* (Cottle, 1993).

Quantitative analysis has shown that the proportion of people of African and Asian descent appearing in British television programmes is generally lower than their proportion in the population at large. For example, Equity's Coloured Artists' Committee's unpublished survey found that, during the week 26 May 1974 to 1 June 1974, out of a total of 891 artists seen on all three television channels, 'only forty-five were coloured, and twelve of these were members of the Harlem Globetrotters team' (Husband, 1975: 29). In 1971 Hartmann and Husband found that during one week in April, there were only one major role and four minor roles for non-white actors in dramatic programmes (Hartmann

and Husband, 1974: 199). In 1982 the CRE found that between 3 and 4 per cent
of dramatic parts on television were played by black actors, which was below the
black representation of 5 per cent of the population at that time (CRE, 1982:
16). There was a general finding in these studies that in dramatic productions,.
black actors were often confined to minor or non-speaking parts.

Qualitative Analysis

In the qualitative analysis of these figures, the authors generally argue that black
representation is characterised by 'negative' images. This term is applied to
characters or situations that represent blacks in a bad light. It includes images of
blacks involved in crime and violence, causing social problems such as housing
shortages or overcrowded classrooms as a result of their immigration to Britain,
carrying out menial jobs in the labour market, or as generally uneducated and
simple-minded. The main alternative to these are images which, when judged by
these criteria, are not overtly 'negative', but which confirm the commonly held
view that blacks are physically gifted but intellectually limited. These include
images of the black singer, dancer or athlete. By implication, if not directly,
these studies suggest that 'positive' images are those where blacks are seen outside of this range and, in particular, where they are shown to be intelligent and
socially responsible members of the community.

   In their study, Hartmann and Husband found that the majority of people of
African descent appeared on television as singers and dancers (Hartmann and
Husband, 1974: 199). Both Hartmann and Husband and the CRE found that
where they appeared in dramatic contexts, they were depicted as disproportionately involved in crime and in menial occupations (Hartmann and Husband, 1974;
CRE, 1982: 19). People of Asian descent were found by the CRE to be under-
represented in all categories, but where they did feature, they were usually in dramatic roles that portrayed them as unable to speak English, giving rise to the view
that they were, as a rule, alienated from British culture (CRE, 1982: 21).

   In both the Hartmann and Husband and CRE studies, the argument held that
although 'negative' images also appeared in the portrayal of white people, for
them there was a far greater variety of images against which to balance these.
The preponderance of 'negative' images in the portrayal of blacks meant that
their representation was stereotyped and, in that it was both distorted and
demeaning, racist.

   The importance of this was said to be that television provided the main or
only contact that large numbers of white people had with any black people,
because of the concentrated pattern of black settlement in Britain. Television
therefore acted as a strong influence on the formation of racist attitudes about
black people. It also helped to reinforce pre-existing stereotypes Europeans had
developed about African and Asian people during centuries of exploration and
colonisation. These, in sum, held that blacks were, variously, dangerous and
violent, 'ignorant savages' or 'happy darkies' – childlike, innocent creatures.
Television's reproduction and reinforcement of these stereotypes then affected
the way that whites treated black people, and resulted in racial discrimination in
employment, housing and other social spheres.

Problems with Evidence

For a variety of reasons, among which is included a lack of consistent institutional backing for the study of race, these few surveys provide the bulk of available hard data for those wishing to study British television and race. The majority of them were carried out so long ago that they are of no help in studying the present day. A further problem, however, is that they provide an incomplete record of television's treatment of race. The reasons for this are that, first, most surveys have relied on either very small timescales or on unsystematic data-collection. The surveys carried out during the 1970s and 1980s above chose a period of time at random, during which some, usually peak-time, television output was viewed and black appearances recorded. Hartmann and Husband's survey monitored programmes for one week in 1971. The CRE's survey monitored programmes for four weeks in 1978, two weeks in 1979 and three weeks in 1982.

In theory, the fact that the viewing periods were randomly selected should have meant that the data was representative of typical or average television output. However, the reliability of the data, or its applicability to television's normal output, is somewhat compromised by these surveys' small timescales.

The CRE's 1982 survey provides an example of problems associated with the use of a small timescale. Its three-week survey carried out in July 1982 coincided with both the Wimbledon Tennis Championships and the World Cup (CRE, 1982: 73). One problem here is that the televising of these major sporting events must have adversely affected the number of black images in dramatic or other contexts, as there would have been extensive coverage of the championships at the expense of other programmes.

Another possible problem is that a short-term survey might miss an important short series in which 'positive' black images are likely to have featured. This in fact happened in at least one case. The CRE's survey of September to October 1978, which included current affairs programmes in its monitoring (CRE, 1982: 14), would not have identified an important educational series, *Multi-racial Britain*, that was shown on BBC2 every evening between 17 and 21 July 1978. In this, academics Stuart Hall, Bhikhu Parekh, Alan Little, John Rex and Archbishop Trevor Huddleston each presented a programme discussing an aspect of contemporary racism.

Angela Barry's 1988 survey covered a much longer period than the aforementioned studies, from 1936 to 1986. The source of Barry's data was the BBC and ITV handbooks for each year (Barry, 1988: 84). However, these are not a good resource for a study of output because the handbooks only provide a summary of the best of each institution's output for the year. On the whole, they concentrate on award-winning productions, those which have generated high audiences, investigative achievements, international co-productions, major costume dramas and other noteworthy programmes. Only a small fraction of an institution's total output is mentioned. The handbooks do not, therefore, provide an exhaustive database.

As an example of the limitations of this method, Barry's conclusion of the 1950s, drawn from the information given in the handbooks, is that 'after the initial enthusiastic welcome for "our Commonwealth friends", few television programmes alluded to anything whatsoever to do with the growing numbers of blacks in Britain. Black issues were articulated with nothing but a deafening silence' (Barry, 1988: 86). However, this is untrue. Black issues were raised many times in the 1950s; for example, in the BBC documentary *Special Enquiry: Has Britain a Colour Bar?* (31 January 1955), the BBC play *A Man From the Sun* (8 November 1956), the BBC documentary series *Meet Us In London* (July 1957), ITV's Armchair Theatre production of Ted Willis's *Hot Summer Night* (1 February 1959), and undoubtedly in news and current affairs coverage of the 1958 Notting Hill and Nottingham riots. The handbooks do not provide this information, nor do they mention any editions of *Panorama* or *This Week* that may have focused on race.

The second reason why published surveys provide an incomplete record of black representation is that they have rarely examined anything other than 'popular' formats such as situation comedy, crime-centred drama and soap opera. Because such programmes tend to rely on stereotyped characters (such as the dumb blonde and the nosy neighbour), research has inevitably found that black characters in 'popular' programmes are made up from popular stereotypes. From there, it has been all too easy to imply that, in any given period, racist stereotypes have formed the basis of television output.

The third reason is that, because the bulk of research discusses the 1970s and early 1980s, not enough is known about the representation of black people on British television during other periods. For example, there has been some discussion of the situation comedies that were popular during these years. However, very little has been written about the plays, documentaries and educational programmes that were produced during the 1950s and 1960s.

The points raised above, although applied to the specific studies mentioned, are symptomatic of the way in which race-related media research still tends to be carried out: either by individuals who have little or no financial support to carry out more widescale surveys, or by an institution such as the CRE, which has limited funds to carry out comprehensive study.

The studies carried out in the 1970s were pioneering. They led to a general campaign against media racism, and brought racism to the attention of academic media studies. They encouraged the media unions to look at their own practices, draw up codes of conduct, and put pressure on management to employ black media workers. They helped bring the issue of racism in the media directly to the attention of institutional executives and policy-makers, and greatly improved the access that black people now have to television, both as viewers and as workers in the industry (Daniels, 1994).

However, there has been very little progress in the field since the early studies appeared. The position today is that, despite the growth in academic media studies, little of the increase in university research funding has found its way to the study of race. The field is still reliant on the work of a handful of individuals with small research grants. The volume and scope of current research output reflect the lack of substantial institutional backing. There have been, at times, individuals researching particular issues, or here and there a research institution providing funds for new research, but not the coordinated effort required to consistently maintain dynamic research that is current, challenging and accessible to the public.

When research is backed by institutions it is often not made accessible to outsiders. For example, the broadcasting institutions regularly carry out their own research on black audiences, and also ethnic monitoring to measure the efficacy of their recruitment and training of black workers, but their findings are not usually made available to outsiders.

Sometimes research intended for publication is shelved or inadequately distributed. For example, the British Film Institute (BFI) has constructed a database that takes a comprehensive view of television output of black images from 1936 to the end of the 1980s. The BFI put substantial financial and personnel resources into carrying out the research. However, the full survey has not yet been published or made accessible to interested parties outside the institution. Its findings have been only partially disseminated in three publications. One of these is an edited transcript of the interviews carried out for the BFI's *Black and White in Colour* television documentaries, first broadcast by BBC in 1992 (Pines, 1992). Another consists of background notes which provide contextual information on the documentaries (Daniels, 1992), while the third consists largely of the proceedings of a conference held by the BFI at which the *Black and White in Colour* documentaries were discussed (Givanni, 1995). However, since they do not attempt a thorough analysis of the BFI's database, but only explain in two 50-minute programmes the material that could be contained, these three publications do not provide an in-depth analysis of the BFI's data.

The inadequate amount of data on television output is compounded by the rather narrow theoretical perspective in which programmes are discussed There has been little British work on the media and race that has been grounded in a theoretical perspective of the role and functioning of the various media. There has been very little attempt to further the discussion begun by the pioneering studies of the 1970s by pursuing issues such as whether there are differences in representation between the various television genres, whether the differences in character between the television channels – BBC, ITV and Channel 4 – has any effect on output, or whether the concept of 'public service' has had any effect on the treatment of race. Neither is there much attempt to analyse images beyond the positive/negative dichotomy. There is very little discussion of the complexities of pleasure and danger involved in representation.

Conceptualising Television and Race

In his article on the construction of racist ideologies in the mass media, Stuart Hall raises some issues that might enable the debate to advance from the positive/negative images dichotomy around which it so often turns. Hall argues for the importance of complexity in conceptualising the nature, roles and functioning of the media. Using racism as an example, his argument is applied to the media as a whole, and is relevant to the many topics that have been the subject of left-wing critique and analysis:

> if critics of the media subscribe to too simple or reductive a view of their operations, this inevitably lacks credibility and weakens the case they are making because the theories and critiques don't square with reality. They only begin to account for the real operation of racism in society by a process of gross abstraction and simplification. (Hall, 1981: 12)

Hall suggests that while simplistic arguments may be beneficial in galvanising black and anti-racist interest in the media, they do not necessarily provide effective weaponry for engagement with and intervention in the mass media.

Addressing the tendency for the left to dismiss the state and its institutions as simply instruments of ruling class political will, he argues that the state and its institutions in the representative democracies of capitalist societies have become 'contradictory formations', representing both dominant class and subject class aspirations. They are neither fully controlled by the ruling class, nor are they the wholly representative institutions that liberal-democratic theory holds them to be. Rather, albeit if in an unequal struggle, they are capable of being shaped by action on the part of either ruling or subject classes.

It follows from this analysis of the state that public service television, although regulated by the state, is not simply and inevitably the ideological tool of the dominant class or race. Neither is it fully independent from government and capitalist interests, but exercises its political neutrality and independence. Hall suggests that the left should not dismiss broadcasting's claims to independence and political neutrality too readily, as these claims can be the basis for raising arguments for social justice. In his article, Hall describes how this was done by the Campaign Against Racism in the Media, which, in a programme in the BBC's *Open Door* series, attempted to show that racist assumptions behind anti-immigration debates were being unquestioningly condoned by television current affairs reports.

Hall's argument is that the relationship between the media and ideology is more complex than crude left or reductionist Marxist analysis allows. This complexity presents problems for the general task of countering racist ideologies. Among the problems is the need to discover how dominant ideologies are constructed and 'naturalised', so that the process by which beliefs become widely accepted can be understood. Such an understanding is a necessary precursor to the task of constructing an alternative common sense which is socialist, democratic and anti-racist.

One way that Hall suggests that the left should confront the complexity of the relationship between the media and ideology is for the left and anti-racists to cease lumping together all kinds of media output, from 'the latest, banal, TV documentary' to 'the TV drama documentary on the General Strike of 1926, *Days of Hope*', on the grounds that all media output inevitably serves to reproduce dominant ideologies (Hall, 1981: 21). Neither can all shades of media coverage of black issues be accounted for by labelling them 'racist'.

However, while proposing that intervention in the media is important for the black and anti-racist struggle, behind Hall's argument is the suggestion that working towards an anti-racist common sense will depend on more than the construction of 'positive' media images of black people. These may be refreshing correctives to 'negative' images, but are based on too simplistic a view of the role of the media in ideological construction. Ideologies are interpretations and explanations of social reality, and are constructed in daily life. Thus television images of black muggers and illegal immigrants may bear some relation to the social structure created by centuries of the social, political and economic subordination of black people. The simple media inversion of these images will not necessarily change popular perceptions of black people; television images of successful black doctors and lawyers may instead be seen as the media's flight from the ugliness of 'real life'. This is not to suggest that all criticism of media 'racism' is therefore unjustified, but that this term must be used judiciously.

In Britain, the debate about television and race has been repetitive and limited. Arguments have tended to proceed from a deterministic view of television's role in producing dominant ideologies and discourses. There is very little discussion of the ways in which the various institutions have an effect on programme-making, of the ways in which media ideologies interact with other ideologies of race, or of the theoretical and practical assumptions behind notions of media 'racism' and 'anti-racism' or a 'black point of view'.

Instead, arguments about race and television tend to assume a theoretical simplicity about the effects of television, suggesting that the main task rests with the production of 'positive' images of black people. There is, additionally, little attempt to discuss the principles and assumptions involved in oppositional practice. So far, the body of work that forms the basis of black and anti-racist analysis of television has barely begun to engage with troublesome political issues, such as the diversity of black identities and aspirations, in the way that black film practice and criticism now do. There is also very little reference to the debates on political strategy that have occupied the left and feminism.

There has instead been what Hall describes as a 'blunderbuss approach' to demonstrating racism in television. The disadvantage of such an approach may be that the possibility of anti-racist intervention from within television institutions is overlooked and television is uniformly condemned as racist. By adopting this approach, nothing can be learned about the way that British public service television operates, and how it could be used to create arguments for social justice.

References

BARRY, A., 1988: 'Black mythologies: the representation of black people on British television'. In J. Twitchin (ed.), *The Black and White Media Book*. London: Trentham Books.

COMMISSION FOR RACIAL EQUALITY, 1982: *Television in a Multi-racial Society*. London: CRE.

COTTLE, S., 1993: *TV News, Urban Conflict and the Inner City*. Leicester: Leicester University Press.

DANIELS, T., 1992: *Black and White in Colour*. London: BBC.

————, 1994: 'Programmes for black audiences'. In S. Hood (ed.), *Behind the Screens: The Structure of British Television in the Nineties*. London: Lawrence and Wishart.

GIVANNI, J. (ed.), 1995: *Remote Control: Dilemmas of Black Intervention in British Film and Television*. London: British Film Institute.

GLASGOW UNIVERSITY MEDIA GROUP, 1976: *Bad News*. London: Routledge and Kegan Paul.

————, 1980: *More Bad News*. London: Routledge and Kegan Paul.

————, 1982: *Really Bad News*. London: Writers and Readers.

————, 1985: *War and Peace News*. Milton Keynes: Open University Press.

HALL, S., 1981: 'The whites of their eyes: racist ideologies in the mass media'. In G. Bridges and R. Brunt (eds), *Silver Linings: Some Strategies for the Eighties*. London: Lawrence and Wishart.

————, 1985: 'The rediscovery of "ideology": return of the repressed in media studies'. In V. Beechey and J. Donald (eds), *Subjectivity and Social Relations*. Milton Keynes: Open University Press.

HARTMANN, P. and HUSBAND, C., 1974: *Racism and the Mass Media: A Study of the Role of the Mass Media in the Formation of White Beliefs*. London: Davis-Poynter.

HUSBAND, C., (ed), 1975: *White Media and Black Britain*. London: Arrow Books.

HUSSEIN, A., 1994: 'Black independents and the marginalisation of Black film and video production in the United Kingdom'. In C. Husband (ed.), *A Richer Vision: The Development of Ethnic Minority Media in Western Democracies*. Paris and London: UNESCO and John Libbey.

MILES, R., 1982: *Racism and Migrant Labour*. London: George Allen and Unwin.

MITCHELL, J., 1966: 'Women: the longest revolution'. *New Left Review*. November–December.

MODOOD, T., 1994: 'Political blackness and British Asians'. *Sociology*, 28, 4, November.

PINES, J. (ed.), 1992: *Black and White in Colour*, London: British Film Institute.

ROSS, K., 1996: *Black and White Media: Black Images in Popular Film and Television*, Cambridge: Polity Press.

SAAKANA, A. S., 1982: 'Channel 4 and the black community'. In S. Blanchard and D. Morley (eds), *What's this Channel Four?*. London: Comedia.

SIVANANDAN, A., 1982: *A Different Hunger*. London: Pluto Press.

SOLOMOS, J. and BACK, L., 1994: 'Conceptualising racisms: social theory, politics and research'. *Sociology*, 28, 1, February 1994.

WADSWORTH, M., 1986: 'Racism in broadcasting'. In J. Curran (ed.), *Bending Reality: The State of the Media*. London: Pluto Press.

8

Audiences and 'Ethnography': Questions of Practice

Christine Geraghty

One of the strongest features of Television Studies in the 1980s was a marked shift to work on audiences. Charlotte Brunsdon, through her participation in International Television Studies Conferences in 1984 and 1986, noted a change in the subjects of the papers presented, 'a clear move in interest from what is happening on the screen to what is happening in front of it – from text to audience' (1991: 121). This is not to say that there had not been work on television audiences or, perhaps more correctly, on television viewing before 1986. Key work like that of Raymond Williams and John Ellis had been premised on identifying a particular mode of television viewing; research into television effects, on children in particular, had tried to assess how television might affect particular audiences; much textual work like Brunsdon's own influential essay on *Crossroads* (1981) had focused on the way in which a particular programme addressed its domestic, predominantly female audience.

Nevertheless, television theory in the 1980s saw a new interest in and a development of audience work[1] which can be characterised, albeit, as we shall see, problematically, by its links with the concept of ethnography. This is one of the points at which the interdisciplinary nature of Television Studies is most heavily marked as approaches developed in Cultural Studies, anthropology and sociology are used to re-frame the questions which can be asked of audiences. The rhetoric of such work shifted the emphasis from work *on* audiences to work *with* audiences and suggested that although television was a mass medium its relationship with its audience was not best understood by studies which assumed a mass response. As David Morley put it, in his comments on the nature of his research for *Family Television*, 'the focus was on the "how" and "why" questions which lie unexplained behind the patterns of viewing behaviour revealed by large-scale survey work' (1986: 17).

This essay, then, has two purposes. I want to indicate what 'ethnographic' work has offered to our understanding of television as an object of study and in particular to our understanding of audiences. But I shall do so by looking at the way in which this research has been undertaken and by focusing on some practical and theoretical issues which are raised by its methodology. I am not offering a guide to ethnographic methods but proposing that, in reflecting on the theoretical outcomes of this work, it is also important to learn something about the practices which produce them. In the interests of clarity, I shall take my examples almost entirely from Television Studies rather than, for instance, from more general anthropological or sociological work which has clearly influenced writers on television audiences. While there are problems in defining the field of study in this way, I hope that the reader will find that dealing with a relatively limited number of relatively limited examples permits a more detailed and comprehensible consideration of what are often rather thorny issues.

The use of the term 'ethnography' is itself polemical. I use it because a number of theorists do claim to be employing ethnographic methods as an important mark of difference from others who study television through examinations of political, economic and industrial practices and/or through textual appraisals. Henry Jenkins, beginning his book on television fans, declares that '*Textual Poachers* offers an ethnographic account of a particular group of media fans' (1992: 1) and goes on, 'I write *both* as an academic . . . and as a fan' (5). Mary Ellen Brown in the introduction to her *Soap Opera and Women's Talk* makes a similar claim: 'mine is an ethnographic study in which I am a member of the group, a fan and also the researcher' (1994: xi). The Tubingen Soap Opera Project team make a more limited claim to be working 'toward an ethnography of soap opera' (Seiter *et al.*, 1991: 225) but associate themselves with 'ethnography's basic interest in an empirical investigation of cultural practices as lived experiences' (227). Similarly, Ann Gray contends that television audience studies in the 1980s had 'not fulfilled the conditions necessary to be described as "ethnographies"' but describes her interview-based study of the use of video in the home as having 'ethnographic intentions' (1992: 32).

Part of the problem lies in the way in which the term 'ethnography' is used. Marie Gillespie in her detailed and vivid study of young people in Southall places emphasis on her use of 'fully ethnographic methods' (1995: 23), which she contrasts with the interview-based approach of the majority of other audience studies. In her definition, she emphasises the method as well as the object or intention of the study: 'ethnography is the empirical description and analysis of cultures based on intensive and extensive fieldwork in a selected local setting' (1). We shall explore what is meant by this later but for the moment it is important to note that Gillespie's definition is much tighter than other more influential definitions in media and cultural studies which, while not ignoring method, have placed more emphasis on the researcher's objectives. John Fiske, for instance, considers that 'the object of ethnographic study is the way people live their culture', but suggests that a variety of methods may be used with the same purpose, i.e. that they 'trace differences amongst viewers, modes of viewing, and the meanings and pleasures produced' (1987: 63). Ien Ang writes of ethnographic work 'in the sense of drawing on what we can perceive and experience in everyday settings' (1991a: 110) and, like Fiske, emphasises the importance of what is produced when she suggests that ethnography is 'not just a research method' but 'a discursive practice *par excellence* that foregrounds the diverse, the particular and the unpredictable in everyday life' (1991b: x).

This emphasis on talking with particular audiences can be traced to a dissatisfaction with theories of the media in 'quite different theoretical debates' from 'mainstream sociology' to 'psychoanalytical film theory' to Marxist analyses of the mass media (Morley, 1980: 164), approaches which assumed that understandings of the audience could be found in studying the television programmes or the economic infrastructure or particular production practices. The work under discussion has therefore a strong pragmatic and empirical base, an interest in 'the social subject' rather than the 'implied reader' of structuralist or psychoanalytic accounts. Henry Jenkins wants to 'counter sweeping claims of ideological critics' with 'empirical reality' (1992: 285). Nevertheless, this work on audiences has always had a strong interest in and relationship with media and cultural theory and should not be thought of as either lacking its own theoretical models or developing separately from other theoretical work. It should be noted that two of the most influential early examples of audience research in this context were developed in relation to theoretical models. David Morley's *The 'Nationwide' Audience* (1980) used 'encoding-decoding' models as the basis for analysing the responses of various groups to an early evening TV magazine programme. Similarly, Janice Radway's *Reading the Romance* (1984) drew on the psychoanalytic work of Nancy Chodorow to interpret the way in which a number of readers responded to their favourite genre. In both cases, the theory was not so much 'tested' as developed through contact with 'the readers'. Thus, in Cultural Studies generally and in Television Studies in particular, while qualitative work has emphasised the importance of being responsive to those being studied and of developing positions out of empirical work, it has always retained close relationships with more abstract and general theoretical accounts.

The tempting promise of ethnographic work is in the pragmatic appeal of its apparent premise. If we want to find out about audiences, why not ask them? Nevertheless, the engagement of Television Studies with qualitative research has meant that work on audience, if it is to be usable, has to address a number of questions and issues which arise precisely from these methods. Unless we are clear about what those issues are, then it is all too easy to assume that a study is telling us something which methodologically it cannot or to believe that one form of audience work must in a common-sense way be better than others. I want to focus now on recent examples of work on television audiences in order to look at how they come to the conclusions they do and draw attention to the way in which practical questions of method shape what can be concluded. I propose to look at these issues under a number of headings which focus on the object of study and fieldwork before moving on to issues arising from relationships between researcher and researched and the problems of generalisation.

The Object of Study

It would seem self-evident that the object of audience studies must be the audience or at least, recognising the way in which qualitative work has been linked to diversity, audiences in the plural. But such an assumption has been and would be dangerous. Under the umbrella heading of 'audiences', a number of different objects of study can be discerned, in each case refining or marking out a particular variant.

A Particular Text

The relationship between the audience and a particular programme or a particular kind of programme has been a popular approach. One of the problems with qualitative work is the sheer weight of data it can produce and one way of making a study more manageable is to narrow the focus by making the text some kind of determinant. Research can be done with single plays or short series as Julie Hallam and Margaret Marshment showed with their study of responses to *Oranges Are Not The Only Fruit* (1995a). More typical is the study of audience involvement with long-running series or serials. One such example would be the work of Henry Jenkins on *Star Trek* and other popular series (1992). Another would be the highly influential work on soaps, initiated by Hobson's study of a single programme, the much-maligned *Crossroads* (1982); this was followed by more general studies of soap viewing in which respondents gave detailed accounts of their engagement with their favourite programmes.

A Particular Kind of Viewer

Very often the study of interaction with a particular text is combined with the study of a particular kind of viewer. Morley's study of *Nationwide,* though much cited, is unusual in that it showed the programme to viewers who did not normally watch it. More common now are studies which try to understand audience interaction from the point of view of a particular kind of viewer, the fan. Jenkins drew on his participation in the conferences and newsletters of television fans while Mary Ellen Brown studied soap opera fans whose networks were 'less formal than groups with membership lists' (1994: 80). Brown, like Hobson before her, combined the fan viewer with another category – that of women – and so focused her study on female viewers of soaps.

Gender and to a lesser extent race and age have been key ways of identifying the particular kind of viewer researchers are studying. 'What I am fundamentally concerned with,' says Ann Gray, 'is the significance of home entertainment technology for one particular member of the household, the adult woman' (1992: 12); Marie Gillespie has studied the role of television in the lives of 'young Punjabi Londoners' (1995: 1); while John Tulloch (1991) has studied elderly people living in a residential home. Class, although it is a factor in work such as that of Andrea Press (1991), has proved more difficult to use as an initial defining category, partly because of problems in classifying audience members according to class.

The Context of Viewing

One of the recent trends in audience work has been to emphasise the context of viewing rather than the activity of particular individuals. This kind of work understands television watching not as a means of watching particular programmes but as an activity which is part of a complex set of domestic relationships. Thus, Morley's study of television viewing habits in families in South London begins with the premise that 'the changing patterns of television viewing could only be understood in the overall context of family leisure activity' (1986: 13). *Family Television*, by trying to take family dynamics into account, can then point to the way in which choice of programmes to view will almost certainly depend on power relations within a family rather than the intrinsic merit of programmes themselves.

It is possible with this focus to shift the object of study away from people to other observable units, e.g. the television set itself at particular periods of time. This is normally the domain of quantitative research; ratings information concentrates on the number of sets tuned in at a particular time. But more qualitative observational work is possible as the work of Collett and Lamb (1986) showed. A camera in the television set showed what was going on in front of the television and in some sense studied the activities which took place in that space rather than following the activities of the people who were notionally watching.[2]

Contextualising Technologies

An extension of this approach has been to emphasise not only the social context of viewing but to de-emphasise the uniqueness of the audience's engagement with television by emphasising the range of 'home entertainment' of which television is but one example. Thus, Silverstone, Hirsch and Morley (1991) placed television within a study of 'communication and information technologies' (204) and studied families' relationship with the telephone, the computer and the VCR as well as the television. Gray (1992) compared the use of VCRs with attitudes to other domestic technology such as the washing machine.

Doing Fieldwork

When a particular object of study is established as central to a research study, issues of how to find appropriate subjects and how to explore their involvement with television then arise. The processes of fieldwork are the subject of specialised literature but some of the problems involved emerge quite clearly from work on television.

Finding the Audiences

There are various methods of finding willing victims to be studied and how they are found and what they are willing to do are intimately connected to the purpose and findings of the research. Advertising, for instance, is likely to attract those who are keenly involved in a particular process and want to talk about it; it is a method appropriate therefore for Ang's work on those who felt strongly about *Dallas* (1985) or Dinsmore's study of film/video collectors in this collection, but not for a project which needs to incorporate the less engaged viewer. Similarly, studies based on the fandom of the researcher, like Jenkins, will draw on certain kinds of viewers and not others.

Researchees are sometimes found through other activity on the part of the researcher. Marie Gillespie argues that her role as a teacher was crucial in giving her access to young people and 'a recognised role in the institution' which 'made it easier for young people to situate me in the dual role of teacher and researcher' (1995: 68). Ellen Seiter (1995) offers an interesting reflection on her use of a parent support group of which she was a member to research attitudes to children's television viewing. While concerned about the implications of the shift from a personal to a professional relationship with the group, she felt the benefits of talking to people with whom she had already established the practice of talking about relationships, work and child-rearing.

Finding interviewees outside these pre-existing settings may be done through less formal social networks. Hallam and Marshment describe how they contacted acquaintances, friends of friends and neighbours; 'we had to feel we liked them enough to spend whole evenings together' (1995b: 175). A popular technique, used by Brown, Press and Gray among others, is 'snowballing' where 'one starts with a member of the desired group and then asks for recommendations of friends, neighbours and relatives to be included' (Brown, 1994: 184). More formal methods include responses to a survey distributed through a video rental shop (Gray) and the use of outside agencies such as the market research agency and staff at local schools through whom Silverstone, Hirsch and Morley identified families for their long-term study

All of these methods of recruitment have their difficulties but perhaps that most remarked on by the researchers is the way in which they lead to a certain homogeneity in the groups being researched. Seiter is not alone in noting that one of the 'glaring limitations' (1995: 150) of her study with the parent support group was the way in which most members of the group were 'highly similar in terms of age, educational level, types of housing' (143) and that it did not include single mothers and women of colour. Snowballing as a technique almost inevitably leads to people who have more in common than simply television viewing. Gray (1995) argues that such homogeneity may be necessary both in terms of easing the sharing of knowledge between the researcher and researched and providing a homogenous base from which comparisons can be made. Theoretically, in qualitative research which is not claiming to be statistically representative, the nature of the group studied is not important provided that the results are not used for more general purposes, but clearly there are political and methodological problems here which will be explored later.

Methods of Fieldwork

As we have seen, methods of fieldwork are at the heart of the claims made by qualitative researchers to be more sensitive to the particularities and contexts of television audiences. But, along with research aims, time, money and institutional support are factors in developing research methods and the popularity of the interview mode may derive as much from these practical factors as from methodological aims. Decisions about method do inevitably have consequences. Participant observation which involves participation for a considerable period of time in the way of life being studied is relatively rare. Gillespie, in a very clear account of her research process, describes the initial stage in which she built up contacts and became, through her school and youth work, an accepted part of the scene, acting as 'the unobtrusive observer' (1995: 62). In the second phase, she became more immersed and more visible, joining in the social life of several families, offering help and support to young people, conducting more formal interviews with them and their families and working with 'key informants' with whom she is in regular contact. Although she uses interviews, Gillespie contrasts that format with the 'spontaneous, genuinely unselfconscious talk in naturalistic settings' (66) which she encountered in classrooms, homes, study groups and celebrations during the years of her research. Gillespie clearly believes that this intimate contact gave her both access to the complexities of her subjects and a means of cross-checking 'the discrepancies between what people say, what they think and what they do' (66) lacking in other approaches.

Silverstone, Hirsch and Morley report that a week's 'participant observation' which was originally part of the research with each family was abandoned after the researchers concluded that the short period of time which could be spent with a family would not allow for a systematic analysis of the families' interaction with domestic technologies nor enable the researchers to 'contextualise families historically and geographically' (1991: 211). Like others, though, they claimed that even without this period set aside for the process, 'a great deal of participant observation took place' through, for example, noting what went on before and after interviews when the researcher might share television watching or a meal and observing the 'arrangement and display of pictures, photographs, objects and furniture in the rooms to which we had access'. This formed again an element in the checking of data, 'a constant check on (and another account of) families' own accounting' (213).

The interview is probably the most characteristic method of work on television audiences thus far. In the majority of cases, the research process is based on interviews of between one and three hours, though these are often buttressed by introductory work, questionnaires and feedback mechanisms. In a number of cases (Brown, the Tubingen Project), group interviews are used while others, such as Hobson's interview with Jacqui (1990) and Dinsmore's with video collectors, are one-to-one. Nearly all take place in the interviewee's homes since, as the Tubingen Group put it, 'the location of the interviews . . . added to the sense of comfort' (Seiter *et al.*, 1991: 226). It is the familiarity of the location which is important, so when the group is one which has its basis outside the home, as is the case with Hobson's work-based group (1991), the venue switches to a bar which is a familiar lunchtime meeting place for the women. Rather than going through a list of prescribed questions, the interview tends to be organised round what the interviewees think is important about a particular topic. Gray describes using 'a loosely structured but open-ended conversational interview' (1992: 32) and Press is 'convinced I would not have gathered the material I did had I created a more closed, structured account' (1991: 180).

Inevitably, the interview format means that researchers are hearing about television viewing rather than observing it; 'I am dealing ultimately with respondents' accounts of what they do,' says Morley (1986: 52). This is less of a problem than it first seems if the object of study is not television watching itself but attitudes to it and the 'rules' which surround it. As Alasuutari puts it, ethnomethodological research in Cultural Studies is concerned 'to study the *methods* or the rules of interpretation that people follow in their everyday lives' (1995: 36). Researchers need to be aware of this distinction and acute enough to realise that what may appear to be irrelevant is actually part of the story. Thus, Gray recalls how 'Above all, the women wanted to tell me "stories", their stories. At first I thought this was going to be of no use . . . but by re-listening to the tapes I realised these stories were an extremely important part of the construction of the interview itself . . . the women were accounting their experiences from particular standpoints' (1995: 164). Morley offers another example of the importance of the telling when he comments on male accounts of watching the news, documentaries and serious programmes: 'even if it could be seriously argued that my results misrepresent the actual viewing behaviour of these men, it would remain a social fact of considerable interest that these were the particular accounts of their behaviour that these viewers felt constrained to give' (1986: 52).

The Research Material

Even when the spoken word is the basis of the research as in the interview format or participant observation, it is almost inevitably the written word which is the outcome of the study. Interviews are made available for study through being transcribed and the spoken comment of the interviewees with all its informalities has to be translated into written prose. Researchers often emphasise their wish to provide enough of the transcribed material to make it speak beyond their particular use of it. Morley hopes that others 'may be able to re-analyse the data supplied in the central section of family interviews' (1986: 175), and Gray also makes use of extended quotations from interviews 'in order to give the reader extended access to the subjects of the study and the process by which the empirical data was obtained' (1992: 35). Very often this emphasis on making material available as well as supplying an analysis of it is sustained by a commitment to giving a voice to those who are not usually given attention – women viewers, fans, 'the ordinary viewer'. 'What I most wanted to do,' says Gray, reflecting on her methods, 'was give a voice to women' (1995: 160); Hobson lets the voice of her interviewee, Jacqui, 'predominate' because it is 'her narrative' (1990: 71); Gillespie tells us that 'I have consistently included the verbatim quotes of informants in order to let young people's voices speak as much as possible' (1995: 74).

Other forms of television research have used accounts written by viewers themselves, in response to specific research requests. Ang (1985) invited *Dallas* viewers to write to her and quotes from their letters. Silverstone, Hirsch and Morley describe a more extended process in which participants were asked to provide a variety of written material to accompany the interviews undertaken. They were asked, for instance, to keep 'time-use diaries' (1991: 214) which provided a record of their use of technologies as well as a basis for discussions about that use; discussion also surrounded another piece of written material which participants drew, 'a map of the internal space of the household', which with its omissions and spatial differences could be interpreted as 'mental maps of the home' (215) in which technology use by different members of the family was given a spatial dimension.

Written accounts of various kinds may offer those being studied a greater degree of control than the spoken word of the interview, the opportunity to present material in a more rehearsed way. They may also, however, present a particular version of their activities which is deemed appropriate for the researcher. Fiske suggests that 'much ethnographic data has been produced specifically for the investigator, which does not invalidate it, but it does urge caution and self-awareness in its interpretation' (1990: 89). Similar care is needed, though, when the researcher makes use of 'found' material, that is material which is produced for purposes other than that of the research. Good examples of this approach can be found in the use made by Hobson (1982) and D'Acci (1994) of the letters written by fans of programmes under threat. D'Acci found in the letters written in support of *Cagney and Lacey* a rich source of material written by women organising in defence of 'their' programme. In letters written for public consumption, there is a different side to the story-telling. The letters need to be read as part of a debate, as the fans' case for protecting the programme, using arguments which they think will be effective as well as disputing (sometimes despairingly) the industry's ability to control their viewing. Letters such as these can say something not just about the viewers' relationship with particular programmes but with television more generally; as D'Acci says, 'the audience letters are potent forces for understanding the viewers' conceptions of audience and of themselves as audience members' (1994: 99). In these cases, the letters are examples of the way in which television viewing, although it takes place most often in the private spaces of the home, crucially interacts with the public spaces of business and production. Hobson and D'Acci, in reading these letters written for public consumption, give them a different and more sympathetic understanding than their original recipients. In a rather different context, Henry Jenkins was aware that in using the 'found' material of his study – letters, stories, artwork and conference discussion – he could be accused of opening the fans up to mockery. He 'had to gain their [the fans] trust' (1992: 6) that he would not misuse their work by bringing it to a wider and potentially less sympathetic audience; instead he hopes that his book will 'provide a record of the accomplishments of remarkable fan writers, artists and performers' (7).

The production of research material is, as this brief account can only begin to show, a complex, difficult and time-consuming task. The different approaches have consequences both for the researcher and the outcome of any particular study. Two common elements are worth picking out from the methodological approaches described above. Firstly, qualitative work on audiences has been concerned to stress its desire to work, as far as is possible, with audiences, to enable participation in the research project to be both conscious and positive on the part of the researchees. 'There has been an attempt,' as Silverstone, Hirsch and Morley put it, 'to shift the status of the researched from subjects to partners' (1991: 222). The researchers are open about their research interests even when they are working in situations which pre-exist the research format. Thus, Seiter asked the parents support group whether it was willing 'to be recorded as a focus group' and was aware that 'I was recasting myself in a new way' (1995: 143–4); the young people whom Gillespie studied knew 'that I was conducting research into young people and television and willingly tolerated my . . . questions and my interest in seemingly irrelevant details' (1995: 62). Gillespie, like others such as Hobson and Jenkins, established key informants with whom she discussed the survey results and the interpretations she was making as the study progressed. Jenkins describes his practice as being 'to share each chapter with all the quoted fans and to encourage their criticism of its contents' (1992: 7). The different methods which Silverstone, Hirsch and Morley employed were discussed with the participants, building up a reflexivity in which 'subjects comment on the research process and their own involvement in it as it progresses' (1991: 222). This emphasis on comment and feedback aims not so much at getting endorsement from the participants as recognition of the researchers' descriptions. As

Silverstone, Hirsch and Morley put it, 'our accounts must be plausible . . . to our subjects, in the sense that they can be persuaded that what we are accounting, and accounting for, in their lives and worlds is recognisable even if they may not in some cases be able to accept our explanations for it' (223).

The second common factor in qualitative studies of television audiences is the willingness of the participants to be involved and the sense that they are getting something out of it. Silverstone, Hirsch and Morley express a common anxiety at the beginning of the research that 'we would be doing all the taking . . . providing very little in return' (221). But generally researchers report on 'enthusiastic discussion' (Tulloch, 1991: 183). Hallam comments that the women they watched *Oranges* with 'all said how much they enjoyed it . . . a few people said to me it really opened their eyes, they didn't realise how much they knew about television' (1995b: 175). Silverstone, Hirsch and Morley realised that they were 'offering a degree of focused attention and interest to families in their everyday lives which was exceptional' (1991: 221), and there is a sense particularly in studies of relatively powerless groups of a pleasure in participating in a project which takes them seriously. Tulloch suggests that the willingness of elderly people to talk to him arose from their lack of economic power and of access to 'formal spaces for wider discussion' (1991: 183). While this sense of reward through sympathetic attention is common in qualitative work generally, it may be that research on television, which is both a common source of conversation and very often a despised one, offers a particularly intense version of it. Seiter notes 'the very ease with which television was accepted as a suitable topic' (1995: 138). Many of the studies under review focus precisely on television talk and audience research of this kind absolves viewers of the guilt normally associated with such discussions by acknowledging the role television plays in modern lives and by taking seriously conversations which, at work and at home, are normally considered irrelevant or trivial.

Power Relations

Concerns about how participants are engaged in and rewarded by research processes are part of a much wider debate about the nature of power relations in ethnographic work which has been taking place in anthropology and sociology. The research process which depends on the objective researcher studying the practices of others and using his/her own framework to provide explanations about them has been challenged by postmodern accounts which emphasise the subjectivity of the researcher, the precariousness of judgements and the complexity of discourses. This work, represented for instance in Clifford and Marcus's influential *Writing Culture* (1986), is concerned to dethrone the researcher as the one who reveals the truth about a culture and to challenge the notion that access to experience (most notably through participant observation) is also access to understanding.[3] This complex debate has left its traces in television audience work and I want to comment in particular on two aspects of it – the positioning of the researcher and the interview as fun.

In nearly every study under discussion, the researcher is concerned to position him or herself in relation to those studied in a way which is additional to or different from that of academic researcher. Sometimes, this positioning is driven by the interviewees as when Dinsmore (Chapter 20) describes the way in which her male interviewees used her gender and status as a student as cues to treat her, not as an academic researcher, but as someone in need of protection. Realising what was happening, Dinsmore decided to allow this apparent reversal of the power relations in the interests of making the interviewees comfortable. Gillespie, too, although she has a position of authority as a teacher, used her reputation as sympathiser to the student underdog to get out of 'some of the more deleterious aspects of teacher–student power relations' and felt she thereby gained access to areas and conversations from which teachers were normally excluded (1995: 70).

Gender and ethnicity are presented as important ways of establishing different kinds of relationships between researcher and researched. The Tubingen Group downplayed their academic status by emphasising both gender and race. The 'foreigness' of three of the researchers meant that they could be understood as lacking knowledge, as 'relatively ignorant but interested "non-initiates" into soap operas' (Seiter *et al.*, 1991: 242–3). As importantly, the women researchers found that 'gender provided a position of "sameness"' (243) which allowed them to share understandings with their women interviewees. Gray is clear that the researcher 'does have access to quite powerful institutions and intellectual capital' but also emphasises 'a very particular level of identification' (1992: 34) with the women in her study, and Seiter recalls the importance of the fact that she was 'accepted as a person with similar kinds of concerns and problems' (1995: 144) by members of the group she studied.

This emphasis on common understandings and experiences contributes to the problem of homogeneity discussed earlier by leading a researcher to draw limits around the kind of audience members who can be studied. Gray understands this problem but felt that the importance of 'shared knowledge' and her awareness of debates about the exploitation of research subjects made her 'unwilling to impose myself and my research on Black and Asian women in a racist society' (1995: 161). Others, however, have tried to investigate groups with whom they had less in common. Tulloch used family relationships as an introduction to the elderly people he studied; 'I was first of all "Douglas' nephew" to the old people I spoke with' (1991: 184); Gillespie, a white Irish woman researching Punjabi youth, used the long process of establishing trust through participant observation to overcome ethnic and gender differences. She claimed that her own ethnic 'liminal insider/outsider status' (1995: 73) encouraged greater freedom in her conversations with young people and their mothers.[4] It was, however, more difficult to establish relationships with groups of boys or individual boys and, despite help from young male key informants, Gillespie alerts the reader to 'the predominance of girls as subjects and informants in this study' (72).

A number of issues around the relationship between researcher and those being studied are brought together in the frequent insistence that the process of being researched can and should be pleasurable. Hallam and Marshment describe their viewing sessions/interviews as 'relaxed' and 'pleasurable' (1995b: 175); Gray recalls that 'many of the conversations were fun' (1992: 33). In part this is pragmatic, since the researcher is dependent on the cooperation of those participating, but this emphasis is worth noting because it gives an insight into a number of factors which are significant in qualitative work on television. The stress on rapport is a sign of the strong influence of feminism in this area of work. The use of the semi-structured interview, the dominant mode here, is strongly associated with feminist approaches to social research. Shulamit Reinharz suggests that as a technique it draws on traditionally feminine skills of listening and empathising and helps to develop 'a sense of connectedness with people' (1992: 20). Gray draws attention to this when she comments on the '*intensity* of the one-to-one conversational interview. The interviewee has the undivided attention of another sympathetic woman who appears to be fascinated by what she has to say' (1995: 163). This is linked to a number of feminist concerns which can be seen at play here: the desire to avoid or circumvent the power relations implicit in more formal methods which are more clearly controlled by the researcher; the use of supportive methods within a homogenous group to share knowledge or experience; the emphasis on personal experience and the re-telling of that experience as a means of moving forward.

In Television Studies, this approach has often been linked to that of the fan; indeed, it is striking that two of the keenest advocates of the fan approach, John Fiske and Henry Jenkins, have been men adopting some of the characteristics of feminist methodologies. As writers on soap opera have indicated, the discourses of women and fans can be understood to have common characteristics. The sharing of knowledge, the establishment of rapport through a common sense of what is valuable and appropriate, the blurring of different relationships to power in the external world through an identification with what is shared in the group, the emphasis on talk as supportive and pleasurable are all characteristics which have been used to describe 'fan culture' (Jenkins, 1992: 6) and 'women's culture' (Brown, 1990). No wonder the key to an approach to such audiences is deemed to be a pleasurable interview.

A mode of research based on identification with the interviewees and the establishment of trust has been both appropriate and fruitful but it has its limitations. It has perhaps led us to underestimate what can be learnt from the difficult interview, the one where rapport is not established. Ellen Seiter draws attention to this in her account of 'a troubling interview' with two 'subjects' who were 'doubly defensive as men and as members of an older generation' (1990: 62). Seiter contrasts her own response to the 'currents of hostility and aggression which ran through Mr H's conversation' with the rapport she had established with all-female groups; far from sharing a pleasurable experience, the interview become a battle for 'control of this verbal "exchange"' and she points to the way in which this forced her to recognise that she was in a more powerful position, culturally and academically, than the interviewee.

The question of the feelings generated by the interview can also be linked to another set of propositions about the trustworthiness of what is being established through the interview. In the interview format, interviewees are generally being asked to describe their own experiences and hence to give an account of those experiences. As Ann Gray makes clear, 'What the women said to me does not directly reflect their experience but is their way of articulating that experience' (1992: 33). But there seem to be limits to the kind of interpretation which interviewees are allowed to give. The 'troubling interview' was rendered difficult by Mr H offering not just his account of his viewing experience but a meta-analysis of television viewing more generally which did not fit his role. Rapport becomes a sign that the interviewee is comfortable with his or her role and will as far as is possible be a reliable witness to their own experience. Andrea Press expresses this link explicitly when she says, 'I sought a relaxed atmosphere because I felt it made our rapport easier to establish, and the women's responses more genuine' (1991: 181). Hallam and Marshment contrast the intimate material the women brought up in their conversations with the more limited responses to the questionnaires – 'they felt relaxed enough to talk about quite a lot of those things' (1995b: 177).

Thus, rapport is deemed important because it allows things to be said which might not otherwise be disclosed. We have seen that researchers in this area recognise that they tend to be reporting on what is said about TV viewing; in that sense, any account is of interest because it offers a particular story about how television is experienced and understood. But the emphasis on rapport seems to indicate that different values are being placed on different kinds of stories and that there is a hierarchy at work which is based on degrees of intimacy, revelation and truth-telling. Qualitative researchers in this area do not necessarily look to their subjects for facts about viewing but in a different way many seem to be looking for witnesses. Perti Alasuutari describes this kind of approach as 'humanistic'. 'It is thought that . . . if the informants trust the researcher, they will also be honest with the researcher' (1995: 52), he goes on. 'In this perspective, honest, confidential, "heart pouring" talk is equated with important information and in-depth analysis' (53).

Alasuutari is not arguing that truth and honesty are unimportant or indistinguishable, and I am not suggesting that work on television audiences should forgo an interest in the intimate detail. But it seems to me not accidental that television ethnography has this tendency to value the revelations of rapport. The dominance of feminism, the practical considerations that make the confession form of the interview the most feasible (and often the only possible) approach, the strong emphasis in Cultural Studies on the politics of the powerless, the desire to assert the resistant possibilities of the mass viewer, the ambivalence of researchers about their own position in relation to ordinary viewers, all have contributed to this mode. And this in turn has consequences for what ethnography, as it has been practised, can say about television audiences.

The Problems of Generalisation

Given its methods and approaches, what can ethnographic work tell us about television audiences, what can we ask of it in terms of knowledge and what are the limits implicit in its objects and methods of study? I pose this as a problem of generalisation because the problem here is precisely one of how far we can take the individual insights of particular studies and build around them concepts of audience which work in the broader context of Television Studies.

The researchers I have been discussing are usually careful to draw attention to the limits of their studies. Hallam and Marshment emphasise 'our sample of eight women was clearly too tiny to generalise from' (1995b: 170) and Morley emphasises of his *Family Television* work, 'I am not arguing that all families in the United Kingdom repeat this pattern. Indeed, I would be amazed if it was repeated among more highly educated professional families' (1986: 53). Even where the disclaimer is not so marked, it is clear that the studies are to varying degrees limited by the number and the nature of the interviews they were able to conduct. In addition, the object of study is not 'the audience' in the abstract but audiences in particular circumstances – in relation to particular programmes such as soap opera, for example, or in particular domestic structures such as the family.

As we have seen, what is being described here is qualitative research which seeks information about audiences not from surveys based on numerical responses or statistical work but from observing and listening to audience members. Such work eschews the generalisations of quantitative work with its emphasis on the 'typical', the 'average' or 'the majority'. Instead, qualitative work looks to explain a particular set of circumstances, to put phenomena in context and to provide interpretations which explain all the elements involved in a situation rather than focusing on one set of relations. David Morley thus talks about approaches which 'are holistic in emphasis and are fundamentally concerned with the context of actions' (1992: 173) and Perti Alasuutari goes so far as to say that 'in qualitative analysis a single exception is enough to break the rule, to show that one has to rethink the whole' (1995: 14). Whereas the quantitative approach relies on samples which can represent the whole and which can therefore be generalised from, in qualitative analysis 'the data are often considered as a totality: they are thought to shed light on a singular logical whole' (Alasuutari, 1995: 11). The move in work on television audiences from looking at individuals to the whole context of the home and the family in relation to television use is thus typical of qualitative work. In this sense, it is not possible to generalise from qualitative work.

The rationale for such work, therefore, cannot be that it tells us about audiences in general. Instead, the emphasis is on the diversity, the particularity of the data. Ien Ang argues this when she suggests that 'ethnographic work is always more complicated and diversified than our theories can represent . . . The critical promise of the ethnographic attitude resides in its potential to make and keep our interpretations sensitive to concrete specificities, to the unexpected, to history' (1991a: 110). This emphasis on the concrete and the capacity to surprise links well with the minutiae of ethnographic work and the openness to the subjects' experiences which I commented on in the last section. It also chimes with postmodernist critiques of generalisation which call into question the capacity for particular instances to inform us about overall structures.

But it is clear that work with television audiences is used to draw general conclusions well beyond the boundary of their study. Hallam and Marshment were led by their interviews to question the whole concept of the ordinary woman viewer which they felt had dominated feminist work in the area (1995b: 170); the Tubingen Soap Opera group use quotations from four interviews to refute Modleski's psychoanalytic model for women's soap opera viewing; both Morley and Gray come to (tentative) conclusions about gendered modes of viewing with, for instance, Gray using her interview material to query some of Morley's conclusions: 'we can see from evidence reported here that women do take pleasure in adopting the concentrated gaze' (1992: 126).

This move to generalisation, even in the most limited studies, seems entirely understandable; academic work is after all concerned with making connections and testing out general propositions. An overemphasis on difference makes it theoretically impossible to move beyond particular instances. If that is the case, however, certain consequences follow. Firstly, it is important to define and respect the object of study and to note that applying findings without taking into account the object of study can produce a misleading picture. The purpose of defining the object of study is not just to ensure that appropriate questions can be asked or manageable parameters set. It also has consequences for what can be said in relation to outcomes. A picture of television viewing based on one category – soap opera viewers, viewers in families, fans, children – cannot be used, as has sometimes been the case, to make general comments about television watching as a whole. Secondly, we need to recognise that there is a difference between the questions to be asked in interviews and the research questions which underpin the study. 'A research hypothesis cannot be tested simply by asking the informants whether your interpretation is right' (Alasuutari, 1995: 169). Interview responses cannot in themselves constitute an argument; they have to be interpreted and set against other material. The counter-checking provided by the variety of methods used by Silverstone, Hirsch and Morley is a good example of this approach. Thirdly, if generalisations are to be made, and it is almost inevitable that they are, some thought has to be given to the problems of representativeness and, in particular, questions of the numbers in a sample.

Concluding Comments

Work on television audiences has been important in recognising that 'television watching' is not simply a question of looking (or not looking) at a screen. It has indicated that there is no one way of viewing which is determined by the television set itself; that television watching makes sense within a variety of contexts which may link it to social arrangements (viewing in a family, discussing it in a work group) or to other entertainment and communication formats (cinema, computers). Ironically, what seems to be missing in this work which attempts to value what different audience members say is a sense of what claims audiences might legitimately make for different kinds of television. While a sense of the public sphere is by no means absent in this work – Morley, in particular, has stressed the way in television can be understood as the means whereby the global becomes local, the public is made private – the concentration on the domestic means that viewers' complaints or frustrations tend to be read by the researchers in terms of broader constructions particularly around gender and the family rather than linked to the political and social arrangements which produce the programmes we watch. If we are not to end up with a stand-off between theories of mass audiences, on the one hand, and increasingly detailed accounts of particular instances, on the other, that gap has to be bridged. Julie D'Acci records the way in which *Cagney and Lacey* viewers entered into a passionate public debate about what kind of representations they wanted. Audience studies more generally need to find ways in which what audiences say can not only be recorded but can find a public voice within discussions about television itself.

Notes

1.   There have been arguments about how 'new' this work on television audiences is. See the dialogue between James Curran and David Morley in Curran, Morley and Walkerdine (1996) for the details of this debate.
2.   An account of this work can be most accessibly found in Root (1986).
3.   See David Morley's *Television, Audiences and Cultural Studies* (1992) for a much fuller account of these debates as they have affected work on audiences.
4.   The difficulty of such claims and the way they relate to issues of power can be seen in Lola Young's (1996) criticism of this and other aspects of Gillespie's work.

References

ALASUUTARI, P., 1995: *Researching Culture. Qualitative Method and Cultural Studies.* London: Sage.
ANG, I., 1985: *Watching Dallas: Soap Opera and the Melodramatic Imagination.* London: Methuen.
———, 1991a: 'Wanted: Audiences. On the politics of empirical audience studies'. In E. Seiter, H. Borchers, G. Kreutzner, and E. Warth (eds), *Remote Control.* London: Routledge.
———,1991b: *Desparately Seeking the Audience.* London: Routledge.
BROWN, M. E. (ed.), 1990: *Television and Women's Culture.* London: Sage Publications.
———, 1994: *Soap Opera and Women's Talk.* London: Sage.
BRUNSDON, C., 1981: '*Crossroads*: notes on soap opera'. *Screen*, 22, 4.
———, 1991: 'Text and audience'. In E. Seiter, H. Borchers, G. Kreutzner and E. Warth (eds), *Remote Control.* London: Routledge.
CLIFFORD, J. and MARCUS, G., 1986: *Writing Culture.* Berkeley: University of California Press.
COLLET, P. and LAMB, R., 1986: *Watching People Watching Television.* Report presented to the Independent Broadcasting Authority, London.
CURRAN, J., MORLEY, D. and WALKERDINE, V., 1996: *Cultural Studies and Communications.* London: Arnold.
D'ACCI, J., 1994: *Defining Women: Television and the Case of Cagney and Lacey.* Chapel Hill: University of North Carolina Press.
FISKE, J., 1987: *Television Culture.* London: Methuen.
———, 1990: 'Ethnosemiotics: some personal and theoretical reflections'. *Cultural Studies.* 4, 1, January.
GILLESPIE, M., 1995: *Television, Ethnicity and Cultural Change.* London: Routledge.
GRAY, A. 1992: *Video Playtime.* London: Routledge.
———, 1995: 'I want to tell you a story: the narratives of *Video Playtime*'. In B. Skeggs, (ed), *Feminist Cultural Theory.* Manchester: Manchester University Press.
HALLAM, J. and MARSHMENT, M., 1995a: 'Framing experience: case studies in the reception of *Oranges are not the only fruit*'. *Screen*, 36, 1, Spring.
———, 1995b: 'Questioning the "ordinary" woman: *Oranges are not the only fruit*'. In B. Skeggs (ed.), *Feminist Cultural Theory.* Manchester: Manchester University Press.
HOBSON, D., 1982: *Crossroads: The Drama of a Soap Opera.* London: Methuen.
———, 1990: 'Women audiences and the workplace'. In M. E. Brown (ed.), *Television and Women's Culture.* London: Sage Publications.
———, 1991: 'Soap operas at work'. In E. Seiter, H. Borchers, G. Kreutzner and E. Warth (eds), *Remote Control.* London: Routledge.
JENKINS, H., 1992: *Textual Poachers.* London: Routledge.

MODLESKI, T., 1984: *Loving with a Vengeance*. London: Methuen.
MORLEY, D., 1980: *The 'Nationwide' Audience*. London: British Film Institute.
———, 1986: *Family Television, Cultural Power and Domestic Leisure*. London: Comedia.
———, 1992: *Television, Audiences and Cultural Studies*. London: Routledge.
PRESS, A., 1991: *Women Watching Television: Gender, Class and Generation in the American Television Experience*. Philadelphia: University of Pennsylvania Press.
RADWAY, J. A., 1984: *Reading the Romance: Women, Patriarchy and Popular Literature*. Chapel Hill: University of North Carolina Press.
REINHARZ, S., 1992: *Feminist Methods in Social Research*. Oxford: Oxford University Press.
ROOT, J., 1986: *Open the Box*. London: Comedia.
SEITER, E., 1990: 'Making distinctions in TV audiences research: case study of a troubling interview'. *Cultural Studies*, 4, 1.
———, 1995: 'Mothers watching children watching television'. In B. Skeggs (ed.), *Feminist Cultural Theory*. Manchester: Manchester University Press.
SEITER, E., BORCHERS, H. E., KREUTZNER, G. and WARTH, E., 1991: ' "Don't treat us like we're so stupid and naive": towards an ethnography of soap opera viewers'. In E. Seiter, H. Borchers, G. Kreutzner and E. Warth (eds), *Remote Control*. London: Routledge.
SILVERSTONE, R., HIRSCH, E. and MORLEY, D., 1991: 'Listening to a long conversation: an ethnographic approach to the study of information and communication technologies in the home'. *Cultural Studies*, 5, 2.
TULLOCH, J., 1991: 'Approaching the audience: the elderly'. In E. Seiter, H. Borchers, G. Kreutzner and E. Warth (eds), *Remote Control*. London: Routledge.
YOUNG, L., 1996: 'Review of *Television, Ethnicity and Cultural Change*'. *Screen*, 37, 4.

9

New Technologies and Domestic Consumption

Eric Hirsch

This chapter is concerned with the relationship between new technologies and domestic consumption. When the editors of this volume asked me to address this relationship, their specific interest was in the way broadcast television is becoming displaced from the centre of domestic culture and consumption by a range of new technologies, including new forms of television. In my previous work in this area it was apparent that the contemporary relationship between new technologies and domestic consumption was part of a long-standing pattern of tension and accommodation (Hirsch, 1992: 211–12). However, in that previous work a sustained analysis of that pattern was not pursued. Such an undertaking is outlined here. I shall argue that there is a clear historical and social connection between the two: domestic consumption for the last 200 years has been sustained (and also continually perceived as threatened) by new technologies. What is meant by 'new' is crucial here. 'New-ness' co-exists in a tension with what is seen as established (or often traditional) – technologies are both established and new at the same time. For example, 'established' forms of computing are nowadays continually perceived as being superceded by 'novel' forms; computing is 'established' and 'new' simultaneously.

Technologies are not alone in being subject to this tension. Forms of domestic consumption are both established and new in an analogous manner: people commonly evoke both old and novel forms of consuming in the domestic context. Moreover, the distinction between old and new which is rendered visible in the relationship between technology and domestic consumption is simultaneously used by people as part of their own self-conceptualisation (Strathern, 1996: 45; cf. Hirsch, 1992). Television, for example, is central to our contemporary everyday patterns of domestic consumption. At the same time personal computers, the Internet, and the 'Information Superhighway' more generally are the 'new' technologies seen as offering novel possibilities for the domestic sphere but also perceived as challenging our conventional or 'established' patterns of domestic consumption centred around broadcast television. A generation and a half ago television would have had the status of 'new' technology positioned on the horizon of the consumer as a novel possibility for domestic use, envisioned as simultaneously supplanting established forms thus rendered as traditional.

My central argument is that an explicit emphasis on domestic consumption – which emerged as a middle-class phenomenon during the late eighteenth to early nineteenth century – has been a project of domestic self-sufficiency.[1] What I mean by this is that this project is sustainable only through an ever-widening and interrelated set of connections with the public, the world of work and 'society', from which it was self-consciously separated. What has become particularly manifest during this period is a mutually constitutive relationship between forms of socio-cultural innovations (e.g. forms of domesticity) and technological innovations (e.g. forms of technology used in or connected to the domestic context) whereby the efficacy of each becomes evident. More specifically, the interests in creating domains of domestic self-sufficiency made manifest the need for connections of various kinds: to goods and services and for communication and transport, each facilitated by new technologies. In a related manner, the new technologies were seen by entrepreneurs and others as feasible avenues for development through their eventual deployment in domestic units requiring various kinds of connections. This essay will therefore look at some examples of these connections in what are now thought of as older technologies, in order to establish the context in which we can begin to understand the family's relationship with new technologies in the domestic sphere (presented as a case study of a family in contemporary Britain).

Although the chapter draws on a range of historical sources (largely from the Anglo-American context), it should not be read as a history. Rather, it is a historically informed account which is deliberately schematic. It is also important to highlight that the mode of analysis used to explore the middle-class project which achieved dominance is, in part, constituted by the project itself: we are constrained to think within its categories. However, when the project begins to unravel, then other ways of thinking about the project become available. It is from this latter perspective that the scheme I present is written.

The 200-year timespan – from the late eighteenth century to the present – can be divided up into roughly five distinct but overlapping periods. Retrospectively, broadcast television is foreshadowed by the relationship between domestic self-sufficiency and the ever more profuse set of connections through which an emphasis on domesticity can be sustained. Throughout successive periods, this relationship becomes more and more close-knit. But as we shall see, the innumerable connections gathered up by broadcast television also foreshadowed its perceived limits and eventual 'undoing', which has become visible during the current phase of socio-cultural and technological innovations, the fifth period.

The first period, from c.1780 to the 1850s, constituted a revolution in speed: the speed at which manufactured goods were produced and transported and the speed with which the consumers of those goods both consumed them and were themselves transported. This first period engendered a crisis of control which provided the contours of the second period. From the 1850s to 1880s a range of social and technical strategies were first formulated to coordinate and integrate the often indiscernible set of connections generated between the production, distribution and consumption of goods and services: between the domestic units and ever more profuse connections. These social and technical strategies were systematised during the third period from the 1880s to 1940s. It was during this time that the cultural ideal, which first emerged 100 years previously, was codified in the spaces of suburbia and became a reality for the majority of the population (in Britain and the USA). This harmonization of 'individual/family' and 'society' entered its 'golden age' during the fourth period from the 1940s to 1970s. Processes of technological miniaturization and the rapid expansion of consumer electronics further enhanced the domestic ideal throughout this period. But the limitations of the systems (both 'social' and 'technical') first codified during the latter part of the nineteenth century became explicit. This sense of limits heralded the period in which we now find ourselves, a period which began during the 1970s and which promulgates a combination of individual 'choice' and technological 'convergence'. This is the long-term perspective that is needed if we are to understand the social and historical significance both of broadcast television – and of the associated range of 'new' technologies which appear to be supplanting its dominance – at the centre of our domestic culture.

Revolution in Speed

The separation of the domestic context from the market was a project that was explicitly aspired to towards the end of the eighteenth century (cf. Stone, 1990: 291; Wahrman, 1995). Domestic life became idealized as a haven from the aggressiveness and uncertainty of the marketplace. But this separation of domesticity both from the perceived harshness of economic life as well as from other domestic units went hand in hand with a range of technical and organizational developments in communication: increasing literacy, the introduction of the postal system, fast and relatively cheap travel by coach, steamer and later railway (Davidoff and Hall, 1987: 321). These might not look like 'new' technologies in the way we currently understand the term, and yet the connections they facilitated were central to the self-sufficiency hankered for by the emerging middle classes: 'The creation of the private sphere has been central to the elaboration of consumer demand, so essential to the expansion and accumulation process which characterises modern societies' (Davidoff and Hall, 1987: 29; cf. Barker and Gerhold, 1993: 41–7, 60). At the same time, novel forms of enterprise, middle-class in emphasis, were created around supplying this private sphere with the goods through which to manifest their newly acquired visibility and distinctiveness. In short, this was the period of the birth of a consumer society: the expectation of novelty and ever-changing fashion came to predominate (McKendrick *et al.*, 1982; cf. Campbell, 1987). The 'novelty' of technologies and of domestic relations in this consumer society was an actualization of speed, which thus became of central importance to both the production and distribution process (Barker and Savage, 1974: 14–15). There emerged, then, a dynamic relationship between an ideal of domesticity and the profusion of connections that at once sustained this ideal and were productive of an industrial economy founded on speed (cf. Schivelbusch, 1986). These connections also led, however, to a crises of control, as the entrepreneurs increasingly found it difficult to manage the products, consumers and connections that had been generated between them (see Beniger, 1986: 227–8). Their control was crucial if the flow between them was to be sustained at an ever-greater pace.

Crisis of Control

The emergence of the department store and the applications of telegraphic communication to the railroads overlapped historically (Chandler, 1984: 474): both developments were significant for the later emergence of broadcast television.

The department store and telegraphic communication were each a related outgrowth of the scale of connections traced both by persons and manufactured goods and the increasing difficulty in controlling their flow effectively. In effect these multifarious connections had grown to such an extent that it became impossible to draw them together within an encompassing form. Both the department store and telegraphic communications were innovations which were designed to transcend this crisis. The scale of capital devoted to production and distribution processes which engendered innovations of control made apparent the requirement to control consumption. Advertising and marketing campaigns through mass-circulation publishing became widespread during this period which, in turn, foreshadowed the development of 'market research': '[m]ass media were not sufficient to effect true control ... without a means of feedback from potential consumers to advertisers' (Beniger, 1986: 284). The current regime of commercial broadcast television is informed by this social innovation.

The new technology of the telegraph helped to make the connections which sustained both the productive enterprises of business and commerce and separate domestic units. The implementation of control on these 'external' connections was paralleled by an emphasis on the control or discipline of the 'internal', domestic environment. There was a proliferation of literature on household management, domestic economy and hints on household taste as an increasing number of new devices required accommodation within the home (e.g. stereoscopes, photographs, gas appliances, etc.) (Briggs, 1990: 217).

This external–internal relationship was soon to be further transformed by the new horizons opened up by the introduction of telephone communication. Alexander Graham Bell's vision was one of universal interconnections over vast distances which were not just for the well-off or for business use (de Sola Pool, 1977: 130). This was not, however, such a far-fetched notion since the telegraph had already established a global system of communication (Headrick, 1988: ch. 4) and the distinct technology of telephone had been isolated as a by-product of telegraphic communication. Just as the technology of the telegraph provided the basis for the telephone, so the culture of the telegraph pre-disposed a particular perception towards the possibilities offered by this new technology. In particular, communication between parties via the telegraph operator was one that took time to wrest away from popular consciousness: '[i]t may be obvious now when the telephone often seems to be an appendage to the mouth and ear how many different uses (and misuses) it has, but those living in the telegraph age had to learn them' (Aronson, 1977: 25).

The widespread delivery of the telephone to domestic as well as commercial contexts was not feasible without a central office system with the connections facilitated by a switching mechanism. As Bell indicated in a letter (of 1878) to the entrepreneurs in Britain charged with developing his invention:

> It is conceivable that cables of telephone wires could be laid underground, or suspended overhead, communicating by branch wires with private dwellings, country

houses, shops, manufactories, etc. uniting them through the main cable with a central office where the wire could be connected as desired, establishing direct communication between any two places in the city . . . I believe in the future wires will unite the head office of the Telephone Company in different cities, and a man in one part of the country may communicate by word of mouth with another in a different place. (quoted by Aronson, 1977: 22)

An analogous relationship during this same period was envisioned for electricity by Thomas Edison whereby electricity was to be delivered into the home (Hughes, 1983; Marvin, 1988; Forty, 1986: ch. 8). In each the notion of a system of interconnections thus came to be of central significance and it was to define the contours of the next period in which first broadcast radio and then broadcast television formally emerged.

System and Simultaneity

The 'systems' approach characterized not only the development and management of technology but it also came to define in a similar manner the analysis and management of 'society'. The crisis of control during previous decades had rendered visible what came to be understood as problems of integration: how was it possible to systematize and thus integrate the various parts to the whole – the individual as part of a wider social reality (Strathern, 1992: 108–9); individual products or services to wider processes of production, distribution and exchange? This was discerned as much as a commercial problem as it was a moral one. On the one hand, Edison's interest in systems was motivated by a desire for commercial advantage, particularly in the development of electricity supply:

> Like any other machine the failure of one part to cooperate properly with the other part disorganises the whole and renders it inoperative for the purposes intended . . . The problem then that I [Edison] undertook to solve was stated generally, the production of the multifarious apparatus, methods and devices, each adapted for use with every other, and all forming a comprehensive system. (quoted in Hughes 1983: 22)

On the other hand, theorists of society such as Durkheim perceived a problem of integration between the individual and society as a consequence of increasing social complexity through the division of labour (cf. Hawthorn, 1987: 123–4, 131). Here was a moral problem that required adequate mechanisms of control if a condition of 'anomie' was to be transcended – the breakdown of norms governing individual and group behaviour: 'Durkheim argued [that] anomie results . . . from the breakdown in communication among . . . increasingly isolated sectors, so that individuals employed in them lose sight of the larger purpose of their separate efforts' (Beniger, 1986: 12). The solution was to be found in public institutions (education, religion, welfare) which engendered a sense of the social whole (system) as integrated and greater than the sum of its parts (individuals/families). Social reform was soon sought through the use of the innovative techniques of social survey questionnaires which were quickly adopted by advertisers and marketers for different but not unrelated commercial problems. The consumer was soon perceived as linked to a number of separately regulated technological systems (telegraph, telephone, electricity), just as the individual/family was linked to the social whole through a number of separate public institutions or systems. Thus was rendered explicit in this proliferation of systems the phenomena of simultaneity: the ability to experience distant events at the same time (Kern, 1983), and broadcasting would emerge as the most powerful form of simultaneity. But its specific form depended on whether it was part of commercial enterprise (USA) or public service (Britain) (cf. Williams, 1990: 326). During the 1920s take-up of radio in the domestic context coincided with the proliferation of the middle-class ideal of domestic living as embodied in the suburban semi-detached house or bungalow (Oliver *et al.*, 1994; cf. Silverstone, 1994).[2] British broadcasters conceptualized their audience not as an aggregate of individuals but as a specifically domestic one – of families (Scannell and Cardiff, 1991: ch. 16). The middle-class values associated with this notion could then be promoted for the whole nation.[3]

Jennings and Gill's investigations on the impact of radio on everyday life were explicitly commissioned for this purpose by the BBC's Board of Governors during the 1930s: 'they concentrated their efforts on a working class district of Bristol, and their report argued strongly that radio had improved the attractiveness of homelife for working class families' (Scannell and Cardiff, 1991: 363). Radio is thus an example of what came into clearer focus during this period between the wars – the advance of the encompassing ideal of the social or collective whole to which individuals/families were related or attached. This was the ethos with which the advent of broadcasting became imbued. A similar ethos existed less visibly in the formation during this time of the National Grid of electricity to which nearly three-quarters of all homes were connected by 1939 (Davis, 1994: 79; cf. Hughes, 1983: 361–2). Many of the new technologies of the home were powered by electricity, and this capacity meant that the pursuit of domestic consumption could be seen at once as an individual achievement and as part of the greater social system (society, culture) of which it was a part: one could now switch on and off at will.

Harmonization and its Limits

Even during the early days of radio broadcasting, television could be envisioned as just around the corner (Briggs, 1985: 155). In Britain at least, its transmission was cut short by the war (Briggs, 1985: 201). With the end of the war the ideal of the suburban semi-detached, middle-class family was ever stronger, but with 'greater security, less responsibility and the assurance of steady material advancement' (Oliver *et al.*, 1994: 194). Broadcast television eventually became synonymous with this advance: it was at once its material embodiment and simultaneously gave audio-visual form to the systematic integration that the individual in the domestic sphere had with this material advancing society. During the 1950s and 1960s this became codified as 'the presumption of the growing internal harmony of a society that was now basically satisfactory, if improvable . . . based on confidence in the economy of organised social consensus' (Hobsbawm, 1994: 286).

This 'harmonization' process was facilitated by the boom in consumer electronics (television sets, hi-fi record-playing equipment and records, tape recorders, FM radios) (Hall and Preston, 1988: 165).[4] General access to these technologies was a visible manifestation of the 'affluence' now seen as prevalent (Galbraith, 1958). At the same time, conceptions of 'harmony' were based on domestic living arrangements envisioned as connected to an ever-expanding sphere of media and communication, as key advertisements of this affluence. Broadcast television became the prime example of these numerous connections, providing the sense of a spatio-temporal flow simultaneous with the flow dictated by a highly rationalized system of industrial production and distribution. The rationalization of television programme content was already prefigured during the early years of radio broadcasting (Scannell and Cardiff, 1991: 374–5): '[I]n the later thirties . . . [t]he Programme Planning Department [of the BBC] was beginning to adjust daily output to chime in with the time routines of day-to-day life through the weekend and working week'.

As we have seen, the use of survey research as market feedback technology for systematizing the production and distribution of individual goods and services enabled the rationalized control of consumption wherever broadcast television figured significantly as a means of advertising (in Britain since 1955). The use of television as vehicle for consumer advertising has come to be regarded as central to its ubiquity in everyday life (cf. Silverstone, 1994). The 'constant presence' of television is both an outgrowth of this rationalization and productive of the sense that we should in some way – often ambiguously – be influenced by it.

The continuing growth in consumer electronics throughout this period was premised on three related technical innovations which all expanded on tendencies present in previous periods (Dummer, 1983), but in its very success this consumer boom also helped to make explicit the limits of 'harmonization'. The first was the transistor, which made possible both processes of miniaturization and an increase in the range of electronic applications (Dummer, 1983: 7). The second was the integrated circuit, which took further the miniaturization process, heralding the establishment of microelectronics and 'the manufacture of many individual electronic components and functions on a single microchip' (Hall and Preston, 1988: 153). The third was the 'microprogrammable computer on a chip' which has the 'capacity to perform the full range of logic functions on every kind of information presentable in digital form' (Hall and Preston, 1988: 153–4).

This 'revolution' in microelectronics was part of the more complete working out of the solutions to the crisis of control that were first proposed over a century earlier (Beniger, 1986: 435). At the same time, the advent of digitization brought into focus the possible 'convergence' of computer, telecommunication and media: it now became conceivable that these separately regulated 'systems' could become part of one fully interconnected network (cf. Nora and Minc, 1980). The possibility of envisioning the eclipse of separately regulated systems coincided with a radical new vision of the individual/family relationship to the shape of these systems: society as regulated by an all-encompassing state. Just as the limits of the period of harmony were increasingly conceptualized around technological convergence, so the individual/family came to be defined less in relationship to an encompassing societal system and more by the exercise of 'choice' (cf. Strathern, 1992: 213, n. 21).

Choice and Convergence

Already by the middle of the nineteenth century, the technology of home entertainment was a well-established industry, first in the form of the stereoscope and
later in the form of the 'instantaneous photograph' (Briggs, 1990: 132, 135). The
notion of the 'spectacle' of a public kind (exhibitions, dioramas) as well as of a
private, domestic kind (delight of the interior surroundings) came to define the
sense of 'separated-connectedness'. This was further elaborated by the advent
of the cinema at the turn of the century and the improvement of the domestic
phonograph.

As we have seen, broadcast media, first radio and then television, were central components in systematizing the relations of this public and domestic culture. But by the 1970s, a new range of technologies and politico-moral ideas
were on the horizon which would re-shape not only the contours of home media,
communication and information, but also the former relationship between
'society' and the individual/family (cf. Williams, 1965: ch. 3). Broadcast television, formerly viewed as almost synonymous with this relationship, was becoming supplanted from this position. At the same time, new configurations of
television (less centred on the broadcast form) in the shape of cable, satellite,
video, the older communication technology of the telephone, and the new technologies of personal computers, were positioning themselves in a politico-moral
environment of 'choice'.

This technological convergence was accompanied by a flattening of the
class-based distinctions that had previously been instrumental in providing
the conceptual and material architecture of the relationship between the
individual/family and society. Now the example being promoted is the
private individual, whether residing in a family-based domestic unit or in a
transnational corporation. The latter are '[s]uper-private, super individualistic,
they seem only larger versions of the private individual' (Strathern, 1992:
141–2).

In this new period of privatized choice, what is potentially emerging are forms
of domestic consumption embodying two screens: the older screen of broadcast
television is now re-figured around a range of new technologies and the screen
of the personal computer. The conventional scheduling structure of broadcast
television has been subject to transformation through the development of the
video cassette recorder (Hall and Preston, 1988: 163) and the use of 'time shifting' and 'zapping' of scheduled programmes (Ang, 1992: 136), alternative media
use (rental movies and video games), and the growth of cable and satellite television from the mid-1980s. What has emerged in this configuration of new technologies and new uses – and this is particularly evident in the British context – is
the movement from 'broadcasting' to 'television' (i.e. a move from an emphasis
on public service to that of commercial profit) (Murdock, 1994: 156): and in
some cases the use of 'television' cable for 'telecommunications' purposes which
is more profitable in the long term (Murdock, 1994: 162–3).

The advent of the personal computer has run parallel with these changes
around the television screen – and initially convergent with them in certain
cases. Its early history during the 1970s and 1980s is in many respects similar to
radio when it first appeared earlier this century – focused as it was on the

hobbyist and organised hobby culture (Pegg, 1983; Haddon, 1992: 94–5, n. 7; cf. Pfaffenberger, 1988). In this incipient market a number of related uses came to the fore, including games, entertainment and education (links between home and arcades; home and school) and homeworking via modems (separating or connecting home and work). To these transformations of the personal computer we must now add the Internet. During the late 1980s and early 1990s this technological innovation (see Rheingold, 1994: 65–88 for historical background) captured the imagination of domestic computer users with its potential for seemingly innumerable connections from the perspective of the individual. More recently, the addition of the World Wide Web has transformed this connecting potential further: 'this hypertext protocol permits people to simply click on highlighted text to be connected to a computer file somewhere in the Web' (Baldwin *et al.*, 1996: 70).

The convergence of information, communication and media, an ideal promulgated by corporate interest and promoted by forms of national regulation, exists in an uncertain relationship with the interests of domestic consumers (the early failure of videotext is such an example) (Baldwin *et al.*, 1996: 65–6; cf. Miles, 1988: 64–9). What is clear, however, is that 'convergence' does not depend on technical innovations alone.[5] Rather, as discussed above, there is a mutually constitutive relationship between 'new' forms of domesticity (based on explicit individual choice) and the connections which such self-sufficiency renders visible for 'new' technologies (based on technological convergence). It has been forecast that even with the implementation of an integrated broadband system, television and computers will not replace one another. Television will continue with its programme format but with some 'interactivity' and the accessing of information. Computers, by contrast, will be used for work, transactional services, e-mail and other on-line services; both will be used for shopping (Baldwin *et al.*, 1996: 156). More precise contours of these socio-technical innovations are difficult to discern from our current vantage point. What is at issue is how these multifarious connections will come to be gathered together in separate contexts of domesticity where the emphasis is less on societal (state) regulated systems, and more on individual choice. At this point we can turn to the case study of one family which exemplifies this engagement with the current range of new possibilities.

Finding a Place for the Modem in the Home

During the late 1980s and early 1990s I conducted ethnographic research with 16 families in inner and outer London.[6] 'One of the families I worked with, which I refer to as the Williams family, lived in a semi-detached house in outer London. Geoff and Maria were both pharmacists and worked in two of the local hospitals: Geoff in a full-time capacity as a Principal Pharmacist and Maria on a part-time basis having recently returned to work after a period away looking after their two children. Heather and Alan were eleven and eight respectively when I first met them and attended a local Catholic school. An explicit concern expressed by Geoff and Maria during my fieldwork with them was the separation of home and work. More specifically, the weekend was a time when the family as a whole would spend time together, not constrained by the dictates of time which govern the working/school week; Geoff would consciously remove his watch at the weekend and not shave.

An important aspect of this weekend period was the time spent watching television together as a family. However, as we shall see below, this sense of togetherness around television, particularly at the weekends, would transform as the children grew older and their concerns for independence and privateness became more explicit. For Heather independence and privateness came to be focused largely around the television, while for Alan the computer became more important, although often in conjunction with television viewing.

The explicit value placed on the separateness of the home came to be, among other things during this period of fieldwork, focused around the computer Geoff had purchased for use in the home. This was an Amstrad 1512 which was initially obtained to encourage Alan to learn how to write his own programmes and to move on from the Sega games console which he used frequently (but more of this below). However, at this time, the computer came to take on a transformed significance in the Williams's home, in the context of constraints now operating on Geoff in his hospital job. As Geoff expressed it at the time:

> A computer to me was a tool I used at work until I got myself into the situation I was working late in the evenings, starting early in the morning and when I actually sat down and thought about it there were things that I could do by finishing off at home. There were things I could start from home by dialling in on a modem and I do all these end of month reports which I can key in at this end and I can go in tomorrow morning . . . For instance tonight was the last night of the financial month and I could key all the information down the telephone and I can go in tomorrow morning and it will be sat there for me when I walk in, whereas otherwise I would have to go in an hour early before I started. So from that point of view it's saving me so many hours a month, probably about six hours a month, and if I have a report to present tomorrow morning and I'm there at 5:30 this evening at work, say, and I haven't quite finished it, rather than sort of sit around for another half hour or hour – well you are never at your best at the end of a busy day – I tend just to bring a floppy disk home, wack it in the computer and just tidy it up. Perhaps the next morning.

Although all the family members were generally happy with Geoff's use of the computer for this purpose, they were less than enamoured with what the modem in the home entailed for their own living space – the lounge to be precise. The computer had to be next to the telephone line in the lounge and this involved it being placed on a coffee table between two of the lounge chairs. Not only this, but it was a central focus of the room when one entered from the front door or came down the stairs. Again, as Geoff put it: 'At the moment, it's not popular there, it's going out of there actually . . . [into a planned conservatory]'.

When I last met the Williams during 1990 the conservatory was completed and the computer had moved into its new home. The modem, however, had not been moved, as a telephone connection point had not been placed there and this entailed a series of extension leads from the conservatory space into the lounge when the modem was in use; it was not a perfect solution in their eyes, but a better arrangement than having the computer and modem together. I recently (1996) re-visited the Williams to find out, among other things, how they had gotten on with the modem in the intervening period.

Death of the Old Modem and Birth of the New

When I returned to the Williams household I was surprised to discover that the modem of old was nowhere to be seen (the Williams had also moved in the intervening four to five years). In fact, the very mention of the old modem provoked laughter from Alan; his father replied defensively: 'In those days it was a fast modem.' Geoff explained that he used the modem for around 18 months and then for a variety of reasons it was no longer needed:

> The security of computer systems have been highlighted in the last 5–6 years ... I would dial from home into the system then, but this is not acceptable now. Some hacker ['cracker', Alan insists in the background] may come in and damage your database. The only safe system today is a dial-back modem with all sorts of security codes on it, but this is big money. Too much money at the moment.

Maria then adds: 'Half of the problem was the way the printer would jam at the other-end ... It was not possible to see what was happening at the other end.' Geoff agreed and added that the system he is using presently is much quicker and more user friendly:

> Time constraints that old one forced upon me during the working day are no longer there ... with the old computer ... if I ran huge reports during a working day it slowed down the speed at which rest of department worked. What was the alternative? ... the alternative was to run those reports outside of working time plugging [the] modem in at work, coming home and waiting until I knew all routine work was finished and then knocking the report out ... System is now 500–1000 times faster.

Alan also interjects with his specific perspective on the matter:

> Seems weird that within my lifetime [he is now 14] you have got modems that have changed from being this big [he motions with his arms spread apart] ... which is like your old black box which you still have lying around somewhere, to something which is like a very thick credit card but 40 times faster.

His parents both respond in kind with the notion of 'progress', Geoff stating that he could remember the wireless.

The demise of this modem in the home, however, did not signal the end of modems on the Williams' horizons. Maria indicated that her hospital is planning to issue modems for those on call in roughly six months' time: 'You would have a laptop at home when on call, doctor can phone up, you can tap into hospital system with [a] modem that does not plug into phone line, but with a card' ('a similar principle to that of a mobile phone', adds Alan) She indicates this modem is still not operational as there are a number of security issues that have to be rectified.

Again at this point Alan offers his perspective to the general direction of our discussion, re-iterating a theme often stressed by his parents in the past. In short, he does not like the idea of working from home: 'There should be a separation ... different mental states'. Geoff replies how this is not an option for those he often deals with through his own work, people who work from home and car. (As we shall see below, this is a possibility from which Geoff now does not preclude himself.)

In the more immediate future another modem is on the horizon. This is the plan to buy a modem for Alan for his upcoming birthday (later in August) and as Geoff puts it 'to go on the Internet'.

Before considering the Williams' conceptualization of entry onto the Internet via the modem, it is useful, I think, to briefly re-trace their more general relationship with computers in the home (while I say 'their', it is more accurate to highlight Geoff and Alan's use, as Maria and Heather showed little interest and/or felt excluded from this domain; although issues of gender exclusion are obviously of importance, due to the limited nature of this paper I do not pursue them here).[7]

A Brief History of Computer Use

Maria purchased the first computer for use in the home. This was a Dragon 32 in *c*.1985. At the time Geoff was taking an evening class on basic computer use and found there was a limited number of computers for the students to practise on. This meant he got very little practice at the keyboard. Maria bought the computer because Geoff continually moaned about this situation but did nothing to remedy it; Maria finally heard enough and went out and purchased what he only talked about getting.

The computer had a 'maze game' which Alan subsequently learned to play. Not long after this Alan also wanted, like others in his peer group, a Sega games console. At the time the family was living in Plymouth. A few years later Geoff took a better position in Slough and the family moved. It was during this time that the Dragon came to the end of its 'life' and Geoff bought the Amstrad 1512. As Alan recalled, the games on the Amstrad were worse than those on the Sega but you could write your own programmes on the former; at this time Alan learned 'Basic' at school and soon became involved in writing his own programmes.

The Williams had the Amstrad for two years and before they moved on to a new 'home', they decided to update the computer for Alan – an Olivetti 386. At the same time Heather was given a new television with teletext and remote control as she was very interested in television in the same way that Alan was keenly involved with the computer. Both were presented as Christmas presents.

As Alan recalls, he bought many computer games to play on the Olivetti for about a three-year period: for two years he bought all the latest versions and then for one year bought the 'budget games'. It was at the end of this period that he discovered 'Visual Basic'. This brief history of the computers in the Williams' home and Alan's involvement with them was glossed by Geoff as follows:

> He moved from games machine which was purely games . . . Sega . . . to the Amstrad where he learned a bit about 'Basic' and how programmes worked, but could still play games, to the Olivetti where games got faster, better and more colourful, to a programming language called 'Visual Basic' which was sophisticated, and last year we got the Pentium.

Maria adds: 'He just grew out of it [Olivetti] . . .'

And Geoff: 'He couldn't do any more with it . . .'

Maria: 'Bit slow for you [referring to Alan] . . .'

Alan: 'My habits changed . . . I developed a hobby – a strange, very sad hobby – I tried to refine it, organize the hard drive so files would be in order I liked them . . . [I wanted to] see how far I could refine the system.'

The move to the Pentium was prompted by these limits and the fact that Alan was receiving money from the BBC for an acting part he had secured on a children's programme. Using also an equal sum from his parents, he acquired a Viglen desktop, Pentium processor, speakers, etc: 'a full multi-task system', as Alan referred to it. Since this purchase virtually all of his free time is spent in the spare room which houses the computer – a routine his parents attempt to monitor and restrict at particular times (e.g. when he is revising for his GCSEs).

It is only recently that Geoff, together with Alan, has rekindled an interest in a modem in the home. The modem will be purchased for Alan's upcoming birthday (see above) and GCSE results. Geoff explains this in the following terms: 'These days keep them up with technology . . . they are going to come across it.'

There are, however, two dimensions to this 'keeping up' idea that Geoff subsequently discloses. The first is related to Alan's involvement in computer use. The second is Geoff's own concern about the security of his position within the 'new' NHS. As both Maria and he indicate during our discussion, jobs are no longer secure in the Health Service; Maria's boss was recently made redundant. For Geoff the interest in the modem is part of an insurance policy in case he loses his job and has to begin to sell his services as a consultant working from home.

Geoff's most immediate interest, however, is the potential he sees in the Internet: 'The Internet is not particularly practical now . . . problem is that it has potential to be very useful indeed but is at its beginning . . . good stuff in there but you have to find it'. By contrast, Maria's major concern is the extent to which her telephone is to be constantly taken up: 'I shall just have to ration you to it . . . '. For Alan the greatest interest lies in e-mail and in particular to a female friend from school who lives roughly 10 minutes away and who already has e-mail: 'The only other instantaneous communication is on the phone, but in a conversation you have to keep to the same topic [in an e-mail message] you can have one paragraph on this and one paragraph on this . . . and then respond and add something else'. 'Surfing the net' does not hold much interest. Rather, he envisions drawing on computer magazines that have regular features about what is good on the Internet 'and we have discovered it'. He predicts his use of the Internet to be similar to his current viewing of television where he consults the *Radio Times* in his sister's room 'when she is not looking' and makes a note of what he wants to watch.

In general, Geoff notes that he has been keeping an eye on the Internet: 'You have got to keep your fingers on the pulse and you have got to know when to jump.'

When to Jump?

I was interested in the way the Williams, and in particular Geoff and Alan, were conceptualizing their moment of truth: when they would make their first connection. It was clear in their minds that all the factors they had some control over had to be researched initially: which modem to buy, which 'provider' to use and what form of access to purchase, which sites to visit, and so on. Each one of these preparatory steps to becoming connected involved a number of elements. For example, Geoff and Alan are currently reading an up-to-date volume on different types of modem. Once they have selected several as suitable ('and cheapest') they will as Alan puts it: 'ask friends, ring the "providers", ring the computer manufacturer to inquire about their preferences and any issues about compatibility'. With regard to the 'provider' a number of factors emerge: should they proceed with a firm like CompuServe which is an international provider and will be more expensive but also more reliable, or with a smaller outfit that is cheaper but perhaps not as reliable? Geoff draws an analogy here with double glazing firms for Maria's sake as she is not clear about the role of the 'provider': 'On the one hand you have Anglia which is a large firm and has an outlet in every town. On the other hand you have "Jo Bloggs" special of five windows for £1000 . . .'. As far as the 'sites' to visit, both Geoff and Alan agree that they will use books and magazines to do the searching for them, although as Geoff observes: 'seems a bit daft . . . all computerised but still using a book to get to it'.

My intention in rehearsing this family's conceptualization of this anticipated connection to the Internet (and there are a number of other details I have left out at this stage for reasons of space) is that it makes visible a series of other related connections: to other domestic contexts (friends), to 'providers', suppliers, libraries and bookshops. And all of these connections are brought into focus at this point in time by a tiny technological object – 'a thicker version of a credit card' – which will enable the initial 'jump'.

Conclusion: Finding a Place for the Modem in the Home

In the half dozen years that I have known the Williams family they have had one modem and are about to purchase a second. There were a number of problems with the first; from their perspective it was the physical place of the modem *vis-à-vis* the computer and telephone line that made it seem so out of place. To help maintain the separation between home and work for which it was summoned the modem did its work, but made its presence visibly felt.

The second, anticipated modem will not, it seems, create the same problem concerning physical presence as did its ancestor. Rather, the problems it will make manifest seem to centre more on the multiplicity of connections that it will enable. This is envisioned as a tremendous potential (Geoff), a threat to the telephone line (Maria), to be weighed against a more intense interest in e-mail (Alan) and of marginal interest in comparison with television (Heather). I would suggest that the anticipated modem has to find its place more in the *relations that constitute the domestic context of the Williams home*, than in its physical location. This was certainly an issue with the previous modem, but the connections and possibilities for connections it entailed were more limited compared to the current version.

In the current period of 'choice and convergence', then, each member of the Williams family perceives the new technology as offering different possibilities, different 'choices'. A number of conflicting interests will have to become reconciled with the advent of the new modem and the multiple connections with the outside world it facilitates. In short, there is uncertainty in what the internal relations around the modem with look like in relation to the outside connections it will enable.

The tensions revealed by this example, although unique to the contemporary period, reoccur throughout the history of the relationship between 'new' technologies and the domestic context which has been surveyed by this chapter. There have been a number of significant transformations over the 200-year period covered which are not simply a consequence of 'new' technologies alone or of 'new' notions of domesticity alone, but of the mutually constitutive relations that each effects on the other. The history of these processes is increasingly being recovered by scholars: around the take-up of television (see Spigel, 1990), for radio (see Moores, 1988), for electricity and telephone (see Fischer, 1988; Marvin, 1988) and for the railroad (see Schivelbusch, 1986), to name just a few examples.

The current debates surrounding broadcast television and its place in the domestic context in relation to a range of new technologies are, as I have suggested, part of a long-standing history where what is new and what is old or established are always co-existent, always define each other. This is as true of the technologies as it is of domesticity and its forms of consumption, and the relations sustained between them.

Notes

1.   The emergence of the middle class, with its emphasis on family-based domesticity and the separation of male (workplace) and female (home) spheres, was one of several ideals (ideologies) promoted during the late eighteenth century. It was not self-evident that the family model of domesticity should become dominant. That it did was in part because of the forceful moral, religious and political arguments orchestrated on its behalf. Other forms of domesticity and of other forms of working arrangements were simultaneously promoted and there was a struggle as to which would be ascendant (see Hall, 1992; Strathern, 1992).

2.   Between 1924 and 1929 the ownership of radio licences in the UK increased from 10 per cent of households to 26 per cent. Over the next 10 years there was a steady increase so that by 1939, 71 per cent of all households possessed a radio (Pegg, 1983: 7, table 1.1).

3.   Simultaneity is more than just people watching at the same time; they must also make similar connections to the media. If simultaneity can only be completed by similarity then the suburban model of living is a perfect exemplar.

4.   In the UK between 1954 and 1968 combined radio and television licences increased from just over 3 million to roughly 15 million (Briggs, 1985: 303).

5.   The most significant technical innovation is arguably the integrated broadband system, based on fibre optic cables, which permits transmission of a large volume of digitized material.

6.   The focus of the research was on the domestic culture of the home in the context of information and communication technologies. The research was carried out in collaboration with Roger Silverstone as part of the ESRC Programme on Information and Communication Technologies. The families involved in the research were recruited through local schools. Fieldwork with each family occurred over a six to nine month period based on eight to nine visits. The research format included structured, but open-ended sets of questions and discussion themes as well as participant observation involving all family members in the home (see Hirsch, 1992 for more details).

7.   Haddon (1992: 90) has documented how the computer game market developed from the male-dominated arcades culture when pinball machines were replaced by video games. It is of note that when the discussion turned to the connections facilitated by the

Internet (e.g. television-related Web sites) Heather expressed an interest in computer use for this purpose.

Acknowledgements

For their helpful comments and criticisms, many of which have been directly incorporated into the text, I want to thank Bryan Cleal, Christine Geraghty, Jordan Goodman, Catherine Harvey and Ralph Schroeder. Errors in fact or form that remain rest solely with the author.

References

ANG, I., 1992: 'Living-room wars: new technologies, audience measurement and the tactics of television consumption'. In R. Silverstone and E. Hirsch (eds), *Consuming Technologies. Media and Information in Domestic Spaces*. London: Routledge.

ARONSON, S., 1977: 'Bell's electrical toy: What's the use? The sociology of early telephone usage'. In I. de Sola Pool (ed.), *The Social Impact of the Telephone*, Cambridge, MA.: MIT Press.

BALDWIN, T. *et al.*, 1996: *Convergence: Integrating Media, Information and Communication*. London: Sage.

BARKER, T. and GERHOLD D., 1993: *The Rise and Rise of Road Transport, 1700–1990*. London: Macmillan.

BARKER, T. and SAVAGE C., 1974: *An Economic History of Transport in Britain*, 3rd edn. London: Hutchinson.

BENIGER, J., 1986: *The Control Revolution: Technological and Economic Origins of the Information Society*. Cambridge, MA: Harvard University Press.

BRIGGS, A. 1985: *The BBC, The First Fifty Years*. Oxford: Oxford University Press.

———, 1990: *Victorian Things*. London: Penguin Books.

CAMPBELL, C., 1987: *The Romantic Ethic and the Spirit of Modern Consumerism*. Oxford. Blackwell.

CHANDLER, A., 1984: 'The emergence of managerial capitalism'. *Business History Review*, 58: 473–503.

DAVIDOFF, L. and HALL, C., 1987: *Family Fortunes: Men and Women of the English Middle Class 1780–1850*. London: Hutchinson.

DAVIS, I., 1994: 'A celebration of ambiguity. The synthesis of contrasting values', In P. Oliver, *et al.*, *Dunroamin: The Suburban Semi and its Enemies*. London: Pimlico.

DE SOLA POOL, I. (ed.), 1977: *The Social Impact of the Telephone*. Cambridge, MA: MIT Press.

DUMMER, G., 1983: *Electric Inventions and Discoveries. Electronics from its Earliest Beginnings to the Present Day*, 3rd revised and expanded edn. Oxford: Pergamon.

FISCHER, C., 1988: ' "Touch someone": the telephone industry discovers sociability'. *Technology and Culture*, 29, 1: 32–61.

FORTY, A., 1986: *Objects of Desire: Design and Society 1750–1980*. London: Thames and Hudson.

GALBRAITH, J. 1958: *The Affluent Society*. London: Hamish Hamilton.

HADDON, L., 1992: 'Explaining ICT consumption: the case of the home computer'. In R. Silverstone and E. Hirsch (eds), *Consuming Technologies: Media and Information in Domestic Spaces*. London: Routledge.

HALL, C. 1992: *White, Male and Middle Class: Explorations in Feminism and History*. Cambridge: Polity Press.

HALL, P. and PRESTON P., 1988: *The Carrier Wave: New Information Technology and the Geography of Innovation, 1846–2003*. London: Unwin Hyman.

HAWTHORN, G., 1987: *Enlightenment and Despair: A History of Social Theory*, 2nd edn. Cambridge: Cambridge University Press.

HEADRICK, D., 1988: *The Tentacles of Progress: Technology Transfer in the Age of Imperialism, 1850–1940*. Oxford: Oxford University Press.

HIRSCH, E., 1992: 'The long term and short term of domestic consumption: an ethnographic case study'. In R. Silverstone and E. Hirsch (eds), *Consuming Technologies: Media and Information in Domestic Spaces*. London: Routledge.

HOBSBAWM, E., 1994: *The Age of Extremes: The Short Twentieth Century, 1914–91*. London: Abacus.

HUGHES, T., 1983: *Networks of Power: Electrification in Western Society, 1880–1930*. Baltimore: Johns Hopkins University Press.

KERN, S., 1983: *The Culture of Time and Space 1880–1918*. Cambridge, MA: Harvard University Press.

MARVIN, C., 1988: *When Old Technologies were New: Thinking about Communications in the Late Nineteeth Century*. New York: Oxford University Press.

MCKENDRICK, N. *et al.* 1982: *The Birth of a Consumer Society: The Commercialization of Eighteenth-Century England*. London: Hutchinson.

MILES, I., 1988: *Home Informatics: Information Technology and the Transformation of Everyday Life*. London: Pinter.

MOORES, S., 1988: ' "The box on the dresser": memories of early radio and everyday life'. *Media, Culture and Society*, 10, 1: 23–40.

MURDOCK, G., 1994: 'Money talks: broadcasting, finance and public culture'. In S. Hood (ed.), *Behind the Screens: The Structure of British Television in the Nineties*. London: Lawrence and Wishart.

NORA, S. and MINC, A., 1980: *The Computerization of Society. A Report to the President of France*. Cambridge, MA: MIT Press.

OLIVER, P. *et al.*, 1994: *Dunroamin: The Suburban Semi and its Enemies*. London: Pimlico.

PEGG, M., 1983: *Broadcasting and Society, 1918–1939*. London: Croom Helm.

PFAFFENBERGER, B., 1988: 'The social meaning of the personal computer; or, why the personal computer revolution was no revolution'. *Anthropological Quarterly*, 61, 1: 39–47.

RHEINGOLD, H., 1994: *The Virtual Community: Homesteading on the Electronic Frontier*. New York: HarperCollins.

SCANNELL, P. and CARDIFF, D., 1991: *A Social History of Broadcasting, Vol.1 1922–1939: Serving the Nation*. London: Blackwell.

SCHIVELBUSCH, W., 1986: *The Railway Journey: The Industralization of Time and Space in the Nineteenth Century*, new edn. Leamington Spa: Berg.

SILVERSTONE, R., 1994: *Television and Everyday Life*. London: Routledge.

SPIGEL, L. 1990: 'Television in the family circle: the popular reception of a new medium'. In P. Mellencamp (ed.), *Logics of Television: Essays in Cultural Criticism*. Bloomington and London: Indiana University Press and British Film Institute.

STONE, L., 1990: *Road to Divorce: England 1530–1987*. Oxford: Oxford University Press.

STRATHERN, M., 1992: *After Nature: English Kinship in the Late Twentienth Century*. Cambridge: Cambridge University Press.

——, 1996. 'Enabling identity? Biology, choice and the new reproductive technologies'. In S. Hall and P. du Gay (eds), *Questions of Cultural Identity*. London: Sage.

WAHRMAN, D., 1995: *Imagining the Middle Class: The Political Representation of Class in Britain, c. 1780–1840*: Cambridge: Cambridge University Press.

WILLIAMS, R., 1965: *The Long Revolution*. Harmondsworth: Penguin Books.

——, 1990. *Culture and Society: Coleridge to Orwell*. London: Hogarth Press.

10

The Popular Culture Debate and Light Entertainment on Television

David Lusted

Introduction

Among elite groups (in the UK, at least), television in general falls into the category of low culture, perhaps even 'despised culture'. Of all the programme categories of television, light entertainment programmes in particular are thought of in this way and not only in the wider culture: within the television institution itself, it is tolerated as a cheap and reliable way of filling the schedules.

For 'despised culture' and light entertainment, read also 'popular culture'. This essay begins by investigating ways in which approaches to television have been historically located within those wider debates about popular culture. In particular, it examines the ways in which a reductive notion of populism has more recently emerged at the centre of critical debates. The essay concludes with an analysis of selected television light entertainment programmes in this context and argues a renewed case for attending to the meanings and values for its audiences of light entertainment in particular, and popular culture more generally.

Popular Culture

Popular culture has been critically regarded (not only in the UK) largely in one of two ways. One body of opinion with a long history constructs the products and practices of popular culture as certainly structurally and probably ideologically complicit with any part of a bundle of economic, political and philosophical categories of disapproval. These include capitalism, commerce, consumerism and conservatism (with a large or small 'c'). Popular culture for such groups can be morally offensive, culturally inferior, it can induce political and ideological passivity and – for the new modernists of postmodernism – its ubiquity can provide evidence of loss of elite status in an increasing process of cultural homogenisation (Baudrillard, 1981; Jameson, 1984). As can be seen from this characterisation, many across the political spectrum of elite cultures share in this hostility to the popular.

The second way in which popular culture has been critically considered is more recent and far less hostile to or suspicious of the popular. There can be a genuine concern here to investigate areas of popular culture with sympathy for the mass audiences who appear its willing consumers. Often, however, that sympathy is extended less towards the forms of popular culture themselves, where residues of suspicion can still be discerned.

Behind even the most celebratory accounts can be discerned a common framework of argument about the actual or potential ideological work of popular culture. Much work focuses on its 'pleasures', which may be seen as harmless or accommodating rather than destructive, but it can also carry more nihilistic associations (especially among certain postmodernists) of a complicity in wider processes of consumerism, of 'amusing ourselves to death'.

I include within this position a critic like John Fiske, even though he paramountly has explored how popular culture (which he distinguishes from mass culture) can offer women (Fiske, 1990) and other marginal social groups (Fiske, 1987) spaces to advance their own definitions of self within cultural forms which are otherwise discerned as plainly patriarchal and consumerist. For Fiske, popular cultural forms are contradictory in their ideological composition. Audiences for game shows, for instance, actively subvert meanings within the dominant ideologies of the popular or, where none are evident, draw upon experiences within their own social formations that enable them to read against the grain of textual meaning, making their oppositional readings – albeit symbolically – as active readers, 'in struggle' with otherwise oppressive texts. Fiske's language is that of 'guerrilla' audiences, 'raiding' game shows to produce their own oppositional readings (Fiske, 1990: 140–1).

I am much more sympathetic to the political and cultural motives of Fiske's framework, and his work is crucial to undermining easy assumptions about the ideological complicity of popular culture. But I want to resist the hunt for progressive or subversive texts, readings or readers as an alternative to a negative view of the popular. Rather more, I am concerned to find out what may be in popular texts themselves that audiences are reading – '*with* the grain' as it were – and from their own sense of active choice.

Populism

The term 'populism' has entered the critical vocabulary in recent years but in quite specific and rather diminishing ways. Some critics (for instance, Williamson, 1986; McGuigan, 1992 in the UK; Modleski, 1986 in the USA, Morris, 1988 in Australia) have labelled the second body of criticism – of which the work of John Fiske is considered a prime example – 'populist' in a number of senses. First, there is the common sense of populism as a political tactic of only an imagined alliance, an ideological construction calling up a mass audience to an identity with ruling-class interests. Historically, this idea of populism has been associated with forms of political demagogy and in recent years embodied in conservative political exponents like Ronald Reagan and Margaret Thatcher.

Second, but exemplified in the practices of the first, there is the sense of a characteristic rhetoric that invokes generalised and conventional cultural mores as 'natural', in a mode of address directly appealing over the heads of representatives to deny sectional interests, specialist knowledge and reasoned argument in favour of amorphous, generalised entities such as 'the nation' and 'the people'. As a rhetorical form, then, populism can cut across otherwise competing political discourses to become a particular mode of popular address.

Third, in cultural studies, but connecting to this political usage, there is the sense of a critical complicity with dominant agencies which manipulate through their control over mass communications. The complicity may be seen as an effect rather than an intent, a naïve response to pressures of the times rather than a reasoned critical position. But it can also imply a thoughtless and wilful act among critics presumed to be natural allies of serious scholarship, of 'giving in' and even 'selling out' political thought and action to the pleasures of the popular. This notion of critical populism, then, is bound up in associations with a common sense of the politics of populism.

What is most interesting here is that, however complex, this set of meanings is ultimately a very narrow, elite (and perhaps very British) notion of populism. Populism has another, more extensive and substantive political and cultural history which troubles those attitudes to the popular reviewed so far.

A little history of populism may be in order. As a political movement in the USA during the late nineteenth century, the key feature of populism was its constituency of disparate groups who came into alliance in the context of collective marginalisation from the political process. What began as an agrarian movement for land reform connected with a proletarian movement for representation and welfare on a platform wide and popular enough to draw sectional groups into common alignment. These groups included traditional labour unions, racial integrationists among the melting pot of new European and Asian immigrants on the East Coast, organised groups of 'emancipated' black indentured labour on the fringes of the South and even a limited incorporation of women's suffrage movements. Populism was formed in political, social and racial combination at a time of massive social transformations connected with European and other migration to America. Its opponents were the political establishment and political organisations (Saloutos, 1968).

But what most interests me about populist politics is its culture (Webster, 1988). This was a chaotic democracy in practice, with decision-making a process characterised by open debate, conflict-ridden exchange, a refusal of hierarchies and an insistence on resolution through collective responsibility. It took literally the plea for 'Life, Liberty and the Pursuit of Happiness' invoked by the Declaration of Independence, although it considered pleasure more a right than a pursuit. Importantly, pleasure was also considered a mechanism in the process of political exchange and reform. Its cultural politics cannot easily be divided from its political practices because they are embedded in the politics of populism.

The more obviously cultural dimensions of populism were as widespread as its political composition, combining folk rituals with country music, mid-West crackerbarrel philosophy with ribald humour of the urban music hall, and satirical song of, especially, urban black 'ragging' music with the sentiment of theatrical melodrama. Political meetings in the frontier films of John Ford (like

The Man Who Shot Liberty Valance), in the small-town films of Frank Capra (like *Mr Deeds Goes to Town*) and in the frantic comedies of Preston Sturges (like *Hail The Conquering Hero*) may most closely evoke the culture of this populism in action.

As a consequence of its social and democratic culture, political populism was founded in an incorporative language, with a transparent vocabulary of inclusion and exclusion. 'In' was good neighbourliness and collective interests. 'Out' were power blocs, elites and other groups claiming special status. A particular animosity was reserved for intellectuals and 'snobs', not so much elites but elitists. Such categories of exclusion pose particular problems for political advance so it is no surprise that populism died as a political movement before the twentieth century, to be integrated in part and in complex ways into configurations of belief and culture spread across the now established political divide of Republican and Democratic Parties. My contention, however, would be that *as a culture* it entered into the mainstream of the American popular at a particularly important moment in its history; at the moment of the rise of the modern entertainment industries and mass communication systems. Populism became inscribed into much of its recorded music, its popular press, cinema and later its broadcasting, all of which media – in their global penetration over the century – have presented a particularly powerful alternative to and within other national cultures and, in Britain, especially to the literary and theatrical cultures which remain dominant among elites there.

Cultural Populism

Hence, much of the antipathy to popular culture in Britain – argued by Dick Hebdige (1987) as elite fears of its 'Americanisation' – is fundamentally an antipathy to its populism. It is amply demonstrated by the long history in Britain of moral panics about: American cinema in the 1920s; American comics in the 1940s; Independent Television – which streamlined light entertainment on the models of American television – in the 1950s; pirate radio and the transatlantic voices of disc jockeys in the 1960s; the demonising of exploitation films as video nasties in the 1970s; and the urban black influence in American popular music from 1920s' jazz to contemporary House.

But the hostility of British elite cultures to the popular is not merely or even *per se* a hostility to its Americanisation. As much as to the act of an invasive cultural colonisation, there is the sense of its foreignness, its alien *feeling*. It is indeed at the level of sensibility – to its affect as central to its feared effects – that the intensity of elite and intellectual objection is best understood. Yet non-elite groups in Britain, especially urban working-class communities, have taken to American and American-derived popular culture as their own, even though they may have little sense of its historical integration into traditional British popular forms and play little part at all in its production.

Why there should be this disparity in reception is bound up in histories of official resistance and common pleasures over popular cultures among elite cultures and their education system. But, more important for the argument here, my contention would be that it is the populism of so much popular culture such as light entertainment that accounts both for antipathies among elite groups *and* its connection to British working-class cultures. As a cultural mode, cultural populism has to be seen to embody the experience and aspirations of socially marginalised groups in its language of collectivity and boundary, and to do so – crucially – at the affective level, at the level not of cognition, of knowledge, but of feeling, including feeling against the exclusions of elite classes.

Television Light Entertainment

I turn now in this context to the case of television light entertainment. In broadcast television in the UK, 'light entertainment' is both a form of programme and the name given to departments producing it. The programme form includes variety programmes, game shows, talent competitions, chat shows and – increasingly among other prime-time programming – 'do it yourself' shows which centre on public rather than professional entertainment.

Light entertainment is a universal television form; examples can be found in any nation's broadcast system. The same programme format can even be found in different national examples: *Dating Game* in the USA becomes the UK's *Blind Date*, for instance, and there are at least three national versions of *The Price Is Right*. Old light entertainment programmes even feature as the raw material of compilation programmes fronted by personalities like Clive James and Chris Tarrant, where Japanese game shows and European variety programmes are regularly singled out for chauvinist fun.

As a cultural form, light entertainment is at least as old as television itself, but it has antecedents in British cultural forms like radio, music hall and parlour games. Its forms are highly conventionalised, drawing on music hall for a structure of variety turns segued by a chairman/host and on parlour games like musical chairs for rule-governed elements such as knock-out competitions for prizes. As in music hall, too, there is an interactive relationship between light entertainment professionals and audiences on- and off-screen. Formats also tend to recur historically, from particular popular games to whole programmes. For instance, the recent *Bob's Full House* is a game show that builds to a climax featuring a crossbow aimed at a target in a game familiar to viewers of the 1950s' *Name That Tune*. Likewise, the contemporary *Beadle's About* modernises *Candid Camera* of the 1950s, in which television professionals conspire with members of the public to play tricks on their friends.

Innovation is also important, though, and light entertainment tends to be quick to deploy new technologies in unexpected ways, providing a twist to the likes of *You've Been Framed*, for instance, where viewers send in and sometimes accompany home videos of accidents and funny moments caught by the camera.

In the UK, every studio-based television company (like the oldest, the BBC) has a department producing light entertainment and every non-studio based company (like the most recent, Channel 4) commissions programmes from independent organisations under this same generic title. Next to continuing serial drama – mainly soap operas like *Coronation Street* and *EastEnders* – light entertainment is the most popular form with television audiences. Weekly game shows like *Strike It Lucky* and *You Bet* regularly achieve top 10 positions in the ratings just behind the most popular continuing soap opera series, with viewing figures of between 10 and 15 million from a potential audience of 45 million.

Light entertainment, then, is a common, varied and popular television form of a wider popular culture, with culturally central antecedents and a site of formal convention and innovation.

Light Entertainment and Criticism

In recent television criticism, much attention has been given to popular television forms such as soap opera and – though, to a lesser extent – comedy, especially situation comedy. These are the major popular television forms in the UK. Much of the attention to soap opera has been inspired by feminist interest in rescuing soaps from cultural disparagement and in investigating its appeal to women (Hobson, 1982; Ang, 1985; Buckingham, 1987; Geraghty, 1990). Comedy has been seen more generally to challenge television's everyday assumptions about its cultural role and its ideal family audience (Cook, 1982; Neale and Krutnick, 1990).

Though comedy is a feature of light entertainment, this larger category has fared critically less well, to some extent in the amount of attention it has received but certainly in the respect it has been granted. Apart from the prolific Richard Dyer and John Fiske – whose work is central to any understanding of popular film and television – and some notable exceptions elsewhere, attention to light entertainment commonly amounts to critical sniping at game shows and quiz shows for allegedly championing consumerism and reductive knowledge (Lewis, 1984; Mills and Rice, 1982), though Garry Whannel (1992) has focused more on processes of game-playing than prize-winning in order to understand the pleasure derived by game show contestants and audiences.

Soaps have been considered a paramountly female genre; and sitcoms have been seen as a comic variant of drama whose audience is primarily, though not exclusively, adult. Light entertainment, however, is habitually watched by both genders and all age groups in television's ideal audience of the family (Ellis, 1982; Paterson, 1980). Most interesting for my purposes, though, is a sense that light entertainment is the programme genre favoured by the broad mass of ordinary viewers who compose regular audiences for television, and one that more than any other brings the urban working-class family together around the TV set rather than sectioning it off in age and gender competition.

By family, here, I do not mean to limit the mental image to the common ideal of two parents with 2.4 children (which anyway only relates to just 12 per cent of households in Britain). Rather, I mean to refer to whatever domestic arrangements a group of people organise within a household – whether that is a single parent family or several adults and children living together.

Unlike most programme forms, then, it is to this extensive sense of the television family that light entertainment seems to appeal, crossing boundaries of age and gender, and to some sense of a common and shared experience of social class position, rather than a fragmented one.

What is it about light entertainment, then, that makes it popular? What makes it connect to such large numbers of otherwise disparate groups of 'ordinary people' (especially to what I would still want to call 'the working class', despite the evident modern fragmentation and dilution of a collective identity more apparent during earlier periods in which, as a class, it was more politically active). What makes them regularly volunteer their free time to it? Part of that concern is to understand how light entertainment can cross generations, especially what its popularity as family viewing means in the production of social identities for old and young alike.

I should admit that this interest is not entirely dispassionate; my first cultural choices tend to emerge from among the popular and I share in those choices socially and most often among a working-class extended family in a very working-class community in London. There is a pressure to understand, arising from experience of a gap between the cultures of groups like these and those organising the elite attitudes explored above which have shaped my own education. If I live in the former and work among the latter, it is largely in the fudged boundaries of the two cultures that I think.

Utopianism and Populism

At this point, Richard Dyer's work becomes inescapable. Dyer's importance lies in the central notion that the pleasures of popular forms lie in their affective rather than their cognitive mechanisms. He has argued that the major characteristic of popular culture is its utopian sensibility (1977 and 1992) through which feelings emerge not just at the representational level (in what people say or do) but also at the non-representational level (in more abstract qualities of movement, colour, music, shape, line, etc.). For Dyer, the meaning of the utopian sensibility lies in its feelings of abundance, energy, transparency, intensity and community.

The utopian sensibility undoubtedly suffuses light entertainment. One example in some depth must suffice to demonstrate its nature and ubiquity. It is evident even in marginal moments such as in transitions from one variety act to the next in variety shows. For instance, in a moment from a British variety programme, *The Joe Longthorne Show*, the eponymous star host joins his guest, Canadian comic Kelly Monteith, at the end of his stand-up comedy routine. Joe, impressionist and singer, thanks Kelly as the audience applause dies down. We watch them talk, they part and Joe is left to sing.

This action, their dialogue and the camera's view of it produce evident qualities of a utopian sensibility. The feelings overlap, but – just to isolate some of them – there is the feeling of abundance in the rich lighting patterns and spectacular design of the set which we see through the eye of a travelling, swooping camera; there is Joe's energy in his song routine; the transparency (honesty) of feeling between Kelly and Joe in their mutual congratulations (and even if the sincerity of the exchange is in doubt – 'This man's marvellous . . . It's been a real pleasure . . . I've heard so much about it . . . ' – it is a *convention* of sincerity); the intensity of emotion in the song, and even in a prolonged handshake; and, finally, the sense of community which we are invited to share with the showbiz professionals ('Yes, I've worked with Tom [Jones] . . . not with Shirley [Bassey], though I've always wanted to . . . ') and the off-screen, applauding audience.

It is clear, as Dyer argues, that the utopian sensibility works to provide a world to escape into, a world affectively different from the the anterior conditions of low-paid wages, long working hours, low status, intensive labour or forced unemployment and uncertain economic futures for most in its audience. But it is not enough to characterise the world that is escaped from entirely in terms of a drab and deficient world of work or unemployment. There are also positive material and affective conditions which characterise the social world of its audience from which they would not wish to escape – for instance, the support structures of family and community; the centrality of home as social and not just domestic space; the emphasis placed on the social relationships that emerge around collective child-rearing; the humour that arises within and despite acknowledged conditions of sacrifice, displacement and resistance; the social role of phatic talk and touch; feelings of location and belonging. This is not a world to escape from into anything more ideal but emphatically a world to be confirmed through its cultural familiarity and its rooted identifications.

In addition to escape from the affective relation to an exterior world, then, light entertainment like the variety show also reproduces in its sensibility a cognitive interior world of social identity, more inclusive than just class identity, providing pleasure through confirming the personal in the collective. Something of Raymond Williams's (1961) notion of 'structure of feeling' is here in the experiential relation between popular cultural forms and the social formations of their majority audiences. Even more, however, the utopian sensibility can be seen not just as a way of understanding the aesthetic pleasures of the popular, but also as a key mechanism within my earlier account of cultural populism, connecting in complex interactions of affectivity and cognition the world of the show to the personal and social world of the working-class family bonded and bounded in community experience.

Populist Heroism

More than a cultural confirmation of working-class social identity, populism is also about drawing boundaries, between us and them of quite other social classes, those who have social power over us, to determine our income or objective conditions. 'They' inhabit a different physical space from us and seem to exist in a different time. Populism was forged on literal frontiers, at the moment of American westward expansion, but the frontier also acts as a metaphor for the lived experience of boundaries between social classes and cultures. 'They' are people with more power, social status and wealth. Having more money is not a problem within populism as long as it is earned, worked for and not inherited or acquired through capital gain. Disparities in wealth can even be accommodated, for the reflexive display of wealth, like celebrity, can provide its own pleasures. But if the wealthier 'they' live out their wealth through a divisive wielding of its power or by their evident discriminatory attitude against 'us', then they find themselves beyond the frontier; 'they' become the felt enemy.

Populism, then, does not eschew but acknowledges and negotiates contest and conflict. Popular figures become populist when, like Joe Longthorne, and despite their showbiz success and wealth, their difference from us is not as marked as their similarity. They are seen to work for their money, like us, not just through the labour of their talent and performances but also through the energy they put into incorporating 'us' with 'them' into a populist continuum and the space of a populist culture.

None the less, the populist hero treads a difficult line and has a dangerous game to play. Populism needs representatives but it is ideologically uncomfortable with leadership. The populist hero must therefore emerge through popular consent rather than nomination (and self-nomination means automatic disqualification). To be (a) representative, s/he must typify and embody the community, be discovered rather than found waiting, be dragged – humbly – kicking and screaming against their will into a limelight which they will then bask in, as if in their natural place. Joe Longthorne is such a populist hero, picked out from the talent competition (that is why talent shows are so popular a form) by popular audience consent (through mechanisms of audience vote) and provided with his own show as if by the will of the people.

As important, however, is that Joe then continues to perform within the populist framework. Once a 'star', Joe lives out his stardom by returning to his audiences again and again to reconfirm that his populist relationship to them is by consent. Joe is special (talented) but common (modest about his talent), performing for the pleasure of self but also for others. We may admire the professional skills of Joe but he is, crucially, just an ordinary Joe.

And these are qualities which are felt in the experience of the show, rather than being the subject of it, which is quite something else. It is this sensibility that the notion of cultural populism locates and which is what for me is the paradigm of light entertainment; what it is 'about'.

I have argued, then, that light entertainment is not just about escape from unpleasant social conditions of deprivation and dispossession, nor just a fantasy that audiences escape into. Its culture is one neither of triviality nor threat, but one that provides pleasures through affective re-location of the private and interior social world of its audiences, in a process confirming social location and identity.

What I would also like to claim now is that, within terms of fantasy, light entertainment speaks to the socially marginalised about the condition of marginality; about strategies and identities of survival within it and forms of resistance to it. In short, it is a culture concerned with the objective conditions, the subjective experiences and social imaginary of working-class social identities.

The Cross-Over Figure

In order to advance this argument, I want now to look at two examples of light entertainment which develop ideas about confirmation and resistance in the populist connection to working-class audiences.

Populism resonates with potential contradictions. Two, I have already mentioned: the matter of inclusion and exclusion, and the problem of leadership in a collective culture. Another arises from it and can be explored in the form of a question: what happens to the populist hero when s/he leaves the populist community to represent a wider collective will? In other words, what happens when you become *different?* Populism can only tolerate difference within unity and community. Step outside community and difference threatens to be deviant. The trick – as with Joe Longthorne – is to be seen to be one of 'them' without losing the sense of being one of 'us'. (The difficulty of sustaining a populist role over time may be the fundamental reason why the popularity of individual entertainers seems subject to fashion, why stardom is often short-lived; audience approval wanes as the one-time star entertainer is perceived to join elite groupings.)

When Joe Longthorne shakes Kelly Monteith's hand as he looks at us, his populism straddles that gap between us and the television institution. But what if someone in the audience were to take the stage at that moment? Would that act be seen as disruptive and transgressive or would that more ordinary some-one represent 'us' more directly in a challenge to Joe's populism? Is populism a relative question of what and how individuals and relationships represent?

This issue of the populist subject is central to game shows and talent shows, where 'members of the public' regularly have the chance to perform. Garry Whannel has also observed how more recent game shows have introduced pop-ulist knowledge into game show formats; where polls are taken and contestants have to guess the most popular – rather than the correct – answers. For the most part, those performances occur within well-defined boundaries, populism seal-ing the joins between the game show team and the public contestants. But often the boundaries are crossed and populist pleasure arises from populist risk. At moments like this, populism presents choices as well as confirmations.

Such moments regularly occur in game shows. An example arises from part of a programme called *The Price Is Right* in which one of the contestants takes on the game show host and the tensions show. Host Leslie Crowther is faced with the chaotic force of a contestant called Maggie whose uncontrolled giggle dis-turbs the normal smooth procedure of the game. Maggie has noisy friends in the audience and appeals to them often for advice and help in the game; she con-stantly talks to Crowther in asides and even addresses the camera unprompted.

First, there is no doubt that Maggie is a populist hero. Of all the contestants, she is the audience's favourite, an archetypal woman of the people. The auto-matic populism of the host is thereby undermined, and in his reaction to Maggie, Leslie Crowther can be seen to acknowledge it. He retains notional control but she seems to be usurping it. His role has been called into question and the conventional populist hero is discomforted by it.

It is true that it is Maggie the person and Maggie's laugh that most disconcert Crowther. She does not so much subvert as personalise the game show, as she takes the microphone and camera in her own time to speak to her 'little boy' at home, puts down what she misinterprets as a sexual proposition ('You've got no chance'), demands a gift she hasn't won (a 'little tea pot') and generally irritates the hell out of Crowther ('Heaven help us ... I could listen to that [laugh] all ... well, the next five minutes'; 'We want you to go home, but not yet'; 'Lovely!' – spoken through gritted teeth and a smile). Maggie is not breaking any rules of the game – she plays it as it should be played – but she is also entirely her own woman, even despite her apologies which seem to function in favour of her modesty rather than to suggest her inadequacy.

Yet, and second, even more than Maggie the person, what makes and keeps her a populist hero is her relation with the often on-screen audience and, through them and the camera, with the audience at home, playing the game with recourse to their advice, sharing with them the pleasure of her exception as performer on stage and taking decisions with their consent. Maggie embodies the spirit of populism and – against the odds of the television institution – is sanctified for it.

Thirdly, Maggie's populism is located in the many ways in which she embodies roles within and thus 'speaks to' the working-class family. She speaks as mother (to her 'little boy': 'Hello, Adam, it's mummy'), her least likely role, as she hardly lives out the stereotypes of the maternal figure or the working-class matriarch. She also speaks as heterosexual partner, sexualised and controlling ('You've got no chance'); as sister, intimate and confiding ('I'm sorry about this . . . '); as daughter and child, irresponsible and self-gratifying ('Can I have that little teapot?'). In other words, one explanation for the family popularity of light entertainment is demonstrated in the way that, like Maggie, it speaks to shifting identities of generations and roles through many familial figures in the multivarious social relations of a populist culture.

A final explanation for Maggie's populism lies in the language and mechanisms of populist inclusion and exclusion employed to establish shifting boundaries of social definition. Maggie addresses the audience as partner and the game show host as outsider, adjusting the relation between them by the semiotic languages of the manner of her speech and body posture.

The Light Entertainment Family

My concluding example is an extract from *Surprise, Surprise*, a show which conspires with families to surprise some of their members. It is of particular interest because it is hosted by Cilla Black, one of the few women hosts in game shows in the UK, where most women, where not contestants, are hostesses, largely silent but decorous assistants to the male hosts. Cilla Black had an earlier career as a pop singer, then a standard singer (a little like Shirley Bassey) and is now one of the most popular and powerful personalities in light entertainment. A case could be made for locating Cilla's populism in the same field of multi-social functions I attributed to Maggie, but my concern now is more with the show itself.

Each week, the routine is that the show culminates in Cilla springing a final surprise in a grand family reunion. The example here, I think, is representative of the programme more generally, yet it is also distinctive and gets to the heart of some commonly felt resistances to – as well as some of the supreme pleasures of – light entertainment and popular culture. Cilla claims a technical hitch will be filled by her talking with the audience. An off-screen voice informs the home audience that this is a ruse to spring a surprise on a member of the audience. Cilla asks who has a birthday and sings 'Happy Birthday' with her choice, Adam. The ruse is exposed and Adam, wife and two daughters find themselves seated on a sofa on the studio stage. Adam's story is revealed through exchange; an evacuee from the volcanic eruption on Tristan da Cunha in the 1950s, he has settled in a new life with his nuclear family in England. The surprise is that the mother and sister he has not seen for 20 years have been flown in for the show.

He breaks down and, in a moment of unease, possibly embarrassment and even humiliation, the spectacle of passion affects everyone around him. While the tearful reunion takes place to one side, Cilla moves to another stage to sing the regular closing theme tune.

One customary way to talk about such a very emotional experience is to distance ourselves from the intensity of the feelings – of those on-screen and off it. The idea of exploitation is often central here. Many times when I have shown this moment, there has been hostility to the show, to the television institution and sometimes to me for producing what is seen as an exploitative experience for both Adam and his spectators, a manipulation of emotion, a moment more appropriate to private rather than public display. It is equated, I suspect, with intrusive and voyeuristic moments in news journalism when the victim of a tragedy is thrust into the spotlight and asked to speak into a microphone about how they feel. Clearly, there are connections here but I would want to argue some important differences in terms of populism.

When Adam breaks down, it is within conditions agreed with – indeed, originated by – the rest of the family, a risk taken by them in a kind of exchange with and for the temporary power of the television institution. It is an ambivalent power 'to be shown'. Our reaction may be to resent the power of the institution, but that need not be confused with a judgement about the public display of Adam's emotion. This also gets to the heart of a problem not just of thinking but also of studying light entertainment; the sense that it is not an appropriate classroom (public) study because of the way it deals with emotion.

There is an interesting relation here to the prevalence of emotional expression in forms of women's cultures, fictions like romance and modes like melodrama, which are also commonly despised cultural forms among elites. In women's cultures, the expression of emotion is seen as a legitimate part of female experience and a proper method of dealing with pain and anger; Christine Gledhill's phrase 'tears and fears' (1987) describes the idea.

Feminist criticism and some psychoanalytic criticism have extended it to analyse both a patriarchal power and a male pathology which validates the cultural suppression of emotion and desire in favour of stoicism and repression as more socially appropriate behaviour (see, for instance, Radway (1984) on romance). I just point to the role of that suppression also in maintaining wider elite cultural controls over the subordination through legislation, censorship and moral disaproval of working-class cultural choices.

The idea that light entertainment may also relate to female culture is attractive, but I want more to invoke class culture here, not least because it is much less critically mapped in television studies. In working-class cultures, too, the expression of emotion is common; a response, perhaps, to the greater emphasis elite groups place on explanatory talk and on language in general (it is no coincidence that elites in the UK refer to themselves benignly as 'the chattering classes'). More than emotion itself, though, it is the *display* of emotion which characterises working-class social interaction. Working-class cultures celebrate sentiment and the display of sentiment (sentimentality?). It is part of popular memory, the cultural equivalent of the museums, libraries, record offices and other monuments to middle-class history. For working-class communities, without resources and organisation to build monuments to their own class histories, oral history becomes crucial in a popular memory which must bear witness through stories of communal traditions and practices. And, within that popular memory, sentiment is the affective agency which works to bind listeners into a common community and class memory. Talk *is* important in working-class cultures, it is just that its substance and objectives are different. Elite cultures value the written word and oration. Working-class cultures favour instead the spoken word and narration. For these features to operate effectively, they require conditions of performance and display – like actors, they require drama – conditions which are echoed in light entertainment.

Surprise, Surprise handles the working-class cultural components of sentiment and display through populism. Cilla calls up Adam's personal narrative but her brief attempt to frame it within a nationalist discourse about the wondrous cultural traditions of Britain ('You decided to stay because you loved Britain so much') is undermined as he insists on his own meanings of distance, separation and loss; 'a little island in the middle of the South Atlantic I went back on the expedition to see was it safe'.

This moment demonstrates instability in the politics of populism. Neither necessarily progressive nor regressive (Ryan and Kellner, 1990; Dolbeare, 1976), populist discourses are as readily available as any other to bind us into the nationalist identities more readily identified in anti-populist assumptions as into the class identities argued here.

It is not false or manipulated emotion that prompts our tears and sympathy. Rather, it is Adam's biography, a particular biography, this personal story, which is what has also prompted the television institution to bring Adam face to face with the family to confront circumstances which have forced them apart.

And maternal Cilla, like the programme itself, well understands (and, unlike Crowther in *The Price Is Right*, can adapt to) the risks in the project. Populist inclusion can easily turn into exclusion: Adam's position could easily turn into embarrassment or humiliation. But I would claim that it doesn't or, at least, that it hasn't with the working-class audiences with whom I have watched it, and also, in mitigation, that the show does its best to control the possibility. That is evident in its use of formal mechanisms which effectively respect personal aspects of the reunion even as they offer us access to it. The camera is not voyeuristic, but hesitantly observant. Cilla's move to a separate stage to sing the programme's theme song, with occasional nods in the direction of the reunion, acknowledges the propriety of distance, taking us out of the programme with promises of more populist surprises next week and the continuity of pleasures from light entertainment.

Furthermore, I would want to claim that for the audience who in any number of ways identifies with the figure of Adam, there is the shock of recognition and new learning here. Adam's story binds him, his family, the on-screen and off-screen audience into a moment of class affiliation through the sentiments and other mechanisms of cultural populism. This is by no means an easy experience or an easy strategy. It is a contested moment and I would not want to dispute with anyone who still understands it, or light entertainment more generally, as manipulative and exploitative. But I would want to contend that there are determinant affective and class-cultural reasons to explain why the audiences who choose to watch light entertainment might find this moment incorporative and not manipulative or exploitative.

Adam is an ordinary working-class man, presumably without the resources to visit his island relatives or to bring his two families together. The lack of material resources for even basic desires to be fulfilled is a class condition that many in the audience recognise. The economics of the case are not unrelated to the celebration of family. The centrality of the family as a primary support structure for working-class communities should not be confused with elite theories of the bourgeois family as a repressive psychic and social force. In working-class cultures, the family is a central economic as well as psychic and social safety net for the kinds of objective political denials such as those experienced historically and currently in Britain, where over the past 18 years government policies have seriously undermined the social safety nets that were once provided by the state, shifting massive resources instead from the poor to the wealthy through discriminatory legislation.

In this political and social context, Adam's story becomes an aspect of the audience's story, an aspect of a class-specific popular memory, reinterpreted through cultural populism. Light entertainment routinely offers these class-specific pleasures. As I have tried to indicate, it also offers contest, food for thinking about those pleasures. It is as important a site for debate about class-specific issues within the classed audiences who watch it regularly and from choice as, say, news and current affairs programmes are for middle-class audiences. And, even despite its mechanisms of class incorporation, it can provoke revaluations of strongly held judgements within it. For regular consumer groups of popular culture, populism is an active cultural process and a site of struggle over meaning and pleasure. To illustrate, let me draw to a close with a story, my own family melodrama.

When I watched this programme with my rather aged parents, the social talk – as always, testy, bordering on insult, but with lots of laughter – all but obscured attention to the programme, except for this ending. My white father, like many in working-class communities in Britain and elsewhere, has an ambivalent relation to the presence of black people around him. In person, they can be the source of friendship but, in the abstract, they often provoke racist fears about their imagined alien ubiquity, especially on television. My mother, far less prone to this kind of talk and, anyway, after so many years together temperamentally antagonistic to everything he says, became increasingly engaged by Adam's story. She silenced us into watching more attentively with her. It was only when Cilla inferred Adam's ethnic origin that my father realised it too, whereupon he rather foolishly complained about yet 'another black face on telly'. My objection silenced him, but the atmosphere grew even darker as we were all moved by Adam's story. As Cilla broke into song, my mother leaned over to my father, who was crying. She shook his arm firmly but compassionately, consoling him with something like; 'There, there, you silly bugger, and black men cry too.'

I do not want to claim too much for this story, but only as much as the meaning and place of television in our lives deserve. The briefest and most ephemeral of experiences in front of a television set provided opportunity for Brecht's 'cheerful, militant learning'. This event redrew boundaries of difference into alliance, and changed consciousness of self and relation to others. It confirmed an idea of family but also redefined relations to others in another idea of family that is more socially expansive and inclusive. It made clear a relation between light entertainment on television and the political meaning and power of populism.

Conclusion

I would hope this essay might invite reflection upon what the forms and processes of populism can mean for those audiences whose personal and class identities may well be bound up in quite intricate and intimate ways with light entertainment and the watching of television, especially if – unlike my parents – we do not quite share those identities. And, if nothing else here, I hope I am raising questions not just about light entertainment or even television, but ultimately about critical responsibilities in approaches to the social groups of ordinary people who compose regular audiences for popular television.

References and Further Reading

ANG, I., 1985: *Watching Dallas*. London: Methuen.

BAUDRILLARD, J., 1981: *For a Critique of the Political Economy of the Sign*. London: St. Louis.

BUCKINGHAM, D., 1987: *Public Secrets: EastEnders and its Audience*. London: British Film Institute.

COOK, J. (ed.) 1982: *Television Sitcom*. London: BFI Dossier 17.

DOLBEARE, K. M. and P., 1976: *American Ideologies: The Competing Political Beliefs of the 1970s*. Chicago: Rand McNally.

DYER, R., 1973: *Light Entertainment*. London: BFI Television Monograph.

——, 1977: 'Entertainment and utopia'. *Movie*, 24, Spring, and reprinted in *Only Entertainment*. London: Routledge, 1992.

——, 1992: *Only Entertainment*. London: Routledge.

ELLIS, J., 1982: *Visible Fictions*. London: RKP.

FISKE, J., 1983: 'Discourses of TV quiz shows, or school and luck = success and sex'. *Central States Speech Journal*, 34: 139–50.

——, 1987: *Television Culture*. London: Methuen.

——, 1989: *Reading the Popular*. London: Routledge.

——, 1990: 'Women and quiz shows: consumerism, patriarchy and resisting pleasures'. In Mary Ellen Brown (ed.), *Television and Women's Culture: The Politics of the Popular*. London: Sage.

GAINES, J. and HERZOG, C., 1990: *Fabrication: Costume and the Female Body*. London: AFI/Routledge.

GERAGHTY, C., 1990: *Women and Soap*. London: Polity Press.

GLEDHILL, C., 1987: *Home is Where the Heart Is: Studies in Melodrama and the Women's Film*. London: British Film Institute.

HEBDIGE, D., 1987: 'Towards a cartography of taste 1935–1962'. In *Hiding in the Light*. London: Comedia.

HOBSON, D., 1982: *Crossroads*. London: Methuen.

JAMESON, F., 1984: 'Postmodernism or the cultural logic of late capitalism'. *New Left Review*, 146: 53–92.

LEWIS, B., 1984: 'TV games: people as performers'. In Len Masterman (ed.), *TV Mythologies: Stars, Shows and Signs*. London: Comedia.

MCGUIGAN, J., 1992: *Cultural Populism*. London: Routledge.

MILLS, A., and RICE, P., 1982: 'Quizzing the popular'. *Screen Education*, 41, Winter/Spring.

MODLESKI, T., 1986: *Studies in Entertainment*. Bloomington: Indiana University Press.

MORRIS, M. L., 1988: 'Banality in cultural studies'. *Discourse X2*, Spring/Summer.

NEALE, S. and KRUTNICK, F., 1990: *Popular Film and Television Comedy*. London: Routledge.

PATERSON, R., 1980: 'Planning the family: the art of the television schedule'. *Screen Education*, 35, Summer.

RADWAY, J., 1984: *Reading the Romance: Women, Patriarchy and Popular Literature*. Chapel Hill: University of North Carolina Press.

RYAN, M. and KELLNER, D., 1990: *Camera Politica: The Politics and Ideology of Contemporary Hollywood Film*. Bloomington: Indiana University Press.

SALOUTOS, T., 1968: *Populism: Reaction or Reform*? New York: Robert E. Kreiger.

WEBSTER, D., 1988: *Looka Yonder: The Imaginary America of Populist Culture*. London: Routledge.

WHANNEL, G., 1992: 'The price is right but the moments are sticky: TV quiz and game shows and popular culture'. In D. Strinati and S. Wagg (eds), *Come on Down? Popular Media Culture in Post-war Britain*. London: Routledge.

WILLIAMS, R., 1961: *The Long Revolution*. London: Chatto and Windus.

WILLIAMSON, J., 1986: 'The problems of being popular'. *New Society*, September.

SECTION III

New Approaches in Television Studies

EDITORS' INTRODUCTION

Section III of this book brings together a number of essays which examine what we have thought of as 'pressure points' in the current study of television. In using this phrase, we refer not just to what the essays say about the experience of television making and viewing but also to what they contribute to the experience of studying television. They offer particularly sharp examples of what happens when the changing world of television is brought up against the concepts and methods of a new and itself changing discipline.

The essays in this section are different in their range, subject matter and approach. Taken together, though, they offer an approach which is questioning and illuminating. They were commissioned with a number of factors in mind. Firstly, each essay offers analysis which is grounded in the kind of specificity which we believe is essential to the production of more general theories about television.[1] In some cases, this specificity may relate to a particular programme under discussion (Kirkham and Skeggs on *Absolutely Fabulous*); more frequently it can be found in the study of a particular genre such as the chat show (Shattuc) or cookery programmes (Strange); in other cases, it may relate to a specific audience group (Dinsmore on video collectors) or production situation (Gaber on news). National traditions of production may be brought into play along with complex positionings across gender, racial and class politics which, as we shall see, feed into broad thematic connections.

Secondly, a number of the essays examine the different kinds of access which audiences have to participation in television. This may be within mainstream programming such as in talk shows, in shows which feature amateur camcorder material and in more formal access programmes (see for instance the essays by O'Sullivan, Shattuc, Humm); it may be outside mainstream television institutions in the different kinds of cable or video distribution systems which Kintz and Freedman discuss. However limited such participation may be and however much on the industries' terms, this work suggests that audiences' familiarity with television forms is leading to a situation in which the possibilities for participation need to be thought about in new ways.

Thirdly, a number of essays examine different kinds of viewing situations and the different understandings which viewers bring to their viewing. Some of this work is explicit. Uma Dinsmore, for instance, talks to film-loving video viewers to try to understand how their particular interest in collecting and watching feature films can throw light on some assumptions about television/video viewing; Jane Shattuc uses the producers' comments about the studio audience's contributions to the chat show format. Other material is more implicit. Aluizo Trinta, for instance, suggests that the programming of the news between *telenovelas* on Brazilian television has implications for the way the programmes are viewed and suggests that, despite different formats, both draw on a repertoire of aesthetic forms that can be understood by audiences in a similar way.

Fourthly, the contributors for this section of the book were chosen because they offer different ways of thinking about and writing about television from particular positions. Contrast, for instance, Kintz and Freedman. Both write about the use of video by activists, but while Freedman is writing from inside the gay activist work he describes, the sharpness of Kintz's analysis of the role women play in conservative educational videos is rooted in her position as a feminist outside the work she is analysing. Gaber writes as a working broadcast journalist for whom questions of balance and control are an everyday concern, while Dinsmore writes as a film lover who is now, through her graduate study, at one remove from that position. The range of positions also means that the contributions can be used to explore a range of methods in Television Studies. The different strands of work on television which Brunsdon refers to in her essay in Section II can be found here: textual analysis is well represented by the very different work of Strange, Kintz and Kirkham and Skeggs, for instance; Freedman, Gaber and Humm in different ways look at the determinants of production; Dinsmore offers an example of qualitative audience research in her detailed account of two interviews; and Kirkham and Skeggs and Trinta are among those who stress the importance of a historical context.

Essays in this section also demonstrate that, while clarity of method is vital, different methods are not exclusive. Thus, Humm tries to relate institutional questions about production to the formal aesthetic qualities of the programmes produced by the BBC Community Programming Office, while Shattuc's textual analysis of the 1990s' chat show is given a context by her illuminating use of information about production. Kintz's detailed work on the narrative and imagery of the videos she describes is placed within a much broader analysis of political debate in the USA and Kirkham and Skeggs situate their textual and generic work in the context of a complex understanding of issues of femininity which owes much to the work done in Women's Studies.

The essays in this section are introduced individually but, taken together, some important themes emerge which tell us much about the new areas which Television Studies is exploring. One such theme is the way in which television needs to be seen as part of the wider social experience of the media and in particular the relationships between film, television and video need to be re-examined. Much of the foundational work on film and television viewing is based on a difference between the cinema spectator and the television viewer, a difference emerging from distinct traditions of theoretical work in the separate disciplines of Film and Television Studies and on the different viewing contexts for film and television. But people's experience of film is now more likely to take place in their own living rooms while, in a reverse move, certain kinds of television programmes, particularly sports coverage, may now, thanks to cable and pay-per-view, be consumed in public places such as bars. The use of video as an educational tool takes television out of the domestic setting into schools, health centres and churches, and the extension of satellite television in countries such as India places emphasis on the public viewing of mainstream television. The interaction between television, video and cinema can be seen in a number of essays in this section: Dinsmore shows that watching films in a domestic context on video is not merely a question of television imposing its mode of viewing by cutting cinema down to size, while Trinta relates the success of Brazilian *telenovelas* to their adoption of certain cinematic modes. Kintz's description of the videos produced by the religious right shows how strongly they rely on the imagery and narrative formats of the horror films they abhor, while Freedman suggests that gay television programmes, for financial and political reasons, draw on the aesthetics of experimental art forms which have also been crucial to independent film-making. Strange continues this cross-generic theme by drawing attention to the interaction of the travel genre in the seemingly straightforward cooking programmes she discusses. This work suggests that in order to understand television viewing we need a more complex account than that which relies on the determinants of the medium or the dynamics of one viewing context (most commonly in the family). Television viewing then becomes a more fluid activity dependent on the circumstances of viewing, the type of programme and the intentions, not only of the producer, but also of the viewer.

A second theme, which is linked to this question of how television is watched, emerges in this section. One of the key features which threads through the essays here is the blurring of the public and private spheres in television's presentation of the world. If one of television's effects has been to bring the public (the global) into the home, one of the ways it has done so has been by making the public personal. Television has been characterised by Brunsdon (1991) and others as a feminised medium both in its address to the feminine consumer and its dominant mode of domestic consumption; much discussion of soap opera, for instance, has rested on the concept of the establishment of a private sphere on television in which women's work in relation to the emotional needs of friends and family is recognised and supported. A number of the programmes under discussion here – cookery programmes, chat shows – would appear to have a fairly clear gendered address, and yet analysis indicates that their address is not necessarily to women but to a more general audience which is interested in the intimate and the domestic. Contributors here draw attention to the development of the confessional mode which is adopted by contributors to video diaries and educational programmes, participants on chat shows and even by the professionals – cookery presenters discussed by Strange who draw attention to their mistakes or actors in the 'out-take' shows discussed by O'Sullivan who allow their mistakes to form the basis of the entertainment. The emphasis on revelation and the intricate discussion of the personal, so characteristic of soaps, have become standard in non-fictional programmes as the division between public and private spheres on television has become more permeable.

In this context, much attention has been paid to the notion that, because of television, the public world of politics, for instance, has become more concerned with the 'trivia' of personal presentation and performance which Gaber describes; the values of the public sphere have been changed and perhaps eroded by translation to a more personal and emotional register (Dahlgren, 1995). This emphasis on the personal in talk shows and other formats has privatised the public sphere, consistently equating individual problems with personal solutions (talking, therapy, emotional display) rather than public action. It is also worth noting, however, as a number of essays here show, that the reverse also applies, that the personal sphere has become more public and so here too more emphasis has been placed on presentation and performance. Shattuc's discussion of the questions raised about the authenticity of certain chat show participants draws attention to the importance of the public presentation of the self in these programmes. In forms like chat shows, video diaries and fly-on-the-wall documentaries, the personal and domestic have been taken over by the public sphere of television so that nothing is free from the eye of the camera. The emphasis on the interaction between the public and personal spheres links back to questions of access discussed earlier. While expertise in the public sphere is deemed to be limited to those politicians, economists and journalists who operate within it, we can all be experts in our own private lives. If nostalgia, revelation and intimacy are, as O'Sullivan indicates, key modes for modern popular television, then the possibilities for participation are opened up to ordinary viewers but, ironically, the possibilities of such participation may be limited by the very modes which have opened them up.

This brings us on to the third theme which runs through the section – the activity of viewers in relation not just to viewing but to establishing meaning. The question of how viewers respond to television, how far they determine their own understandings rather than accepting those imposed from above, has been a key point of debate within television studies; it is a debate which has drawn on a wider discussion within Cultural Studies about how far popular formats are popular precisely because they have to allow space for people to recognise and talk about their own struggles, oppressions and pleasures. It was through the study of television by writers such as Hobson (1982), Ang (1985), Fiske (1987) and Brown (1990) that this argument extended beyond subcultures and into discussions on mass culture, into the analysis of programmes like soap opera and quiz shows which had no apparent connection with youthful rebellion. Television studies now has to take on the critique of 'cultural populism' (to use Jim McGuigan's term (1992)) which has suggested that audiences are less resistant and by implication are more vulnerable than had been proposed. This debate, which is discussed in Lusted's essay in Section II, can also be seen at work in a number of pieces in this section. Shattuc, for instance, suggests that the US chat shows do offer space for disreputable, 'outlaw' culture, a space for groups – women, gays, black people, the young – to discuss issues on their terms and break through some of the restrictions of white middle-class good taste. Kirkham and Skeggs also point to the ways in which *Absolutely Fabulous* appears to offer support to those who feel oppressed by the limits of appropriate feminine behaviour; they go on to argue, though, that these transgressive possibilities are bound up with questions of class and that resistant readings may be limited for working-class women.

Each of the essays in this section deals with an issue which is of current concern in Television Studies and we have not attempted to force them into a particular approach or style. They may be read individually and used to study a particular aspect of television at the moment. We do believe, however, that, as in the best academic work, studies of particular instances also comment on more general issues, and in this introduction and in those to the individual essays we have indicated how these essays speak to each other and participate in the debate about Television Studies which this book seeks to encourage.

Note

1.   Corner and Harvey refer to the problem that 'much previous theory was insufficiently connected to specific analysis' and suggest a need for ' "lower"-level analysis' (1996: xvi). While the description is somewhat derogatory, we would agree with the emphasis on particularity and specificity.

References

ANG, I., 1985: *Watching Dallas: Soap Opera and the Melodramatic Imagination*. London: Methuen.

BROWN, M. E. (ed.), 1990: *Television and Women's Culture*. London: Sage Publications.

BRUNSDON, C., 1991: 'Text and audience'. In E. Seiter, H. Borchers, G. Kreutzner and E. Warth, (eds), *Remote Control*. London: Routledge.

CORNER, J. and HARVEY, S., 1996: *Television Times*. London: Arnold.

DAHLGREN, P., 1995: *Television and the Public Sphere: Citizenship, Democracy, and the Media*. London: Sage Publications.

FISKE, J., 1987: *Television Culture*. London: Methuen.

HOBSON, D., 1982: *Crossroads: The Drama of a Soap Opera*. London: Methuen.

MCGUIGAN, J., 1992: *Cultural Populism*. London: Routledge.

INTRODUCTION TO CHAPTER 11

As a number of essays in this collection illustrate, questions about the nature of television as a medium continue to be debated. Tim O'Sullivan draws on Umberto Eco's notion of a shift to 'Neo-TV' in which the focus is not on the external world beyond television and viewer but on the relationship between viewer and television itself. O'Sullivan contributes to this debate by analysing three types of programmes which cannot easily be fitted into the old categories such as drama, documentary and outside broadcasts. He looks at programmes which use a variety of footage – archive material, out-takes, amateur footage, candid camera set-ups – and, while he analyses only British programmes, many of the formats he describes originate in the USA and will be readily recognisable as the basis for popular programmes elsewhere.

O'Sullivan's analysis is rooted in the notion of flow which organises television's output not only over a particular period of viewing but across its own lifetime and that of any particular viewer. The archive programmes remind us, often with particular vividness, of the flow of our own viewing and call on our memories of what it was like to be differently positioned – as children, adolescents, fans – in that history. O'Sullivan links this to notions that television has shifted from being a special or privileged site to one which has become part of the domestic clutter of everyday life. The barriers between television and its audience have been breaking down as television competition has forced it to become more user-friendly. Television seems to have become less pompous: the out-take programmes are, indeed, based on professionals agreeing to acknowledge their mistakes. Viewers participate, knowingly or not, as 'actors' in comic scenarios and submit for public viewing their own tapes of domestic accidents in which subject (falls, trips, spills) and form (sudden camera movement, odd angles) are equally haywire. Video diaries in which viewers report on their own private lives breach the divisions between the public and private and have an intimate quality, engendered as much by cramped camera work as by personal confession. In these programmes, and in those which reconstruct 'real events' such as crimes and accidents, television's own codes and rules emerge from hiding; enjoyment seems indeed to depend on conventions being understood, followed and occasionally flouted.

It is significant, though, that O'Sullivan's textually based essay stops short of telling us what the audience can be assumed to think about these forms of television. O'Sullivan criticises those who claim the high cultural ground by criticising these programmes despite the lack of ethnographic work which might give more insight into their appeal, but he does not go on to celebrate unproblematically the participatory possibilities he sees in the programmes. It is significant also that, while O'Sullivan clearly believes that light entertainment programmes on television merit serious consideration, he finds it hard to elaborate the criteria by which they might be judged. This awareness is based on an understanding that high culture values cannot simply be reversed in the name of populism. With commendable honesty, O'Sullivan illustrates the way in which Television Studies has opened television itself up for study but is still grappling with questions of quality, perspective and control.

11

Nostalgia, Revelation and Intimacy: Tendencies in the Flow of Modern Popular Television

Tim O'Sullivan

Television in Trouble?

The 1990s have witnessed a general quickening of the competitive pulse of television. At an institutional level, policies of deregulation – as made manifest in Britain in the Broadcast Bill (1990) and its springboard, the preceding White Paper 'Competition, Choice and Quality' – have forced a reassessment of established notions of public service broadcasting and sought to make television companies more competitive and more efficient. Not surprisingly, the search for large audiences and hence for the currency of popular programmes has emerged as one of the key themes for debate during this period. High ratings have been invoked by some as the ultimate index of the success of the new television regime in an era 'democratised' by market forces with liberated viewers – consumers – 'voting' with their remote control buttons and their satellite cards. For others, this scenario has in fact removed some of the key obligations and safeguards which have distinguished the qualities of national, publicly provided television in the UK since it began. From this point of view, television as a cultural system is becoming steadily less democratic and accountable; less able to contribute to the cultivation of a viable, modern public sphere. In this vein, some have suggested that changes in the organisation of British broadcasting in the late 1980s and early 1990s have to be understood as part of a general erosion of the rights of modern British citizens, especially in terms of their access to certain cultural resources, diverse forms of information or entertainment programme services.

Two further points should be noted in this brief introduction. First, as broadcast organisations themselves have acknowledged, UK research indicates that television appears to be losing its grip on its viewers. People in general seem to be spending less time watching TV. It is arguable, therefore, that television has to work harder to find new ways of soliciting viewers whose fragmented and fickle appetites are more demanding and whose finger on the remote control button appears more ready to press for channel change or 'off'. Second, the recent period has also been characterised by the development of other forms of television, notably those which are not based on terrestrial broadcasting and reception, but which come from 'the skies', down the cable or from the local video rental outlet. Conventional broadcasters have seen in these new forms part of the reason for their declining audiences and ratings. Satellite, cable and video have clearly become recognised as new sources of 'interference' and competition. Given the nature of these and other shifts in the period, it is not surprising that the 'quality' of television has emerged as a highly contested sign for the state of contemporary culture as the end of the twentieth century fast approaches. Television has often in its history performed this 'condensing' function. However, there appears to be something fundamental about the current phase and the changes taking place which goes beyond much of the rhetoric which has accompanied it.

In assessing these and related issues, it is important to remember that television broadcasting in Britain, as within many other national cultures, was once marvellous and novel, its spectacle a sign of postwar modernity and 'the new'. In its early days, it was formal, mannered and inhibited in its address to the unknown viewer citizen. Writing of the ways in which television invaded and reshaped the private space of the home, Todd Gitlin (1982) has noted that 'television suffuses the private domain with a new order of experience'. This 'new order' was achieved initially in the novelty that television offered, especially over the pre-existing forms and relations of cinema, newsreel, radio and the press, in terms of its abilities and efforts to connect and mediate between the public 'world out there' and the private, domesticated world 'in here' – 'at home'. The modalities and agenda of television have changed, however, and have had to change considerably in its 50-year history. In the drive for viewers and in the points of view and modes of address currently constituting the flow of modern, popular television, a number of significant shifts have taken place. As Paddy Scannell (1989, 1996) has suggested, these may be part and parcel of the new, gradually more egalitarian and democratic communicative relationships which have been created by broadcasting more generally. They also relate to the logic of what Anthony Giddens (1991) has referred to as 'high modernity'. In short, television no longer has its earlier spectacular power or presence. As a result and in contrast to earlier moments or periods, TV is now a part of the profane, personal and everyday, characterised by self-reflexivity, self-parody, informality, knowingness and familiarity – part of what Joshua Meyrowitz (1985) has referred to as the 'electronic placelessness' of modern times.

This essay sets out to develop some ideas concerning the current phase and state of transformation, in the ways British television addresses us now. It is an attempt to recognise history and historical process in the present tense and, although it has already been overtaken by new, ever more hybrid programmes, its focus is on the last ten years, the pre-digital era.

Neo-TV – 'The body becomes useless, and the eyes are all you need'?

For Umberto Eco, commenting on developments in Italian television in the early 1980s, the distinctions and forces at work here involve a fundamental shift from what he terms the old, established regime of *Paleo-TV* to *Neo-TV*:

The principal characteristic of Neo-TV is that it talks less and less about the external world. Whereas Paleo-TV talked about the external world, or pretended to, Neo-TV talks about itself and about the contact that it establishes with its own public. It does not matter what it says nor what it might be about (especially now, as the public, armed with remote control, decides when to let it speak and when to switch channels). Neo-TV, in order to survive this control, tries to hold viewers by saying to them: 'I am here, it's me, I am you'. (1992: 247)

Eco proceeds to provide a guide to the distinctive features of Neo-TV: these relate to changes in the classification and framing of television as a cultural system, including a process of weakening and merging of genres, changes in modes of address and the construction of the 'truth', the emergence of the 'hold all programme', the frequent appearance on screen of the boom-mike, the TV camera and the telephone. He notes in particular a new interactivity and knowingness which have accompanied and driven recent changes in the relationships television now actively cultivates with its viewers.

Pre-Eco – Television Flow

From an earlier (and perhaps with hindsight a more secure) television time, Raymond Williams suggested that the 'central television experience' was 'the fact of flow'. In this formative discussion, Williams sought to emphasise that television as a cultural form was not watched as a set of discrete, bounded items or programmes but rather as a 'flow sequence'. As he noted,

hardly anything is said about the characteristic experience of the flow sequence itself. It is indeed very difficult to say anything about this. It would be like trying to describe having read two plays, three newspapers, three or four magazines, on the same day that one has been to a variety show and a lecture and a football match. And yet in another way it is not like that at all, for though the items may be various the television experience has in some important ways unified them. To break this experience back into units . . . is understandable but often misleading. (1974: 95)

It is important to note a number of points here. As Stuart Laing, for instance, has argued in his helpful commentary: 'The problem with "flow" is that it is a concept which was asked to do too much – to cover too many diverse aspects of the contemporary situation as well as to be the defining characteristic of the (television) medium' (1991: 155). While this analysis usefully contextualises and provides a detailed breakdown of the concept, there are two particular strengths which I think make it worthwhile persevering with – especially in a period of change. First, it directs our attention to the holistic contours of TV output: to the characteristics of television as an overall cultural system of communication with distinctive features which cut across generic divisions. It is therefore an encompassing concept and foregrounds an understanding of the dynamics and modalities which are dispersed throughout and constitute the TV 'flow' relationship. Second, 'flow' refers to the viewers' lived experience of and with their televisions and their activities in relation to the TV interlocutor. Increasingly, television has to be seen not just as the singular 'box in the corner', but as the diverse screens which now characterise the myriad of private and public situations and contexts, from multi-set, multi-screen homes to screens in pubs, clubs, schools and workplaces.

It is in the light of these contextualising notes that I want to address a number of tendencies which seem to have become more pronounced in the flow of modern television. Each prompts intriguing questions about the changing relations of TV in current times and I hope briefly to sketch some of these. They can be located in specific programme formats, or items, but more generally they have emerged as constitutive elements within and across the flow of evening, night-time, daytime, weekly, weekend, seasons of television. Each has a particular historical dynamic, and they are in important and hybrid ways interrelated. First, I want to assess the growth of television programmes and forms which I have grouped under the label 'nostalgia TV' – in the main, selected, repackaged archive materials – an extension of the conventional policy to recycle 'repeats' of relatively recent, successful programmes. Second, I want to suggest some issues concerning the 'out-take' format, those programmes composed of the 'revealing' bits culled from the editing desk which once were waste but have now become international 'hot property' in the entertainment economy. Finally, the discussion concludes by posing some questions about what I have called 'Candid Video', embracing programme forms which in Britain have become almost synonymous with the name and TV personality of Jeremy Beadle but which also extend from light entertainment to embrace new types of documentary programmes, 'reality programming' and the 'reconstruction' form. The common features of these latter two seem centrally to involve novel and greatly expanded forms of revelation and intimacy.

The 'Rear-View Mirror' – Nostalgia TV

In the 1960s Marshall McLuhan wrote of the apocalyptic impact that electronic media – especially television – had on modern consciousness (1964, 1970). In pursuing this theme, he employed the idea of a car's rear-view mirror to characterise the ways in which television and other media profoundly shape and structure our sense of history, our collective ability to 'look backwards' at the past. In making this point, he was in part drawing attention to the power of television images in the construction of a view of historical events and processes, in documentaries or dramas, for instance. Furthermore, and in parallel with more recent postmodern assessments of TV culture, he suggested that contemporary understanding of history has become rooted in the mish-mash of representations and images provided by television. The 'real' history is both lost, replaced by and translated into the simulated, the imaginary or illusory. For some of these recent writers, this absence of a real sense of communal history has contributed to the growth of forms of collective nostalgia for the past, and this has been identified as a defining feature of postmodern culture.

This perspective may offer one way to start to understand the more self-conscious fashion in which British television companies have recently begun to recycle and re-present their archive resources. TV began as a medium without a memory and with little regard for the value of archiving or systematically storing and preserving its output. Steve Bryant (1989) has valuably documented some of the variable forces at work in the preservation of a British TV archive, highlighting the significance of what he terms the 'Television Heritage'.

In recent years, archive footage has punctuated and entered the flow of television in a number of ways, most obviously perhaps in the form of the British Channel 4's *TV Heaven* series which strip-scheduled Saturday evenings with blocks of programmes from yesteryear – 1959 one week, 1971 the next, and so on. Episodes from series and serials, single plays, documentaries and other surviving 'oddities' were packaged for consumption 20 or 30 years on. With Frank Muir hosting the evenings, these appear to have been targeted at older, more nostalgic viewers. Not to be outdone, the BBC countered with its *TV Hell*, scheduled across the August Bank Holiday evening prime-time. Featuring Angus Deayton and Paul Merton as presenters, this montage of clips and archive moments aimed at younger, more cynical audiences represents television apologising for its embarrassing past, rather than eulogising it. In the recent past, the BBC has also enlisted Philip Schofield to present *TV Hits*, a kind of archive 'chart' format, as well as employing a thematic approach in the *Black and White in Colour* series, selecting programmes to illustrate representations of black experience from the 1950s to the present day. One of the best-selling video packages for BBC Enterprises in the early 1990s was the *Watch with Mother* selection of surviving children's programmes from the 1950s and early 1960s.

As television has become more conscious of its own past, its own history, archive material has been harnessed as part of 'TV on TV' quizzes, on chat shows and in other formats of popular programming. Repeats of early *Coronation Street* episodes (1960 to date), notably one of the weddings of Elsie Tanner (1967), coincide with actuality celebrations, stretching back a little further and involving the replay of the television Coronation (1952–92). With the *Lime Grove Story*, repeats of *Dr Who* and *Thunderbirds*, *The Alan Bennett Season*, montages such as the *A-Z of Television* and *1001 Nights of TV*, the bricolage of *The Astounding Tales of Ferdinand de Bargos*, with the Victor Lewis-Smith shows and the Harry Enfield Mercury advertisements, it would seem that the 1990s has witnessed the triumphant return of old television, sometimes in new clothes.

At one important level, it is clear that the development of these types of programming in a period of economic stringency makes good commercial sense, especially when they perform creditably, as they have done, in the ratings. The ex-controller of Channel 4, Michael Grade, for example, has noted that it would be madness on the part of broadcasters not to exploit what he termed 'this sleeping asset'. But the logic of the commercial equation – the relative economy of production costs – does not fully explain these programmes' popularity, the deep nostalgic pleasures they appear to be capable of activating. How can we understand their popularity?

I have noted elsewhere that most people have memories of their early encounters with television. Many of these recollections function as quite powerful points of symbolic, biographical and generational reference. Many consist of memories of the 'live', televised event: the Coronation, the assassination of Kennedy, the election of Harold Wilson, the Beatles or Rolling Stones, sporting, space and other spectaculars, and so on. One of the levels of satisfaction in watching archive programming is rooted then in the positions they offer on the recent past, the 'rear-view mirror' which allows both a social and personal perspective on 'how things were' and at the same time 'how we have changed'. A number of pre-recorded video packages have been released in recent years to capitalise on this market – *'1950'*, *'Where were you when . . . ?'* etc. These and other, non-actuality programmes also function as points of reference for remembered domestic biography, relations with people, situations, places and stages of life that surrounded the old sets and constituted the viewing cultures of the time. It is important to note that old programmes do not mean the same things to all people. In fact it makes decided sense to think of 'audiences' for these forms of output, noting the importance of the generational cycles which have marked the development of TV since the 1950s. For instance, the television critic Mark Lawson has, as an aside in this context, remarked that people divide according to the *Blue Peter* presenters they remember most vividly.

There is a final and fundamental issue that deserves to be raised here. The very idea of nostalgia implies a harkening back to a sentimentally remembered age. In this case, not a 'golden' but a monochrome period of more restricted TV, when television viewing became 'the essential social habit of the age'. There are deep forms of cultural and emotional (in)security in play here, often in tension with the 'kitsch', slightly disturbing or comic–archaic qualities revealed in the juxtaposition of the 'dated' old within the flow of the new. Quite how long these archive elements will retain their attraction and popularity remains another question.

Out-takes, Mis-takes and Behind the Scenes

The out-take format is another relatively recent development which has rapidly gained currency in the flow of television. By comparison with TV which invites us to celebrate the varied aspects of our public and private television histories and biographies, the appeal of programmes such as *It'll Be Alright On The Night* (LWT) or *Auntie's Bloomers* (BBC) resides in their revelation of the unexpected and the often undignified or comical spectacle. Here is another side to the normal, professional performance and the flawless, controlled flow of pro gramming. Occasionally, the routine, anticipated flow sequences of TV are unintentionally disrupted: by technical fault (studio light dropping onto newsreader's desk during bulletin); or continuity error (incorrect tape sequence, caption or studio camera control); or in some instances, other forms of unplanned external or human agency (Sue Lawley reading the news during an 'invasion' of the studio by gay rights activists). These slightly unsettling, often magnetic or comical occurrences have always happened and, precisely because they disrupt the normal flow of events, they are often memorable television. Most viewers have their own stock of particular favourites. As television production has become a technically and professionally more sophisticated business and given the decline of genuinely 'live', simultaneous broadcasting, they occur with much less frequency now than in the 'early days'. While their possibility is distributed across the flow of TV, their appearance in recent years has been guaranteed in specially packaged programmes. In Britain, the presenter Denis Norden, with his particular style of delivery, has in large part become a modern television personality on the basis of fronting subsequent series and seemingly endless repackagings of (The very, very worst of) *It'll Be Alright On the Night* (ITV). These programmes have entered the ritualised flow of seasonal TV. American in origin, the programme concept entails recognising the value of the out-take as a segment of popular comedy entertainment rather than a professional or organisational aberration to be discarded, junked or suppressed. Once again, the logic of relatively cheap packages of television, often drawing on archive recordings, and the production of large popular audiences have proceeded hand in hand.

The programmes in this format present audiences with segments which in broad terms appear to be selected to offer two types of appeal. The first can be likened to the long tradition of slapstick comedy. As viewers, we are able to witness the actuality of accidental or coincidental things happening to people, usually television presenters or performers, and their resulting indignities are 'captured live' by the camera. Unplanned, unexpected interventions from nature – wind, water or animals, for instance – physically or otherwise disrupt the action. In some instances these types of disruption are the product of human agency, as in the case of the 'vox pop' which goes wrong because the particular member of the public chosen does not conform to the rules or codes of the street interview. The second source of the popularity of this kind of programme concerns what Denis Norden in his inimitable style of presentation often refers to as the 'cock-up', usually professional problems in production. The professional is revealed as fallible. These would typically include presenters or actors forgetting their lines, missing cues, 'drying' or giggling uncontrollably. Scenery collapsing or props malfunctioning also figure in many of these segments.

The popularity of these shows has been accompanied by the growth of an international import and export trade in out-takes, most obviously from Australia and the USA. From an organisational point of view, the packages offer popular, relatively cheap and hence effective television entertainment. The clips themselves serve to humanise the presenters and performers featured by locating them in a 'funny old world' which we are all assumed to share – a world of random, mundane fallibility, where chance events triumph rather than the 'serious', seamless and professional machine of television production. 'We' are allowed behind the scenes, invited to guess and predict 'what happens next' and assumed to be united in our appreciation of the comic spectacle. In this sense, programmes of this type often reveal the artifice of 'normal' TV and encourage identification with the human, individual, everyday, 'accidental' out-of-control nature and scale of things. It is significant, however, that the out-takes 'disruption' itself has, with repetition, rapidly become somewhat clichéd, predictable and anticipated. Once you have grasped the idea and context, the pleasure lies in spotting what is going to 'unexpectedly' happen. In this area of television entertainment, the requirements are not just for more out-takes, but for more shocking spectacles or comical novelties caught in front of or behind the camera. There is presumably a limited amount of usable out-take material available. Even in the light of the recent discovery of their entertainment value, they cannot really be 'performed' or manufactured. To find developments of this nature, we need to shift across to consider another related set of elements constituting and interrupting current TV flow.

Candid Video, Voyeurism and Vérité

In this final section, I want to give some speculative attention to an allied but distinctive recent tendency in the flow of TV, the candid video format. On the one hand, this undoubtedly offers various forms of voyeuristic pleasure – both the securities and insecurities – associated with a kind of televisual equivalent to 'eavesdropping' on events. Significantly, these programmes also rely on portable video cameras and, coincident with the rapid expansion of the domestic camcorder market, these are operated not only by professional producers but also by 'ordinary' or 'real' members of the public. These are their and our 'very own' out-takes. In varying ways, as John Dovey (1996) has noted, they have been hailed as new forms of 'people's' or 'interactive' television, home movies for the modern age.

Camcorder Comedy

In the mid-1980s, the 25-year-old formula of *Candid Camera* was given a new and profitable lease of life in Britain in the form of programmes like *Game for a Laugh* (ITV) and *Beadle's About* (ITV). The success of the format continued to rely on the conventions of providing a privileged and hidden view of unsuspecting victims reacting to a 'set up' or 'practical joke'. The camera secretly records and televises 'real', actuality instances of embarrassment, anger, bewilderment and other reactions to the absurd, bizarre or apparently catastrophic and transforms them into public spectacles. The audience experience, at a safe distance, the tensions of narrative build-up and the relief and 'canned laughter' of resolution, when all is revealed as a TV stunt, rather than real life. The significant additions to the format in the late 1980s over the 1960s were initially technical – use of more easily disguised, more portable cameras – and presenter Jeremy Beadle, who has become a British television personality of some repute. For many critics, he has performed the function of perfectly embodying and condensing the 'vulgar' or 'barbaric' values of today's television, and wider media responses to his television career and personality make for an interesting subject in their own right. From this point of view, he has been taken to represent a kind of televisual victimisation, a peculiar medieval type of torture made modern, wherein audiences ('the mob') are encouraged to laugh at the misfortunes of others, and all this justified in the name of 'popular entertainment'. The claim of such critics to the high moral and cultural ground, it should be noted, has been accompanied by an absence of any serious ethnographic research which might actually shed some light on how and why diverse groups of viewers relate to and engage with this kind of television – and what, if anything, they get out of it.

This is also the case with programmes which have shifted to encompass actual instances of everyday, private aberration, captured this time by 'you the viewers'. *You've Been Framed* (ITV) and *Caught in the Act* (BBC) represent programmes which capitalise on and serve to index the rapid growth in domestic, personal ownership of the video camcorder. Television advertisements have also made use of these kinds of 'home movie' type segments; Scottish Amicable, for instance, selling insurance by making dramas out of these moments of everyday crisis. Once again, the programmes appear to offer an 'unmediated' view of the taken-for-granted, commonplace absurdities and disruptions to the normal in family and social life, wherein personalised, private experiences and emotions are revealed. Domestic settings, family leisure and other routines form the backcloth for the quirky, zany, anarchic tribulations in these archives of everyday life. A good recent example of the 'shock-live-intrusion' has been demonstrated on *Noel Edmond's House Party* (BBC). The domestic and private unknowing scene around the screen is suddenly on the screen and made public. It has been televised. These kinds of 'frames' and the diverse points of view they make available have been extended recently to encompass more fully developed, but less comical, more 'confessional' modes of revelation.

Put Yourself in My Place: Developments in Documentary

If the portable camcorder has provided the impetus for new types of light entertainment and comedy programmes or relationships to emerge in the flow of television, as Peter Keighron (1993) has noted, they have also had implications for the TV documentary feature. Most obviously, perhaps, this has been the case with *Video Diaries* (BBC) and more recently with the *Video Nation* (BBC) project. Since the early 1960s, with long-running series like *Man Alive*, British TV documentaries have always made use of 'real people' and told, or used, 'their' stories. The trend now, however, is towards an accentuated personal, direct and intimate address which, when combined with the camcorder, can in certain instances 'short-circuit' the historical relations which have regulated the power of those behind and those in front of cameras. From the chilling surveillance images of the Bulger or Rodney King cases, to the compressed everyday records of the *Living Soap* or *Sylvania Waters*, the video camera has made available new kinds of revelation and intimacy within the documentary and current affairs economy. As a result, the 1980s and 1990s have seen a realignment of the documentary enterprise and a concern to foreground the personal, observed and intimate experience, live/life stories in private spaces.

In their recent and illuminating commentary on Italian television, 'more consciously organised around self-reflexivity than other television networks', Iain Chambers, Lidia Curti and Anna Marie Morelli refer to allied developments. They note the growth of new genres: the 'television of suffering' (inside stories of addiction, prostitution, abuse, illness, etc.) and 'confessional TV' (personal stories of sexuality or criminality, for instance, etc.). These 'tales of lived experience', of 'ordinary people', are significant, they suggest, in their appeal:

> this kind of narrative . . . is presented and received as something made by 'one of us'. In other words the author of the script is or appears to be the viewer herself/himself . . . The process at work in these present-day Italian programmes emerges quite clearly: a public that is transfigured into authorising, both individually and collectively, the television event.' (1993: 277)

Overall, these and other shifts in contemporary TV fundamentally involve this realignment of what they see as the traditional transmitter–receiver roles:

> the receiver simultaneously slides through the TV membrane into becoming a transmitter in a dissemination of authority that not only punctuates the sense of

television flow as being something that is unilaterally directed from above, but also raises the intriguing question of whose television it is anyway. (1993: 284)

And Finally – A Note on 'Reconstructions'

There is an interesting relationship here with the ways in which other non-documentary, hybrid TV formats have also begun to foreground the 'reconstruction' scenario. In the absence of a video camera capturing 'live' action, in either professional or amateur hands, television now supplies the 'reconstruction', the 'enhanced documentary'. Initially this occurred in *Crimewatch* (BBC) and the updating of the discourse of public information-appeal crime programme. More recently the format has been developed, as John Corner (1995a) has suggested, in programmes like *999* (BBC), *Crime Stories* (LWT) or *Michael Winner's True Crimes* (ITV), which have attempted by dramatic reconstruction to position the viewer in a real, recent situation or event. *Caught on Camera* (LWT) promises to televise viewers' own video footage of rescues, dramas or tragedies. On the one hand, these have been justified and publicised in the interests of crime detection and awareness; on the other, as a celebration of escape from disasters or potentially life-threatening circumstances – seen 'with your very own eyes'. In both cases, programme-makers have drawn on devices which simulate the real by the revelation of personal and actual details of incident and intimate, lived emotion. Docu-dramas, drama-documentary and 'factions', those other 'little chinks' between fact and fiction, have previously stimulated debate similar to that which has accompanied these developments. The reconstruction format, however, stands in an interesting relationship to the footage from surveillance cameras which is also 'leaking' into contemporary television flow.

Critical Fictions?

This discussion has sought to highlight the emergence of several interrelated and novel shifts in the flow of contemporary television in Britain. Popular culture in general and popular television in particular have often been regarded and dismissed as 'formulaic' in their structure and appeal. While this is arguably the case, it is important to note that such formulae change and, in this case, flex *across* the flow of television. Perhaps the most important questions concern the interpretation of the significance of these shifts. In crude terms, should they be condemned or celebrated – and what kinds of criteria should we employ in judgement? Undoubtedly these programmes represent important elements in the commercial operation of currently popular TV as it 'desperately seeks the audience'. In addition, however, they are popular precisely in that many people actively choose to watch them, enjoy them and talk about them afterwards. In the search for viewers, they appear to offer a kind of participatory TV – television which, by its mode of address and subject focus, attempts to do away with the distance between itself and its viewers, reflexively marvelling and poking fun at its own 'artificial' history, its own abilities to reveal the private ups and downs, the pathos of identifiable, everyday existence.

As I suggested at the outset, pre-millennial times have been characterised by highly charged debates about the place and quality of television and its obligations in present and future national cultural life. In his recent analysis, Jim McGuigan (1992) has provided a framework for assessing what he terms 'cultural populism'. In this discussion, he outlines the major dilemmas facing attempts to assess and analyse popular cultural forms and their dynamics in the current period. In particular he warns against: 'the drift into populism focused more or less exclusively on "popular readings", which are applauded with no evident reservations at all, never countenancing the possibility that a popular reading could be anything other than "progressive"' (1992: 72). In other words, the analysis and evaluation of the types of television which have figured in this discussion need to be tempered and driven by more than a simple, uncritical celebration of their popularity in a kind of 'mirror image' of more traditional forms of unexamined, elitist dismissal. As a result, these remain significant programmes for analysis and consideration, partly because of the difficult problems they pose (see Corner, 1995b). In the shifting cultural economies of the present times they provide an important – if problematic and at the same time revealing – focus for renewed forms of critical engagement and cultural analysis.

References and Further Reading

ANG, I., 1991: *Desperately Seeking the Audience*. London, Routledge
BONDEBJERG, I., 1996: 'Public discourse/private fascination: hybridization in "true-life-story" genres'. *Media Culture and Society*, 18: 27–45.
BRYANT, S., 1989: *The Television Heritage*. London: British Film Institute.
CHAMBERS, I., CURTI, L. and MORELLI, A., 1993: 'Italy and biodegradable television'. In U. Bechdorf et al. (eds), *Watching Europe: A Media and Cultural Studies Reader*. Amsterdam and Tubingen, Cultural Studies Foundation/Tübinger Vereinigung für Volkskunde E.V. 274–84.
CORNER, J., 1995a: *Television: Cultural Form and Public Address*. London: Arnold.
———, 1995b: 'Media Studies and the "knowledge problem"'. *Screen*, 36, 2: 147–55.
DOVEY, J., 1996: 'The revelation of unguessed worlds'. In J. Dovey (ed.), *Fractal Dreams: New Media in Social Context*. London: Lawrence & Wishart, 109–35.
ECO, U.,1992: 'A guide to the neo-television of the 1980s'. In Z. Baranski and R. Lumley, (eds), *Culture and Conflict in Postwar Italy*. London: Macmillan, 245–55.
GIDDENS, A., 1991: *Modernity and Self-Identity*. Cambridge: Polity.
GITLIN, T., 1982: 'Television's screens: hegemony in transition'. In M. Apple (ed.), *Cultural and Economic Reproduction in Education*. London: RKP, 202–46.
GOODWIN, A., 1993: 'Riding with ambulances: television and its uses'. *Sight and Sound*, 13, 1: 26–8.
KEIGHRON, P., 1993: 'Video diaries: what's up doc?'. *Sight and Sound*, 3, 10: 24–5.
KILBORN, R., 1994: 'How real can you get?: recent developments in "reality" television'. *European Journal of Communication*, 9: 421–39.
LAING, S., 1991: 'Raymond Williams and the cultural analysis of television'. *Media, Culture and Society*, 13: 153–69.
MCGUIGAN, J., 1992: *Cultural Populism*. London: Routledge.
MCLUHAN, M., 1964: *Understanding Media*. London: RKP.
———, 1970: *Culture is Our Business*. New York: Ballantine Books.
MEYROWITZ, J., 1985: *No Sense of Place: The Impact of Electronic Media on Social Behaviour*, Oxford: Oxford University Press.

O'SULLIVAN, T., 1991: 'Television memories and cultures of viewing 1950–1965'. In J. Corner (ed.) *Popular Television in Britain*. London: British Film Institute, 159–82.

SCANNELL, P., 1989: 'Public service broadcasting and modern public life'. *Media, Culture & Society*, 11: 135–66.

———, 1996: *Radio, Television and Modern Life*. Oxford: Blackwell.

WILLIAMS, R., 1974: *Television: Technology and Cultural Form*. London: Collins.

Jane Shattuc provides a detailed account of a television phenomenon of the 1990s – the personal problem talk show. These talk shows, like the programmes which O'Sullivan describes, are participation programmes and Shattuc's discussion raises questions about the way in which divisions between viewer and programme are breached through the undisciplined mode of debate and the invitation for viewers to participate as guests or members of the studio audience. Shattuc describes how the 1990s' talk shows differ from their predecessors in their determination to break the rules about taste and behaviour and hence scandalise Middle America. In some senses, she suggests, the scandal is as much about the way in which debate is conducted as it is about the ever-more risqué subjects discussed. For a non-US viewer, this sense of scandal is reinforced by the way in which talk shows have become one of the most derided of America's television exports, alleged evidence of the depths to which popular culture can sink.

Shattuc's account is informed by both textual analysis and work on production. In her textual analysis, Shattuc offers an account which reads against the grain of the liberal moralising sometimes provided by the host and looks to understand the programmes by analysing the excessive overplaying, the visual spectacles and narrative rituals, the flamboyant style and the emphasis on breaking taboos of performance as well as subject matter. Linked to this textual analysis is commentary on production in which she looks at the construction of the studio audience not just by the producers but by its members' knowledge of the programmes' conventions. She suggests also that we need to think beyond the common question about the status of the guests ('Are they just actors?') in order to analyse the pleasures and possibilities of participation and performance.

Shattuc brings both these aspects together in a case study which reflects on a number of important issues which are of current concern in Television Studies. She comments, for instance, on the way in which these shows breach the conventions which reserve some debates for the public and some for the private sphere by hauling emotional problems and personal feuds into a very public arena. Taking feminism's emphasis on self-expression to extremes, the talk shows celebrate the triumph of the personal sphere in which issues are debated within an entirely emotional register. Like Kintz, Shattuc draws attention to the way in which some order is sought through the application of a rigid moral code based on binary oppositions but suggests that in this case carnivalesque excess is too strong to be controlled. This is particularly so since the shows, in the way in which they deal with participants and audience, privilege performance over truth and style over moral correctness.

Shattuc suggests that the 1990s' talk shows draw on discourses of identity politics and, in differing degrees, owe their emphasis on expression and confession to modes taken from feminism, black culture and, in particular, the aesthetics of gay camp. In this, like O'Sullivan, she joins the debate about whether popular television can be explained as a site in which those without power can begin to forge their own cultural understandings. Shattuc is somewhat wary of celebrating this example of popular television as a form of resistance. Nevertheless, she suggests that the scandal caused by the shows is linked to the way in which they gave space to the disrespectful and aggressive voices of 'outlaw culture' and argues that their demise may have as much to do with the re-assertion of social power as with good taste.

12

'Go Ricki': Politics, Perversion, and Pleasure in the 1990s

Jane Shattuc

Today, we turn our attention to television. Now these days there is a lot of criticism directed at television – the casual cruelty, the rampant promiscuity, the mindlessness of sitcoms and soap operas. Most of the criticisms are justified. But this is not the worst of it. The worst television is the day-time television talk shows we have identified. In these shows, indecent exposure is celebrated as a virtue.

William Bennett, former US Secretary of Education[1]

Today's talk shows celebrate the victim and the victimizer equally; they draw no lines and have no values except the almighty dollar. And as cheap as they are to produce, they pay: Over the past decade, television talk shows have proliferated like roaches in the walls of a New York apartment.

Jill Nelson in *The Nation*[2]

I think the show is almost gay sometimes.

Viewer, 'Ricki Lake' Computer Message Board, *America On Line*, 7 April 1995

Introduction

After a decade of four programmes with some political commitment – *The Oprah Winfrey Show*, *Phil Donahue*, *Geraldo*, and *Sally* – talk shows seemingly lost their tie to the public sphere in America in 1995. Scores of new talk shows aired: *The Jerry Springer Show* (1991), *Maury Povich* (1991), *Montel Williams* (1991), *Jenny Jones* (1991), *Ricki Lake* (1993), *Gordon Elliott* (1994), *Carnie* (1995), *Tempestt* (1995).[3] Topics moved from personal issues connected to a social injustice to interpersonal conflicts which emphasized only the visceral nature of confrontation, emotion and sexual titillation. The expert disappeared as the number of guests proliferated – each programme staging a whirlwind succession of five-minute sound-bites of conflict, crisis and resolution.

Everything also got younger – the guests, the studio audience, the host and even the demographics. The hosts – Danny Bonaduce (*The Partridge Family*), Gabrielle Carteris (*Beverly Hills 90210*), Tempestt Beldsoe (*The Cosby Show*),

Carnie Wilson (*Wilson Phillips*) – came out of the entertainment industry instead of news. Suddenly they were nominated as 'experts' based on claims of their 'averageness' as products of middlebrow commercial culture. The studio audience moved from the role of citizens making common-sense judgements to spectators hungering for confrontation. Talk shows seemed more like a tele-vised coliseum where the screaming battles of an underclass are carried out as a voyeuristic spectacle rather than a venue for social change. 'Go Ricki!!' had become the rallying cry for not only the death of the public sphere, but the pri-vate sphere – nothing seems taboo.

Reacting to this shift towards greater tabloidization, both the political left and right in America exploded in anger. Liberal to left magazines (*Ms.*, *The New Yorker* and *The Nation*) decried the lack of social consciousness of the pro-grammes. William Bennett, the neo-conservative former Secretary of Education, launched a campaign against the new talk shows through his think-tank 'Empower America' in October 1995. He labelled them as a form of 'perversion' while oddly praising the old liberal programmes *The Oprah Winfrey Show* and *Phil Donahue* (once considered purveyors of abnormality) as upholding family values. How could talk shows have come to this contradictory moment?

Such a significant difference in programme content and reception allows us to examine not only the historical change within the genre, but the role that iden-tity politics played as it was popularized within a commercial medium. Talk show history paralleled America's shift from a broad institutional definition of politics based on citizenship (e.g. the party system, Congress and the Bill of Rights) to a narrower notion of politics based on sectarian needs defined by cul-tural and psychological identity of the individual or the 'personal as political'. And into the fray rushed commercial television, ready to stage this newest def-inition of 'the people' and exploit its potential sensationalism by presenting pri-vate acts as socially relevant.

Traditional theories of generic evolution argue that a genre begins in a naïve state evolving towards greater awareness of its own myths and conventions.[4] Here, a self-consciousness of the medium has produced programmes in the 1990s that communicate at a number of levels commenting on TV's own history and methods. Due to the phenomenal popularity of *The Oprah Winfrey Show*, the programmes of the 1990s emerged out of the historical need of commercial television to repeat success. In an attempt to create a different market the new programmes reached out to a younger audience and constructed a new form based on the sheer pleasure of breaking social taboos – especially those main-tained by an older generation of 'serious' talk shows.

TV talk shows are dynamic cultural objects; they have signalled major changes in the American culture, the television industry and other programmes. In the 1990s they abandoned the unwritten guidelines that identity politics once provided for talk shows in defining social injustice in terms of race, gender, class and sexual preference. On one hand, these new programmes stem from a gen-eral shift in the American political temperament as gay rights, affirmative action and abortion rights had come under fire with the neo-conservative attack in the 1990s. But, on the other hand, they spring from the voracious appetite of com-mercial television where innovation has led to a self-conscious gutting of the feminist notions of empowerment based on confession, testimony and social conversion. Rather, *Ricki* et al. attest to the power of the broader pleasures of

youthful rule-breaking and renegade individualism in the face of the social regulation imposed not only by identity politics in the 1990s, but the established talk
shows of 1980s.

The Mode of Production of Talk Shows in the 1990s

It is too simple to paint the change in production between the early talk shows
and later ones as the loss of social scruples under the corrupting influence of
profit and competition. Oprah Winfrey's astute announcement in September
1994 trades on this assumption when she declared she would no longer do 'trash
TV'. In a cover story in *TV Guide* she 'confesses':

> I understand the push for ratings caused programmers to air what is popular, and
> that is not going to change. I am embarrassed by how far over the line the topics
> have gone, but I also recognize my contribution to this phenomenon.[5]

On one level, she fails also to confess that her pledge to take the high road
serves as a shrewd business move to differentiate her talk show in the face of
indistinguishable tabloid shows. She will reign over her self-created moral uplift
market for talk shows while the other shows will take a small share of the
crowded tabloid market.

On a more important level, Winfrey's statement perpetuates the myth that television merely follows popular tastes toward tabloidization instead of creating
tastes. However, she promises to create a new market with her oath to create
'shows with images of what we would like to be'.[6] As a result, the *Oprah Winfrey
Show* has turned to bourgeois knowledge as the source of programming; the programme is now based on upbeat interviews with 'exemplar' celebrities and self-
help discussions with experts with a quiescent audience nodding in approval.[7]
However, the youth-oriented talk shows continue the tradition of soliciting the
active audience by constructing their vision of a younger more fun-loving consumer. This process has been vaguely termed as 'sensationalizing' the medium – a
rather inexact term given that the genre has always been sensational.

A more exacting analysis of the production and publicity process in the 1990s
reveals the construction of what I would call an implied 'self-conscious' or 'playful' viewer/consumer. I argue that present talk shows are unusually polysemic.
On one level, they can still be read as straight talk shows offering 'individual'
solutions to the lower classes' everyday personal dilemmas. Both Jerry Springer
and Ricki Lake end their programmes with the host moving off to side to comment on the conflict and offer advice. After the angry programme on unwed
parents-to-be (9 September 1995) Ricki Lake offered:

> It is difficult when the one you love is hated by everyone else in your family. It is
> important not to close the doors on your family because they do love you and want
> the best for you. But they just may not be able to express their feelings.

Platitudes and biblical style commands ('honor your mother and father') have
replaced the socially conscious language of Freudian therapists as talk shows
have sought to broaden the serious appeal of their audience.

However, these newer shows invite a second reading which deconstructs the
serious or liberal 'do-good' intentions of 1980s' talk shows by inviting an ironic
reading. Here, the methods of the earlier programmes are so excessively over-

played that they highlight the contradictions of any talk show – particularly the first generation of Oprah Winfrey and Phil Donahue (even Geraldo Rivera) – which unctuously attempts to help disadvantaged people while simultaneously profiting from the act. Although these new programmes flaunt their asocial values to the point of a callous lack of care, they cannot be subsumed within right-wing ideology. Their style and content derive from the sexual liberation movement of identity politics (gay, lesbian and bisexual culture and feminism).

The topics for a majority of these shows are not new; they recycle the old talk show topics with a bolder and more direct approach. Reunions, secret crushes, meet a celebrity, confronting the perpetrator, return guests, and makeovers are all staples of the new shows – established successful topics borrowed from the established shows. However, instead of labelling the programme in terms of a social issue to be debated or investigated neutrally – e.g. 'A Rare Look into the Lives of the Obese' (*Oprah Winfrey*, 2 February 1994) or 'Sexual Harassment Among Teens' (*Sally Jessy Raphaël*, 7 March 1994) – the 1995 programmes have shifted to more first- and second-person exclamations or imperatives to increase not only personal identification but to move away from the 'pseudo-seriousness' of third-person objective distance of the programmes associated with identity politics. Here are some titles for one week in November 1995:

Gordon Elliott:
'Gordon: Hook Me Up with a Hollywood Hunk' (20 November)
'Incredible Twin Reunions' (21 November)
'Relationship Rehab' (22 November)
'Big, Bad, Beautiful Babes' (24 November)

Carnie:
'Your Flirting Has Gone Too Far' (21 November)
'Left at the Altar' (22 November)
'I Know That I Shouldn't Want You, But I Do' (23 November)
'Dream Come True Makeovers' (24 November)

Ricki Lake:
'Listen, Family, I'm Gay ... It's Not a Phase ... Get Over It!' (20 November)
'Girl, You're Easy Because You're Fat ... Respect Yourself ASAP' (21 November)
'My Family Hates My Friend Because She is Black' (22 November)
'Someone Slap Me! Today I Meet My All-Time Favorite Star' (23 November)

Gone are the talk show topics that were tied directly to explicit public sphere debates such as 'Press Actions on Whitewater' with reporters (*Phil Donahue Show*, 16 March 1994) and 'Strip Searching in Schools' with school administrators (*Sally Jessy Raphaël*, 13 March 1994). Nor does one see personal topics presented as general social issues such as 'When Mothers Sell Babies for Drugs' (*Geraldo*, 17 March 1994), 'Custody Battles with Your In-Laws' (*Sally Jessy Raphaël*, 22 April 1994) and 'Domestic Violence' (*Phil Donahue Show*, 1 February 1994). Rather, the topics are narrowed to an interpersonal level. They are presented in colloquial or imperfect English to signify that the discussions will not be refined, but casual among friends. And finally, they are written as directives which implies a certain amount of humorous hyperbole, but more importantly there is a level of aggression in their urgency that signals potential conflict.

There are two broad types of programmes: the tongue-in-cheek just-for-fun kind and the do-gooder interpersonal variety. The new variation tends to recycle stars from 1970s' middlebrow TV culture such as *Ricki Lake*'s 'Someone Slap Me! Today I Meet My All-Time Favorite Star' (23 November 1995) where guests meet their favourite star such as Gary Coleman (*Different Strokes*) and Debbie Gibson. Consider the *Gordon Elliott* programme, 'Gordon: Hook Me Up with a Hollywood Hunk'(20 November 1995), where audience members go on dates with look-a-likes and the talk show cameras follow them. In general, the audience members participate much more directly, becoming part of the drama. However, these programmes have become preconstructed from beginning to end. There is much less spontaneity; the surprise and pleasure come from the gamble whether the audience member/guest will be embarrassed or play into the forced role. As in the old celebrity shows, these programmes function as comic relief from the 'heavier' topics about relationships.

The more frequent type of programme (and the object of public ire) is the interpersonal or relationship conflict show. These topics are about the emotional conflicts involved in breaking sexual and social taboos. In a study commissioned by the Kaiser Family Foundation, Bradley S. Greenberg and Sandi Smith (Michigan State University) broadly evaluated 200 videotapes and transcripts over the 1995 summer. They found that the hosts and guests talk mostly about family, relationships and sex. The most common disclosures per hour were five of a sexual nature including one of sexual orientation and four about a personal attribute such as addiction or health. The report also described that 16 disclosures per hour were of what it typed as 'ambush disclosures' where a guest surprises an acquaintance, a friend or family member with a secret.[8]

Although the salacious content of older talk shows (*Geraldo*) looks indistinguishable from the new programmes, there are still important differences in the shift in the 1990s. The newer programmes maintain the six-segment programme structure, but instead of three guests discussing an issue in some depth, the programmes time each segment around a new guest pair. The performance is choreographed around the introduction of the complaining or aggrieved individual while the problem person(s) wait 'unknowingly' off stage with a camera trained on him/her. Under the host's prodding the complainant reveals a series of intimate details about the other's deviant sexual activity. Together the host and the guest come to the mutual conclusion that this person has a problem and the programme has its necessary 'conflict'.[9]

'Ambush disclosures' (or making the private public) are carried out as an extension of a therapeutic logic: privacy is a sign of repression. The host calls the person out onto the stage and begins to investigate if her/his story parallels the first guest's and then begins to admonish him/her for breaking the social rules, causing emotional pain and not being open. This scenario is usually repeated six times with six different guest pairs. This duplication results in slight variations on a dysfunctional norm. The degree of similarity between couples feels like a sociological revelation: 'Given many duplicate problems it *must* be truly a social issue'. But their parallel acts and their unexpected differences are labelled harmless entertainment; the programme invites the audience to chortle at the repeated foibles and acts of the human experience. The fact that the programme and the host so obviously construct these stories through the guiding hand of the production process does not matter. These parallels in behaviour and the telling of their life stories repeat the predestined logic of a lower-class culture which historically does not have the power to control.

Aesthetically, what is important here is the form not the content of these scenarios. One waits to see how *Ricki Lake* varies the presentation, the graphics and the narrative set-up. The programme focuses on visual spectacles: entrances of guests, audience reaction and a set of rituals comparable to game shows' use of weddings, proposals, punishments and contests. In fact, rituals of other television TV genres have been incorporated into the talk shows, demonstrating that not only do genres become more self-conscious as they age, they hybridize with other genres in search of innovation. Cameras furtively follow guests in to public situations (*Candid Camera*); romantic problems are worked out by dating games (*The Dating Game*); a guest will often have to perform as if in a talent show (*Star Search*). The pleasure comes from recognizing the original TV sources and how 'badly' its conventions are mimicked.

Ultimately, these programme topics are staged by the talk show on the pretext of doing social good. (Ricki often coos: 'We are here to help you.') They offer advice and solutions for day-to-day problems such as promiscuity, betrayal and lack of self-esteem. They are the children of the therapeutic programmes which defined the first generation of talk shows, but they have lost any sense of difference between social identity and private emotions. And like good children they have learned so much from the parental generation that they rarely use a therapist. The host takes on the role of therapized individual dispensing commonsense advice.

When the earlier programmes did relationship programmes – e.g. 'You are not the Man I Married' (*Geraldo*, 14 February 1994), 'Broken Engagements' (*Oprah Winfrey Show*, 31 January 1994) – there was a sense of objectivity and detachment as both sides of the conflict were presented. The new programmes are based on a bias from the start: the programme will side with one person – usually the 'I' of the title (typically a woman). That person will confront the 'you' for his (most often) or her moral failings and demand a change. The following *Ricki Lake* titles baldly reveal this preconstructed dramatic structure: 'You Act Like You Don't Want Me . . . But I Know That You Do' (18 December 1995), 'Yeah Mom, I'm 13 . . . But I am Going to Make a Baby!' (20 December 1995), and 'Yeah, Mom/Dad, I'm Marrying "That Jerk" . . . Whether You Come to the Wedding or Not' (27 December 1995).

The morality play of talk shows has a heavily controlled logic: there is no nuance. There are clear victims and clear victimizers. The victims are accusatory and aggressive; they want justice and often revenge which the talk show gladly enacts. Retaliation is a frequent form of closure. *Richard Bey* takes such acts to their absurdist conclusion where an errant male is put into stockades by his girlfriend on an entire programme devoted to the ritual of reprisal: 'Yo! You're Busted' (5 October 1995). In another example, *Carnie*'s 'Left at the Altar' (22 November 1995) allows each rejected spouse-to-be to play out a mild form of revenge on the partner who left. On a certain level, the world of new talk is much more moralistic than the 1980s' style. There are clear right and wrong acts and there are clear penalties to pay for such acts. The humour often lies in knowing that inevitably justice will prevail. These talk shows deny restraint; they are more theatrical and self-conscious than any nineteenth-century melodrama. They are closer to highly controlled game shows or WWF wrestling matches in their excessive style, their emphasis on ritual and, most importantly, the participation of the audience. Roland Barthes writes that the attraction of wrestling was once the 'spectacle of excess' evoked through grandiloquent gestures and violent contact. It was a lower form of tragedy restaging the age-old battle between 'the perfect bastard' and the suffering hero.[10] Like wrestling, talk shows celebrate the self-consciousness of the drama where the performance breaks through the orienting boundaries of stage theatrics into the audience.

If the studio audience member represents the ideal viewer from the programme's point-of-view, the viewer is a woman of colour under 30. However, these audiences have noticeably more men than the first-generation shows. Moreover, these newer programmes demand an active studio viewer, in the words of *Ricki Lake* producers. These are not the nice middle-class white women who populate *Phil Donahue*'s studio, nor even the tasteful rainbow of women at the *Oprah Winfrey Show*. Rather, the *Ricki Lake* guests are streetwise. They must go through a metal detector and guns are routinely confiscated. Security guards sit anonymously through the audience, ready to spring if an audience member becomes too aggressive. It is not that *Ricki Lake* is beset by aggressive viewers; the show actively constructs them.

To warm up the audience and rehearse its temperament for the programme, a producer asks the studio viewers to be like a 'Ricki audience'. He picks out a random member of the audience to read a fake talk show statement such as an outrageous revelation by a guest: 'I have been impregnated by aliens'. In a highly theatrical manner a producer scolds the audience 'for sounding like a Donahue audience' by reacting too genteelly. When the woman reads the cue card again, the audience reacts uproariously – 'huge, loud, almost crazed'[11] – and the producer congratulates it on the correct 'Ricki' response. Where once audiences applauded lavishly to signal segment changes, the 'Go Ricki' chant with the arms swirling over members' heads has replaced the clapping. It causes a new level of emotional and physical response from the studio; the producers want what they call an 'edgy' feel. It is full of nervous energy which is emotionally reactive, perhaps a bit unstable, not intellectually contemplative.

Nevertheless, this new talk show audience is not undisciplined nor slow-witted; it participates and takes great pleasure in the outrageousness of the prescribed rituals of the programme. Not only do they chant, applaud and react as the show asks them, many audience responses have become ritualized set-pieces with preordained gestures, wild boasts, warnings and exclamations. The studio audience knows the show's rules; they have come prepared to out-perform the show.

For example, a *Ricki Lake* (5 October 1995) did a programme entitled 'I Talk Virgins into Sleeping with Me . . . And You May Be Next'. When Charles, the perpetrator, comes on stage, the audience unleashes a torrent of warring boos and applause from women and men respectively. As each of three former virginal women testifies as to his 'lying' ways, the audience hoots and howls with glee and anger at the man's hubris. When the audience later questions the man, many (both black and white) perform homilies with which to lecture him or to lend support to his epic conquests. A man starts by addressing Charles: 'You represent to the fullness' – to indicate a coded notion of respect. A woman audience member retorts:

> I have a comment for Charles. You should not go around hurting people and taking girls' virginity . . . because, remember this, the world is not flat and it is round. And what comes around goes around. And someday you may have a daughter and she may run into a dog just like you.

Quite pleased, Charles flashes her a smile and a victory sign. This is not the image of a sad underclass easily swept up in the programme's predatory needs of which much of the press speaks. Nor are these people with small egos in search of 15 minutes of fame. The show's need may be exploitative, but the audience is amazingly proud of and creative in their responses. They usually outclass the host's uncomfortable performance; they reveal a flair for drama, a poetic cadence and an outrageous pleasure in performance.

Beyond the producers and the studio audience, the authenticity of the guests has been a central issue in the debate about talk shows in 1995. The new talk shows make headlines for their duplicity for not only coaching real guests to repeat word-for-word/act-for-act the drama that the producers want, but for manufacturing guests. For example, the *New York Post* on 4 December 1995 announced in a headline: 'Daytime Talk Shows: Fake Guests Common in Battle for Ratings'.[12]

However, talk shows in the 1990s have changed: they are not concerned about social truths; they reveal the performance behind the notion of truth. The credibility of the older daytime talk shows depends on the legitimacy of the guests and their stories. Day after day *Phil Donahue*, *Geraldo* and the *Oprah Winfrey Show* stage the stories of the underclass. These programmes are predicated on the clear societal boundaries between victims and victimizers. The *Donahue* programme on 'Crooked Attornies' (9 February 1994) 'works' because we can identify with detailed and idiosyncratic stories of victimization at the hands of lawyers. The logic is that here is a social group with a shared problem. Yet the programme allows the guest to construct her/his own story. Sometimes it is boring and the host hurries it on, but it is their story. The signs of authenticity empower the melodrama (the tears, emotions and physicality) of these talk shows.

By 1995 talk shows produce episodes having actors or imitation guests. With eight programmes located in New York City the programmes are in a highly crowded competitive industry that thrives on innovation. The shows are in search of good 'acts' or actors who can stylistically spin a good story. The general public pronouncement by the talk show producers about their process of verification is that they attempt to cross-check the guest's story, but in the rush of the production schedule inevitably fake guests slip through. Garth Ancier, executive producer of *Ricki Lake*, argues that it results from the differences in generational ethics: 'Younger audience implies a different ethical mix, we have had to be extremely tough on the veracity of the stories.' Generally, if a talk show needs a certain kind of guest, its producers will look the other way if they have the sense that the potential guest is a poseur. The controversy over fake guests has functioned as an advertisement for viewers to try their hand at acting by calling the constant 1–800 numbers of the programmes that travel across the TV screen. Now the request appears continually during the programme like a weather alert. The shows have a voracious appetite for any American willing go on 'stage'.

By December 1995 newspaper articles were appearing stating that the talk shows were paying 'stringers' who created cattle calls for actors to 'play' lesbians and motorcycle bikers. These players would receive money indirectly from the talk shows through the stringer's fee.[13] The concept of fake guests has been part of the popular press about talk shows for over a decade. The audience has slowly grown to question the 'truth' of talk. Questions have shifted from 'Where do they get those people?' to 'Are those people real?'.

The authenticity of the stories is not as important to the success of a *Tempestt*, a *Gordon Elliott* or even a *Jerry Springer* as is the ritual of performance. 'Left at the Altar' (*Carnie*, 22 November 1995) reveals what seems to be actors playing out rather ungraceful performances of jealous lovers. Stacy, aggrieved bride-to-be, narrates in a highly rehearsed style how she discovered that Jason, her ex-fiancé, was cheating on her. Nothing is spontaneous. Her delivery style is clipped; her story smacks of the worst romanticized clichés I have seen on a talk show. And when Jason comes on, he gets the story wrong several times and becomes silent. And when the 'other' woman Jacqueline appears, a theatric rendering of a catfight takes place. The audience loves the game. They hoot when Jason comes out. They groan when the story becomes convoluted and embellished. There are shots of them shaking their heads. They laugh continuously; they are not respectful. Even when Jason proposes (a common ritual on such shows) and Stacy throws the ring into the audience with the aplomb of a bad version of Alexis Carrington, the audience goes into a frenzy – laughing and cheering. The following three pairs of guests are equally self-conscious and clumsy in their performance.

Even guests who are 'authentic' often use the occasion to be more theatrical. Typical is a *Jerry Springer* programme 'Couple in Crisis' (5 October 1995). The show's first half is devoted to the accusations between a 'redneck' wife and her cheating best friend and the inevitable physical fight that breaks between them. Then a punk couple, Mike and Dementia, are added to the stage. Mike blames Dementia (who is in complete gothic regalia with white face and lips framed by jet black and red dreadlocks) and her style for their problems. Not only is Dementia all theatre, but her friend, Ollie, who is there to support her side, is a performance. He too is gothic (white make up with blue lips), but he is also over six feet tall and two hundred pounds, sporting a black patent leather jumpsuit, five-inch platform shoes, and short-cropped bleached hair. As he enters, he parades sashaying to the rhythmic beat of the audience clapping while tossing confetti. They love him. Jerry Springer, like all hosts, plays straight to Ollie's outrageous drag queen performance, asking him what he thinks about the couple's problem. Not only is the contrast between the 'rednecks' and the 'gothics' incongruous, the difference between the straight performance of the programme which must maintain its sincerity and the theatrics on the stage is even more absurd. By 1995 almost everyone 'acts' on talk shows breaking the realist ideology that fed its identity politics beginnings and now is frustrating the viewing public's desire for social truths.

Talk in 1995: The Triumph of the Camp Aesthetic

Gay camp is the aesthetic that underlines the new talk shows in the 1990s. I expect that many people might balk at such an assertion. Camp 'exists in the besmirk of the holder'.[14] It sets up a cultural distinction between the ignorati and the cognoscenti: those who do and do not recognize the ironic attitude that is struck in talk shows. Gays have fashioned their own subversive style that serves as a dissonance critiquing the seriousness of the cultural object on display. It is a complex concept; it involves an attitude – a way of seeing the world as an outsider that refuses to take dominant tastes seriously.

Ever since Stonewall – the first public rebellion by gay men over discrimination in 1969 – gays have slowly become an unspoken taste-making culture in
America. Certain 'style professions' – ballet, musicals, interior design, fashion
design and most recently television design and production – are dominated by
gays. In my interviews in the talk show industry, I ran into two kinds of producers: straight women and gay men. Martin Berman, executive producer of
Geraldo assured me: 'Gay men are some of the best producers in the talk show
industry.'[15] As Richard Dyer points out, much of this professional work is clearly
marked as the acceptable kind of gay camp in that

> they are style for style's sake, they don't have 'serious' content (a hairstyle is not
> about anything), they don't have a practical use (they're just nice) and the actual
> forms taken accentuate artifice, fun and occasionally outrageousness . . . all that
> paraphernalia of a camp sensibility that has provided gay men with a certain
> legitimacy in the world.[16]

But as much as camp can revel in a mindless pleasure with style, it has also been
marked as a form of social commentary. Such a sensibility comes from a gay critique of the dominant 'straight' tastes of a culture and how those tastes repress
others. In his essay 'Camp and the gay sensibility' Jack Babuscio writes that it is
'a creative energy reflecting a consciousness that is different from the mainstream; a heightened awareness of certain human complications of feeling that
spring from the fact of social oppression' for gays.[17] It springs from the identity
politics movement of the 1970 as gays finally found a public identity that was
their own.
    Along with feminism, gay camp is a thorn in the side of macho male hetero-
sexuality. However, as a political tactic, it has always had an uncomfortable relationship with conventional activism. It has divided the gay community as
'straight' gays disagree with the tactics of the more rebellious and proudly
'queer' (replicating a generational split within many of identity politics groups).
They refuse the 'straight' gay his closet by publicly outing him. Michelangelo
Signorile, the *OutWeek* warrior who outed many celebrities, even appears on
Ricki Lake as an expert on gay teens (20 November 1995). Additionally, gay
ACT-UP, Queer Nation, Lesbian Avengers and Guerrilla Girls have turned
around the dominant homophobic notions of gay as 'queers' or the 'good' gay
that passes as 'straight'. These organizations have used camp – flaming queens,
macho man costumes, drag balls, queer die-ins and even guerrilla masks – to
politicize the notion of the 'acceptable' gay and lesbian. However, they have
alienated other political groups who seek to work within the dominant system
which camp parodies.
    How are talk shows themselves camp? First, contemplate the 'queen' of new
talk: Ricki Lake. Her fame is based on her roles in the films of John Waters –
the 'straight' originator of the camp sensibility for feature film. In contrast to
Oprah Winfrey's acting career in middlebrow do-good films, Lake played the
archetypical American teen in *Hairspray* (1988), *Cry Baby* (1990) and *Serial
Mom* (1994) – all send-ups about the icky-sweet family values in America. Her
supporting role on a 1970s' and 1980s' TV programme (*China Beach*) unites her
with a number of the new talk show hosts as part of retrieving marginal figures
from past popular culture and giving them a 'false' celebrityhood as hosts of
lowbrow talk shows. Mark Booth comments that camp strategy is often 'to

present oneself as being committed to the marginal with a commitment greater than the marginal merits'.[18] Here, camp takes pleasure in the self-consciousness of their wooden acting not the earnest content of the programme.

Moreover, these talk shows use style to critique the 'seriousness' of the old talk shows and their pretension to therapeutic help. Here, their style can be seen as a form of defiance – a refusal to be moral when the concern with identity politics of the old talk shows is so fraught with self-gain and market strategies. Fake guests reveal the inauthenticity of any claim of truth on talk shows. Camp reacts against puritanical morality of the identity politics of the Oprah Winfreys and the Phil Donahues. Susan Sontag argues that camp 'neutralizes moral indignation'.[19] At its best, it celebrates the outlaw nature of a people who are repressed by the dominant ethos of 'thou shall nots' while it pleads for a certain sympathy and consideration for the differences and inequality in social circumstances.[20]

Herein lies the political contradiction of camp on talk shows: it is both progressive and reactionary. At its best, the camping on talk show turns around the rhetoric of old talk shows where people of colour, women and gays were seen as victims; talk becomes a celebration of rule-breaking. The guests and audience members of *Carnie, Ricki, Tempestt* or *Charles Perez* no longer sit in long sober sad conversations about discrimination, sexism and homophobia. Rather they now play act, applaud and revel in their difference. The seriousness is intercut with colourful and often silly graphics, the shriek of audience members, or mock fights between guests.

Decorum and civility are not the mode of new talk. These programmes are upbeat, fun and 'in your face', much like the tactics of an ACT-UP demonstration for more AIDS funding. They talk about multipartner sex, promiscuity and the body without much apology. It is no wonder that conservative America is appalled. These people are out of control – their control. *Ricki Lake* and the others have not only incorporated the outrageousness of camp; they have added the language, gestures and rituals of poor black and Hispanic America as black and white guests and audience members use the street language and gestures of the African-American. The programmes encourage the use of black signs. The topics are in street vernacular (e.g. 'Yo! You're Busted', *Richard Bey,* 5 October 1995). Ricki Lake is famed for her appropriation of 'girl!' from black feminine culture as a tease for the programme. The guests and audience respond by willingly signalling their racial otherness through jewellery, gang colours, and clothing. There is an aggressive refusal to be proper as revealed through boasting of heroic sexual conquests and a pleasure in the excessiveness of the body.

Generally, the press has reacted in horror to the racial and class stereotypes being played out on these talk shows. However, the 'outlaw' type has had a long and celebrated history in American media and concepts of freedom. bell hooks argues that blacks have learned gangster culture from white society watching white gangster mythology play out in films and television. The issue for her is the white misogynist society which produces black popular culture. She writes that the American outrage at black transgression is duplicitous in that the misogyny of the black form is conditioned by the prevailing sexism of that 'white supremacist capitalism' that produces and encourages such cultural expression for profits. In fact, the press's anger at talk show representations only encourages greater interest in and therefore more profits for the white-produced programmes.[21]

Henry Louis Gates argues that representation of black outlaw culture is even more complex. On one level, he suggests, much of the black celebration of the O. J. Simpson acquittal stemmed from not only the subversion of a white justice system which has failed blacks repeatedly, but the display of black prowess during the trial. But on another level, he warns about the tendency of ' "outlaw culture" which unites our lumpenproles with postmodern ironists – to celebrate transgression for its own sake'.[22] On talk shows the guests and audience members have triumphed in the rebellion against the social and sexual civility of the white middle class that characterized 'advice' in America since the latter half of the 1800s. But Gates worries if such displays of being *bad* have lost their attachment to a social agenda and are now merely playful.

However, this sensibility is also reactionary; it stops political change. If nothing is to be taken seriously, then nothing needs to change. Yet these new talk shows still depend on real social issues as fodder for their content. Their programmes are about unprotected sex with AIDS (*Jerry Springer*, 2 October 1995), women with little or no self-esteem (*Ricki Lake*, 21 November 1995), black women who get beaten up by their gangsta boyfriends (*Richard Bey*, 5 October 1995) and drug users (*Montel Williams*, 22 November 1995). They parade the underclass on the shows – often missing teeth, drugged, unable to talk, and/or intimidated by the television process – all marked by an unjust social system. But then the production process camps it up, leaving the sensibility that you cannot take anything too seriously – not even the poverty and physical abuse suffered by these people. Not everything is a joke; we need to know about the social logic of this repression. The camp aesthetics stops the questioning. This is why the left has reacted so angrily to talk shows.

Conclusion

In many ways these new talk shows can be read as a celebration of outlaw culture – gay, black and/or female. None of these new talk shows were as simplistic or mindless as the established press said. They may be amoral, but the shifts in tone, political points of view and styles are vertiginous and contradictory. At their worst they exploited and made people inured to social injustice. But at their best, they finally offered an active, even aggressive 'in your face' identity to people who have been represented either as victims or perverts by a dominant culture.

On one level, this argument supports a classical reading in cultural studies: the carnivalesque. Through their emphasis on the physical excesses, scandal and their offensiveness to the *status quo*, talk shows reproduce much of the same liberatory pleasures that carnival provided in Rabelais's world. Bakhtin writes: 'Carnival celebrated the temporary liberation from the prevailing truth of the established order: it marked the suspension of all hierarchical rank, norms, and prohibitions.'[23] However, Umberto Eco cautions how such rule-breaking could also be a form of 'authorized transgression'. He argues that although comedy is built around breaking rules, the rules are always in the background. Eco writes: 'Our pleasure is a mixed one because we enjoy not only the breaking of the rule, but also the disgrace of an animal-like individual [the transgressor].'[24] Talk shows repeat this form of law enforcement because we are able to play out our transgressive desires through identification with this 'low' culture of talk show guests without ever having to leave our orderly complacent world.

Nevertheless, *Richard Bey* stopped airing in Boston in December 1995. In January 1996 *Gabrielle* and *Richard Perez* were cancelled. That month Phil Donahue quit. Geraldo Rivera also announced he would like to be a network anchorman and changed the title of *Geraldo* to *The Geraldo Rivera Show* featuring more hard news stories. With programmes entitled 'Advice to Oprah Letter Writers' (1 December 1995) and 'Tipping and Gift Anxiety' (29 November 1995) Oprah Winfrey had gone on a 'spiritual quest of moral uplift' – returning to the values associated with the bourgeois tradition of feminine advice. There is even a suggestion that talk shows are going to return to the *Mike Douglas* style of the 1960s as the light entertainment of celebrity talk. It appears that we have gone full circle; talk is returning to the banter of an apolitical America in the mid-1960s.[25]

There is now less bad taste and incivility on television. But who or what has Bill Bennett's Empower America campaign protected? The disenfranchised from exploitative convoluted images of itself? Or the American middle class from dealing with the impolite and impolitic behaviour of its underclass? What is sadly lost is an important venue for average people to debate social issues that affect their everyday lives. Those discussions may not have taken place in total freedom as in the idealized public sphere as imagined by Jürgen Habermas. Nor did they follow the language and habits of civil debate. But with talk shows, we have only begun to consider how our notions of 'good taste' mask power and stop debate.

Notes

1.   Statement by William Bennett in press release from Empower America, Washington, DC, 26 October, 1995, p.1

2.   'Talk is Cheap', *The Nation*, 5 June 1995, p. 800.

3.   Other talk shows in 1995 are *Danny!, Gabrielle, Charles Perez, Marilu, Shirley* and *Mark*. Shows that were launched in the early 1990s are: *Bertice Berry, Vicki!, Les Brown, Jane Whitney, Leeza, Dennis Prager* and *Rolonda*.

4.   Jane Feuer, 'Genre and television', *Channels of Discourse: Reassembled* (Chapel Hill: University of North Carolina, 1985), p.156.

5.   Oprah Winfrey, 'Truth, trash, and TV', *TV Guide*, 11–17 November 1995, pp. 15–16.

6.   Ibid., p. 18.

7.   As evidence here is a week's worth of her programme titles from October–November 1995: 'Oprah's Child Alert: Children and Guns, Part I' (30 October), 'Are You Still Haunted by Your First Love?' (31 October), 'Caroline Kennedy on Privacy' (1 November), 'Loni Anderson' (2 November), and 'What Your House Says about You' (3 November).

8.   Bradley S. Greenberg and Sandi Smith, 'The content of television talk shows: topics, guest and interactions', Report prepared for the Kaiser Family Foundation, Michigan State University (November 1995), pp. 1–7.

9.   The competitive pressure for new and more revelatory conflict has led to a series of ongoing confessions by ex-producers of talk shows. For example, Joni Cohen-Zlotowitz (former *Charles Perez* producer) states: 'We were told by the corporate people

we had to put conflict into every segment . . . And the conflict had to be wild. Get a fight going the first segment or you're going to lose [the audience]. Those are the guidelines.' She also recalls producing a show called 'I Have a Surprise I Want to Tell You' in which a young woman told her father that she worked as a stripper. She said that she refused when she was told to have the woman perform in front of her dad. The supervising producer screamed at me: 'That's what makes this show'. Chuck Sennett (lawyer for the *Charles Perez* show) 'acknowledged conflict is a key element in the program, noting that it "is a part of every talk show from *Charles Perez* to *The McLaughlin Group*"', Meredith Berkman, 'Liars send in clowns for sicko circuses', *New York Post*, 4 December 1995, p.8.

10.　'The world of wrestling', in Susan Sontag (ed.), *A Barthes Reader* (New York: Wang and Hill, 1982), p.23.

11.　Traci Grant, 'Ricki Lake's TV talk-show formula', *Boston Globe*, 18 December 1994, p.B5.

12.　Meredith Berkman, 'Daytime talk shows: fake guests common in battle for ratings', *New York Post*, 4 December, 1995.

13.　Berkman, 'Liars send in clowns for sicko circuses', p.8.

14.　Thomas Hess, quoted in Andrew Ross, *No Respect: Intellectuals and Popular Culture* (New York: Routledge, 1989), p.145.

15.　Interview with Martin Berman, New York City, 6 March 1994.

16.　Richard Dyer, 'It's being so camp as keeps us going,' *Only Entertainment* (London: Routledge, 1992), p.138.

17.　Jack Babuscio, 'Camp and the gay sensibility', in *Gays and Film*, ed. Richard Dyer (New York: Zoetrope Books, 1984), p.42.

18.　Mark Booth, *Camp* (New York: Quartet, 1983), p.18.

19.　Susan Sontag, 'Notes on camp', *Against Interpretation* (New York: Octagon, 1978) p.288.

20.　Babuscio, 'Camp and gay sensibility', p.42.

21.　*Outlaw Culture: Resisting Representation* (New York: Routledge, 1994), p.118.

22.　'Thirteen ways of looking at a black man', *New Yorker*, 23 October 1995, p.60.

23.　*Rabelais and his World* (Cambridge, MA: MIT Press, 1968), p.10.

24.　Umberto Eco, 'The frame of comic "freedom" ', in *Carnival*, ed. Thomas A. Seboek (Berlin: Mouton, 1985), p.6.

25.　Fred Biddle, 'TV new shocker: the talk turns tame', *Boston Globe*, 5 January 1996, p.1.

INTRODUCTION TO CHAPTER 13

Like some other contributors in Section III, Peter Humm turns his attention to the question of access and the relationship between 'real people' who for various reasons want to appear on television and the professionals who enable that to happen. Humm concentrates on access programming which, unlike the programmes discussed by O'Sullivan which are produced as light entertainment, hand over a degree of editorial control to the amateur maker. Humm reminds us that this drive to let people make programmes is not new and he traces debts to North American programmes of the late 1960s and 1970s, while at the same time recognising that in a British context the BBC's legal and public services commitments to education and to representing a cross-section of Britain are also important factors. Humm's account of the BBC's Community Programme Unit which lets the less powerful in to make television contrasts vividly with Freedman's notion of activists demanding air time.

Humm focuses in particular on the way in which the amateur television maker has to be fitted in to the institutional arrangements for production and reception. He examines the views of producers who act as mediators between the film-makers and the institutional expectations about production, organisation and quality. He looks also at examples of how this access programming is received by critics who are uneasy about what the combination of education, representation and entertainment can deliver.

Humm takes up two major themes in his essay. Firstly, he reflects on how the difference between the amateur and the professional has to be marked through a style which privileges the signs of inexperience – wobbly camera work, lack of narrative focus and technical disasters which are not completely edited out. Humm suggests that these formal marks are required less by the film-makers (who are increasingly becoming more professional) but by producers and critics who need them to mark out the authenticity which is the premise of this programme-making. In a reverse strategy, of course, those who are interested in making cheap programmes can claim that their technical roughness is in the interests of authenticity rather than cost.

Secondly, Humm draws attention to a shift in access programming from the community-based projects of the early years to the personalised, diary formats; he suggests here a move from the public to the private sphere, a change from programmes which made a public case for representation on the part of a particular group to those which reveal the everyday intimacies and accidents of private lives. In part, Humm attributes this to changing levels of access which give individuals personal control of their own camcorders rather than having to rely on group access. More generally, he suggests that the change is linked to broader changes within television generally, which downplay the importance of communal activity and emphasise the private and the personal. The attempts to turn access programmes into soaps following the lives of real people are entirely logical in this respect. Humm closes with an account of the way in which particular interest groups, like environmental activists, have used video to both record and act as witness to their campaigns against road-building. In this instance, the groups follow the route of the groups who feature in Kintz's study; they make the material and distribute it through an alternative news service, refusing the 'open door' of mainstream television.

13

Real TV: Camcorders, Access and Authenticity

Peter Humm

Among the current nightly offerings on Sky One, Rupert Murdoch's most cheaply available British cable channel, is a programme called *Real TV*. It mixes together camcorder footage of police drug busts, skidding car wrecks, tourist encounters with threatening wild life and all the grainy, unrehearsed collisions with reality that have become a staple of contemporary television. Sky provides a tabloid version of the 'real people shows' defined by Sue Dinsmore as those featuring anyone who appears on television, but does not make their living out of producing television programmes (Dinsmore, 1994).

Such shows appear in many television genres. In British television alone there is weekend light entertainment in *Blind Date* or *You've Been Framed!*, daily polemic in *Your Shout* or *The Slot*, as well as *Video Diaries*, which make up the BBC's *Video Nation* and stand in that long documentary tradition of representing 'real lives'. Channel 4 has been particularly generous in handing over camcorders to members of the public, be they the lager lads mocked by *The Girlie Show* or the holiday-makers whose taped adventures abroad make up *The Real Holiday Show*.

You've Been Framed! ends each week with Jeremy Beadle's encouraging promise to his viewers: next time, 'the star of the show could be you'. The tensions implicit in making a spectacle out of the ordinary run through this entire tradition. One way of interpreting these programmes and their histories is to consider the various roles of the real and ordinary person as star performer, as reporter, as author or even maybe as *auteur*.

Even the most showbiz spectacle of *Blind Date* or *You've Been Framed!* is structured around a contest for authorial control. Just who is telling these stories – real people or the television professionals? One of the cruel pleasures of *Blind Date* is hearing the edgy voices of the contestants perched on their shiny stools as they negotiate the narrative puns and innuendo imposed by the rehearsal scriptwriters and by Graham's avuncular voice-over. There is a similar nervousness in Beadle's manic hosting of stars whose twinkle is never allowed to outshine Jeremy.

The punning ambiguity of *You've Been Framed!* emphasises the extent to which these predictable scenes of domestic mishap are set up, not by the amateur camcorder operator who lures the family cat into a plausible collision, but by the man whose television career is founded on ambushing the gullible. But even in the Reithian outpost of the BBC's Community Programme Unit, there is an uneasy tension in the representation of these videotaped lives, which are meant to both inform and entertain the viewers. Take a brief pre-title sequence from a programme shown in 1995.

> A grandmotherly figure sits down in her garden chair, drops the clip mic, pins it more firmly to her dress and then mouths soundlessly at the camera; a couple on a sofa groan that once again the battery has betrayed them; another couple anxiously admit they should know by now that if the red light goes out they're in trouble. The red light goes out.

This display of engagingly amateur incompetence is how BBC2 chose to introduce a 'bumper collection of the best entries to our Video Nation Diary 1995'. It is, of course, a rhetorical trick; television's equivalent of abandoning the written text to demonstrate that this time the speech is from the heart, not the auto cue. The clumsiness is a ploy designed to prove that what we are about to hear and see is real, authentic, unmediated by what professionals call over-fondly 'the magic of television'. But it is those professionals, not the silenced fumbler with the clip mic, who decided on this teasing introductory device. What, then, does the popularity of real people shows tell us about the contemporary rhetoric and aesthetics of television and, in particular, about politically charged issues of authorship and control?

Such questions have both a formal and cultural significance; they also have a long history dating back to the first experiments in access television. In 1972 a small group of programme-makers attached to BBC2's *Late Night Line Up* established the BBC's Community Programme Unit. They had been impressed by programmes developed in North America in the late 1960s: New York's *Open Channel*, Canada's *Challenge for Change* and especially WGBH Boston's *Catch 44*, set up in 1970 to operate a studio in which the public could make programmes on a first-come, first-served basis.

On one improvised occasion in 1971, *Line Up* took a film crew to a Guinness factory canteen to record workers' views on television programmes. Tony Bilbow, the presenter, was told firmly by the Guinness workers that the BBC would not be interested in the opinions of ordinary viewers and that anything they did say was bound to be edited to fit BBC prejudices. *Line Up* answered the challenge by showing the film in a deliberately rough editing style, which included in the final credits the film clapper boards.

In this dry run for *Open Door*, which began two years later, two key tenets of access philosophy were established. As Jeremy Gibson, a former head of the Community Programme Unit, said in 1992, ' the maxim that we exist by has not really changed. We exist to represent the under-represented, the mis-represented or the non-represented' (Dovey, 1993: 164). Giles Oakley, the present head of the Unit, describes their philosophy in similar terms:

> Access to the airwaves is not a simple business ... not everybody has an equal chance of getting representations of their lives, accurate or fair in their own terms ... our department exists, to some extent, to redress that imbalance, to try and hold the ring to the advantage of those people who are not already powerful and don't have a virtually automatic entry into the media. (Evans, 1996: 12)

What is evident in these statements of mission is that access programming, historically and presently, is led by the professionals. It is the professional programme-makers looking at the work of other professional programme-makers in North America who push open the door. Pressure does not come from people demanding air time for films they make at home on a Bolex or camcorder. The emphasis from the start is on a traditional notion of advocacy – the *bourgeoisie oblige* of the BBC producer.

At the same time, there has been a historical commitment to the formal consideration of how that presentation is to be made. *Radio Times*, in its launch publicity for *Open Door*, promised that in this programme, 'people and groups are given a chance to have their own say in their own way'. Compare this emphasis with a key phrase in the 1977 Annan Committee Report recommending a new channel which would 'say something new in new ways' (Jivani, 1990: 22).

When Jeremy Isaacs recruited his first staff for Channel 4's launch in 1982, several, including channel controller Paul Bonner, and Mike Bolland, in charge of youth programming, had worked for the BBC Community Programme Unit. In September the following year, Channel 4 began *People to People*, which ran for seven years. The 'crucial idea' of this series was: 'collaborative production, the making of television programmes with and by members of a community, which truly reflect their ideas and experiences and not that of the professional programme makers' (Oakley, 1990: 17). In this first decade of access programmes, there is a tension between the commitment of television professionals to broaden the range of those represented on television and the search for new modes of expression. At the centre of this debate is what can be called the aesthetics of authenticity, that particular style through which we are accustomed to equate the shakiness of the camera with the truth of what it records.

In 1985, *People to People* broadcast *The Battle of Orgreave*, a film commemorating an epic occasion in the previous year's miners' strike. The 90-minute film mixes together interviews with miners and their supporters, archive footage and historical narration, reconstructions of particular incidents and immediate news coverage of the battle between police and miners, some shot by ITN and some by members of a local community action group.

The professional footage is credited to ITN while similar scenes recorded by Steel Bank Film Co-op are labelled 'Amateur Video'. Both show shocking incidents of police cavalry-charging the lines of miners while individual strikers are chased and beaten by supporting policemen in armoured riot gear. But where the ITN crew with their costly Betacam stand back at some distance, the non-professionals with their hand-held camcorders are caught up in the middle of the action. The steady professional camerawork of ITN provides us with the detached viewpoint of the reporter; the amateur video forces us to be jostled with the camera. ITN makes us see their footage as a witness; the community group makes us into a participant.

In *Storm Over 4*, his personal account of Channel 4's foundation, Jeremy Isaacs describes his ambition that 'somehow new ideas, wonky ideas ... would be put forward. I was after a combination of professional experience, of relevant but disparate disciplines and of innocent inexperience, if there was invention to go with it' (1989: 35). It is the wonkiness of ideas produced by inventive yet innocent inexperience that interests me. As Jon Dovey, among other critics of access television, has pointed out, 'the camcorder's aesthetic depends on our tendency as viewers to interpret low resolution as veracity; the "amateur video" tag on newscasts signals subjectivity but also immediacy and truth' (1993: 168). There is throughout the history and continuing practice of access television, a marked assumption that an innocent, subjective veracity is most convincingly conveyed wonkily.

In America, with its 14 million camcorders, there are weekly networked shows such as *I Witness Video* and *Hard Copy* broadcasting the news stories sent in by those patrolling the mean streets with their amateur equipment but increasingly professional sense of what the market will pay for an up-close and personal report. The beating of Rodney King by members of the Los Angeles Police Department in 1991 – on 3 March at 12.53 a.m. as the date on the video tape tells us – has become iconic. The presenter of *I Witness Video* introduces each week's reports against a video-wall background repeating in merciless slow motion the clubbing which fuelled the Los Angeles riots.

The subsequent trial of the four police officers prompted considerable debate over the credibility of George Holliday's clumsier footage: the defence made much of these moments when the camera zoomed out of evidentiary focus. Alongside these legal arguments, however, goes a popular questioning of the apparent connection between wobbly focus and a believable report. As camcorder operators discover the steadying virtues of a tripod and learn the grammar of television composition, they give rise to questions about framing and intent which nervy hand-held footage does not allow. When 'amateur videos' are sent in not by accidental, once-in-a-lifetime witnesses but by dedicated pursuers of hard copy, those filming and directing the stories become open to the questioning to which every professional reporter is properly subject.

The most Americanised of current British access programmes is Channel 4's *Takeover TV*, whose pitch proclaims its promotion of 'Television of the people by the people'. This television revolution is made possible by the fact that 15 million British citizens have access to home video equipment. The tension here between the camcorder user as public citizen and a chronicler of private family life is a significant one. There has been a marked shift in the 25-year history of access programmes from those made by community groups to the individually authored stories featured in *Free for All* or the pointedly named *Video Diaries*. Now that camcorders are more often privately owned than shared among those meeting after work in the community centre, there is a far greater concentration upon the personal witness.

Open Door had invited 'grass-roots' organisations to submit programme ideas, to be selected by an editorial group, which democratically included the Unit's secretaries. Channel 4's *Free for All*, which ran for over 50 editions between 1991 and 1994, described its relationship with its sources in a more individual fashion. As John Samson, the head of Filmit Productions and series editor of *Free for All* put it:

> people come to you and say I don't want to be a one-off article in a newspaper; I actually want to say it myself the way I want to say it. Because I don't want a story about me by somebody else; I want a story by me. (Dovey, 1993: 170)

Filmit gives each prospective author a 12-point statement describing their rights. These include the right to have their view, opinion or story told in an unmediated way in a form they choose and under their control; to take joint responsibility with Filmit for the creative realisation of the item; to be involved in the off-line edit.

In describing its authors as 'viewers turned reporters', *Free for All* was clear about its status and function as 'a current affairs programme where you call the shots'. Its weekly broadcasts in the prime slot of 8.00 on Thursday evenings were backed by a regular newspaper providing further information and contacts. The emphasis on creating a dialogue with its contributors was designed to distinguish *Free for All* from what Roger Shannon, one of its producers, described as:

> traditional notions of access [which] seemed to always be about a series of victims with a particular genre and styles attached to that. We wanted to celebrate people's diversity. Access is too often about putting gripes on TV. A sense of being neglected isn't always about gripes. Someone's sense of achievements are often neglected also and sometimes that's what people want access for. (Evans, 1996: 29)

Free for All assured its potential contributors that 'no television experience is necessary – a TV production team is standing by to help you put your case'. Most of its broadcast stories were accordingly shot by a professional crew on Betacam and edited with full use of graphics, music and a fast-moving sharpness with 'no professional presenter to get in the way'.

This carries the risk that evident high production values undermine rather than enhance the credibility of the case that its campaigning reporters are presenting. The tension between a professional sense of what contributes 'good television' and the demand for authenticity is revealed again and again in the comments of programme-makers and critics alike.

At the 1995 Edinburgh Television Festival debate on DIY TV, the producers of *Video Diaries* and *Video Nation*, *The Real Holiday Show* and *Takeover TV* made their case against a barrage laid down by critics in the press:

> for the cost of a tape and Hi 8 camera, producers get cheap as chips telly which they pass off as being edgy and innovative. (Paul Ross, *The Tatler*, May 1994)

> What irritates is that the whole thing pretends to be a spurious democratisation of the film-making process without actually delivering it, because you can't. (Andrew Davidson, *Guardian*, 14 November 1994)

> *Takeover TV* is like all DIY – enormously rewarding for those banging in the nails. It leaves onlookers with the feeling it might have been better to pay someone who knew what they were doing. (Allison Pearson, *Independent on Sunday*, 14 May 1995)

Television critics are notorious for preferring the flashing pleasures of their own style to the daily grind of studying television schedules, yet this rhetorical salvo is understandable when set against the solid simplicities of professional presenters. Robert Llewelyn, who introduced *I Camcorder*, assured his audience that the camcorder 'has given every living human being the chance to make their own television programmes every bit as good as the real ones'. Gaby Roslin, the presenter of *The Real Holiday Show*, shares a similarly untroubled notion of real television:

> Welcome to the first of a new series: *The Real Holiday Show*. It's real people on real holidays. We gave them a camcorder and with our help they recorded an inside view of what went on. They let us have the tapes and our tape editor Lucy and a producer put them together. It's as simple as that. (Edinburgh Television Festival, 1995)

David MacMahon, the programme's Executive Producer, knows that it is not quite that simple. In that same Edinburgh debate, he described the camera training given to the holiday-makers by the Associate Producer, who joins them for the first couple of days:

> 'Try to keep the camera still, don't zoom in and out of the place and make sure that if you're talking about something you show us what you're talking about.' That's the sort of process we do simply because we did a pilot and we didn't give that sort of instruction so we got three hours of wind-surfing holiday, which didn't mean anything. That's the problem. It's all about telling the story properly. (Edinburgh Television Festival, 1995)

Fenton Bailey, the Executive Producer of *Takeover TV*, has an even sharper notion of how to tell stories on television. He describes how items for the show are chosen from the thousands of tapes sent in:

> There was only one concern ... was it compelling? does it make good TV? ... A genuine valid concern about issues wasn't enough to guarantee a space in the show. We felt it had to be done in a compelling and entertaining way ... A good example of that I think is Daisy Witch, who protested against the Criminal Justice Bill by removing her clothes. Although we had lots of tapes about the Criminal Justice Bill, this was one which really popped and really stood out. I thought it made a great piece of TV and made a point at the same time too. (Edinburgh Television Festival, 1995)

Not surprisingly, then, selection and edition are still critical processes in the making and broadcasting of access television. *The Real Holiday Show* attracted 9000 applicants, the BBC's *Video Nation* is very carefully composed by those choosing whom to let in. As Bob Long, producer of *Video Diaries*, explains:

> We've only got eight slots a year so we have to choose ... We don't have a set figure but about half of the people who do *Video Diaries* are people who have written in. So that's about 4 out of 3,000 [applicants]. The others are people who we've set down and talked about ... Last year we decided we ought to dip into mental health. Therefore we did and got a very good diary out of that. (Edinburgh Television Festival, 1995)

David MacMahon is equally concerned to achieve what Long calls 'a very broad sense of Britain':

> One of our most difficult processes in ... selection is to make sure we've got the mix of people; not only the obvious ethnic, age mix, sexual orientation mix, but it was a question of 'Where are they going? Are they going on cheap packages? ... on luxury holidays? Are there families who may have a disability in the family?' ... the selection process is part of the question: 'Are we going to make balanced programming?'
> (Edinburgh Television Festival, 1995)

The shooting ratio on these programmes would exhaust any fly on the holiday villa wall. The average on *Video Diaries* is 180 hours' filming for a one-hour programme: the record is 500 hours. The resultant need for frequent contact between the diarist and the producer – four to five phone calls a week – as well as intensive editing underlines once more the anxieties over authenticity. In a review of *My Demons*, a Video Diary broadcast in 1991, the *Independent's* anonymous critic commented that 'the diary was just a bit too polished (even amateur television seems too slick these days) ... The juiciest, truest diaries are those not meant for publication' (29 July 1991). John Naughton in the *Observer* was fiercer: 'like any diary written for publication, these home movies are unreliable if not downright incredible. Seeing is not believing, even when the camera shakes' (26 May 1991).

In 1994 Jonnie Turpie, who had worked on the pilot for *Free for All*, and Tony Steyger from the BBC's Community Programme Unit founded Maverick Television. They produced four series of *Video Diaries*, which were screened during BBC1's *Good Morning with Anne and Nick*. These diaries were filmed on Hi 8, which has become Maverick's favoured format. As Claire Welch, Maverick's production manager explains:

> Hi 8 is not a replacement for Beta or film. It's just a different format. The reason for doing things on Hi 8 is to get the immediacy, the intimacy and the reality. Hi 8 is reactional. (Evans, 1996: 30)

Jonnie Turpie emphasises the aesthetic advantages of using a camera which costs one-tenth of professional Betacam equipment:

> A Hi 8 camera is part of the action rather than being outside the performance. You get the feeling of truth. There's great direct eye-to-eye contact. It's more engaging. People *want* to tell you what they feel. (Evans, 1996: 30)

Maverick's latest project is *Celebrity Diaries*, which will rely heavily upon the strange urge of the famous to reveal themselves in the sanctuary of a television confessional. A Hi 8 diary will, we assume, provide the authentic revelation that the sofa-managed conversation with Oprah or Vanessa or even the hard chair of Jeremy (Paxman and Isaacs) never quite achieves.

And yet these films will need to employ those now recognised codes of authenticity – unsteady cam; sharp swings in mood and focus; with luck, some breakdown in front of the camcorder – to convince us that we are encountering the real person beneath the celebrity image. It will be the editor and producer who will have to persuade the celebrity that truthful television, good television requires the viewer seeing all those moments that any agent might prefer to leave out. Otherwise, we will be back to the soft puffery of *Hello*.

Maverick are also involved with APT productions in the Hi 8 us Project, a mobile TV unit taking accessible facilities on the road. But generally, the resistance to this politically charged shift from the collective to the individual is led by production companies, who are no longer interested (if they ever were) in attracting the support of Commissioning Editors from the big four channels. Small World Video produce *Undercurrents*, 'the first ever alternative news service on video. Published every few months, it challenges the mainstream media's definition of news' (blurb).

The five editions of *Undercurrents* produced in the last three years include stories such as: 'The Buck Stops Here – using camcorders to stop hunting'; 'Welcome to the Jungle – DIY Pirate Radio in the council estates of London'; 'Barbie Liberation Front – Barbie dolls give themselves "corrective surgery" to confront sexism'. The commonest subject is reporting the many anti-road campaigns from the M11 to Skye to Newbury and stopping *en route* with 'The Green Man – wassailing to stop road building in Coventry'. Thomas Harding, a director of Small World, has set up a Camcorder Action Network of a hundred or so activists ready to provide the videotaped evidence that is increasingly called upon to contest the official version of events recorded by the Group Four security guard or the police. Harding is concerned not just with radical content but also the form of these alternative reports:

Some people might consider it a backward move shifting to camcorders from Betacam gear and switching to more localised concerns but they would be missing the point. It's effectively getting issues across. Development in camcorder technology, coupled with falling prices and therefore easier access to the tools of exposure, meant activists were more capable of getting down to the nitty gritty. (*Camcorder User*, August 1995)

Getting to the nitty gritty calls for a particular camera style, which in turn forces questions of political change on to the schedule. As Harding explains:

Another good reason for having a camcorder around is you get that visual appreciation ... Camcorder footage is more immediate and emotional. It gets you involved. Our criteria is whether it will bring about change, the concrete political effect of the film. (*Camcorder User*, August 1995)

In films such as *Unreasonable Force*, a 12-minute account of the contest between security firms and campaign groups, there is, in Dinsmore's phrase, a 'simultaneity of action and record', which breaks against the conventional grammar of television reporting and thereby increases its political impact (Dinsmore, 1994: 45). The camcorder operator swings between an alarmed anti-road campaigner and the advancing security guards marching up the hill to put an end to the interview being recorded. Authenticity is guaranteed by the wavering inaccuracy of the camcorder's panning and zoom. As the camera is pushed back, we retreat on the side of the campaigners.

At one point, the activists are themselves videotaped by Group Four's own camcorder operator who is asked 'Have you had much training in photography?'. That question has a particular resonance in understanding the effectiveness of such alternative video. It is because these reports disrupt the conventions of politically detached documentary – the training that keeps interviewers from cutting in or allows editors to insert answers recorded later – that they are so revealing.

There are two obvious dangers here. One is over-aestheticising a style of filming prompted not by debates in media studies but by the very real threats of helmeted bullies landing real punches as they drag people down from the trees at Newbury. The other is ignoring mainstream television's use of similarly dodging camera work as Roger Cook or Joe Layburn is pummelled by those they seek to expose. This is where questions of form become linked with those political questions of authorship and control that began and now end this essay. Mainstream television is increasingly appropriating the shaky, skewed style pioneered by access programmes and those maverick organisations such as Small World and the Camcorder Action Network. Comedians such as Mark Thomas or Steve Coogan produce their own camcorder investigations or parody video diaries while Radion soap powder, Pot Noodles and Corsa Vegas from Vauxhall are advertised in the grainy lurch of Beadle vision.

This sophisticated quoting of the familiar aesthetic of the domestic camcorder disguises important issues of cost and, crucially, distribution. Details of programme financing are difficult to discover but there is no reason to disbelieve those working for the Community Programme Unit or Filmit or Maverick when they say that their budgets are comparable to any other form of current affairs production. But the use of Super VHS or Hi 8 in *Video Diaries* or *Moving People* increases not only the range and number of programme-makers but also the viewing public's tolerance of lower definition videotape and poorer picture quality. This widening definition of what is acceptable as broadcast standard allows *The Real Holiday Show* to equate the cheap with the authentic.

The Beadle Company has produced another camcorder series besides the ever-repeated *You've Been Framed!*. *Beadle's Hot Shots* introduced short home movie features revealing their makers' enthusiasm for dressing up family and friends as the cast of their tribute to Steven Spielberg or James Cameron.

This move from documentary to fiction can be read as a significant step in the creation of a society confident enough in its media literacy to produce as well as consume television narrative. As Fenton Bailey suggested at Edinburgh, the next technological advance will be in cheaper home-editing systems:

> We're getting more and more tapes that are already edited and all we have to do is drop it in. Maybe sometimes we'll tighten it up and make it a little bit sharper ... but more and more people are editing their own materials and sending us completed edited pieces. (Edinburgh Television Festival, 1995)

Home-editing may demystify the magic of television but only in a narrowly formalist fashion. Helen Fielding, who worked for *Nationwide* explained the corrupting effect of television's mystique:

> Its obvious power and the notion of apparently unfathomable technological skills behind it has created a particular atmosphere which still lives on in the industry: a ridiculous self importance, the notion of Us and Them – we in the know and they, the punters who admire and envy us and long to get in front of the lenses.
> (*Independent*, 15 September 1994)

We punters may be beginning to fathom the technology but we will remain excluded as long as they in the industry control access to the key power of distribution. Mike Fentiman of the Community Programme Unit sees the history of access programming as a slow change from a process of mediation by the professional broadcaster to a more open dialogue between the professional and amateur would-be broadcaster: 'It then depends entirely on the conscience of the professional broadcaster as to how far he/she lets go of the controls ... if I was writing a thesis, having worked in this business for 30 years on and off, my title would be "Better Than Nothing"' (quoted in Evans, 1996: 39).

That is a depressing if honest statement from deep within the television industry. One of the pioneers of community programming was the Dutch broadcaster Liebje Hoekendijk, who said that the trouble with television is that it always has the last word – Good Night.

I do not want to end with any professional mediator between those viewing at home and those invited, just for a moment, to star on the screen. Instead, I would like to leave the last word to my favourite contributor to that 1995 anthology of *Video Nation* – Lauren Bateman of Wallington, Surrey.

Lauren and her mother are arguing over Lauren's deeply felt wish to have her hair purple. Just as things are getting heated, Lauren notices the camcorder in the corner and demands it be turned off. The Video Diarist goes on filming; so Lauren pulls the plug.

Acknowledgements

I first presented some of these ideas at a lecture in the National Film Theatre in March 1996;. I would like to thank Carole Walker of the British Film Institute for her help in tracing the archive material whose unseen presence flickers through the chapter.

I owe particular thanks to Sue Evans, whose dissertation provided me with valuable material from interviews conducted in her research.

References

DINSMORE, S., 1994: Introduction to *Watching Ourselves: Real People on Television*. National Film Theatre Conference, May.

——, 1996: 'Strategies for self-scrutiny. *Video Diaries* 1990–1993'. In Colin McCabe and Duncan Petrie (eds), *New Scholarship from BFI Research*. London: British Film Institute.

DOVEY, J., 1993: 'Old dogs and new tricks: access television in the UK'. In Tony Dowmunt (ed.), *Channels of Resistance*. London: British Film Institute.

EDINBURGH TELEVISION FESTIVAL, 1995: Transcript of debate on DIY TV, 28 August.

EVANS, S., 1996: *To what Extent is the Camcorder enabling Access, Participation and Control to the Ordinary Citizen in the Broadcast Environment?* Birmingham: University of Central England.

ISAACS J., 1989: *Storm Over 4: A Personal Account*. London: Weidenfeld and Nicolson.

JIVANI, A., 1990: 'Making a difference: the impact of Channel Four'. In Janet Willis and Tana Wollen (eds), *The Neglected Audience*. London: British Film Institute.

OAKLEY, G., 1990: 'Opening up the box'. In Janet Willis and Tana Wollen (eds), *The Neglected Audience*. London: British Film Institute.

INTRODUCTION TO CHAPTER 14

Linda Kintz's essay, as she suggests, looks at a neglected area – the videos produced for education and proselytising work by religious conservative groups in the USA. She looks at the way in which educational videos like these can be used in a variety of contexts – the home, schools, community groups, cable access channels – and can indeed be tailored for their particular audience. In Cultural Studies work, the active reader who is resistant to the ideological claims of the mass media tends to be understood in progressive terms as someone who works on the text to create meanings which support or even empower those who are oppressed. Kintz reminds us of the activity of the conservative right who seek both to restrict what can be shown on television and video and to provide their own versions of popular imagery and narratives. She suggests that the imagery and language of the videos, far from being outside the mainstream, can be found also in political debates in the USA, The videos thus speak to anxieties and needs within American society and provide an organised response to the uncertainties and instabilities of postmodernism. Kintz writes as a feminist who is deeply critical of these videos but points to the crucial importance of the way in which women are given a key role in their textual and emotional organisation.

Kintz's method is to analyse the form and mode of address in three videos in order to see how they construct a world in which their arguments make sense. The imagery she describes has much in common with that of the media they are criticising – children under threat, Halloween monsters, the links between sexuality and death. The videos try to make literal what is feared, creating dramatic and compressed metaphors to arouse horror about what must be opposed, whether it be sex before marriage or AIDS. The argument is made through a single narrator who places these stories in an educational context, calling on experts and witnesses and controlling what we see. Kintz suggests that the often unstable visual material is organised through a set of binary oppositions – the godly/the rest, inside/outside, good/evil, purity/promiscuity – which work to provide a desired clarity in an unstable society. Furthermore, she suggests that the videos draw consistently on metaphors which combine religious and financial discourses, metaphors of payment, cost and price in a way which inextricably links the market of the fiscal conservatives with the salvation of the religious right.

At the heart of this is the figure of the woman who acts as narrator and transforms that role into one of nurturing and mediation. Kintz points to the way in which the private, domestic role of the mother which is such a strong feature of conservative ideologies is deployed here in a public space, though a public space which is rather hidden in the personal networks of home, school and church. This 'modern traditional woman', who can be found in political parties and PTAs as well as in the videos, mediates between impersonal fiscal systems based on the market and the sexual and emotional concerns of the domestic sphere. To miss this dimension of emotion and feeling is, Kintz suggests, to miss an important element of economic as well as cultural activity.

14

The Simple Care and Feeding of the Economic Apparatus: Videotapes of the Modern Traditional Woman

Linda Kintz

I

Television studies has generally dealt with the influence of mainstream television, both in terms of its effects and the resistances to those effects. However, its dominance has, at least in the USA, been increasingly challenged by the proliferation of cable outlets targeted to specific demographic groups and by the growth of other forms of popular media. One of these is the production and distribution of videotapes for private and group viewing by religious conservatives who are highly critical of mainstream popular culture. The increasing availability of such videotapes is part of a resistant subculture that uses the sophisticated resources of media technology to oppose a mass-mediated public culture it considers to be unacceptably secular and immoral.

Three videotapes produced in this context, *Sex Has A Price Tag*, *No Second Chance* and *Halloween, Trick or Treat*, will be discussed in this essay, all made available for purchase and distribution by Concerned Women for America (CWA). These tapes are used in a number of contexts: they are bought by Christian families who homeschool their children because of their dissatisfaction with the public schools, used by teachers in private religious schools, shown on public access cable television as well as on such conservative networks as Paul Weyrich's National Empowerment Television, and featured by churches in their youth education programmes. Sometimes two versions of abstinence material are produced, one available without explicit religious material for showing in public school sex education classes, the other including such material. These latter are occasionally, if illegally, also shown by sympathetic public school teachers.

Concerned Women for America bills itself as the largest women's organization in the USA, claiming 600 000 members, though exact documentation of that number has never been made available. Its structure consists of 1100 prayer action chapters across the country, which provide 'informed prayer for our nation and its leaders' as well as a venue for organizing (LaHaye, 1984: 14).[1] The videotapes circulated by CWA also foreground the importance of the relation between emotions, women, religion and politics. As Lawrence Grossberg argues, it is the popular culture of everyday life that affects the public language of what matters, the term 'matter' here referring, on the one hand, to the way we conceptualize materiality and our relationship to the real, and on the other, to the ways emotions and intimacy are taught and learned so that certain things, and not others, come to matter deeply and passionately. Because the political is increasingly defined as the history of the struggle within and on the plane of emotions, the 'feeling of life' is of great importance. And those feelings about what matters most in postmodern America are being framed in terms of the absolute morality of traditional values, which now saturate not only conservative religious discourses but secular public policy language as well.

Contemporary conservatism's reaction against postmodernity, drawing on its best technological resources, is also part of an attempt 'to regulate the possibilities of pleasure and identity as the basis of political opposition and to dismantle the cultural and political field constructed in the 1960s . . .' (Grossberg, 1992: 10–11). In part, this depends on producing different *kinds* of pleasures, for example the passions of family, religion, patriotism and property within a satisfying cultural homogeneity. That homogeneity gains coherence through a set of homologies that fit together like Russian dolls, loosely guaranteed by the Judaeo-Christian Book of the World: God as Creator; the traditional family; a divinely inspired Declaration of Independence and Constitution; a nation characterized as God's unique experiment in human history; a belief that the free market is inherent in human nature; and the claim that, because it has been specially graced by God, America has a God-given responsibility to spread free market democratic capitalism around the globe.[2] This passionate, mass-mediated, hyperreal structure thus links meaning from womb to Heaven, and though it might seem to harbour too many contradictions to bring diverse groups together, in particular social conservatives and economic libertarians, its most important characteristic is its ability to remain both vague and passionate, while also producing fears against which the clear structure will offer itself as inoculation. And while secular analysts have often trivialized religion, regional identifications and emotion, religious conservatives have built an intensely passionate national popular movement out of precisely those resources.

Gluing together these various elements depends in large part on the work of modern traditional women, their construction of the 'matter' of absolutist intimacy grounded in the lesson – either through natural law or biblical mandate – that a woman's identity is fundamentally that of mother. The mediation of modern traditional women helps construct the biggest prize of contemporary American, mass-mediated politics – the feelings of life.

II

From among the videotapes, some produced, some only marketed by Concerned Women for America, three are of interest here because they foreground uneven developments within popular culture, with popular culture referring in this instance to the variety of books and videotapes sold at both conservative religious conventions and religious bookstores. These follow a similar format, relying on a pseudoscholarly use of footnotes in the case of books or interviews with experts in the case of videotapes to legitimate their arguments, even though when one tracks down the documentation, it is often spurious, obscure or anecdotal. They are, however, becoming increasingly sophisticated.

These particular tapes deal with abstinence, on the one hand, and Halloween celebrations, on the other. Though the abstinence tapes, *Sex Has A Price Tag* and *No Second Chance*, are heavily infused with absolutist morality, they might have some appeal to secular parents worried about sexually transmitted diseases, pregnancy and rape as their children enter adolescence. The appeal of *Halloween, Trick or Treat*, on the other hand, is much narrower, but it provides an allegory of the powerful anxieties aroused by postmodernity, a term used here to refer to the historical era of rapid change brought about by a globalized information economy and the shift from industrial to financial capitalism. Several themes are common to all three videotapes. One is a focus on the dangers of secular culture to children; another has to do with the difficulties of adolescents who are just entering puberty; yet another firmly situates death within any kind of sexuality outside of marriage. And finally, all suggest, in one way or another, that public education, with its lessons of tolerance and diversity, is at the very heart of the dangers facing children, teens, the American nation and, ultimately, all of civilization.

Sex Has A Price Tag organizes its lessons to a young audience by combining the language of born-again evangelism with that of buying and selling, its principal lesson that sex outside of marriage is not only sinful but dangerous. The only thing that will protect a young person from sexually transmitted diseases and AIDS is waiting to have sex until after marriage, then remaining monogamous after that. This does not remove pleasure from sexuality, but constructs sacred intimacy as the site of intense pleasure without guilt because it is blessed by God, an important attraction for women, for whom sexuality has always been associated with guilt. The unspoken implication here is a message of homogeneity, and a lesson that is both remarkably exclusive and remarkably trusting, for it requires no discussions of the precautions one should take, just in case temptation cannot be resisted, nor a recognition that even one's Christian partner might, in fact, not be so pure.

Produced by Youth for Christ and Twin Cities, the tape begins with a brightly coloured shot of teenagers on a ferris wheel, as the voice-over describes the excitement and beauty of true love. Immediately, the picture changes to black and white, and the narrator distinguishes between the emotion of love and the much more common, less sacred experience of making love. We then find ourselves in what appears to be a church auditorium, where Pam Stenzel, who travels around the country speaking to church youth for Straight Talk, Inc., addresses an audience made up mainly of young teenagers.

Stenzel is a lively, emotional speaker, with an easy rapport with students, although she later becomes overly moralistic. First she acknowledges how pleasurable sex is: 'It is a beautiful thing. God created it. If it felt like hacking your hand off, you wouldn't be here.' She then begins to separate sex from sex-within-marriage, for as she tells it, God created sex only for the very specific context of marriage. She then establishes the metaphorical frame for her lesson: 'If there is one thing I want you to remember, it is this – if you have sex outside of marriage – *you will pay* . . . What is it going to cost you and is it worth it?'

The talk will later return to this collapse of sacred language into the language of the market, but first Stenzel takes her audience through a list of ways they will pay, drawing on vague statistics without verification. These include abortion, poverty and disease: 87 per cent of women who have had an abortion, she says, regret it; 87 per cent of girls who have a child alone live below the poverty level; and herpes, gonorrhoea, syphilis and genital warts threaten those who do not wait, the most serious consequences being conveyed in her melodramatic story of a 13-year-old girl who contracted gonorrhoea: 'She will *never have children.*' From there, Stenzel turns to AIDS, citing the failure rates for condoms and ridiculing the claim that condoms make safe sex possible.

She then acknowledges that her audience may, in fact, be mature enough to handle abstinence: 'You should be offended when adults tell you you can't control yourself', and describes what her cat is like when she is in heat. Though the cat could not control herself, these young people can: 'You are better than the family cat. You can say no ... Saying no to sex will never hurt you. Once you say yes, you have lost all guarantees.' Saying no to sex is not even very radical, but simply an example of the kind of discipline required after marriage: 'If you can't practise discipline before marriage, what makes you think you can after?'.

Stenzel then turns to God's view of sexuality outside marriage, eliciting the sense of a deeply loving, fatherly God, not an angrily judgemental one: 'God is saddened. He sees what you could have had, what your relationship could have been.' Sexual sins are, in fact, different from all other sins because they relate so directly to His presence: 'He who sins sexually sins against his own body ... Your body is the temple of the Holy Spirit. Your body is not your own.'

The sense of the holiness of the body is then jarringly interrupted; the body as sacred temple has become the body as object of exchange: 'You were bought with a price. Therefore honour God with your body.' The sensual saturation of the body by a loving God now disappears in a transaction that is simultaneously commercial and sacrificial. The sensual emotions of sacred intimacy are now, without apology, linked to the sensual emotions of the sacred free market and its economy: 'You will pay' if you have sex outside of marriage. This rhetoric also unites the notion of judgement and an all-seeing God, no longer quite so gently loving: 'You cannot run from God. We will all stand before Him some day ... The wages of sin is death, but the gift of God is eternal life through Jesus Christ our Lord.'

Stenzel ends the talk with the obligatory evangelical appeal to those not yet saved: 'If you are here today and have not yet accepted Jesus Christ as your personal saviour, you need to do that.' The other steps you must take include: delay dating until you are 16; date in groups while you are still in high school; decide with your head what you want to do before you go on a date; take a quarter on every date so that if your date pressures you, you can tell him to call your dad and ask his permission for whatever he is pressuring you to do; and finally, find a Christian friend with whom you make a pact, and ask that friend, 'Will you help me save myself?'.

In the face of temptations to be sexually active before marriage, Stenzel suggests a response to peer pressure to have sex: remind them that 'any day I could be like you, but you will never again be like me ... Once it's gone, it's gone.' She also takes another step characteristic of lessons about abstinence, connecting the purity of abstinence with opposition to abortion, again in the style of high melodrama: 'Today before you and I go to bed, 4400 babies will be ripped apart in their mother's womb, torn limb from limb because somebody made a wrong sexual choice.' She connects the act of abortion to the larger question of nationality morality: 'That's the kind of country you and I live in today.'

As in most abstinence videotapes, the lesson about abstinence becomes the occasion for the mandate to be active in the public sphere. God is looking for young people to stand up in a nation where morals have deteriorated: 'Who will stand up and say "I'm going to be different and I'm going to make a difference"?'. The question of sexual intimacy is now situated not only within a homogenous Christian community, but within a homogeneity unambiguously demanded of the public sphere. After asking them if they are going to be the ones to whom God is speaking tonight, she prays that God will 'raise up a mighty army, a mighty generation'.

III

A second tape, *No Second Chance*, produced in Hemet, California, by Jeremiah Films, also focuses on children and teens, while introducing another common theme, the idea that sex outside of marriage is like Russian roulette, a gamble with death that gives you 'no second chance'. This time the opening sequence shows bright, happy young people in a suburban mall, as they visit and flirt; it is immediately followed by a shot of a young boy of about six, James, who walks slowly and painfully outside his grandparents' home. James's father, who had had sex outside of marriage, contracted AIDS, as did his wife. Both parents died within a year of becoming ill, leaving James seriously ill, the tubes and catheters taped to his body and visible as he walks. This is followed by shots of dying AIDS patients in hospital beds, as a voice-over reminds the viewer that sexually transmitted diseases are no longer simply about a shot of penicillin.

Then we find ourselves in a classroom, where a nurse, Cathy Kay, R.N., representing a group called California Health Care Advocates, formed to educate teenagers about the risks of sexuality, speaks to a high school class. While we are shown clips of young people dancing in darkened rooms, a number of experts talk about AIDS and the fact that it takes years to develop. In another theme common to these tapes, its threat is characterized by invisibility; one need not look sick or infected to pass AIDS on. Its symptoms and complications are then discussed, while shots of talking heads are interspersed with those of dying AIDS patients, and finally, a body in a coffin.

As the lesson continues, the invisible nature of the disease is again stressed: 'No one knows who and where [the carriers] are', and often they do not even know they are infected. Because of AIDS, she tells students, their 20-year high school reunion will be marked by many empty chairs. The screen is then filled with the terrifying phallic image of a pistol, eerily shaded in black and white, implying that using a condom to protect against an invisible killer like AIDS is like playing Russian roulette with this ominous pistol. When you have sex with someone, it is as if you are packing along a loaded revolver, as if you are crawling into bed with a whole group of people you do not know.

But if people just stopped having sex, there would be no babies and no fun, so what to do? Here the lesson takes the same turn as Stenzel's, for the solution is monogamy. But if you have already had sex, there is also such a thing as secondary virginity. You can make a decision never to do it again until you meet and marry that one special person. By now, death has been installed within intimacy with such intensity that sexuality saturated with death can only be purified by God. The only safe sex is sacred sex. When one of the young man asks, 'What if I want to have sex before I get married?' she replies, 'Well, I guess you just have to be prepared to die. You'll probably take with you your spouse and one or more of your children.' And the viewer sees a photo of little James dressed in cowboy clothes, sitting painfully, miserably on a horse.

Cathy advises the students to resolve never to have sex until their wedding night, for death lies in sex outside of marriage. We then return to the AIDS patients in the hospital, one of whom has become a Christian and says of his sexual behavior: 'I was actually hurting God's feelings. I would rather have AIDS and have the relationship with Jesus Christ than not have AIDS and not know Jesus at all.' Cathy now insists that her young audience not alienate those with AIDS and encourages them to show compassion and understand that they will not get AIDS by hugging, holding, or sitting and reading to those dying of AIDS.

The lesson about abstinence ends with another picture of James, the child whose fate is now linked to the pleasure that lies outside of Christian marriage. A few moments of such pleasure, the lack of discipline to wait for sacred intimacy, can lead to a lifetime of regret, as he and we now know: 'Those are not just empty words.'

IV

A third videotape, *Halloween, Trick or Treat*, produced by Cutting Edge Films International, with Jeremiah Films, seems far more eccentric and marginal, but it provides an allegory of the structure of homologies with which this essay began. Part of a 13-part series entitled *The Pagan Invasion*, it illustrates the pastiche of postmodernity made apparent in the juxtaposition of sophisticated computer graphics with versions of the occult and the Satanic that seem almost medieval. This involves the paradoxical interdependence of two things: exponential *instability*, or the infinite possibilities of change; and exponential *stability*, the most simplistic repetitions of rigid binary structures.[3]

We find ourselves, at the opening of the videotape, moved dizzyingly and frighteningly by computerized graphics through glittering crystals, then through labyrinths and castle walls, inside the game of Dungeons and Dragons. Finally we enter a room in the middle of a castle and watch documentary footage of witches, the diversity and festivity of urban street scenes, and a pagan workshop. The first thing we are warned about is the public school system.

The female narrator enters, and far from looking like the stereotypical Southern churchgoer or an older matron one might expect, she is a typical straight, white, educated, middle-class, articulate suburban wife, though she speaks with a British accent. She begins to describe the dangers of Halloween: it is big business, a major marketing opportunity for department stores that sell costumes, for farmers who sell pumpkins, for those who make horror movies and videos, for entrepreneurs in general. The success of special effects in horror movies has allowed the video industry to link together their two biggest sources of profit: horror and pornography, with Hollywood, in particular, capitalizing on this craving for the occult and demonic. And she informs us that Hollywood even hires practising witches or Satanists as technical advisers to assure the authenticity of reproductions and performances of sacrifices, spells and curses, producing movies that include depictions of violence and cruelty, sexual activity, cannibalism, rape and the drinking of blood.

The viewer is then shown an interview with Glen Hobbes, a young man who tells the interviewer that he was initiated into a Satanic coven as a child. His grandfather initiated him, and his whole family was involved in the coven. Hobbes describes his first Halloween ritual, when he and a little girl named Becky were 'married together in the beast', sexually abused while blood was spilled over them. Then they were involved in rituals that began at the end of September; their clothing was removed, they were left in a shack, animals were sacrificed, and Lucifer was summoned. As Hobbes talks, grotesque paintings of Satanic creatures are flashed on the screen, with no acknowledgement of their source. On Halloween night, he tells us, he and Becky were drugged, put in a van, and taken to a place with an outdoor altar. The little girl was placed on the altar, her feet were bound, she was roped to the altar with arms and legs apart, and finally the bottoms of her feet and her wrists were slit. Then a high priest forced Hobbes to hold a knife in his hand, which the priest pushed into her chest. We are given no information whatsoever about the credibility of this interviewee.

From this nightmarish story, the narration returns to the significance of Halloween, informing the viewer that this kind of ritual abuse and murder 'is happening every Halloween. Children all over the world are losing their lives every Halloween, yet we celebrate.' And with no documentation, the viewer is told of police reports from all over the world that tell of heinous crimes in which the occult plays a part.

The pedagogical intentions of the narrator take over to reveal 'the historic roots of this mayhem' through clips of interviews with practising witches and druids in England, part of a revival of Druidic and Celtic culture that involves witchcraft and nature worship. These people seem to be ordinary, New Age, middle-class Britons, who cooperate with great candour, as if they have no idea that their interviews will be used in this way. Philip, an Arch Druid in London, tells us that Halloween marks the time when the dividing line between the dead and the living is at its thinnest, when contact with the dead is easiest. Another women interviewed says that 'if you sacrifice an animal, you want to do it again'.

After this clip, the narrator shares her derivation of the word 'witch,' which is from the Saxon 'wicca', one who practises sorcery. As the Oxford Dictionary defines it, 'wiccan' means twisted, bent, or warped in reference to a practice that cannot be divorced from demonology. Because of this derivation and because of an overall rhetorical frame in which absolute binaries drop down to eliminate ambiguity or complexity, what now becomes apparent is the rigid concept of language at the bottom of this belief, the fact that once a word has been contaminated with the Satanic, it will retain that contamination forever.

She continues her history lesson, informing the viewer that though Halloween is often confused with All Saints' Day, it is actually linked to the ancient Festival of the Dead, when the gates of the underworld open, and witches, druids and

Satanists make contact with the spirits of the dead. (In the background, while she speaks, more grotesque paintings of Satanic figures appear, again with no indication of where they come from but implying that these kinds of creatures actually appeared on those nights.) Halloween, she tells us, is actually part of an anti-religion, a religion of Satan in which the trances that are invoked turn into Satanic possession. And the viewer is brought back to her real concern, children, for in this neo-pagan revival, 'children are going to lose their lives'.

What business, then, do churches and schools have in sponsoring Halloween parties when they should be battling against them?: 'The fact is that a highly organized network of Satanists are operating in America and Europe today.' Thus it is not only mortal danger that threatens children, but the danger of spiritual possession. This fear becomes an allegory of the fears many conservative religious people have about public schools in general, for secular schools threaten to 'possess' children by means of liberal indoctrination which turns them against their religion and their parents. In her history of the concept of Satan, Elaine Pagels cites the fact that Satan turned from angel to 'intimate enemy' of God, from 'us' to 'them'. This pattern suggests why the most dangerous place in modern America has been the public school, for that is precisely where our children – 'us' – are being turned into 'them'.

Closely related to Halloween and its pagan history are the environmental and ecology movements, also considered to be pagan forms of nature worship. The widespread interest in both environmentalism, with its worship of nature, and in pagan rituals so closely linked to Satan, are signs that we live in a 'post-Christian era' of 'neo-paganism'. Hal Lindsey, famous for his best-selling book, *The Late Great Planet Earth*, now appears to bring his apocalyptic warnings to bear on the dangers of Halloween. He is shown standing near a shack in the California desert east of Los Angeles to show the viewer a place where the ritual worship of Satan has taken place, as evidenced by the candles, upside-down crosses, bones, Satanic symbols, and, ominously, the diaper of a very small baby.

Lindsey worriedly elicits the terms of the apocalyptic discourse of his earlier writing, in which anti-communism and the nuclear threat were at the centre. With the communist Anti-Christ gone, the threat is displaced elsewhere: 'You know, I believe that this country is experiencing a pagan invasion.' The upsurge in the practice of witchcraft and outright Satanism are all part of this new apocalyptic threat, which he believes is openly glorified on Halloween: 'Halloween seems to be high holy day for the Satanists and the occultists . . . when all across the country in secret places, in the dark there will be little babies sacrificed to Satan.'

A voice of legitimacy is then added to the discussion when Detective Kurt Jackson, of the Beaumont, California, Police Department, is interviewed, once again with no verification. Jackson describes killings in which bodies were marked with Satanic symbols, his ominous tone and frightening information immediately juxtaposed to everyday life, as the viewer is situated firmly within the phobic rhetorical frame. Fear is first produced, then a particular belief is offered as the cure for that fear. Danger is again characterized by invisibility, and as in the discussion of AIDS, both the urban landscape and the suburban mall teem with invisible danger. When an ordinary street scene is shown in slow motion, the viewer is warned that this is where the greatest danger lies: 'The real

Satanists, the hardcore Satanists, are involved in criminal activity. They are going to try and look as ordinary as possible. They're doctors, they're lawyers.' And with almost mechanical predictability, the viewer learns that 'they're oftentimes people who are in positions of great influence over small children'. A playground scene, coded both in terms of absolute danger and absolute innocence, then fills the screen.

Finally we return to the narrator in her pink dress and pearls, as she stands in front of the computer-generated interior of the castle to make the link to children even more concrete by clarifying the occult origins of Halloween practices. Trick or Treat, she tells us, was originally associated with giving food in return for the blessings of the spirits of the dead. Jack-o-lanterns came from the practice of carving laughing faces of demonic spirits on turnips as symbols of damned souls. If one left a carved turnip or pumpkin outside of one's house, that meant that the occupant was sympathetic to Satan and would receive mercy from trick or treaters. Bobbing for apples was part of a ritual to divine fertility, and witches' hats and broomsticks were originally considered to be phallic symbols. She also tells the viewer that because transformed sexual and psychic energy was released during orgasm, the sexual nature of Halloween rituals was especially dangerous; here Satan, death and sexuality are joined in a tidy structure.

Yet as she reminds the viewer, these Satanic and pagan elements are celebrated even by Christian churches, which participate in Halloween parties and celebrations in spite of the fact that they are 'occultic celebrations which glorify the powers of darkness'. Just as words once contaminated by Satan are always contaminated, so too are these customs, which are contaminated by their consecration to Satan. And though Christians, either out of fear or ignorance, have allowed these celebrations to continue, it is time for them to 'gather together to educate themselves and pray against the forces of darkness', time to worship, pray and give thanks for Jesus's victory over Satan, death, and hell.

The structure of clarity that organizes the comforting simplicity of this videotape and eliminates ambiguity is grounded in the biblical text of Deuteronomy 18: 9–13, which warns that:

> There shall not be found among you any one that maketh his son or his daughter to pass through the fire, or that useth divination . . . or an enchanter, or a witch, or a charmer, or a consulter with familiar spirits, or a wizard, or a necromancer. For all that do these things are an abomination unto the Lord: and because of these abominations the Lord thy God doth drive them out from before thee. Thou shalt be perfect with the Lord thy God.

The videotape ends with words of solace that return the viewer to the theme of economic exchange: 'If you accept the fact that His death and resurrection is payment in full for all of your sins, you will have everlasting life.'

Though, of course, most religious conservatives do not oppose Halloween nor do they take witches literally, nevertheless this passage reveals an interpretive structure that can accommodate a wide variety of different contents: the binary division between godly people and all the rest, the coding of those outside this group in terms of purity and abomination, and a belief that the abstraction represented by spiritual purity will transcend nature, materiality and death.

V

Connecting these videotapes, which may seem marginal, even bizarre, to the passions that help bring together market fundamentalism and religious absolutism shows how important the motherly face of the modern traditional woman has become. For the symbolism of her face, joined with her activism, helps seal the emotional truth of an organizing structure that can admit wildly different contents – the stability of its forms joined to the instability of their contents. That motherly face becomes the pivot that mediates between the public and the domestic spheres because it generates the kinds of passions that are felt to be immediate, natural and spontaneous. In an important way, these 'spontaneous' passions leave us at a kind of zero degree of conservative politics, where the needs of the market now match the needs of conservative religion. Or as Fredric Jameson argues, conservative politics have increasingly become 'simply the care and feeding of the economic apparatus' (Jameson, 1994: 283).

And yet the word 'simply' brings me suddenly to a halt here. It is too casually thrown in, its usage strangely dismissive of the curiously domestic terms, 'care and feeding'. What the description of zero degree politics misses is the entire middle section of this essay. These videotapes, like the activism of conservative religious women, are still too often off the radar of analysis, an oversight that not only robs the analysis of important information, but also provides an invaluable invisibility for conservative religious activism.

What hides within the word Jameson slides over, 'simply', is in fact not trivial at all but is at the very centre of politics. For as Plato long ago showed in the *Timaeus*, if the Father's word is to be enforced, it must be inscribed *in* something. What Plato found necessary for the power of that word was the amorphous matter that had no identity in and of itself, but even though it was formless, it was nevertheless indispensable. Plato called this formlessness matter and identified it as feminine, maternal. Analysing the conservative popular by overlooking the matter of the tablet upon which the forms of the market and absolutist religion are written, as Jameson does, misses the very evidence we need to understand how this kind of politics works, how it comes to function in the matter and senses of the body.

For while modern traditional women agree to be written on, they also demand to do some of the writing. And because they have had to decipher conservative belief from the inside, their texts and videotapes provide a first-hand reading of the way that belief is constructed, even if these videotapes also show how these women's own self-empowerment dangerously displaces the social contract's sacrifices away from them and onto others. By so doing, they help push the social contract toward its most violent edges.

Understanding the appeal of the conservative national popular and the way it targets those onto whom the sacrifice of women is redirected, as well as the way it settles the market into the depths of intimacy, of 'biology', means learning what the modern traditional woman already knows – that the feelings of belief are not trivial. In the face of a long tradition of dismissing religion, women and emotion as unpolitical, the modern traditional woman knows very well that there is nothing more political than what matters.

Notes

1.   LaHaye writes this in a letter that accompanies the Concerned Women for America organizational manual. Energized by conservative religious women's angry response to the National Women's Convention in Houston in 1977, CWA was founded by Beverly LaHaye and modelled on a story she read in *Reader's Digest* about the role played by women in Brazil in the military coup against Joao Goulart in 1964. The women 'formed cell groups to organize prayer meetings, patriotic protest marches, and the purchase of television airtime and newspaper space to proclaim their anticommunist message ... the efforts of these anticommunist women ... made the businessmen successful' (LaHaye, 1984: 13–14).

What she does not tell us is that the military dictatorship installed in 1964 led to the exile of many priests and Catholic lay people involved in Peasant Leagues in the Brazilian countryside, one of whom was Paolo Freire. It also led to a police state characterized by media censorship, death squads and torture, the shutdown of Congress, and the elimination of the right to elect mayors and governors.

2.   The phrase 'Judaeo-Christian' is regularly used by the religious right to emphasize the inclusiveness of statements about the biblical intentions of America's Founding Fathers. Israel has also long been an important issue for conservative religious people, in part because of its importance to apocalyptic prophesy, in which the Book of Revelations is interpreted to mean that Israel will be the site of the Battle of Armageddon, which will precede the Second Coming.

In spite of diplomatic attempts by Ralph Reed, Jr., to monitor the public discourse of the Christian Coalition, individual members frequently give a narrower picture of the Coalition's base. As one of the speakers at the 1995 Christian Coalition convention in Washington, DC, Peter Marshall, Sr., told his audience, 'America is God's project ... the only nation in the world deliberately founded on the Bible'. Dedicated to Jesus Christ by the Pilgrims, America is now threatened with the disintegration of that godly culture, the greatest crisis the nation has ever faced. Calling for a 'national revival and restoration of Biblical prinicples in every area of life', Marshall advises that such revival must be the goal of Christian activists, for whom there is 'no King but King Jesus'.

3.   Jean Baudrillard develops this argument in *The Illusion of the End* (1994).

References and Further Reading

AMMERMAN, N., 1991: 'North American Protestant fundamentalism'. In M. Marty and S. Appleby (eds), *Fundamentalisms Observed*, Vol. 2. Chicago: University of Chicago Press.

BAUDRILLARD, J., 1994: *The Illusion of the End*, trans. Chris Turner. Cambridge: Polity Press.

DIAMOND, S., 1995: *Roads to Dominion: Right-Wing Movements and Political Power in the United States*. New York: The Guildford Press.

GROSSBERG, L., 1992: *We Gotta Get Out of This Place: Popular Conservatism and Postmodern Culture*. New York: Routledge.

JAMESON, F., 1994: 'Postmodernism and the market'. In S. Zizek (ed.), *Mapping Ideology*. New York: Verso.

LAHAYE, B., 1984: *Who But A Woman?* Nashville: Thomas Nelson Publishers.

MOSSE, G., 1985: *Nationalism and Sexuality: Middle-Class Morality and Sexual Norms in Modern Europe*. Madison: University of Wisconsin Press.

O'LEARY, S., 1994: *Arguing the Apocalypse: A Theory of Millennial Rhetoric*. New York: Oxford University Press.

PAGELS, E., 1995: *The Origins of Satan*. New York: Random House.

ROSE, J., 1993: *Why War?: Psychoanalysis, Politics, and the Return to Melanie Klein*. Cambridge, MA: Blackwell.

US television is usually characterised as unashamedly commercial in contrast to European systems which have (or had) strong state or public service elements. Eric Freedman's essay reminds us that the USA too has its public service element, proportionately very small, but subject at least periodically to debates about how it should be controlled and what it should show. Freedman's essay looks at programmes made for and by gays and lesbians; like Kintz's study, though with a very different subject, it explores the ways in which cable television and video have been used to try to make an intervention in public debate and to challenge ideas and images deemed to be dominant in mainstream television.

Freedman deploys two discourses in his analysis. The first is that of civil rights, in which it is argued that access to the public sphere of television is a question of freedom of speech. This is a particularly resonant argument in the USA where it can become a question of Constitutional protection but it is relevant to any discussion of the relations between mainstream television and audiences. The second discourse is that of queer theory with its emphasis on shifting identities, permeable boundaries and coalition politics. In this context, Freedman is concerned to look at programming across the categories of education and entertainment, at the borrowings and transformations of mainstream genres and at the interaction of these access programmes with and beyond their target audiences.

In both education and entertainment programmes, Freedman identifies the disappearing boundaries between producers and audiences as a key factor. Medical hierarchies are challenged when members of the audience give advice from their own experience; entertainment shows in New York feature well-known personalities in the gay community; chat shows and magazine programmes depend on inside knowledge and active dialogue.

Following the arguments of O'Sullivan, one could see this greater interaction between audience and programme as generically determined by the type of programmes produced for gay viewers, and Shattuc interestingly ascribes changes in the mainstream talk show to the influence of a camp aesthetic. Freedman, however, goes on to make a connection between the formal qualities of gay access programming and independent producers operating in television and other media. Deploying an argument more prevalent in film than television, he suggests that the rough aesthetic of at least some of the programmes – simple lighting, improvised dialogue, raw sound, minimal editing, for example – challenges the smoother conventions of mainstream television and connects them with radical politics in the widest sense.

The vulnerability as well as the possibilities for non-mainstream programming are clear in Freedman's analysis. He identifies the dangers of censorship, on the one hand, and incorporation into mainstream modes, on the other, but finishes with a strong call for continuing to press for public access television as a site of struggle.

15

Producing (Queer) Communities: Public Access Cable TV in the USA

Eric Freedman

I question what community I belong to. On a fundamental level, do I define myself by race, gender, sexual preference, class, nationality? Am I part of an academic community? Indeed, are the borders of these communities mutually exclusive or even clearly defined? I want to explore the notion of community, and challenge any presupposition of an inherent unity. 'Community' is a term under which we can speak of collective involvement, or even unified resistance, while at the same time respect (and expect) difference.

I watch network television. I know there are other people who watch network television. I am part of a community of viewers. I am one member of an audience, but I would certainly not call my involvement with my fellow viewers 'collective'. My intuition tells me that there are striking differences among us, some of which have demographic indices. Of course, there are certain factors that cannot be measured, one of which is fantasy, constructed around *how* and *to what end* I consume (what pleasure I derive from a given programme).

Yet fantasy itself is not a free radical; it is regulated. Indeed it is the mass media which serves as a linchpin in the construction of fantasy, for we are constantly mediating, or negotiating, between our desires and images provided to us in culture. By extension, only by inserting our own bodies into the flow of representations, into the discourse of the media, can we take control of our desire. If fantasy lies at the intersection of desire and image, we can attempt to reconsider and enlarge the lexicon of images if we choose not to limit the realm of desire (for setting limits amounts to setting margins, a way of signifying 'deviance' or defining 'non-normative' behaviour).

Access to the media can be equated with access to history, for representations provide a site for negotiating a position within a continuous discursive flow. This is not to suggest a desire for the creation of an archive, a testament to the diversity of human experience as evidenced by a warehouse of images and assorted by-products, whatever those would be (for images in themselves are not agents of action). Rather, it is to suggest that individuals do indeed negotiate positions in relation to the images that surround them as part of an active social process.

This essay will address issues of marginality made manifest through cable access programming and consider public access as a performative space for subcultural work, investigating both the politics and aesthetics of this form of independent media production. In particular, the focus here will be to examine the use of access programming in the queer community, activity that simultaneously functions (as a tool) to negotiate cultural difference, to edify a polymorphous sexuality, to visualize coalition politics and to formulate new histories. Ideally, the methodology incorporated in this study can be used to investigate the manner in which other forms of cultural difference (for example, difference based on race, class, nationality or gender) are negotiated through specialized and localized access programming. In every case, the question of what pleasure a viewer derives from a given programme is made much more complex; no longer limited to choosing among network offerings, a viewer can make a programme that is intimately linked to his or her own fantasy. This is perhaps the primary reason that public access is a highly charged space, positioned at the centre of public debate about censorship and First Amendment rights in the information age.

In the history of alternative modes for securing access to the media, public access cable television is only one site of intervention, a method framed by the era of television and the systematic introduction of televisual practices (including, but not limited to, regulatory and station practices). The introduction of cable television in the early 1970s was accompanied by an FCC (Federal Communications Commission) mandate for new (cable) systems in the 100 largest television markets to include provisions for public, education and government (PEG) access channels, suggesting, in fact, that cable systems should make available a total of three public access channels: one for state and local government, one for education, and one for community public access use. 'Public access' was construed to mean that the cable company should not only make available airtime, but also make available equipment so that literally anybody could make and broadcast programmes on a first-come, first-served basis, with a freedom of speech and action subject only to standard obscenity and libel laws. In some cases, a local organization was set up to manage the access system, while in others the cable operator itself assumed these duties (Kellner, 1987: 610).

The availability of access channels depends, for the most part, on the political savvy and/or clout of committed community groups and local government (Kellner, 1987: 610). The privately owned cable company must make a bid to each region that it intends to service, and as part of its franchise agreement it must pay a franchise fee to the city (in effect, to justify its monopoly over a given geographic radius). A percentage of this fee can then be used to fund public, education and government (PEG) access channels; the extent to which fees are used for public access as opposed to more general community services is determined by the city itself. In addition to a public access channel, most cable operators also offer leased access channels (that are made available for a programming fee), and local origination channels (that are run by the cable company itself, typically for its own community affairs programmes or other in-house productions).

Although a 1979 Supreme Court decision struck down the aforementioned 1972 FCC mandate (construed to be a violation of freedom of speech, for cable companies claimed they were 'forced' to air programming over which they had little or no editorial control), by this time cable had expanded so rapidly and become such a competitive industry that city governments were able to negotiate for access channels as well as financial support to maintain and operate public access systems; contracts went to those companies that could meet city demands, and resources for access continued to grow throughout the early 1980s (Kellner, 1987: 611). Unfortunately, numerous cities in the United States committed to extended contracts prior to 1972; as these have yet to expire, many areas are still several years away from renegotiating with local servers for, among other improvements, public access channels.

Public access cable stations are non-commercial enterprises (though governed by private business – cable operators). The public access programming day is not divided into traditional scheduling blocks – it has no inherent 'prime time'. Public access station operators do not engage in strategies to keep viewers from channel-surfing, simply because there is no programmer's logic in the mapping out of the broadcast day. Public access producers do not reserve blocks in the weekly schedule; time slots are assigned only after producers complete their programmes, duplicate their tapes and deliver them to the programming office. Typically, producers look over the schedule for what they deem to be the most appropriate spot for their programme (a logic perhaps dictated by their experiences with the network schedule), and quite often must wait weeks before they can get their programmes aired at a desired time (because the schedule tends to fill up rather quickly) – unless they want to choose a 'less desirable' time slot and get their programme on the air sooner. For this reason, the daily schedule is composed of rather unrelated blocks of programmes; a producer has no control over what airs before or after his/her show. Thus it does not make sense to speak of 'flow' in a conventional sense, though one can invariably speak of incorporating the selected viewing of public access as part of a larger pattern of active television watching (most likely dominated by encounters with network texts); indeed public access channels oftentimes interrupt that flow, because of their distinctive 'low tech' surface (the 'rough spot' in a smooth surface of network texts). I would call these shows 'counter-media' or 'counter-television', not because they intend to interrupt the flow of network television and/or the inherent ideologies of the network text, but because they *do* – the effect is largely due to audience response/reaction and not directorial intent. Although many directors actively choose to map out a space in public access that is markedly different from network television (both in form and content), an equal number of directors use network television as a model for their own programmes (thus the proliferation of generic forms).

To many of us, public access cable channels are those annoying channels that we have to flip through as we make our way to network fare; for some of us who are more technically proficient, we have programmed these channels 'out' of our remote control devices so we no longer have to bother with them. Populated by members of our local community – though commonly people we do not know – the public access channels of local cable television are littered with shows in which we may personally have no interest. Regardless, these programmes are a fundamental part of a local politics, and in my pursuit to examine public access cable television as a 'public sphere' of production (programming produced by, for [in the interests of], and starring members of a local community – community in a physical sense referring to *individuals* residing in a particular geographic radius) I do indeed want to privilege the local over both the national and global. Though local station operators are asked to act in the 'public interest' (and cases such as WLBT in Mississippi have tested this FCC mandate – though as cable becomes deregulated such guidelines will most likely be ignored), the abstractness of this term needs to be foregrounded. To whom are public access cable operators (a subsection of the cable franchise) responsible: those community producers who choose to make use of the station, those who regularly view the station (and thus demonstrate an 'investment'), or those who may not view the station but nevertheless receive their cable services from the same operator? Public access television viewing is difficult if not impossible to gauge. Ratings systems do not measure use (on the production or reception end); local and national television guides (i.e. *TV Guide*) do not and cannot provide listings of public access programmes (it would be a logistical nightmare), and cable operators themselves do not monitor community viewing patterns.

Network television standards, though certainly ill-defined, are more clearly national standards, given the size of the network viewing 'community' (and again it is problematic to off-handedly talk about a 'community of viewers'). It is not economically feasible for networks to be accountable to their more localized constituencies. I call for a proliferation of viewpoints or at the very least a proliferation of opportunities for alternative views to come to fruition and be voiced (and hopefully heard). I am mindful that although the texts I am writing about are largely 'progressive' or 'liberal' in their politics, that I must also take the bad with the good, that I cannot deny voices on the right their freedom of speech, their freedom of access. What I call for is not a mandatory policy of inclusion, of a quota of representation(s) on network television, but rather a more general awakening of the importance of 'micropolitical' action, of a community politic(s) that is just as vital, and perhaps distinct from, a national politic(s); and for a turn toward local action and a concern for the use-value of local media. I am not espousing isolationism, but rather the increasing vitality of a bottom-up approach in a nation which is (as I write) becoming ever-more global, ever-more interconnected, as our 'communities' continue to expand over the contested terrain of the Internet and we are asked to monitor our actions in light of potential audiences across the globe.

The technological apparatus of broadcasting has not in itself guaranteed democracy, and the idea of democratic video as taken up by corporate television (in programmes such as *America's Funniest Home Videos*) is quite different from that espoused by access producers working on the margins. In his essay 'Alternative television in the United States' William Boddy recounts that:

> The new delivery technologies were widely hailed in the popular press of the 1970s as harbingers of a 'media revolution', bringing diversity and new viewer sovereignty to television in the home. In the popular press, cable television was the chief public benefactor, promising not only more channels of conventional programming, but specialized cable networks for diverse tastes. (Boddy, 1990: 94)

The degree to which public access has succeeded or failed in delivering the revolution to the people depends on one's expectations. For those to whom public access signified an 'electronic soapbox', access channels can be considered successful, if measured simply in terms of the sheer number of new voices. For others, though, including many of the earliest advocates of the new technology as well as those working in activist video, who had envisioned access as something more cosmic, it can only have proven to be a disappointment. For them, access was a way to decentralize communication, to revive a sense of community through a new forum – an attempt to replace passive consumership with 'active citizenship' (Stier, 1982: 9).

'Amateur' video productions can provide a means of access (to power) for those interest groups who both create and consume them.[1] On a fundamental level, the videos serve to counteract increasing censorship and, more specifically, to provide positive representations of alternative cultural identities seemingly at odds with and therefore absent from the familial moralism of the mass media, functioning outside and therefore against the entire structure of 'official' representations afforded by Western society. 'Access' implies not only access to the resources needed to produce programming, but also access to the same civil rights heretofore restricted to the prevailing hegemony.

Access programming is necessarily politicized through its alternative modes of production, distribution, exhibition and reception. Low-end production values (commonly referred to as a 'cheap-media' aesthetic) can be equated with a subversion of the broadcast medium itself and the production standards of network programming; and unlike network fare, many access shows circulate outside of the traditional channels of broadcast television, achieving international recognition through closed-circuit distribution among localized interest groups. Live shows are taped for distribution and are made readily available by their producers for distribution or 'bicycling' (an informal distribution system among fellow viewers) at a nominal fee (normally the cost of a blank videotape).

As part of its development through the late 1980s and early 1990s, access programming has become increasingly stratified; current community-based programmes are developed by and for rather specialized interest groups within quite restricted geographic radii. Despite the emergence of programmes with a unique community focus ('community' in this sense refers to a particular geographic boundary and demographic constituency), there are numerous examples of fairly similar programming developments in rather diverse areas of the nation, perhaps signalling a similarity in user demographics (and user concerns).

While surveying work produced by gay and lesbian public access users throughout the USA, I have found a definitive number of programming strategies. Public access is being used in one or more of the following ways: 1) as a vehicle for the distribution of information (on public affairs broadcasts and through community-based coverage of newsworthy events); 2) as a forum for media analysis and intervention; 3) as entertainment. More importantly, in terms of understanding public access and its role in defining a community, all of these processes can be fundamental parts of a coalition-based politics.

As one of several activist media strategies, public access is being used as a tool to take control of the discourse surrounding AIDS and to empower those populations who aim to redefine their relationship to the disease through the acquisition of scientific knowledge. Since the early days of ACT-UP, a video collective called 'Testing the Limits' (formed in 1987) has been documenting demonstrations and creating a public archive. Its six members produced the 28-minute documentary *Testing the Limits: NY* in 1987 as well as several programmes for the weekly New York cable network show *Living with AIDS*. There are many educational aspects of AIDS activist video production, all of which can be related to the Brechtian notion of radio communication, the prime objective of which is 'turning the audience not only into pupils but into teachers' (Brecht, 1986: 54). In recent years, the New York-based cable network programme has been joined by a host of other community-based productions providing support for local communities affected by the disease – in Los Angeles alone there are at least six such shows, including the *Being Alive Medical Update*, *AIDS Vision*, *AIDS Update*, *HIV Update*, *Positive News* and *Heart to Heart*.

The *Being Alive Medical Update* is a monthly event sponsored by Being Alive, an independent organization of and for people with HIV/AIDS. In addition to the medical update, Being Alive provides a number of services to its members and the community including: roommate referral, peer counselling, neighbourhood networks, a research library, support groups, newsletters, advocacy, social events and a speakers' bureau. The medical update takes two forms, a written column and a live public address, both of which are presented by an affiliated medical doctor (Mark Katz, MD); Dr Katz presents general information on HIV/AIDS epidemiology, transmission and history, with a focus on treatment issues. The column is published as part of Being Alive's monthly newsletter, while the public address is presented as part of an open forum at West Hollywood's Plummer Park on the third Monday of every month. The forum is a two-hour session – the first hour is dedicated to general treatment issues, as well as the announcement of clinical trials, research projects and conferences, while the second hour features a guest speaker addressing a specific topic (including opportunistic infections, malignancy and Kaposis Sarcoma, oral and dental conditions, skin manifestations, psychology, minority patient history, immune-based therapy, etc.). Time is allotted at the end of each session for questions and answers. The public address is videotaped and broadcast on public access on a weekly basis both in the Los Angeles area (on Century Cable, Continental Cable, United Artists Cable, and West Hollywood Public Access Channel 36) and in neighbouring communities (including Ventura, San Diego, Santa Barbara and Palm Springs).

At a time when network news programming has for the most part dropped its coverage of HIV/AIDS treatment issues (while it nevertheless continues to report the more sensational AIDS-related stories), it is significant that centres such as Being Alive, APLA and the GMHC are still providing outreach for the general population. While information has always provided a framework for the more expressly politicized actions of groups such as ACT-UP, it is evident that the distribution of information has itself become a significant feature of a contemporary activist position; although programmes such as Being Alive's *Medical Update* are not of an expressly politicized form, they are nevertheless political. These programmes are political in the sense that they invert traditional hierarchies and/or knowledge-formations. Firstly, medical information is given out freely. Secondly, individuals are given the tools to perform self-diagnosis or, at the very least, are informed of their treatment options and able to review medical research prior to visiting a physician (and in many cases informed of new clinical trial opportunities). Lastly, while these programmes are aired on cable access, tapes are often made available for a nominal fee (or free of charge) for individuals who are not cable subscribers.

The existence of an access programme devoted solely to issues of HIV/AIDS must be considered within the context of the origin and evolution of activist strategies with respect to this specific disease (dealing with both misinformation and a general lack of information). These activist strategies need to be understood within the framework of 'the queer', and the unique position in which a marginalized group is placed when it is underrepresented by the media.[2] When placed at the margins, a group must formulate alternative routes to accessing information. At the same time, these activist strategies need to be understood within the framework of medical knowledge, which is itself an area of contestation. Many groups have contested the privileged status of medical doctors (for example, consider the recent investigation, led by former patients, of breast implant surgery). With each of these frames in mind, the existence of HIV/AIDS programming on public access is undoubtedly symptomatic of a larger problem in reportage.

Developing alongside these more politically engaged or information-based programmes, there are numerous access productions created by and for the queer community that, though certainly not disengaged or apolitical, are first and foremost entertaining; and in terms of defining a constructive televisual aesthetic, one that demonstrates a hegemonic resistance of marginalized groups against mainstream broadcast television (shows that 'look different' from network farc), the most progressive work is still found here. These programmes include a trio of shows produced as part of the New York-based Gay Entertainment Network (*Party Talk*, *Makostyle* and *Inside/Out*) and four shows produced by the New York-based Total Entertainment Network Plus, Inc. (10+, Inc.) (*The Gay 90s*, *The Barry Z Show*, *Drag Talk* and the *Gay Fashion Club*).

The Gay Entertainment Network is the brainchild of Marvin Schwam, which he formed to fill a media void in gay television. *Party Talk*, the network's flagship programme, began as an infomercial on NYC's commercial cable access channel 35 for a bulletin board Schwam had started about where to go out and where to party. About four months later, Schwam added more diverse personalities as spokespeople in order to more truly represent the gay community. In its current form, *Party Talk* showcases local gay and gay-friendly talent in a familiar format (with segments anchored by hosts), yet at the same time attempts to highlight what is happening in gay culture on a national level. Unique not only for being America's first soon-to-be syndicated gay/lesbian-oriented TV programme, *Party Talk* also enjoys the financial advantages of having acquired a rich, powerful, and hitherto mainstream corporate sponsor, Miller Lite.[3]

The Gay Entertainment Network's assault on the nation's commercial cable access channels also includes the shows *Inside Out*, an Oprah/Donahue-esque programme exploring subjects such as gay relationships, the corporate closet, and gay parenting; and *Makostyle*, hosted by photographer Christopher Makos (of *Interview* magazine fame), a show whose focus is on style, in its many yet mostly queer forms. The Network's shows are now airing in New York, Chicago and Miami, but will soon be appearing in other cities.

While the programmes of 10+, Inc. are currently being broadcast only in New York, they too encompass a broad range of formats and subjects.[4] *The Gay 90s*, like *Party Talk*, features a variety of segments, yet for the most part covers local events and celebrities. *The Barry Z Show*, like *Inside Out*, follows a more traditional one-on-one interview format, with the host Barry Z speaking with celebrated members of the local gay and lesbian community. *Drag Talk* follows a slightly altered talk show format, as the hostess Hedda Lettuce opens with a monologue, banters with other local drag divas, and closes with a solo performance. Lastly, the *Gay Fashion Club* (GFC) is modelled after the Home Shopping Network, but features clothing specifically for the fashion-conscious gay man.

The motivation of both network producers is to provide programming made *by* gay people and *for* gay people 24 hours a day, seven days a week. Yet is gay television simply symptomatic of the current proliferation of alternative cable networks in the USA such as a sports channel, CNN, a weather channel, Court TV, and an entertainment channel, joining the ranks of Black Entertainment Television and women's programming on LIFETIME?

Let us turn for a moment to the lessons taught to us by queer theory. The interdisciplinary nature of queer theory (as an approach that can be applied to a variety of subjects and that can incorporate a variety of critical vocabularies) has, so far, not prevented it from residing in the ghetto. Queer theory is a mode of inquiry that seeks to transgress borders (if not erase them altogether); the shift in terminology from 'gay and lesbian' to 'queer' was a strategical move that sought to both acknowledge and eradicate the internal 'differences' or margins established in traditional discourses surrounding alternative sexual practices and their respected communities and localized politics (differences, again, based on race, ethnicity, class, gender, and so on). Like other marginalized groups, queers have been asked to weigh the pros and cons of integration and segregation as part of their everyday lives. Securing the representation of difference should not be an end in itself. More important than token representation is the possibility of opening up a space in which a dialogue can occur; for *representing* difference does not necessarily guarantee *understanding* difference. Moreover, *how* can difference be represented in a manner that seeks to obscure its very nature (of being different)? Television producers need to think about more than content – they need to think about form.

The expansion of the number of broadcast channels (made possible through cable delivery) has not resulted in a correlative expansion of the diversity of available programmes. Most examples of narrowcasting have amounted to little more than extensions of specific pre-existing programming categories into entire channels, and access programming may itself be interpreted as the most extreme manifestation of narrowcasting – serving up shows that cater to a very select (and localized) demographic (Walden, 1991: 22–3). Furthermore, many access programmes rely on generic formulas derived from network television (though their production values are quite distinct).[5] What does it mean for a gay-themed talk show to adopt the already established conventions of the network talk show?

Do the formative networks of Gay Entertainment Television and 10+, Inc. want to be transgressive (a question of intentionality)? Does the content of their shows (despite and in spite of their respective forms) make them in some way transgressive? Does the eroticism of the *Gay Fashion Club* in some way 'pervert' one's reading of the Home Shopping Network (or bring to the surface an already existing subtext)? Does Hedda Lettuce appear to be (to use Dick Hebdige's phrase) 'consigned to a place beyond analysis' (being queer, being on cable), or does she, by virtue of her active dialogue with the space of access and her reflexive acknowledgment of the sphere of network television (both in the content of her work – which is littered with pop culture references – and in her method of presentation) actively adopt and appropriate it, marking it as her own? (Hebidige, 1979: 97). Though the content of these shows is notably different from network fare, the formats (genres) are quite similar (predominantly talk shows and variety/magazine shows).

Yet genre and content are only two variables at work here. The third, and perhaps most important variable (one that allows us to expand our consideration beyond the boundaries of the 'queer' text and into the realm of the 'independent' text) is execution or 'style'. The producers of many access programmes are unapologetic users of cheap media, with a commitment to making alternative media which directly counter and interfere with dominant media assumptions. One could argue that the more potentially subversive programmes adhere to a number of identifiable aesthetic principles, foremost among them 'showing the seams'. Using a relatively unpolished style (an aesthetic dictated by its limiting conditions), these programmes, in effect, demystify the processes of live television and suggest that making shows need not be prohibitively expensive. The 'style' of such shows is commonly marked by a simplicity of design and lighting, a single stationary camera and a static wide angle shot, in-camera effects, a minimum of editing, low end graphics and a raw sound quality. By virtue of their departure from network standards, most of these programmes have an immediately discernible visual quality and by using improvisation (with a minimum of scripting) many have an immediacy in their narrative format akin to a guerrilla-*verité* style (and Agitprop theatre). Certainly, there are two tendencies at work here; on the one hand, the *Gay Fashion Club* tries quite hard to mirror the look (and harmonious narrative flow) of the Home Shopping Network, while both *Party Talk* and *Drag Talk* combine an impromptu nature with low-budget sets and cheap special effects in a remarkably effective manner. Like all gay camp, the amateurishness of both *Party Talk* and *Drag Talk* could be the secret of their success in challenging the assumptions of dominant television.

However, this binary of alternative and mainstream reifies the alternative text and only engages us in a formal analysis of programmes, reading their surfaces to determine their differences. As intervention, as access, as a form of securing or rethinking media discourse, how does one gauge the use value of these texts? What is their effectiveness? Where is their subversiveness?

Artist and activist Gregg Bordowitz has noted that television is a 'situation' that can be used in directed pragmatic ways as a means of defensive action; however, if made in the interests of community, it can also be pro-active. The fact that some of the programmes used in this analysis are engaged in a critique of the media (most often through satire) is in part the result of the inherent character of queer-aligned strategies, and not necessarily the result of any directed political action.

Regardless, the 'work' done by these programmes is tied to their production, distribution and exhibition. Created *by* and *for* a more localized community (more localized than the network text), these programmes approximate collective involvement (between producers and viewers), if not unified resistance. First and foremost, public access programmes are made in the interests of a particular audience, an audience of which its producers and performers are also a part.

The 'community standards' under which local access stations have been operating are perhaps the last holdout of an ever-shrinking 'public sphere' of community-based communications systems; and as we enter the digital age, public access and community video have once again landed at the centre of a debate about censorship and the First Amendment. Several recent cases clearly illustrate that public access is quite a contested terrain:

In mid-August of 1993, Colorado Springs Cable Vision (located in Colorado Springs, home of numerous right-wing religious groups and a population that overwhelmingly voted in favour of Amendment 2, a ban on gay right's laws) refused to air *Sacred Lies, Civil Truths*, a pro-gay video.

On 16 August 1993 the American Civil Liberties Union filed a lawsuit against Denver Community Television, a cable television firm, for violating the free-speech rights of' the host and producer of the public access programme *Magazine* by refusing to air one of its programmes. (The company contended that the programme contained obscene footage that suggested a man was performing fellatio.)

On 26 August 1993 the producer and host of the Austin, Texas public access programme *Infosex* was indicted on charges of promoting obscenity and exposing minors to prurient material for airing a programme that included footage from a safer-sex video.

As information has become a profitable commodity, access to it for free has become considerably more difficult. The cable corporations are attempting to use the First Amendment as a means of protecting their corporate profits, and to reclaim channels that are devoted to access so that they may be used for profitable ventures; and the 'public interest' (as it relates to media) is being defined and redefined by politicians, lobbyists, commercial networks, executives, analysts, critics and academics – by everyone, it seems, but the public itself. If community-based programming is to survive at all, it cannot afford simply to follow the lead of network television, but rather needs to serve as a forum for envisioning the future of the medium. Community-based programming, however, does not generate itself. It requires not only an active base of producers, but an active base of viewers – informed citizens who know how much they can demand from their cable operators and their elected officials (many of whom do not support public access programming and feel no need to ask local operators to provide channel capacity and/or equipment for it). With this in mind, we cannot wait for television to fall into our hands. We need to take it with whatever force is necessary.

Notes

1.   In this context 'amateur' is not a derogatory term; it does not signify a lack of proficiency but simply a lack of resources. The 'amateur' vs. 'professional' distinction is, as defined here, only an economic one.
2.   Representation is itself a highly charged subject. A group can be marginalized yet have high media visibility, or a group can be marginalized and have no media visibility at all. Furthermore, underrepresentation cannot simply be positioned as the consequence

of marginality, but invariably a cause as well. In each case, it is not simply the act of being (or not being) represented, but more importantly *how* one is represented. I do not have the space here to speak at length about the politics of representation with respect to positive and negative images, and have limited myself to speaking about having the *opportunity* to represent oneself as well as the choices that are made in constructing a representation of self.

3. These shows appear on leased access, not public access; while commercial sponsorship is not permitted on public access, it can be used on leased access to offset programming fees. Though the support of a corporate monolith like Miller may seem surprising, it is in fact perfectly in synch with numerous other national advertisers who have begun courting the gay discretionary income. Most sponsors, however, appear to be more comfortable in gay publications than on gay television. Perhaps this is because print advertising is literally bound to a particular context and audience, while broadcast advertising is more likely to be picked up by anyone and everyone within the open flow of television. But more likely the absence of widespread corporate sponsorship on gay television is simply due to the (perceived) absence of gay television (though there is an acknowledged presence of gay-friendly television).

4. The programmes of the Gay Entertainment Network and 10+, Inc. had been airing on leased access in Los Angeles until 1995. Their disappearance from the Los Angeles market can be attributed to 1) a lack of regional sponsors (advertising dollars are necessary to offset the cost of leasing time), and 2) the increasing editorial control certain cable operators have exercised over programming on leased access.

5. The most distinguishing feature of drag programmes is also what is most problematic about them: the persona of the hostess. Public access shows such as *Drag Talk*, *Brenda and Glennda* (produced in New York), *DeAundra Peek* (produced near Atlanta), and *Decoupage* (produced in Los Angeles) are true to form to network talk shows in the credence that each gives to star power, for each show is only as successful as its hostess.

References and Further Reading

BODDY, W., 1990: 'Alternative television in the United States'. *Screen*, 31, 1: 91–101.

BOYLE, D., 1990: 'A brief history of American documentary video'. In Doug Hall and Sally Jo Fifer (eds), *Illuminating Video: An Essential Guide to Video Art*. New York: Aperture Foundation, Inc. and the Bay Area Video Coalition, 51–69.

BRECHT, B., 1986: 'The radio as an apparatus of communication'. In John Hanhardt (ed.), *Video Culture: A Critical Investigation*. Layton, Utah: Gibbs, M. Smith Inc., Peregrine Smith Books and the Visual Studies Workshop, 53–5.

GOLDBERG K., 1990: *The Barefoot Channel: Community Television as a Tool for Social Change*. Vancouver: New Star Books.

HEBDIGE, D., 1979: *Subculture: The Meaning of Style*. London and New York: Routledge.

KELLNER, D., 1987: 'Public access television: alternative views'. In Donald Lazere (ed.), *American Media and Mass Culture: Left Perspectives*. Berkeley and Los Angeles: University of California Press, 610–18.

MARCUS, D., (ed.), 1991: *Roar! The Paper Tiger Television Guide to Media Activism*. New York: Paper Tiger Television Collective.

ROSLER, M., 1990: 'Video: shedding the utopian moment'. In Doug Hall and Sally Jo Fifer (eds), *Illuminating Video: An Essential Guide to Video Art*. New York: Aperture Foundation, Inc. and the Bay Area Video Coalition, 31–50.

SHAMBERG, M., 1971: *Guerrilla Television*. New York and Chicago: Holt, Rinehart and Winston.

STIER, K., 1982: 'Tangled tactics: Big Apple cable franchise'. *Independent*, 5, 1: 9–12.

WALDEN, J., 1991: 'Unpacking the revolution in a box'. In Daniel Marcus (ed.), *Roar! The Paper Tiger Television Guide to Media Activism*. New York: Paper Tiger Television Collective, 22–4.

Getting on television is commonly seen as crucial if you want to communicate your views. Television has been characterised since the 1950s as a powerful manipulator and mediator and, as the essays by Freedman and Kintz show, activist groups often feel that access to television is a necessary way for them to establish a presence with the viewers (and the voters). Struggle for access goes on in a rather different way in mainstream television and Ivor Gaber's essay looks at the way in which mainstream politicians and their organisers try to organise their television appearances to their best advantage. The debate about how political control is or is not exerted in the media has been a long-standing topic not only among academics but among practitioners and politicians, and the 1990s saw an increase in complaints that political debate was increasingly dominated by the demands of the media and particularly of television.

Gaber writes as a journalist who has worked extensively in British television on political and parliamentary issues. His account is based therefore on his own experience of production since his work brings him every day under the pressures he describes in his essay. Television news requirements for immediacy mean that decisions have to be made quickly – hence the importance of the production framework which Gaber describes. He argues forcefully that politicians still control television's news agenda since, although they like to complain about how they are treated on the news, the mechanisms for control lie with them. At the micro-level, Gaber describes the day-to-day efforts which political parties make to control how they are represented – efforts which have resulted in a new language of 'spin doctors', sound-bites and 'terms of engagement' in which it is agreed what issues an interview can and cannot cover. More broadly, Gaber describes how British television's requirements for balance and objectivity favour the two main parties by locking them into a binary opposition which makes it more difficult for other voices to be heard. This is consolidated by the establishment of permanent media teams to act as filters and controllers for the political parties in the organisation of access. The case studies with which he concludes his essay, particularly the account of Mrs Thatcher's handling of environmental issues, give evidence, Gaber argues, of the success of the politicians' strategies.

Gaber also draws attention in his case studies to the complex interaction between different media in establishing how and when a news item will run. In particular, he looks at the way in which politicians can choose between the press, radio and television for their outlets; like other contributors, Gaber looks at changes in technology and argues that the proliferation of media outlets for news, particularly through cable and satellite television, has increased the competition for media access to the key figures in any story and given the politicians the opportunity to go to the reporters or programmes who give them the most sympathetic or 'soft' coverage.

Gaber's essay is written from inside television's institutions and deals therefore with what he knows most intimately – the television reporting of British parliamentary activity which provides his source material. Nevertheless, his contribution has resonances with news reporting in other arenas. Much of what he describes, for instance, is deemed to be US in origin (unlike the tabloidisation of the press which is characterised as a British phenomenon) and the assumption that television has changed politics for the worse is part of the more general world-wide association between television, US culture and a threat to national standards and values. Gaber clears the way, perhaps, for a more informed debate about how we should understand television's news agenda.

16

Television and Political Coverage

Ivor Gaber

> It would be a shocking thing to have the debates of Parliament forestalled on this new robot organisation of television! . . . The rights of M.P.s have to be protected 'against the mass and against the machine'.
>
> Winston Churchill MP 1946

Winston Churchill was prescient, although not necessarily right. Just after a war fought against dictators who had made skilful use of the new means of mass communication – film and radio – Winston Churchill was acutely aware that the even newer medium of television had to be treated with caution. He feared that television, even more than radio or film, represented a real threat to the political system under which he had prospered – a system based on a national press, the London Clubs and above all the House of Commons.

Today he would no doubt be a horrified observer of the current British political scene, in which No. 4 Millbank, a mock-Edwardian building across the road from Parliament, stands as the symbol of what for many is the electronic media's dominance of current day politics. For it is here that the radio and television studios of all the major British broadcasting networks are now housed. And it is in these studios, it is argued, that the real political dramas of the day are played out, rather than on the floor of the House of Commons.

Even on those few occasions when the media's attention is focused on events inside Parliament, such as the now weekly ritual of Prime Minister's Question Time, critics claim that the real power still lies with the broadcasters. 'Any M.P. can stand up in he House and say what he or she likes', one Member of Parliament told the author, 'but it's you guys, who decide whether anything that he's said is worthy of putting on the national news, who've got the real power.'[1]

On both sides of the Atlantic television news is now the major source of information for most people. In the UK, large numbers of people watch television news on a daily basis – consistently seven to eight million each evening for the main bulletins, and slightly fewer for the early evening bulletins. On days of real political significance, for example when Margaret Thatcher resigned, those audiences can rise to 12 million or more – one in three of the adult population.

On the other hand, we need to keep these figures in perspective, for with 10 million reading the daily tabloid the *Sun* and around eight million reading the *Daily Mirror*, those two papers are reaching more people on an average day than television news bulletins.

Nevertheless, people certainly believe they rely more on television for their national and international news than any other medium. The Independent Television Commission has been monitoring people's news sources since the early 1970s and their most recent data show that 62 per cent say that television was their preferred source for keeping up with national news compared with 17 per cent who say they rely on newspapers. It is hardly surprising: whatever the limitations on the number of stories and lack of detail, broadcasting's immediacy and vividness cannot be matched by the print media. Television – and to a lesser but still significant extent radio – therefore keeps us informed and provides us with the informational sustenance that we need as citizens in a democracy to hold considered opinions and make intelligent decisions about which representatives to elect.[2]

The broadcast media are the engine room of an informed democracy, but an engine room which is undergoing rapid and not always predictable change. And the focal point of this change is the relationship between politicians and the broadcasters – a relationship which is usually tense, sometimes abrasive and always subject to the most intense public scrutiny. But it is not an equal relationship. This is because politicians keep tightly within their own control a whole panoply of controls. These range from the highly formal, such as the awarding of the BBC's charter and licence, through the slightly less formal, such as the power to appoint members of the Boards of Governors of the BBC and ITC, through to the highly informal myriad of pressures that politicians bring to bear on broadcasters to secure favourable coverage. But despite the politicians' dominance, the relationship is one that never ceases to attract public interest and argument.

The BBC's Director General, John Birt, weighed into the debate in 1995 when he appeared to criticise the way broadcasters, and in particular the BBC, were covering politics. Birt argued that broadcasters were having a negative effect on the democratic process because of their apparent ability to control the political news agenda. Some of his thinking was informed by the work of Steve Richards, then one of the BBC's own political correspondents,[3] who has argued that because of the rapid expansion of broadcast news and current affairs outlets, broadcasters had been able to seize the news initiative. 'The endless round of political interviews,' he wrote, 'sustains stories that would otherwise have faded away. As such whenever a politician is in trouble, he tends to stay in trouble for much longer' (Richards, 1995: 60–5).

In his research Richards looked in detail at how this process could be seen at its clearest as a result of the mushrooming of political interview programmes which are transmitted on radio and television on Sunday mornings. He argued that the process ran thus: television (and for that matter radio) producers decided whom to invite onto their Sunday morning interview programmes. These programmes are then avidly watched, if not by the general public, then certainly by the political correspondents who, in the absence of other material on a Sunday, fell upon these interviews as manna from Television Centre. In this situation any politician deviating from the accepted party line received a quantity of coverage which bore no relationship to the substance of the story. In support of his thesis Richards provides a number of examples from the divisions over Europe and his own leadership which had dogged the Conservative Prime Minister John Major in the period 1994–95. These he compares with the relative ease with which, he argues, Labour Prime Minister Harold Wilson was able to deal with a potential leadership challenge back in 1968 when, in the absence of today's range of broadcasting outlets, he only had to worry about a hostile press and recalcitrant colleagues.

In the light of the new-found media phenomenon of the 'gaffe' – in which politicians are pilloried for alleging straying from the perceived party-line – the Richards thesis has much to commend it. But it also presents certain difficulties. First, it is difficult to sustain the notion that politicians are wholly passive participants in this process – the result of some arbitrary exchange of telephone calls responded to, or not, as the case may be. In fact politicians end up in television studios as a result of a ruthless process of management and manipulation by the parties' media machines. The 'terms of engagement' behind the agreement of a politician to appear on a radio or television programme are usually the end product of tough negotiations. And the greater number of broadcasting outlets with which politicians and/or their advisers are now able to negotiate actually increases the power of politicians and their advisers to set their own terms of engagement, since they are able to negotiate with producers with the implicit, and sometimes explicit, threat that if the terms are not satisfactory then they will take their 'business' elsewhere. And even once an agreement has been reached, the words that politicians say, and the nuances they appear to offer, are in the main far from spontaneous. Andrew Lansley, Head of Research at Conservative Central Office between 1990 and 1995 and now a Conservative MP, has noted: 'I have observed the care that politicians take in preparing for interviews and nothing that they don't want to be said is said' (Lansley, 1995).

Another difficulty raised by the Richards thesis is that it is dependent on the notion that it is possible to make a meaningful judgement as to whether a story has originated from a politician or the media. Such distinctions are, at the very least, problematic since the political news agenda is influenced by a myriad number of factors which are almost impossible to isolate; and even if such isolation was possible it is still difficult to sustain the argument that it is largely the broadcasters who are in control. For example, a few days before the British Chancellor of the Exchequer's annual budget statement, a story appeared in a Sunday newspaper claiming that the Chancellor was going to introduce a windfall profits tax on the public utilities – gas, electricity, etc. (*Observer*, 19 November 1995). It was a major story on that day's television and radio bulletins and the following day the story moved on (*Guardian*, 20 November 1995), with newspapers suggesting that opposition to such a move was building on the Conservative back-benches. The interesting point about this story, apart from the fact that it turned out to be totally untrue, is who ensured that it became and remained one of the top political stories in the broadcasting media in the two days leading up to the Budget. There are six possible 'culprits' who are relevant not just to this story but to the wider political agenda-setting debate.

First, the press ran with the story on two consecutive days and they, it is claimed, set the agenda for the broadcasters; in this instance they amplified it by putting it at the top of their budget stories (as Roy Hattersley, a former deputy leader of the Labour Party, has said: 'Broadcasters feel an irresistible desire to follow the lead of the newspapers' (Hattersley, 1993: 78)). The source could have been the politicians – Labour, who for long have been campaigning in favour of such a tax, or a Conservative, perhaps from the Right of the Party, hoping that leaking might spike the Chancellor's guns; it could even have been the Chancellor himself who wanted the story set up as an Aunt Sally, so that he could knock it down, as he did, two days later. It could have been another media source such as a civil servant perhaps, hearing the wrong end of a conversation; or maybe external agencies – the utilities themselves hoping to deflect public criticism, or perhaps it was that most elusive of concepts, public opinion, which although unable to initiate stories in the first place does play a major role in heightening their salience and, in the case under consideration, was clearly antagonistic to the way the utilities were conducting themselves, making such a tax appear to be a popular option to pursue. Thus one could identify six factors which contributed to this particular item rising up the political agenda – the press, the broadcasters, the politicians, other outside sources, external events and public opinion.

All these factors play their role in building the political news agenda; they are involved in a dynamic and constantly evolving relationship with each other. However, despite the complexity of the relationship, it is possible to detect within this constantly changing matrix the dominating position held by the politicians in the process and this control comes about because of the political environment within which the game is played.

This environment buttresses the power of the politicians from the two major parties over the broadcasters. The British political system is highly polarised which, despite the efforts of the present-day Liberal Democrats, the SDP and others, has been a constant in the political culture for the past 250 years and is even reflected in the confrontational layout of the House of Commons. Confrontation and bipolarity are endemic to the British political system. Broadcasters are going to reflect that bipolarity in their political coverage, but it also serves their purposes. This is, first, because straightforward conflict creates entertaining and exciting television but, secondly and more importantly, because the partisan nature of British politics is ideally suited to enable broadcasters to claim that they are meeting their legislative commitments to demonstrate impartiality and balance. Complex issues can be difficult to cover from 'all sides', but if they can be reduced to a basic 'Labour says this, the Tories say that' then both the broadcasters and the politicians are satisfied – at least the politicians from the two main parties are, which, whilst they remain the realistic contenders for power, is all that really matters as far as the broadcasters are concerned.

Another aspect of the political environment is that it is now dominated by a growing army of professional 'spin doctors' (formerly known as press officers) making the role of the parties (not to mention the government's) media operations a major factor in the political landscape. For example, a few years ago it would have been inconceivable for broadcasters to feel that they had to make their 'bids' for political interviewees to anyone other than the politician him or herself; today it is almost inconceivable that such bids would not go through the relevant press officers. (The situation with ministers is somewhat different in that the activities of Whitehall press officers are not a new phenomenon, although the degree of their control is.) This gives tremendous power to press officers to grant or deny access, depending on how satisfied they are feeling with the coverage they are receiving from the particular outlet in question. Denial of access is a relatively minor nuisance for a newspaper, but for a broadcaster it is potentially disastrous – for a political report that does not contain the voice or picture of the central characters is, to say the least, less than satisfactory. At the other end of the spectrum there is the growing practice of party machines making spokespeople available to programmes uninvited, thus putting the producer in the unenviable position of either broadcasting an interview which he or she had not sought or sending the politician away and risking a major row with its resultant negative consequences.

And the parties are now *all* giving a far higher profile to media activities. Looking at the Labour Party, for example, in the early 1980s the Labour Party's media team consisted of a press officer, a broadcasting officer and two others. Today it is a many-headed operation, operating out of party headquarters, the regional offices, Parliament, the Shadow Cabinet offices, the Deputy Leader's Office and the Leader's Office. There are now around 50 people involved in Labour's media operations, with a doubling of that number once an election campaign gets underway. Given the sheer quantity, experience and energy of such a team it is hardly surprising that their impact is so observable.

Both major parties now openly acknowledge that they see control of the political news agenda as central to their objectives. Conservative Andrew Lansley has written: 'For a political party the primary objective is to control the agenda, by determining the issues of political debate . . .' (Lansley, 1995). Such sentiments are echoed across the political divide. Joy Johnson, a former Labour Party director of media and campaigns, has written: 'The party that captures the news initiative will both dominate the agenda and wrong-foot their opponents' (Johnson, 1995).

An account of the unfolding of the British political day well illustrates this point. For the staff of BBC Radio's *Today* programme, seen by many as the primary political agenda-setter, their day in fact begins the night before when the following morning's political coverage is planned between *Today* producers based at Broadcasting House and the BBC's political staff. This usually involves one of the BBC's political correspondents going into Broadcasting House at 6.30 a.m. for what is known as the 'early two-way' – a semi-arranged conversation between the *Today* presenter and the correspondent about the key political issues of the day. Much of this conversation will have been based on the intelligence that the correspondent had gathered from talking to politicians or press officers, by considering the day's diary of parliamentary and political events and by reading the first editions of the national press – most of these activities being heavily biased towards the politicians' view of the news agenda.

This will probably be followed later in the programme by political interviews developing the theme or themes of the 'two-way'. These interviews will be monitored and responded to by other broadcasters and the evening newspaper journalists. In the course of the day the national print journalists will join the fray to add their own contribution to the mix. At the same time the broadcasters will have had in front of them that morning's papers and will be working out how, if at all, they should be reacting to the national newspapers' political coverage. In addition there are various fixed points in the political day. There are the twice-

daily briefings given by the Prime Minister's Press Secretary at which government announcements are foreshadowed, the Downing Street 'line' on current
issues presented and political gossip exchanged; the twice-weekly Prime
Minister's Question Time which, apart from providing a story or stories in itself,
gives lobby correspondents a chance to buttonhole MPs, who tend to be a little
more elusive at other times of the week; and during a normal parliamentary day
there will be other occasions when correspondents will go into the chamber to
hear a specific debate or attend a meeting of a committee. However, their main
activity is talking with MPs in the House of Commons lobbies, bars and tea-
rooms and conducting conversations among themselves and with the parties'
media teams.

These media teams follow a daily routine which almost mirrors that of the
journalists. They might well have been involved in negotiations with *Today* or
other broadcasting outlets about the 'terms of engagement' for the morning
interviews, including arguing for one of the prime spots. They might also have
been on the phone to the broadcasters 'advising' them on developing stories.
Party media teams, like news organisations, have their own daily editorial meeting where they look at the issues that have come up so far and are expected to
come up later; at these meetings they plan their own media initiatives and work
out how to respond to opposition moves and to other news developments. This
sort of operation is what one might anticipate during an election period but is
now a permanent feature of the political scene.

All of this enormously enhances the ability of politicians to dictate the
media's news agenda. This proposition can be illustrated, if not actually proved,
by reference to two very different case studies.

The first relates to the history of environmental coverage in Britain.[4] Interest
in the environment always scores highly when people are asked to state their
major political concerns[5] and yet only intermittently does it surface in a major
way onto the media's agenda. There was, for example, a brief burst of media
interest in the environment as a result of the activities of Greenpeace in places
as diverse as the North Sea and the South Pacific, but when no major party or
politician took up the issue, that interest died. Prior to this flurry the last time
the British media evinced any interest in environmental issues was in the second
half of 1988 – a wave of interest that lasted through until 1990.[6]

At the time, there was both an overall rise in awareness of issues such as
global warming and the hole in the ozone layer, but there were also specific
stories which attracted significant media and hence public attention. First, there
was an outbreak of an unknown illness in the North Sea in the summer of 1988
which was killing seals at an alarming rate. Then in September environmental
interest was further stimulated by the story of the *Karen B*, a freighter that was
bound for Britain loaded with toxic waste; following a high-profile media campaign, the government was forced into refusing the *Karen B* permission to
unload its cargo in Britain.

Research conducted among environment reporters identified these two
issues as particular significant moments in the conversion of Margaret
Thatcher, then Prime Minister, from, as one put it, 'the iron maiden to the green
goddess'.[7] Mrs Thatcher went publicly 'green' in a speech to the Royal Society in
London in September 1988. But in fact this transformation was a more gradual
process for Mrs Thatcher, as she later revealed in her memoirs. She claims her

interest in the environment was first stimulated in 1987, before the 'seals' plague' and the *Karen B*, in response to what she saw as legitimate concern about the environment being used 'to attack capitalism, growth and industry' (Thatcher, 1993: 639). As a result, she set about reclaiming the issue for the Conservatives. And despite the fact that environmental correspondents believe that the turning-point was her speech at the Royal Society,[8] Mrs Thatcher recalls that in fact media interest in that speech was at the time negligible. She recalled the problems caused by the absence of that interest:

> It broke new political ground – but it is an extraordinary commentary on the lack of media interest in the subject that, contrary to my expectations, the television did not even bother to send film crews to cover the occasion. In fact, I had been relying on the television lights to enable me to read my script in the gloom of the Fishmonger's Hall, where it was to be delivered; in the event, candelabra had to be passed up along the table to allow me to do so. (Thatcher 1993: 640)

However, following the positive reception given to the speech, a month later she used her address to the annual Conservative Party Conference to reiterate her new-found interest in environmentalism. Following these two interventions there was a huge increase in the amount of space devoted to environmental coverage in the national media . For example, references to 'global warming' in a sample of national newspapers were three times as frequent in the 12 months after Mrs Thatcher's speech as compared with the 12 months before.[9] And, in the year following Mrs Thatcher's two speeches the number of environment correspondents employed by national newspapers increased from one to 12.

However, this new-found political interest in environmentalism came to a shuddering halt following the elections for the European Parliament in June 1989. These saw the hitherto minuscule Green Party win 2.3 million votes or 15 per cent of the total vote. Mrs Thatcher believed that virtually all those votes had come from the Conservatives (Thatcher, 1993: 750). And that was the last time that the Conservatives, or for that matter Labour either, put green issues at the top of their agendas – and the media appeared to follow suit. Over the next 12 months all the tabloid newspapers and Independent Television News dispensed with their dedicated environment correspondents and, by 1991, references in the British press to environmental issues had returned to the levels that existed prior to Mrs Thatcher's 1988 intervention.

The second case study involves an examination of BBC Television's *Nine O'Clock News* and ITV's *News at Ten*. The study was an attempt to examine the extent to which the political stories covered by the two main news programmes on British television were generated by the media, the parties or came from elsewhere. The BBC's *Nine O'Clock News* was monitored between July and August 1995; in that period Parliament was in session for only two and a half weeks out of the ten and the period had been immediately preceded by John Major's successful attempt to have himself re-elected as Leader of the Conservative Party. Hence, if the media could be seen to be driving political agenda, then a period of low parliamentary activity should be a good moment to observe the phenomenon.

The *Nine O'Clock News* is the BBC's flagship evening news. If something significant has taken place during the day then, so the theory goes, it will be on the programme. When Parliament is sitting there is normally an average of 10 main stories, called reporter packages, on each bulletin, of which one or two would normally come from Westminster. In July and August of 1995 there were 22 political packages on 40 editions of the *Nine O'Clock News*; seven of these were directly attributable to initiatives by the government or Conservative Party, four to initiatives by the Labour Party and one to the Liberal Democrats, six were stories about events such as parliamentary debates or by-elections and four were reports of Labour Party criticism of Tony Blair.

A similar comparative exercise was undertaken in March and April of 1996, this time monitoring ITN's flagship programme *News at Ten*. In that period, in which apart from Easter, Parliament was in continuous session, the following breakdown of political packages was observed: of the 36 reports emanating from ITN's political staff, seven related to one particular event, the outbreak of BSE or 'mad cow disease', six were reports of continuing European differences within the Conservative Party, five resulted from initiatives by the Labour Party, two were reports of government announcements, one was an account of Prime Minister's Question Time (a lower figure than most observers would have predicted) and just two resulted from journalistic investigation.

No major theory can be postulated on the basis of such a limited sample. However, the observation can be made that in this particular period, and perhaps it goes for other times as well, it is difficult to sustain the argument that the broadcasters were setting the political agenda. The argument is reinforced by the fact that many of the other stories that ran in the periods monitored could also be traced back to the activities of politicians but were not covered by political correspondents – these ranged over issues such as rail privatisation and water shortages. These latter stories also raise some interesting questions about provenance; for often stories that look like they have resulted from old-fashioned journalistic enterprise have in fact been fed to the journalist by the parties. The Labour Party, for example, in the 1995 period under consideration, devoted considerable time and attention to digging out instances of mishaps in the newly privatised utilities – whether they were the inadequacies of the ageing water supply system, rail safety, or the alleged iniquities of share option schemes. Several of the stories that appeared on these subjects were prompted by Labour Party press releases or news conferences; some had been 'leaked' to sympathetic journalists by the Labour Party in the hope that as 'exclusives' they would receive more exposure; and just a few have been as a result of genuine journalistic enterprise – but even then, it could be argued, these entrepreneurial activities have been undertaken only because Labour had made these issues salient.

In other words, whether looking at the presence or absence of whole categories such as the environment, or looking at specific stories on specific days, it is difficult to deny the argument that it is politicians, and equally importantly their media teams, who are driving the news agenda. Speaking after the 1992 General Election, former Conservative Party Chairman Norman (now Lord) Tebbit, said: 'It doesn't matter how hard the broadcasters try they will, on the whole, be pushed back on to the issues on which the . . . politicians, the most powerful group, has decided it wants to address' (Tebbit, 1993). And he went on to state explicitly that he believed that the driving force behind the creation of this agenda was and remains the strength of political ideas that are driving the parties and politicians: 'Let me make one important point about agenda setting and the power of the media,' he said referring to the impact of Thatcherism on

British politics in the 1980s, 'Who changed the agenda of the seventies into the agenda of the eighties? Was it the broadcasters, who took the lead and produced that profound change in British politics, which began with the election of 1979 and has run through into the nineties? No, it was the people who had ideas' (Tebbit, 1993). Lord Tebbit's logic is difficult to refute.

Notes

1. This information is based on a private conversation with the author who is currently (1997) based at Westminster, overseeing political coverage for Independent Television News.
2. See for example Wober (1992) which demonstrates that around 80 per cent of the viewing public were satisfied or very satisfied with the quality of political coverage they saw during the 1992 General Election campaign.
3. This is based on private conversations in 1995 when the author was a member of the BBC staff.
4. This case study is based on work undertaken by the author as part of an Economic and Social Research Council research project into the media and the environment. The results of this research are due to be published in Chapman et al. (1997).
5. In response to a Gallup question in 1993 'What do you think is the most important issue affecting the world at the present time?', 28 per cent responded 'War', whilst 26 per cent identified environmental issues. This, at a time when the level of coverage in the national press of environmental issues was running at a level of barely one-quarter of its 1990 high point. And research undertaken by Research International for the Henley Centre in the same year revealed that environmental issues came out as the number one priority in terms of respondents' interests in local and national news items.
6. See Anderson (1993).
7. See Chapman et al. (1997).
8. Ibid.
9. Ibid.

References

ANDERSON, A., 1993: 'The production of environmental news: a study of source-media relations'. Unpublished Ph.D thesis, University of Plymouth.
BRIGGS, A., 1995: *History of Broadcasting in the United Kingdom*, Vols 1–5. Oxford: Oxford University Press.
CHAPMAN, G., KUMAR K., FRASER C. and GABER I. 1997: *The Mass Media, Environmentalism and the North-South Divide*. London: Routledge.
HATTERSLEY, R., 1993: speaking at 'The Westminster Consultation'. Unpublished transcript, Goldsmiths College, London.
JOHNSON, J., 1995: 'Driving the News'. Unpublished Labour Party strategy document.
KELLNER, P., 1993: speaking at 'The Westminster Consultation'. Unpublished transcript, Goldsmiths College, London.
LANSLEY, A., 1995: lecture given at the London School of Economics.
LINTON, M., 1996: 'Maybe the Sun Won it After All'. *British Journalism Review*, 7, 2: 20–6.

RICHARDS, S., 1995: 'Soundbite Politics'. Reuter Foundation Paper 14, Green College, Oxford.

TEBBIT, N., 1993: speaking at 'The Westminster Consultation'. Unpublished transcript, Goldsmiths College, London.

THATCHER, M., 1993: *The Downing Street Years*. London: HarperCollins.

WOBER, J. M., 1992: 'Televising the election: a preliminary report on knowledge, news use and attitudes in the United Kingdom'. London: Independent Television Commission.

INTRODUCTION TO CHAPTER 17

In his examination of Brazilian *telenovelas*, Aluizio Trinta looks at a phenomenon which has spread well beyond Latin America. *Telenovelas*, massively successful in their country of origin, have been exported not only within Latin America but also to the USA, Europe, Africa and Asia. Trinta focuses on production context and text to trace a history of the format in Brazil and to analyse the implications of some of the changes that have taken place.

There is a tendency in academic work on *telenovelas* to measure them against the definitions of soap opera which have figured so strongly in Television Studies and are discussed in Laura Stempel Mumford's contribution in Section I. Trinta, while he acknowledges that relationship, stresses also other factors. Firstly, he comments on the way in which the increasing popularity and marketability of the programmes were sustained by a visual style which owes more to cinema in its emphasis on camera technique and action scenes on location than to the domestic interiors of daytime soaps. Secondly, Trinta argues that while *telenovelas* clearly draw on the complex traditions of melodrama, it is important also to recognise their realist components. Trinta describes the way in which the programmes have shifted from a preoccupation with romance to the dramatisation of contemporary problems in a recognisable world in which the acting style, script and dilemmas parallel or mimic the events and conversations which the audiences experience in their own lives.

Trinta's analysis contributes to wider debates about television as a medium. While soaps have been studied in terms of their gendered audience, Trinta argues that the audience for *telenovelas* is more mixed in terms of both gender and class. It may be that this shift to a more respectable audience is figured in the emphasis on the high production values associated with cinema and the traditions of education and information associated with realism. In both cases, television is moving outside its pejorative associations with low budget entertainment.

Trinta goes on, however, to argue that this 'borrowing' is not all one-way. Drawing on arguments about television flow, he suggests that the news and *telenovelas* share certain common formal characteristics – an emphasis on immediacy, the use of pictures and images as visual, emotional stimuli, the establishment of a repertoire of familiar images and stories which allows for explanations to be offered and accepted. Trinta suggest that both *telenovelas* and news items demand an emotional response and a symbolic framework which allows them to be understood within a national context. Significantly, Trinta's discussion closes with a description of a mixed genre programme – a news programme in which a true story is re-enacted with all the codes of realism to produce the impact of real life, or of melodrama.

17

News from Home: A Study of Realism and Melodrama in Brazilian *Telenovelas*

Aluizio R. Trinta

Television is arguably the most important mass media communication system in Brazil, where television broadcasting began in the early 1950s. Since then, *telenovelas* have gradually grown to be a specific feature of the television system in Brazil. In general, the *telenovela* (or 'television novel') is a genre developed with success by Latin American countries, particularly Mexico, Venezuela, Argentina and Brazil. The origins of Latin American *telenovelas* can be traced back to the *roman feuilleton*, the 'chap book' style mass literature, which was so esteemed by the end of the nineteenth century in France. More importantly, Latin American *telenovelas* have a great deal in common with the theatricality that defines the melodramatic genre. Common elements include emotional entanglements involving well-established characters and the traditional romance plot with true love triumphing over adversity; characterisation is clearly subordinated to plot and spectacular physical action predominates. The plot is developed around a sad 'love story', whose end is reached by resolving a certain number of interwoven situations. In this way, affectionate and tender devotion always wins a victory over evil. Happiness to be found in love is obtained only through high moral purpose. As in the purest melodrama tradition, music plays a large role in creating mood, and 'incidental music' adds to the dramatic climaxes. Through such devices, melodrama makes a sentimental treatment effective for every social problem.

The Development of a Genre

Telenovelas were created, given a recognisable style and made memorable through the technical tools of first radio and then television. Initially presented in Brazil as a radio drama in 1952, the original Cuban script *O Direito de Nascer* (The Right to be Born), could serve as an emblem of Latin American *telenovelas*. It was a melodramatic story about a handsome young doctor trying to find out who his parents were and it met with a resounding popular success in

1964 on Brazilian television. The Brazilian *telenovela* – henceforth referred to as *telenovela(s)* – differs in many aspects from the French *feuilleton télévisé*, the North American 'soap opera', and the Italian *teleromanzo*, a popular genre, which in Italy, is based on literary works. It differs also from its Mexican or Venezuelan counterparts, in that *telenovelas* produced in Brazil are distinguished by a higher degree of artistry in which the skilful audio-visual composition is used to display the fine settings, the exterior scenery and well-designed costumes.

It would seem that, on the whole, Brazilian *telenovelas* have gone a step beyond the traditional paths followed by American soap opera. In Brazil, *telenovelas* made remarkable progress in both thematic and aesthetic terms, developing into a new form of dramatic expression. The borrowed foreign plots were gradually abandoned by the end of the 1960s to pave the way for subjects such as current life in the Brazilian middle class, historical and regional topics, as well as serious social and political themes. From 1981, real national issues were being dealt with in a straightforward manner on a television show. (This is what critics call the 'Brazilianisation' of *telenovelas*.) In addition, by the mid-1980s, *telenovelas* underwent a notable transformation into a sort of cinematic genre, in terms of style, technical devices and the rhythm of production. Some of the best actors, playwrights and directors in Brazilian cinema and theatre were called upon to work in *telenovelas*, raising them to a higher grade in artistic quality. These dramatic evening shows thus became financially rewarding since they excited an agreeable anticipation in the audience and promoted advertisers' interests.

No one can deny that television, as an electronic medium, does benefit from an extraordinary immediacy and an unprecedented effect of reality. Television tends to impose upon a country an amazing simultaneity, if not a visible oneness. This powerful means of communication acts as a mediating influence in the way in which it tells stories to a national audience and in affecting everyday attitudes and morals. Playwrights and film scriptwriters have always processed political or cultural events into various forms of entertainment. In a number of ways, television hastens the process of turning reality into fictional art as *telenovelas* writers developed similar reflexes.

As a mimetic form of communication, soap operas, as well as *telenovelas*, do reflect ordinary life. In addition, *telenovelas,* like soap operas, deal with 'love triangles', but soap operas are continuing serialised daytime dramas whereas prime-time *telenovelas* are programmed at early evening (from 6.00 to 9.30 p.m.) and thus can be followed by all members of the family.[1] Furthermore, in the USA, it is assumed that soap operas are basically aimed at women, getting their name from the detergent companies which sponsored the programmes in order to advertise to housewives. Of course, the 'gendered spectatorship' of *telenovelas* is predominantly a female one, but men watch them too and *telenovelas* aim to cater for a wide audience. Once on the air, soap operas are likely to remain there for many years. (One of the oldest CBS soap operas, *As The World Turns*, celebrated its 35th birthday in 1992. Similarly, the British soap opera *Coronation Street* has been on the air continuously since 1960.) In contrast to other kinds of television soap drama, especially daytime serials, *telenovelas* are not on the air for more than six months; a *telenovela* broadcast consists of daily episodes of an hour's duration divided into six ten-minute segments. The number of episodes ranges between 120 and 140 at an average cost of US$30 000 per episode.

Telenovelas in Brazil are broadcast Monday to Saturday in the evening. In comparison with the long-running soaps, *telenovelas* are faster in pace; the divisions created by commercials permit *telenovelas* to concentrate on small, but intense dramatic scenes as the audience thoroughly enjoys unexpected twists in the plot. In the soap operas, most of the action takes place indoors; a few, inexpensive sets are therefore needed, and they rarely change. This stands in contrast to the *telenovelas'* exterior shots which have an artistic quality quite similar to that of cinema pictures. The high production values are evident in superb location scenes which were made possible by access to gigantic studios with well-furnished and very realistic sets. There is also an emphasis on action so that, unlike the conventions of soap operas, not all the action in a *telenovela* is reported through dialogue.

Changing production methods have enabled these characteristic features to develop. In the early 1950s, *telenovelas* used to be produced like theatre performances on television; they were studio-bound, both in concept and execution, taking for their model the theatre rather than the cinema. Before the videotape was introduced, *telenovelas* were aired twice a week and went out live. In 1962, with the introduction of videotape, the production of the shows could benefit from the adoption of film-making techniques. The possibilities of film drama have driven cameras out of the studio and into a well-finished imitation of 'real life' aided by exterior settings and external shots. The recording sequence was established in accordance with the possibilities of the set rather than the detail of the script as it had previously been. In addition, a greater number of episodes could be recorded per day, allowing the producers to present *telenovelas* on a daily basis and definitely influencing the final quality of this variety of television drama. *Telenovelas* players became well-trained television professionals thus adding to a higher standard of acting. At present, screenwriters write almost exclusively for *telenovelas* and they are expected to abide by the network's concern for entertainment – better described as 'infotainment', as we shall see – in the form of evening serials. The traditional melodrama where romantic love is at the centre remained, but it has been modernised and updated and the characters are no longer flat, detached from the real world and its daily concerns.

In its early days, the *telenovela* appeared to be a unique blend of the *feuilleton* drama presentation and North American radio plays which gave birth to the commercial production of basic plots and simple drama. As I have pointed out, this characteristic television genre has evolved, in both aesthetic and thematic terms, shifting from oversentimental romanticism to a greater realism and even to a sort of naturalism of dashing appearance, supported by the shift out of the studio and the use of realistic settings and dialogue which is comparable to daily conversation. Full-bodied acting tends to be kept to a minimum by the extensive use of medium shots and close-ups which focus on the facial expressions. Close-ups show faces in detail and therefore are a potential source of information because of the audience's ability to draw inferences from the outward appearance of the character. In addition, close-ups dominate the scene to emphasise emotion, to reflect intimacy and to capture dramatic conflicts. It is important to note, however, that close-ups are also used extensively in news stories; people identified as newsworthy display physical features so distinctly that viewers are allowed to make personality judgements and, for the same reason, get emotionally involved. As a result, as we shall see, many *telenovelas* are comparable to, and seem to have the same impact as, documentary film; in both cases, strong messages about drama and emotion are readily conveyed to the public

From their earliest days in the 1950s, *telenovelas* had centred on the continuing drama of idealised or archetypal heroes. Most of the conventional characters tended to be less interesting and the issues raised in the *telenovelas* were not yet the social and political debates that really concerned the viewers. As the form developed in the 1960s, *telenovelas* writers turned to these controversies as a source of current issues or questions that presented themselves for discussion. Now, plots must always be related, in one way or another, to what is about to happen or has already happened in society. New material, however, has to be introduced with care. Of course, plots and characters are submitted to change but they become different slowly, at a pace which does not disrupt viewers' comfortable recognition and immediate identification. That is why production staff are careful not to create scripts too far in advance. Although a *telenovela*'s summary or outline has to be sketched before the actual production, individual episodes are written as the show is in progress, thus giving writers a chance to suitably comment on current issues. This also accounts for the fact that some significant events in the narrative are 'foreshadowed' before they take place. If necessary, entirely new material can be added right up to air time, so that a *telenovela* can keep up with what is happening across the whole range of what is of most concern to the audience.

A *telenovela* is an open-ended play in the sense that, due to daily transmission, it is subject to a great variety of influences and action can be reconstructed since the story can be redirected. Moreover, its text is not at all closed to a range of referential readings which deal with real life. Viewers habitually create the meaning of television plays through their competent decoding. *Telenovelas* adopt a realistic mode in which the characters behave as real people do in a very nearly naturalistic setting and thus provide endless opportunities for audience identification; indeed, it is frequently taken for granted by producers and critics that regular viewers will be inclined to interpret the plot in a veristic manner. Each episode – in Brazil, we call it 'chapter' or chain of events: the last scene sets up the opening of the next 'chapter' – is produced according to patterns of audience reception as well as to narrative progression. *Telenovela* is then a relatively 'open' television genre that invites its audience to become involved as regular viewers through identifying with characters. In fact, *telenovela* viewers often know in advance what will happen but, even so, they get involved in seeing how it happens. In some degree, this kind of drama grew from the opportunities of the moment and from improvisation; actors and actresses are encouraged 'to become' the characters and eventually invent both their speech and action.

Telenovelas as Mass Cultural Products

It can be argued that the *telenovela* is now a highly processed media product expertly designed to appeal to large audiences. Great consideration has therefore to be given to the supposed desires of all those who watch such programmes. Certainly, the success of *telenovelas* requires careful targeting to suit culture and taste. So while a format or concept may have universal appeal, the execution of that format ensures that shows speak to audiences in their own language, both literally and figuratively. By means of public opinion research, TV Globo Network, for instance, can always determine themes that will arouse the audience's curiosity or issues that the audience wants to see covered; a character can be given greater or lesser prominence depending on the reaction from viewers. Public response has always been a source of new material for *telenovelas* in Brazil. In accordance with traditional customs of melodrama writing, these evening dramas involve viewers as participants and so writers and production staff are used to adjusting plots to satisfy the public. Suggestions for new plots and characters are commonly drawn from market research into audience ratings. With these evaluation techniques, for instance, TV Globo Network anticipates audience's preferences and expectations and it would seem that audience involvement does produce more audience interest. This work with audiences by the producers of *telenovelas* tends to mean that, to a large extent, *telenovelas* can be said to be coherent and consistent with the viewers' social identities.

In television fiction dramas such as *telenovelas*, the role played by advertisers and sponsors has always been a decisive one. In Brazil, up until 1965, the British advertising agency Lintas was keen to reach housewives through *telenovelas*. In the late 1960s, American ideas about commercial broadcasting for extensive audiences were put into use by TV Globo, which is by far the richest television station in Brazil. As a result, a decade or so later *telenovelas* were no longer simple evening versions of daytime serials. In a sharp contrast with soap operas, which remain confined to afternoon viewing and are usually limited to a domestic market, *telenovelas* began to be a mass cultural product with standardised production, marketing strategies and viewing schedules, a production for national consumption that came to be a commodity for export. Part of the success of this strategy rests on the idea that human conflict is very much the same the world over and *telenovelas* do not convey purely idiosyncratic meanings. In addition, TV Globo Network has indeed attained a high degree of technological proficiency in, for example, its production techniques and runs *telenovelas* on very efficient and professional lines. Furthermore, should *telenovelas* be syndicated, additional profit is guaranteed for the production companies. Thus, due to the fact that in most cases *telenovelas* meet international standards of television production, TV Globo Network is at present exporting its entertainment programmes to over 50 countries and syndicating *telenovelas* around the world.

As a rule, *telenovelas* pay for themselves through advertising (e.g. 'merchandising') revenues. The 'merchandising' of products in *telenovelas* is indeed an ingenious promotion of brand names as if they naturally belonged to the dramatic action. In other words, 'merchandising' is consumer product advertising built into the script, thus becoming part of the narrative structure. 'Merchandising' practices not only create or encourage new habits of consumption and consumer demands but also pay approximately 35 per cent of the total costs of producing the episode. In general terms and despite the depth of social content which is a characteristic of *telenovelas*, it cannot be denied that lifestyle exhibited in *telenovelas*, mostly in contemporary urban middle-class settings, is organised around a conspicuous consumption of material goods as a means of attaining perfect happiness. It should be noted that the so-called 'qualified' or 'specific' audience of Brazilian television networks is formed by socio-economic groups with great purchasing power who represent 40 per cent of the total television viewing audience.

The most important factor for the professional success of a commercial television network is that the best possible level of audience be achieved. We should bear in mind that profit motive, the rating systems, the sharply defined cost–profit margin and so on, are innate to the contexts of commercial broadcast. However, being sensitive to the market economy of ideas and entertainment preferences, television naturally represents various points of view, seeking the widest possible audience. Thus, Globo's dominance of broadcasting in Brazil is probably due to its Hollywood mode of production and particularly to its splendid technical resources (although critics claim that, aesthetically, this same 'standard of quality' is, in its luxurious images, an attempt to portray a society with no real social conflict). A broadcaster such as TV Globo Network which commands greater audience shares has consequently a larger slice of the advertising cake – and an increasing interest in maintaining this position. In order to do so, this Brazilian television network has established audience ratings, on the basis of surveys, as a regulatory mechanism of the quality of the *telenovelas* it produces.

Storytelling and Myth

People invent stories in order to explore their customary manners (either good or bad) and to become aware of their own habitual way of acting or doing things. Whenever mere habit no longer suffices, people require the stabilising and instructive influence of human tales, that is, the surrounding atmosphere of myth. We have to think about this when considering televisual narrative and television drama as entertainment made with the supposed audience's needs very firmly in mind. It can be argued that television's storytelling has become a contemporary form of symbolic democracy. In every culture, the process of myth-making is ongoing, since myths are forms of public imagination or symbolic narratives about deep-seated concerns of particular collectivities; a myth is operative in the sense that it provides an emotionally and ideologically valid interpretation of real facts. Myths are realised in or through ritualistic behaviour, such as devoutly watching a favourite long-running soap opera. In Brazil, viewers have long been addicted to *telenovelas*. The public drama of ritual is therefore a way to reaffirm a collective identity, to be imagined in national cultural myths. As will be pointed out below, the broadcasting media has been central to the mediation of this ritual, and, in various ways, has itself assumed a ritualistic character. Also, the maintenance of mental cohesion and continuity is the most significant role performed by television as cultural institution for storytelling in Brazil. In fact, much folklore and myth may be embedded in the stereotypes, propagandas and customary practices of *telenovelas*.

Although the overwhelming bulk of a *telenovela* is devoted to romantic love, and the compelling passions of the characters dominate the action, the symbolic democracy of the *telenovelas* allows for a broad spectrum of social problems to be touched on at various times. The mixture of various plots and the juxtaposition of several storylines is responsible for much of the *telenovela*'s unique appeal to millions of viewers. With different stories (or plot lines) unravelling at the same time through the careful alternation of different stories in different scenes, viewers have always to make thematic connections between dramatic sections and to organise the action into meaningful patterns. Undoubtedly, *telenovela* is an imaginary representation in that it is not intended to present an exact description of reality. However, it involves an important range of different real life situations, as every *telenovela*, as we have seen, refers to reality in some way. A *telenovela*'s head writer and his or her collaborators are permanently turning to real life for feedback, and off camera there have always been specialists on hand to advise writers and actors on specific matters. Critical commentaries should then focus on the relation between the fictional nature of *telenovela* and its role in the 'melodrama' of everyday life, regarding this genre as one which by every means tries to balance social demands for fantasy and realism.

Every *telenovela* is built upon a deliberate enactment of a wide range of social and personal problems which draw on a sense of what real life is like. In this sense, *telenovelas* may have a redeeming value because many of them feature socially aware stories about interracial romance, administrative corruption, marital break-ups, individual ethics, and social problems. Modern *telenovelas* can also be seen as an intellectual tool for cultural criticism, as they relate themselves to another Brazilian reality by attempting a more tentative rescue of traditional customs, political practices and moral values. The *telenovela Roda de Fogo* (Circle of Fire, TV Globo, 1987) introduced situations and characters which closely resembled the political reality of the country in a recent period. It was perhaps the first programme to present such facts for fictional purposes: corruption of businessmen, the hardships of military dictatorship and, on an interpersonal level, sado-masochistic behaviour. This commentary on reality is reinforced by the way *telenovelas* emphasise the para-social interaction or interpersonal relationship between fictional characters on air and members of the audience. Family members as well as romantic partners tend to converse in a casual style on interpersonal topics and discuss domestic matters. This exchange of routine information is also the chief material of our everyday activities, and accordingly the use of conversational styles in *telenovelas* is a thorough imitation of real life, adding further strength to an illusion of reality. Similarly, in so far as viewers regard fictional characters as 'real people', *telenovelas* are likely to be perceived as an extension of the real world. The use of mimetic characters and plausible plots cannot but add to the portrayal of a world 'just like ours'. Even though segments of every episode are taped, they seem to have the effect of live performance, mostly because they are carefully edited and actors are sometimes free to *ad lib* lines 'in character'. In general terms, ways of using words, music, lighting and the frequent use of close-ups, create an aura of intensity and familiarity on the part of the viewer. *Telenovelas* deserve to be noted for their apparent realism, as if real life created needs that could be addressed and fulfilled . . . by the storytelling of *telenovelas*.

It is thus possible that many viewers watch *telenovelas* because they perceive them as resembling their everyday lives. These viewers are in search of both entertainment and advice on how to handle satisfactorily interpersonal relationships. Taking everything into consideration, *telenovelas* and their manner of presentation give the viewers something to be concerned with and talk about.

Telenovelas may therefore act as a 'school of life', where moral standards are often taught and learnt by example. A certain 'illusion of reality', of realities and feelings conveyed through pictures and found in the catchy storylines of *telenovelas,* provides millions of viewers with a kind of 'social knowledge' required to live in the modern world. The aesthetic experience of such a subtle blend of the real and fictitious permits the audience to watch patterns of human behaviour carefully, thus enabling the long-term viewers to give passionate attention to attitudes and values concerning what is considered 'proper' in society. In this *telenovelas* may have more in common with the social realism in British soap operas such as *EastEnders* than with their US counterparts which seem more directed at an instant emotional involvement through a close connection with the viewers' fantasies.[2]

Telenovelas and Documentary News

As we have suggested, *telenóvelas* gained part of their popularity from the dramatic treatment of what is presented as the immediate realities of life. Of course, problems are dramatically useful in creating conflict. Even though their dramatic solutions tend to be conventional, topical issues may be exploited for their narrative interest as if day-to-day life were (or could be) serialised. In this sense, *telenovelas* can be seen as representing strong tendencies in television more generally and having striking resemblances to non-fictional formats. Television as a form makes it possible to see events happen, immediately or after only a little delay; viewers are quick-witted in learning television codes and arguably have a better grasp on reality than ever before. The strong impression of television news stories on the viewers is enhanced by their comprehensive pictorial content, the abundant visual scenes and film clips. Television news language is based upon a rather stereotypical verbal and visual discourse that is designed to be promptly understood because viewers concentrate only on the basic meanings made known to them by audio-visual messages.

Since coded verbal and visual contents of television news stories are presented to vast and diverse audiences, these same viewers must be capable of easily discerning the intended meanings. As the average news broadcast offers a great number of continuously changing pictures, many involving movement, the viewer learns to make meaning from the televisual presentation. This means that audiences are likely to pay more attention whenever fine photographic techniques (e.g. camera angles and a variety of coded shots, such as close-ups) are employed in order to convey visual information. Familiar pictures make it easy for viewers to relate the message to information previously stored in their memories and to capture a story's inner meaning. The visual elements of television news may be used for establishing an atmosphere rather than ensuring referential development. Ordinary viewers rarely think about the contribution made by the visual aspects of television; they take it for granted because moving pictures always elicit a high level of attention or a greater care about the issues, in addition to making information transmission accurate and realistic. People gain a keen sense of being spectators of both genuine and imaginary events, when they see them presented in moving pictures on television.

News stories, in Brazil as elsewhere, often have familiar scenarios but may feature different 'actors' in distant locales. Some of these stories exemplify the so-called 'heart throb' genre, i.e. upright, ordinary citizens suffering misfortune and making great efforts to cope with forces beyond their control. Furthermore, news stories shown by major networks have a large number of visual scenes (as happens in *telenovelas*), possibly on the assumption that they make all these stories more meaningful. The generation of densely packed pictorial information, by means of a flood of scenes that follow each other in rapid succession, conforms to the logic of the medium, regardless of the fact that picture choice and framing may give a false account of facts.

Social issues of the present time are pursued both in the news and current affairs programmes and at times are clearly expressed in the dramatic format of *telenovelas*. Curiously enough, *Jornal Nacional* (TV Globo Network evening national newscast) is aired right after the end of a *telenovela* and shortly before the beginning of another. It is not surprising that some of the news stories it brings forward have in common with *telenovelas* interesting arguments, remarkable dramatic performances and a fine artistic production. It is also the case that the basic device on which all varieties of story-telling depend is continuing narrative. News stories are a symbolic system, a narrative ordering and simplified explanation of complex phenomena. In other words, the news is understood as constructing meaningful totalities out of scattered events in the way that myths do. It is often assumed that news discourses command a relatively greater power over imagined narratives but it is the range of opinion offered on topical issues that is important when it comes to comments on the news.

In the rapid flow of events that can be observed, either on TV screens or in real life, too much happens, too fast. Thus, television networks bring home news about culture and society, focusing habitually on their 'novelty' or else their 'rareness'. This may fall into the realm of 'infotainment', a term which so well defines the pervasive presence of television in society. At every turn, one of the potential sources of inspiration for works of fiction is what the French call *fait divers* or 'man-bites-dog-items'; these are essentially melodramatic stories as they intentionally put a stress on the deviant or transgressive acts, and for this very reason they refer not so much to the sphere of true facts as to the domain of fiction. Some other occurrences are singled out for their inherent 'fictionworthiness' in so far as they seem to arouse the interest or curiosity of the viewers. Moreover, these 'bad news' stories – in the sense of bizarre, very strange or unusual stories – may be deemed to relate to an alleged topical interest so that they can be used to refer to current social controversies.

Since viewers are exposed to both fiction and news stories (e.g. the day-to-day events or exciting reports upon important issues faced by Brazilian society), *telenovelas* can always draw their inspiration from real facts which have recently happened. Interestingly, though, the 'reality' displayed in television news is comparable to drama in the sense that the intense flood of new current information is transformed into an entertaining story. Themes may vary in their importance and attractiveness for the audience but they are plainly valued for their undeniable emotional impact. Television news, like television fictional drama, seeks to create emotional concerns and day-to-day suspense. The action (as in *telenovelas*) is cut at a crucial moment and points forward to the next episode. Fantasies may seep into facts. Entertainment and journalism drift back and forth across the borders. The plot is not always totally fictitious; the characters are not at all times unreal.

One example of this is the most spectacular newscast in Brazilian television which bears the descriptive title of *Aqui Agora* (Here Now). Presented daily by Brazilian Television System or SBT, which seems to specialise in lower-class-orientated entertainment, this programme, as its advertisements proclaim, purports to bring before viewers 'life as it really is'. Thus, by adding to the value of reports of what has most recently happened, this newscast intends to portray aspects of real life and, as in a drama, have them arranged for enactment. In the news stories of *Aqui Agora*, the sense of reality is sometimes almost unbearable: the camera is hand held, the scenes brought before the camera are so marked by realism that the audience is tempted to forget it is watching something 'constructed', not something truly taking place before its very eyes. The camera becomes part of the ongoing action to such an extent that it seems impossible to tell what has been 'scripted' and what has happened for real.

Conclusion

As we have seen, *telenovelas* dominate the prime-time hours, attract the widest attention, and have become a major artistic force that consolidates the cultural identity of the audience. The prime-time *telenovela* at 8.30 p.m., as presented by TV Globo Network, gathers and uses for dramaturgic purposes all sorts of news information. As a television genre, *telenovelas* have flourished chiefly because of their ability to meet the emotional needs and express the usual attitudes of the audience. Besides excitement and passionate involvement, suspense provides the 'hook' that keeps viewers interested. Many *telenovelas* ingeniously combine realistic portrayals of everyday life and the narrative conventions that preside over this genre: realism and fantasy are here two halves of the same whole. The specific organisation of signs and dramatic symbols that constitutes every sort of artistic fiction – *telenovelas*, as well as docudramas – is here treated as completely transparent for the viewers. They are supposed to understand the plot and 'read' its impossible meanings according to their 'cultural competence'. In the process of reception, individual perceptions may always differ, but certainly are influenced by common cultural factors. In sum, *telenovela* narrative promotes a remarkable sense of concern in its viewers, a concern which is part of the experience of being a *telenovela* fan.

The story of almost every successful *telenovela* is perhaps the story of many people in Latin America, not to mention Brazil. In spite of its consummate artistry, this noteworthy television spectacle is neither plain melodrama nor straightforward audio-visual fiction. *Telenovela* is then a creative version of a possible Brazil's national story, where the clear-cut historical reality gradually merges in the faint half-light zone of imagination. *Telenovelas* stand for a fantasy of what Brazilians might be; a kind of driving myth or a self-image of some sort; they are like the lives of many viewers or else how would they like their lives to be.

Notes

1. See Laura Stempel Mumford's *Love and Ideology in the Afternoon; Soap Opera, Women and Television Genre* (Bloomington: Indiana University Press, 1995) for a definition of soap opera which stresses the importance of daily scheduling in understanding US daytime soaps.
2. For a discussion of the realism of British soaps in the 1980s, see Christine Geraghty's *Women and Soap Opera* (Cambridge: Polity Press, 1991).

Suggested reading on Brazilian *Telenovelas*

FADUL, A. (ed.), 1993: *Serial Fiction in TV: The Latin American Telenovelas*. São Paulo, SP: ECA / USP.
HEROLD, C. M., 1988: 'The "Brazilianisation" of Brazilian television: a critical review'. *Studies in Latin American Popular Culture*, 7.
JOHNSON, R., 1988: 'Deus e o Diabo na Terra da Globo [God and the Devil in the Land of Globo]: *Roque Santeiro* and Brazil's "New Republic"'. *Studies in Latin American Culture*, 7.
MATTELART, M. and A., 1990: *The Carnival of Images. Brazilian Television Fiction*. New York: Bergin & Garvey.
STRAUBHAAR, J. D., 1982: 'The development of the *telenovela* as the pre-eminent form of popular culture in Brazil'. *Studies in Latin American Popular Culture*, 1.
———, 1988: 'The reflection of the Brazilian political opening in the *telenovela* 1974–1985'. *Studies in Latin American Popular Culture*, 7.

Situation comedy has been one of the great staples of television broadcasting and Pat Kirkham and Beverley Skeggs analyse an example of what might be seen as a new brand of comedy. *Absolutely Fabulous*, which became a cult success in the USA and Australia as well as Britain, is a world away from the family-on-the-sofa comedy still associated with television sitcoms. It had its irreverent roots in the independent comedians' circuit and, as Kirkham and Skeggs argue, took as its target the individualist politics of the 1980s and the lifestyles of the rich and famous. In their essay, Kirkham and Skeggs offer a textual account of the programme but also place a strong emphasis on context. In this case, they seek to place *Absolutely Fabulous* in the political context associated with a ruthless Thatcherite emphasis on individual advancement and in the comic traditions of disruption and burlesque in which US programmes such as *Roseanne* and *The Golden Girls* are also important. Kirkham and Skeggs work with a variety of sources, drawing on Television Studies (in the analysis of comedy, for instance), Film Studies (in the discussion of the disruptive potential of the female gaze) and Women's Studies (in for instance, the emphasis on unruly women and masquerade).

Kirkham and Skeggs raise a number of issues which resonate with other essays in this book. Like O'Sullivan and Shattuc, they are concerned with the way in which television handles personal and private issues by making them public. *Absolutely Fabulous* mocks the way in which personal angst is paraded for public consumption and satirises the world of media and public relations which precisely relies on this blurring of distinction. The queue of media personalities wanting to feature in the second series indicates how difficult it is to keep such satire sharp in a situation in which, as O'Sullivan describes, television continually reflects itself back to the audience.

Kirkham and Skeggs's essay is also an example of the feminist contribution to Television Studies described earlier by Brunsdon and Stempel Mumford. They suggest that for women, in particular, *Absolutely Fabulous* offers the pleasures of transgression as feminine ideals of beauty, motherhood and proper behaviour are exploded by its two heroines. But Kirkham and Skeggs also point to the way in which feminist assumptions about female friendships, the relationship between the personal and political and women's pleasure are also the subject of comedy in the programme.

A feminist reading tends to emphasise, as Kirkham and Skeggs show, the transgressive possibilities of Edina and Patsy's rebellion, the sense that their refusal of femininity's straitjacket may empower the female audience to do the same. Kirkham and Skeggs do, however, suggest that an emphasis on class position as well as gender may complicate such a resistant reading. They argue that for women who have no access to the world of champagne and vodka, beauty treatments and fashionable restaurants, the programme may actually work to reproduce the very desires it purports to mock. To criticise Thatcherism for being vulgar may work only for those who have access to the lifestyle which is under attack; for working-class women, the programme may actually reinforce a painful feeling of exclusion.

18

Absolutely Fabulous: Absolutely Feminist?

Pat Kirkham and Beverley Skeggs

Much work on television fiction has focused on questions about the ways in which programmes appeal to and affect different audiences. Feminist work in particular has focused on the way in which the soap opera genre has appealed to both feminine and feminist feelings to develop its pleasurable possibilities. Less work has been done on comedy and this essay therefore offers a study of a popular British television comedy which features four women characters spread across three generations. We are interested in the possibilities opened up by a situation comedy and in particular we want to explore the complex pleasures for women viewers which this conjunction of femininity, feminism and comedy offers.

This essay will first interrogate the contexts of the textual production of *Absolutely Fabulous,* outlining the historical positions and traditions on which it draws and the knowledge(s) required to understand it. It will focus on a number of interlinking areas: conduct and behaviour; responsibility; femininity and masquerade. In doing so it will draw attention to the central motifs through which the programme explores these issues: mother/daughter relations, the relationship between female best friends, and comedy based on women's appearance, the body and ageing.

Written by the comedian Jennifer Saunders (who achieved fame and commercial success in Britain in a comedy partnership with Dawn French), directed by Bob Spiers and produced by Jon Plowman, *Absolutely Fabulous* is a situation comedy based on four central women characters. Saunders herself stars as PR executive, Edina Monsoon, with Joanna Lumley as her best friend and fashion editor Patsy Stone, Julia Sawahla as her school student daughter Saffron, and June Whitfield as her mother. The series is set mainly in the 'designer' kitchen of Edina's large London house, which is equipped with 1980s' and early 1990s' designer gadgets and furniture as well as examples of 'ethnic chic' and modern art. The other main location is Edina's equally 'designer' office, although there are occasional location episodes based on holidays in Provence, Marrakesh and skiing in the Alps.

First broadcast in Britain in the autumn of 1992, the series began in a mid-evening slot (9.30–10.00 p.m.) on the more 'highbrow' of the two BBC channels and attracted audiences of up to 10 million, winning somewhat unusually (for such a large audience) a cult following and high critical praise. It won the 1993 British Film and Television Award for best comedy series. This popularity ensured that the second series in 1994 was moved to the same time slot on the more popular BBC1 channel, where it retained audiences of 11 million and quadrupled its budget. Guest appearances from celebrities such as Germaine Greer, Britt Eckland and Miranda Richardson confirmed its cult status. The third and final series began in April 1995 on BBC1, although two 45-minute 'special' episodes were shown on BBC1 in November 1996. Jennifer Saunders has sworn this is the end for Patsy and Edina, though a final, final comeback would be welcomed by fans.

Plans to show the series in the USA met with problems because it was regarded as too vulgar and too pro-drug, as were the scripts for an 'American re-make' submitted to ABC TV after Roseanne Barr acquired the rights.[1] In the end, the first British series was screened in the USA in 1994 and met with success, winning two Emmys (television's equivalent of Oscars). It achieved a cult status in the USA, as it did in Australia where 'Patsy look-alikes' first appeared in the Sydney Mardi Gras parades in 1994.[2]

Historical and Socio/Political Contexts

The original idea for the programme came from Ruby Wax (famous for her irreverent, anarchic, surreal humour) who wanted to interview Joanna Lumley on her TV programme by setting her up (obviously with her knowledge) as a completely drunken cook. The basic structural gag was thus initiated around a woman who refused to accept the need to behave 'appropriately'. The series draws on 1960s' hippydom, 1970s' hedonism, 1980s' Thatcherism and 1990s' righteousness. The central character, Edina, is allegedly modelled on a very successful PR executive, Lynn Franks. Edina and the hard and cynical Patsy represent aspects of 1980s' Thatcherism: they are bullish, selfish and hideously materialistic. This aspect, however, is set against the remnants from their late 1960s'/1970s' laid-back and lazy lifestyle, represented mainly by Buddhist chanting and the use of drugs, both 1970s' 'dope' and 1980s' 'coke'. The past and the Thatcherite present are, at times, played off against each other to produce comedy and social comment while at other points they meld together in hilarious confusion. Even Edina's surname – Monsoon – with its connotations of hippie Eastern travels is also the name of a fashion retailer of middle-of-the-range hippy clothes. Patsy's name – Stone – refers both to the past (to being stoned and the Rolling Stones) and to the present hardness of her character.

The critique of the materialist values of Thatcherism is made apparent in most episodes. As a PR executive it is Edina's job to work out the marketing angles on ultimately non-functional commodities, such as 'pop specs'. This emphasis on profits at all costs is taken to its limits in the Romanian baby episode, where she imports Romanian babies and works out the sales angles available as if they were simply another commodity. This lack of ethical and collective values, arguably a central Thatcherite project, is made explicit by setting it against the characterisation of the daughter Saffy, who is used to represent a caring 1990s' student, anti-materialist, into ecology and social issues. 'Mum,' she comments in a typically exasperated moment, 'people don't get more interesting the more money you spend'.

The fit and muscular values of Thatcherism are also associated with the current preoccupation with health and care of the self and body. This enables the body to be more Darwinistic ('survival of the fittest') and hence more productive in the labour market, but in *Absolutely Fabulous* it is ridiculed through the excessive drinking and drug-taking of Edina and Patsy, which again is set against lemonade-drinking Saffy.

The other acquisitive Thatcherite and neo-colonial value exposed in the programme is the use of ethnic objects to signify distinctive taste and thus a lifestyle. This is expressed in the decor of the set and is made obvious in lines by Edina such as :

> I got a load of those lip plates from dead Amazonian Indians, I thought could be ashtrays. [*to Saffron*] Don't look at me like that, we can take the lips off. Lots of kitchen pots and pans from Somalia. They don't need them, they've got no food to eat. But, best news of all, you know all the villages that were deserted by the Kurds . . . *I've* got the franchise. (Saunders, 1993: 144)

This delight in 'Third World chic' and global commodification not only suggests that nothing is sacred from capitalism ('the franchise') but also that nothing is sacred from comedy.

Finally, but crucially, feminism of the 1960s and 1970s provides the context for much of the humour of *Absolutely Fabulous*. Again this is handled through contradiction and contrast. The emphasis on women as best friends, the flirtation with lesbianism, the way in which Edina and Patsy pursue their own goals seem to stem from feminist positions of independence and female worth, but in their obsession with fat (featured in an episode actually called 'Fat' but present throughout in comments and jokes) the two central characters continually fly in the face of the notion that 'fat is a feminist issue'. The feminist context also helps to explain the way in which the obsession with fashion (Edina literally prostrates herself before a fashion designer in the final episode) is offered both as a source of identification and mockery.

Comedic Traditions

The historical and social contexts of *Absolutely Fabulous* operate within the wide range of comedic traditions on which the programmes draws. Much of the originality and freshness of *Absolutely Fabulous* lies in its particular mix of comedic devices. Visual, verbal, physical, situation and character comedy are all present and the interplay between the different aspects is important. The verbal jokes about hedonism are frequently played out in the physical – a device which works, for example, to highlight the tensions between smoking and drinking as sophisticated social tools and as indulgences which wreck the mind and body. Similarly, narrative situations such as moments of crisis which disrupt the normal are made the more comic by the additional elements of visual and physical humour. The visual parody of fashion is made largely through Edina's clothes (the ridiculousness of her outfits contrast with Saffy's unassuming dress and the sophistication of Patsy's). This is augmented by physical comedy, most notably when Saunders uses her 'too large' body to fit into 'too small' clothes, clothes that were deliberately bought a size too small in the manner of Charlie Chaplin and Norman Wisdom.[3] The wearing of clothes is also a comic device in the treatment of Patsy. She wears beautiful and expensive clothes which hang and fit perfectly on her model size body, but this image is deflated when they become out of place, disrupted and dishevelled, drawing attention to her feminine constructions. One episode involves a scene of arrival at Marrakesh airport in which the comic effect is based on this contrast. Patsy, beginning as the model of sophistication, gets progressively drunk and aggressive on the plane and, in a brilliant piece of physical comedy, she gets stuck on the revolving luggage deposit. She finally emerges from the airport as a complete mess with clothes dishevelled and high hair lopsided.

As this incident shows, at the heart of *Absolutely Fabulous* is the question of 'making a spectacle' of oneself and the show can be seen to operate within the general modes of ritual spectacle, comic verbal compositions, curses and oaths, disruption of order and general unruliness reminiscent of those described by Bakhtin (1984) in relation to carnival. A central feature of *Absolutely Fabulous*'s comedy is what happens to people when they step outside of their place, when they transgress the social limits which circumscribe their actions. Banks and Swift (1986) argue that for humour to be maintained, characters can never achieve their ideals and are always reminded of what they really are. Much of the verbal interplay of *Absolutely Fabulous* consists of reminding characters of their place. This form of wit could not be achieved without the buddy relationship of the two female central characters. Patsy and Edina encourage each other to reach for impossible desires, neither exercises a limit on the other and they turn to each other for bickering solace with every failure.

Other long and rich traditions on which the programme draws include ridiculing the rich and the ruling classes, political and personal satire, unruly women, 'the Fool', the 'kill joy', the dupe, role reversals, juxtaposing the unexpected, anarchic comedy and comedies of manners. The play on the 'grotesque woman' is frequently used (Russo, 1986). The 'one liners' of *Absolutely Fabulous,* including quick put-downs, sharp and often vituperative satirical stabs, verbal deflations and repartee which approaches mutual heckling, and the double acts of comic and 'straight guy', naïve simpleton and clown (Edina and Saffy, Edina and her mother, Patsy and Saffy) can be traced back to and contextualised within these traditions.

Many of these older aspects of comedy were given more specific configuration within the nineteenth- and twentieth-century traditions of music hall and variety shows which featured individual performers and double acts. In the overall narrative, therefore, individual set-pieces such as Patsy's drunkenness or Edina's self-denigration are important elements in the comedy. More recent influences include the British comics Tony Hancock, Harry H. Corbett and Wilfred Bramble (Steptoe and his son) and John Cleese. The Cleesian influence is most apparent in the physical clowning and the comic use of the body. The send-up of bourgeois pretensions draws on the famous *Hancock's Half Hour* radio series and the subsequent television shows; the gag of the grown-up child playing parent to the disreputable parent was the basis for the television series

Steptoe and Son. Although it is not unusual to have women as the focus of comedy of middle-class pretensions, the Cleese and the Steptoe comparisons remind us that the effect of making oneself ridiculous through the body or behaving in other vulgar and outrageous ways when old is all the more striking when the protagonists are women.

Until recently there has been very little comedy on our television screens of women behaving in vulgar and unruly ways, and the debt of *Absolutely Fabulous* to Roseanne Barr should not be ignored. It was she who, writing and playing in the US sitcom *Roseanne,* made a comedy heroine of the unruly and irreverent woman and broke down many of the unwritten codes about the comic depiction of the behaviour of mothers and of women over 30 (Rowe, 1995). A further influence is another US sitcom *The Golden Girls,* which features four or five older women, some of whom seriously transgressed 'appropriate' behaviour in relation to age. It contained a brilliant example of a mafia-style mother whose long-suffering daughter tried to keep her out of trouble – surely one model for the mother–daughter role reversal which is at the heart of *Absolutely Fabulous*.

Absolutely Fabulous also needs to be contextualised against the phenomenal growth of alternative comedy in Britain in the 1980s and the space created within that by and for female and feminist comics; Jennifer Saunders came up through that route to *Absolutely Fabulous,* as is indicated by her previous television shows, *Girls On Top, French and Saunders* and *The Comic Strip Presents.* Her presence reinforces the use of sketches and draws on traditions established from variety performances and radio shows which used 'real' characters alongside recognisably straight actors in supporting roles. *Absolutely Fabulous* is clearly alternative in its use of one-liners, its social observation and its political comment.

Saunders's very presence announces the fact that *Absolutely Fabulous* is a 'comedian's comedy' (Jenkins, 1992: 232); her being there signals for us to laugh. Yet intriguingly she is the one character who is cast neither for nor against type, probably because her chameleon-like ability to take on a huge variety of roles means that she is not type-cast. By contrast, Joanna Lumley, the epitome of upper-middle-class British white femininity, was cast against type to great comic effect. This former boarding school girl from a colonial family, a former model (with a passing resemblance to Princess Diana) and a reputed supporter of the Conservative government, plays the ageing, dissolute and drunken best friend who not only burns the innocent Saffy with a cigarette but also sells her off in Morocco because she spoils the fun Patsy likes to have with Edina. Neither her role as Purdy in *The New Avengers* nor as a 'James Bond Girl' prepared the public for this role and the juxtaposition of the haughty 'English rose' image with the outrageous character of Patsy creates a frisson which is absolutely central to the comedy.

June Whitfield and Julia Sawahla were by contrast much more in tune with the parts they played. Part of the strength of Saffy's 'straight guy' character comes directly from Julia Sawahla's previous television roles, particularly the squeaky clean teenager in spectacles in *Press Gang.* June Whitfield is a famous comedy actress. She performed in the BBC light entertainment programmes such as *Love From Judy* and *Take It From Here* in the 1940s and was probably best known for her television role as the sweet and innocent suburban woman in the sitcom *Terry and June.* However, there is another side to Whitfield – she played Margaret Thatcher on the radio and this dualism is cleverly developed in

Absolutely Fabulous. Gran is an older 'straight' character whom Saunders could use in a second-layer of the mother–daughter reversals and also a character who on occasions matched her daughter, Edina, for maliciousness.[4]

Some humour which results from the programme's roots in situation comedy comes from working within those traditions, but much comes from stretching them to their limits. The family is central to situation comedy but the family presented here is strange both in its structure and the degree of its dysfunctionality. Firstly, Edina is a single parent and Saffy's father is gay. Secondly, the traditional roles of mother and daughter are reversed in Edina and Saffy, and Edina's relationship with her own mother is shocking in the lack of filial affection. Juxtapositions, oppositions and role reversals all work to heighten the bizarre nature of the family which is never as strong a unit as the best friend dyad of Edina and Patsy. The main 'outsider' role of Patsy is a co-starring one which thus de-centres the family, as does the way in which she constantly pulls Edina away from the home to indulge in non-domestic pleasures.

Another outsider to the family, Bubble (Edina's assistant played by Jane Horrocks), strengthens this depiction of Edina's world beyond the home, the world of fashion at which Saunders's scripts take numerous swipes. Like Gran, Bubble is in the tradition of 'the Fool', part of whose function is to expose the pretensions of the serious. Like Gran, though, Bubble is a hybrid character incorporating aspects of the village idiot, clown, working-class and dumb blonde stereotypes – all of which add up to a general whackiness. Nevertheless, the very battyness and naïveté of both these characters is used to highlight the constructed nature of all claims to seriousness. Bubble and Gran represent different generations and embody different value systems which, together with Saffy's moral code, work as foils to expose the more preposterous values endorsed by Patsy and Edina. Saffy's moral positions point to the immorality of her mother and Patsy. Bubble's naïveté points to the calculating manipulations of Edina and Patsy, and Gran's innocence points to their knowingness. Juxtapositions have long been a staple of comedy and here they enable ethical explorations to be made.

Comedy, particularly that in which the freedom of the clown to act outrageously is usurped by women, can be liberating (Jenkins, 1992), but these effects can be dampened and closed down by censure such as that exercised by Saffy and Gran. The liberating effect can also be counter-balanced by closure, by the programme returning the viewer to the safe values of the *status quo*. However, *Absolutely Fabulous*, more than most comedies, rarely achieves closure; the viewer is only ever given a glimpse of normality for it to be ripped away again. We wait for Edina to be nice to her daughter, but if we get such a moment occasionally it is only to have it immediately snatched away. The degree to which the programme resists closure is new and accounts in part for its impact. It continually shifts between liberation and censure and moral closure is rarely achieved. The codicils at the end often put a final sting in the tale; Edina and Patsy save Saffy from a disastrous marriage and promptly steal the tickets for her honeymoon trip . . .

Feminine Conduct

As the previous section has indicated, much of the comedy of *Absolutely Fabulous* centres on questions of female conduct and appropriate behaviour.

Debates over correct conduct with women as central signifiers have been waged for centuries in England. These struggles are based on establishing and marking the distance between the 'respectable women' and the sexualised others, whose behaviour was so lacking in respectability and authority that they could have no claim to power and authority. Black and white working-class women (usually signified as prostitutes, malignant and contagious) have been used as the deviant others against which correct and appropriate feminine behaviour could be defined (Gilman, 1992). Vron Ware (1992) notes how definitions of white femininity were generated through the designation of the black sexualised other and Lury (1993) argues that the ability for women to comment or look, particularly in a sexual context, was compromised and circumscribed by an adherence to feminine characteristics of respectability. She traces the emergence of gendered notions of propriety in the late eighteenth and nineteenth centuries, which suggested that women's respectability would be compromised by their ability to look, to use their gaze. The promotion of feminine characteristics was re-produced through representations of women's bodies. As women's bodies came to signify femininity, so notions of appropriate feminine conduct operated as processes of monitoring and self-surveillance which enabled distinctions between different groups of women to be maintained.

This was further consolidated by the responsibilities which women were given. Women could show their respectability by carrying out particular responsibilities but not others, and labour and self-regulation were tightly linked to self-presentation. It was not just the dispositions and characteristics of respectability which signified an appropriate femininity but the performance of duty and obligation (Skeggs, 1997). As part of this process, sexual behaviour had to be placed and contained within family values, as Foucault notes:

> the first figure to be investigated by the development of sexuality, one of the first to be 'sexualised', was the 'idle' woman. She inhabited the outer edge of the 'world', in which she always had to appear as a value, and of the family, where she was assigned a new identity charged with conjugal and parental obligation. (1979: 121)

In the moralising of the social order which designates care for others and care for self as feminine responsibilities, new guilts and new shames are produced (Elias, 1982). It is these (self and other) controls and responsibilities which *Absolutely Fabulous* irreverently addresses.

As a mother, Edina constantly refuses maternal responsibility: 'As your mother I cannot be responsible for your well being' she tells Saffy. The whole programme is structured around the irresponsible mother and best friend. A whole sketch centres on Edina's refusal to take responsibility for family finances. When she misses Saffy's birthday, she remonstrates with her saying, 'Don't get at me darling, I'm the one who gave you birth, I'm the one who uncrossed her legs for you.' This is not just a refusal of maternal responsibility, but also of the guilt that usually accompanies it (Wearing, 1984; Donzelot, 1979). Edina also fails to respect the maternal position more generally. When a friend who is a new mother (Miranda Richardson) comes to stay, Edina has sex with the husband (the audience hear it over the baby intercom), whilst the mother/wife bemoans her maternal duties. Edina is thus completely amoral in the face of possible pleasure. In addition, she ignores her duties in other relationships, refusing to behave responsibly towards her own mother and her friends. After a call from a distressed friend, she complains, 'she was crying so much I had to put the phone down'.

Edina, however, does not completely eschew responsibility for herself, but pays for it rather than labours at it. She pays for self-care, whilst refusing to take care of the self. Although she is locked into the discourse of the care of the self, anything which takes time from shopping or drinking is considered a distraction. She is constantly finding new schemes, such as Japanese chanting or crystals, which will enable her to get in touch with some spurious notion of 'herself'. The whole discourse of feminine self-care is thus sent up and trivialised through Edina's many attempts to try on new forms of self-understanding. She continues to drink and take drugs in vast amounts, whilst also having colonic irrigation, undergoing fat-reducing sessions by being wrapped in mud, and trying aroma-therapy and rebirthing. Edina's responsibility for her body is explicitly commod-ified. At the same time, Patsy exemplifies the excessive self-regulation encouraged by dieting. In one sketch, Patsy holds her stomach and Edina asks 'have you eaten something?'. 'Not since 1973', replies Patsy. This points to the differences between the two women's bodies. Patsy is the 1970s' model, who has retained the same body, controlling it through drugs and cigarettes; Edina's body, in the tradition of grotesque realism, is completely out of control; both are a response to political contexts and interpretations of femininity.

Regulation is constantly set against the hedonism in which Patsy and Edina delight. They are rarely in control and their excesses make explicit the controls and regulations upon women's conduct. They drink too much and take drugs in inappropriate places, places of labour and responsibility, such as the office and the kitchen. Patsy and Edina are unashamedly hedonistic, not a term associated with women, for as Kaplan (1992) notes, women's love of pleasure is deeply stig-matised as the sign of their degradation. Patsy's and Edina's hedonism provides commentary not on just regulations, but also on pretension. Although the two claim to be knowledgeable consumers, the audience is encouraged to find their excessive expenditure and their Thatcherite hippydom vulgar. In Bourdieu's terms, they operate at the level of the profane; while they claim to be culturally superior, theirs is hardly 'the sacred sphere of culture . . . of those who can be sat-isfied with the sublimated, refined, disinterested, gratuitous, distinguished plea-sures for ever closed to the profane' (Bourdieu, 1986: 7). Thus it can be argued that the programme offers to certain viewers the satisfaction of looking down on this vulgar hedonism, a satisfaction largely based on the viewer's own access to the cultural capital derived from 'high' culture. Many viewers, however, may not have access to this 'high cultural' knowledge to be able to critique it.

This commentary and comedy is thus double-edged. The textual critique of pretensions is contradicted by the display and use of what are already coded as desirable objects. What Patsy and Edina hedonistically consume – whether it be designer clothes, holidays or drink (characteristically referred to as 'Bolly' and 'Stolly') – is very desirable to most viewers. As Patsy and Edina playfully try to pass as knowing, consuming, global bourgeoisie and as successful, cultured, glamorous women, they laugh at themselves. But the comedy of all this depends on whether the audience is positioned to read their pretensions and passings as ironic. For those who have yet to gain access to time and space to play, playful-ness around consumption may remain unthinkable, the clear parody of exces-sive consumption coming up against the reality of viewers' lives and experiences.

Access is the key issue and here we come up against the limits of textual analysis; further work is needed to analyse how different audiences handle such issues.

The parody of consumption may also have backfired in another way. *Absolutely Fabulous* was lauded and hyped by the very world it sought to satirise, as was evidenced by the stars and celebrities queuing up to make guest appearances. It marketed as desirable the very objects it sought to deride. Whilst *Absolutely Fabulous* may serve to legitimise women's refusal to fit into appropriate modes of conduct, it can also be seen as presenting traditional femininity and excessive materialism and greed as desirable.

Despite this, we would suggest that that the programme does adopt a feminist mode in the way in which it contests the male view as dominant. It contributes to the challenges of the male gaze that are being made across the various sites of popular culture. In *Absolutely Fabulous*, use is made of the female gaze to scrutinise, assess and humiliate in a humorous tradition which can be found in many areas of women's culture outside of the visual (Skeggs, 1991). Patsy and Edina look, they laugh, they judge and are irreverent about the male gaze. It no longer has the power, once suggested, to control and fix women as objects to be looked at.

Femininity as Masquerade?

The feminine masquerades of Patsy and Edina are a humorous exposé of the impossibility of femininity. Their efforts show that it is impossible to 'do' femininity properly. It is significant that both have female names and nicknames based on male forms (Pats and Eddy) and use a variety of endearments and modes of address; both have moments of self-doubt which they occasionally reveal to each other but which are soon covered up, both display an endless concern for presentation and appearances while being aware always that they are playing. Even sexuality is a form of teasing as the hints about a lesbian relationship are undercut by arguments about who puts out the light when they share a bed. Edina and Patsy's spectacular displays challenge propriety, care of the self, female responsibility and respectability by parading femininity as a mode to be put on and off rather than something which comes naturally. But, as with the parodying of consumption, this presentation of femininity as masquerade has its limitations which we can see by contrasting the two main characters.

Patsy represents an old symbol of old white English femininity, the vain, sexually frank, non-income generating, decadent, licentious female that disrupts the domestic containment of women in particular and the social order in general. But with her imperious presence, she also resembles the form of white English femininity given renewed symbolic legitimacy through, for example, Princess Diana. Joanna Lumley's connections with the British aristocracy are well publicised. In a deeply class-divided society, Patsy represents aristocratic femininity. Because of her class, she has fewer constraints on her behaviour than other women and because of the associations between feminine and aristocratic modes of behaviour (see Nead, 1988 and Ware, 1992), Patsy can achieve the feminine standards established. She has access to the 'right' accoutrements of femininity and the styling of her body. In this sense Patsy is a sign of femininity as simulation. She presents her body as if she (and it) has submitted to ideas about what a certain kind of upper-middle-class women should be.

This simulation is made especially apparent when we learn in the second series that Patsy had a sex change in Morocco in the 1970s and was previously a man. Patsy is able to flaunt femininity in order to hold it at a distance and make it an object of ridicule whilst being very successful at it. However, setting up femininity as a masquerade to be laughed at only works with Patsy because she operates as such a strong signifier of upper-class femininity, and the strength of this signifier cannot be destroyed through the way in which it is played with through her performance. Her glamour overrides ridicule and even if it is a masquerade it is a very good one, one to which many would aspire and one which has been promoted as ideal in women's and TV listing magazines.[5]

Edina is not in the same position. Her social and cultural location is not of the aristocracy, but of lower middle class made good, precisely the social location that was offered inducements through Thatcherism in return for its votes. Edina cannot successfully play at femininity because she does not begin from the right location with the right objects and the proper body. Edina repeatedly gets it all wrong. For her femininity is a form of visible labour. She works at it continually but fails to get it right. Her body is out of control, her accoutrements are over the top. Even though she wears the 'right' designer labels, she puts them together in such a way as to look ridiculous. Her knowledge is not the right class-based knowledge. Watching Edina, we feel embarrassed by her very performance, the masquerade made explicitly spectacular by the colours and tightness of her clothing. Femininity as masquerade may only operate as a critique for those who can actually access it effectively when necessary. As Tyler argues:

> Theories of mimicry reinscribe white, middle-class femininity as the real thing, the (quint)essences of femininity . . . Miming the feminine means impersonating a white middle-class impersonation of an 'other' ideal of femininity. . . Feminist theorists of mimicry distinguish themselves from 'other' women even as they assimilate the latter by romanticising them, assuming the other has a critical knowledge about femininity because of her difference from what counts as natural femininity: white, Anglo, bourgeois style. It is only from a middle-class point of view that Dolly Parton looks like a female impersonator. (1991: 57)

Both Patsy and Edina make visible the invisible, the masquerade, the labour and ridiculousness of femininity, but it is only in Edina where femininity is made really undesirable. Because Patsy is so close to ideological ideals and representations of femininity, she does not generate distance from it and her character therefore hinges on a critique of a particular form of conduct rather than on femininity itself. Although in both cases femininity is presented as a construction, it is never entirely undermined. Edina's pathetic attempts and Patsy's assured assumptions of the trappings may ultimately make achievement of the feminine ideal more distant but also more desirable.

Conclusion

Absolutely Fabulous has been understood to offer a mocking critique of both the greed and commodification of 1980s' Thatcherite political values and a celebration of unruly women who kick against the restrictions of British society.

But the critiques of the vulgarity of Thatcherism and the follies of the class system work only if the objects used in making the critique are not still seen as desirable by those not privileged enough to abandon them. The programme may in fact serve to reproduce the very desires and longings it mocks and works against, desires and longings in the audience based precisely on their persistent exclusion from the possibilities which Patsy and Edina parody. This is why it needs to be studied within its historical and national context. It is a programme that could only have been generated from the class-divided 1980s when aristocracy and anarchy, feminism and femininity, contributed to produce a form of comedy which enabled the pretentious not only to laugh at themselves but, in the strong traditions of British comedy, to be laughed at by others.

Notes

1. See *TV Guide*, Indiana Edition, 23–29 July 1994. Thanks to Ellen Seiter for information.
2. We are grateful to Jackie Cook and Karen Jennings for information.
3. For a discussion of dress and *Absolutely Fabulous* see Angela's Hogan interview with costume designer Sarah Burns, 'Dressed to Spill', *TV Times*, 22–28 January 1994, pp. 8–9.
4. For an indication of June Whitfield's persona during the period of the programme, see Vanessa Berridge, 'June Whitfield', *Women and Home*, February 1994, p. 56 and Alan Franks, 'Sainted Aunt', *Times Magazine*, 11 January 1997.
5. See *TV Quick*, 22–28 January 1994, Issue 3; *TV Times* 22–28 January 1994.

References

BAKHTIN, M., 1984: *Rabelais and his World*, trans. H. Iswolsky. Bloomington: Indiana University Press.

BANKS, M. and SWIFT A., 1986: *The Jokes on Us: Women in Comedy from Music Hall to the Present Day*. London: Pandora.

BOURDIEU, P., 1986: *Distinction: A Social Critique of the Judgement of Taste*. London: Routledge.

DONZELOT, J., 1979: *The Policing of Families: Welfare versus the State*. London: Hutchinson.

ELIAS, N., 1982: *Power and Civility: The Civilising Process, Vol. 2*. New York: Pantheon Books.

FOUCAULT, M., 1979: *The History of Sexuality, Vol. 1: An Introduction*. London: Penguin.

GILMAN, S., 1992: 'Black bodies, white bodies: towards an iconography of female sexuality in late nineteenth century art, medicine and literature'. In J. Donald and A. Rattansi (eds), *'Race', Culture and Difference*. London: Sage/Open University Press, 171–98.

JENKINS, H., 1992: *What Made Pistachio Nuts? Early Sound Comedy and the Vaudeville Aesthetic*. New York: Columbia University Press.

KAPLAN, E. A., 1992: *Motherhood and Representation: The Mother in Popular Culture and Melodrama*. London: Routledge.

LURY, C., 1993: *Cultural Rights: Technology, Legality and Personality*. London: Routledge.

NEAD, L., 1988: *Myths of Sexuality: Representations of Women in Victorian Britain* Oxford: Blackwell.

ROWE, K. K., 1995: *The Unruly Woman: Gender and the Genres of Laughter*. Austin: University of Texas Press.

RUSSO, M., 1986: 'Female grotesques: carnival and theory'. In T. de Lauretis (ed.), *Feminist Studies/Critical Studies*. Bloomington: Indiana University Press, 213–29.

SAUNDERS, J., 1993: *Absolutely Fabulous*. London: BBC Books.

——, 1994: *Absolutlely Fabulous 2*. London: BBC Books.

SKEGGS, B., 1991: 'A spanking good time'. *Magazine of Cultural Studies*, 3: 28–33.

——, 1997: *Formations of Class and Gender Becoming Respectable*. London: Sage.

TYLER, C-A., 1991: 'Boys will be girls: the politics of gay drag'. In D. Fuss (ed.), *Inside Out: Lesbian Theories, Gay Theories*. London: Routledge.

WARE, V., 1992: *Beyond the Pale: White Women, Racism and History*. London: Verso.

WEARING, B., 1984: *The Ideology of Motherhood*. Sydney: Allen and Unwin.

The turn to lifestyle issues was, as Kirkham and Skegg's essay on *Absolutely Fabulous* shows, a widespread phenomenon in the 1980s. Cookery and eating out, home decorating, fashion design, travel, gardening, all moved out of their specialist arenas, particularly in women's magazines, and were given space in newspaper supplements, television programmes and beautifully illustrated books. Television programmes which were part of this process, including the cookery programmes Niki Strange studies in her essay, no longer had to be caught during the flow of an evening's viewing: they could be found in videos; recipes from them were reprinted in magazines; books were linked to them; and featured dishes and ingredients turned up in kitchens and restaurants throughout the land. In an example of synergy to rival Disney, the BBC, in particular, turned cooks like Delia Smith into a piece of television mythology.

Strange indeed begins with Barthes and her essay, although it deals with cooking programmes, ranges well beyond that apparently restrictive genre. She demonstrates that even the most straightforward 'show-tell' demonstrations carry connotations which root them in discourses of nationalism, colonialism and gender. Strange adopts a structuralist approach, drawing out a series of binary oppositions which give her the terms of her argument; she combines this with an analysis of formal elements such as mode of address and shot sequences in an account which is rooted in careful attention to detail. This gives her a firm basis for exploring the way in which broader cultural elements work in the programmes. Her discussions, for instance, of Rhodes's tour of British food and Jaffrey's presentation of Indian cookery offer elegant examples of the way in which the identification of ingredients for a recipe and the manner of cooking and presentation relate to questions of nationality, tourism and ethnicity. Presenters show us how to prepare food but they are also involved, often quite consciously, in the re-presentation of our own and other cultures.

The cookery genre offers another example of the way in which what might previously have been seen as women's matters have been transformed into mainstream television. Unlike some daytime shows, Strange's examples are taken from prime-time viewing and do not assume a gendered spectator. Nevertheless, Strange reveals clearly the different ways in which gender underpins the organisation of the programme and illustrates vividly that, while the women presenters are at ease in their educative and nurturing role, the male presenters have to work hard, using emphatic gestures, physical display and an irreverent approach (not to mention alcohol) to ensure that their role as cooks does not undermine their manly status. This often involves breaking the rules of the format and it is interesting to note that the cookery programmes – like the programmes described by O'Sullivan and Shattuc – depend on the audience understanding the conventions well enough for the presenter to break them.

Strange demonstrates that cookery programmes are cross-generic in that they emphasise the light entertainment as well as education, the sensual beauty of food and landscape as well as information about weights and measures. She argues that some of these generic requirements are dictated by their production roots in, for instance, the BBC Education Department or the Multicultural Programmes Unit. It could also be argued, though, that it is around programmes like this that the public service mandate of the BBC is most heavily compromised, with the programmes becoming extended advertisements for the (BBC-produced) video and book. Strange's analysis extends beyond the remit of public service broadcasting and offers a rich set of explanations which could inform an examination of any of the lifestyle genres.

19

Perform, Educate, Entertain: Ingredients of the Cookery Programme Genre

Niki Strange

Food, at the most fundamental level, is a biological necessity for life. At a more sophisticated level, cultural work such as Roland Barthes's semiological analysis of food advertising (Barthes, 1973) and Pierre Bourdieu's studies of 'taste' (Bourdieu, 1984) has acknowledged the profound significance of food.

One area within which the general cultural concern with food and cookery is manifest is the media. Indeed, cookery programmes have long formed a staple of the televisual diet fed to viewers. By contrast, the genre, as an object of study, has remained absent from the academic menu. This neglect suggests the assumption that cookery programmes (and other lifestyle/leisure genres such as gardening and home decoration) are transparent: that they are merely about food and the instruction of cookery methods and, as such, do not merit closer examination. Influenced by the existing rich cultural work about food, I turned a long-overdue critical eye to four cookery series (*Delia Smith's Christmas, Far Flung Floyd, Rhodes Around Britain* and *Madhur Jaffrey's Flavours of India*) and have developed the following terms which broadly characterise the main ingredients of the cookery programme genre and offer a framework for its study:

- 'Cookery-Educative' (Cook-Ed.): The most easily identifiable element, this term refers to instruction through cookery demonstration. It consists of an instructor; a verbal, written or visually articulated instructive discourse; and a textually inscribed tutee to whom the discourse is addressed.
- 'Personality' (Per.): Refers specifically to the instructor/presenter who is placed within the format and beyond it. I have used the term personality rather than instructor because of the useful connotations of entertainment.
- 'Tour-Educative' (Tour-Ed.): Travelogue aspects are often evident in cookery programmes. The Tour-Ed. category may serve as a channel for wider educational projects of a series.
- 'Raw-Educative' (Raw-Ed.): This category refers to the way in which the food's journey from raw state to finished dish is accommodated within a series. It may also act as a cipher for wider educational projects.

Though identifiable in their own right, these elements often interact, inflecting, affirming and sometimes short-circuiting each other. A particular construction of Per., Tour-Ed., and/or Raw-Ed., for example, may significantly alter the mode of Cook-Ed. While cookery programmes have common characteristics, their configuration may thus dramatically differ. It is at these points that the programmes offer fascinating insights that serve to problematize any charge of 'transparency'.

All programmes contain some element from all of these categories, though some will be more evident than others. I intend, therefore, to explore the genre by analysing these categories more fully, using examples from particular programmes to demonstrate both the paradigm itself and the way in which it is deployed in particular instances.

Cookery-Educative: *Delia Smith's Christmas* and *Far Flung Floyd*

The average number of cookery demonstrations in each of the six-part series studied is four per programme. In *Delia Smith's Christmas* (or *Delia*), the length of each demonstration tends to be five minutes, whereas in *Far Flung Floyd* (or *Floyd*) it is three minutes. This broad survey indicates, firstly, the contrast between the time that may be given over to Cook-Ed.: over two-thirds of a typical *Delia* is taken up by demonstration; for *Floyd* it is under one half. Secondly, and as *Floyd* illustrates, substantial parts of a cookery programme may consist of non-demonstrative, and even non-cookery related items – something that will be explored in the following sections.

A characteristic *Delia* demonstration features in programme one in the series. The item – about Christmas cakes – opens with a sequence introducing three cakes in turn. The audio-visual repertoire is made up of medium close-up, close-up and extreme close-up shots of each of the cakes, laid out as parts of a tableau with dishes of selected ingredients and table arrangements, accompanied by Delia Smith's voice-over comments about ingredients, look, texture and taste. Three-key lighting works with the beautifully constructed tableaux to articulate that time has been spent to create an appealing context for the demonstration, working with the Cook-Ed. in two ways. By underlining that time, labour and presentation skills are fundamental to cookery, and by showing the 'finished dishes' before the demonstration, the programme reassures us that it is possible for the viewer/cook to recreate such pleasing dishes if they carefully follow the ensuing demonstration.

This sequence dissolves into a mid-shot of Delia Smith standing in her kitchen. Addressing the camera she says, 'Now if you've never made a Christmas cake before, a classic Christmas cake, and you're a little bit worried about it, what I'd like to do first of all is just go through the basic principles with you.' Following her speech are a series of inset images showing the step-by-step preparatory stages in making a classic Christmas cake. Smith's hands occasionally enter the frame: otherwise her only active participation is via voice-over, telling of precise measurements, timings and methods.

Here, the mode of Cook-Ed. address – the comforting and encouraging register of Smith's dialogue and delivery, and the chronological simplicity of the step-by-step demonstration – serves to textually inscribe a viewer/cook whose knowledge of cookery is elemental. If the aim of Cook-Ed. is to teach the viewer how to cook, then this demonstration exemplifies Cook-Ed. proper, though the real proof is in one's recreation of the 'pudding'. Even so, the Cook-Ed. is disrupted by the programme's use of elliptical editing to negotiate time constraints and lulls in action – literally watching a cake rise doesn't tend to make for entertaining television.

'Lesson two' follows immediately, with a return to Smith's kitchen. Smith addresses the camera, saying, 'Well, those were some of the basic principles of classic cake-making. Now we're going to move onto something completely different and that's a new Christmas cake called Creole cake. It comes from Trinidad . . .'. The viewer/cook has been promoted from beginner to intermediary level, without shifting from armchair to kitchen. Assessing her viewers to be advanced enough to follow, and potentially at least to recreate the 'new' recipe, Smith introduces an 'exotic' twist on the standard fare. In actuality, the ingredients are typical cake ingredients; the differences occur in her use of certain alcohol, and in the particular amalgamation of those ingredients. That this recipe uses readily available raw materials typifies those featured by Smith and, in the somewhat rare instances that Smith uses ingredients that are not commonly accessible to the viewer/cook, the stampede that has ensued on the days following the broadcast has ensured that the product will be stocked on supermarket shelves from thereon.

The easy-to-follow visual and verbal instructions and relatively simple recipes that characterise the mode of Cook-Ed. in *Delia* sharply contrast to those of *Floyd*. Whilst Smith's recipes are largely selected from a menu composed of a normative British conception of a Christmas feast, Keith Floyd's dishes are drawn from a range of foreign cuisine, relating to the specific location that he is visiting on his journey. His recipes thus involve ingredients that may be less familiar and accessible to the viewer/cook: 'If you want to do this at home, cook your cobra for at least five minutes.' In the unlikelihood that the intrepid viewer/cook managed to obtain a cobra, the next obstacle in their path would be to follow Floyd's demonstration.

In order to capture the 'authenticity' of the dish, and of the place that it represents (and here, characteristically, we see an example of the Tour-Ed. element that will be discussed later), Floyd's demonstrations often use temporary 'kitchens' set up on boats, on bustling street-corners and outside village huts. Whereas Smith's demonstrations are predominantly shot in MCU, CU and ECU, with wide-shots merely utilised to establish her location and to take us into and out of a demonstrative sequence, Floyd's consist of many more wide shots to allow for the camera to capture his surroundings. The action is thus spread across the frame; cookery is not the focal point. Indeed the demonstrations tend to be punctuated with scenic cutaways to, for example, onlooker's faces (registering their often bemused reaction to Floyd). The combination of wide-shots and scenic cutaways serves to distract the viewer/cook, and also Floyd himself, from the cooking and influences the character of the Cook-Ed.

Illustrative of this is a sequence featuring Floyd in the jungle, cooking a curry for a regiment of Vietnamese soldiers who are playing football in the background. At one point, there is a crash caused by something off-screen, and Floyd says 'That's fine. That was just a ball hitting me. You didn't see that, did you? I was injured by an enemy b- by a ball, [he giggles embarrassedly] depending on which side you were on. B-Team got me there, you see. I'm hoping the reds will win [laughs and covers mouth with hand]. Sorry . . . [another crash]. There goes the whisky.'

Despite these, albeit entertaining, distractions Floyd completes the curry and offers plates of it to the surrounding soldiers to taste. Their local knowledge enables them to assess his cookery skills and how well he has learnt about local cuisine. Such a process of judgement tends to conclude Floyd's demonstrations: in programme six, for example, he is observed by four chefs who bear testimony to his knowledge. Thus even though Floyd's demonstrations are instructive in that he talks the viewer/cook through the ingredients he is adding, and the processes by which he is creating a dish, his position as authoritative tutor is ultimately short-circuited by his construction as tutee.

My analysis of the two series demonstrates that, whilst cookery programmes may share common elements: presenter/cooks and demonstrations, they may involve dramatically different modes of Cook-Ed. In *Delia*, priority is placed upon the communication of cookery methods to the viewer/cook, with the relatively simple menu and verbal and visual clarity of demonstration designed to ensure this. In *Floyd*, the viewer/cook is not the object of the Cook-Ed., but rather the observer of Floyd's culinary adventures. As Pearson Phillips writes from an interview with Floyd: 'There are apparently people who watch Floyd with a pencil and paper at the ready, hoping to note down a recipe. "That's not what it's about", he (Floyd) says. There is one thing that he is not trying to do and that is to give cookery lessons' (Phillips, 1991: 23).

As Floyd himself asserts, his series is not about giving cookery lessons. This raises the issue that if we concentrate only on cookery we may actually miss other crucial aspects of a programme. This is even true of the most normative – by virtue of its prioritisation of the Cook-Ed. – of the series I have looked at, *Delia Smith's Christmas*.

Personality: *Delia Smith's Christmas* and *Far Flung Floyd*

In both *Delia Smith's Christmas* and *Far Flung Floyd* the presenter lends their name to the title, implying that they are judged to be of sufficient popularity to entice viewers familiar with them as personalities. The presenters of cookery programmes may thus operate generically, as conventional sites for viewer expectations. An exploration of the genre, commonsensically and historically defined by its subject matter, should acknowledge and account for the role of the personality presenter within and beyond the immediate text.

One of the ways in which a presenter's personality is inscribed in a programme is location. The vast majority of *Delia* is set within Delia Smith's house. In the opening sequence of the series, Smith stands on her doorstep and, addressing the camera, says that by sharing her own Christmas with the viewers she hopes to help with their Christmas preparations. She even regrets that she cannot take the panic and pressure away. As she speaks, the camera zooms in from a wide-shot of Smith and her cottage to a mid-shot of Smith, doubly framed by the doorway. After a cut-away of trees gently bobbing in Smith's garden, there is a cut to Smith walking into her kitchen, the camera panning to follow her movement as she says: 'In this series I'm very pleased to be able to invite you all into my own home . . .'.

From the outset the register is of domestic intimacy; the viewer is welcomed into Smith's personal space. Her verbal articulation of this is compounded visually by the closing-in movement of the zoom, added to the framing within a frame expressive of enclosed space. Here, Delia Smith as televisual construct is conflated with Delia Smith as 'real' person via a shared *mise-en-scène*. The specificities of this *mise-en-scène* – domestic, private, enclosed and secure – serve as an extension of Smith's personality, reinforcing her solid, rooted and reliable presence. These characteristics in turn resonate within her mode of Cook-Ed. As Matthew Fort describes (Fort, 1995: 22): 'Short of charisma maybe, but much more importantly, you feel that Delia will never let you down. She is completely reliable, and given the anxiety – nay, terror – most of us feel when boiling an egg, having Delia at our side is very comforting.'

Unlike the static setting of *Delia*, *Far Flung Floyd* is structured around Keith Floyd's journey through the Far East. The opening sequence features Floyd at the airport, addressing the camera-operator, trying to persuade him to come on the trip: 'We'll have wonderful fun, you know. There are wonderful curries and rice dishes. We can go fishing, we can go into the jungle, we can even eat coconut milk!' Floyd's discussion of the 'wonderful fun' that he will have sets up the Personality/Cook-Ed./Tour–Ed. configuration as being framed by his role as *male* adventurer, as traditionally masculine in its dynamic journey through the public sphere as Smith's private sphere stasis is traditionally feminine.

The contrast between Smith's 'interiority' and Floyd's 'exteriority' – manifest in the different locations of the series – is also present in their verbal and gestural repertoires. Whereas Smith's delivery is measured and methodical, Floyd's is flamboyant and chaotic. Moreover, whilst both presenters directly address the camera, Floyd actively directs it. In programme six, for example, he directs the camera-operator on some 13 occasions, with comments such as 'Follow me please, Paul . . . good close-up on that please . . . Paul, back to there . . . okay, that's long enough'. His transgression, as registered by both his exposure of the mechanics of television and his disruption of the Cook-Ed. discourse, is subsumed to become a trait of his televised personality. In this way he stamps his authority within the format, with the demonstrations functioning as sketches (as he himself terms them, with all the connotations of comedic entertainment) in which he performs.

A significant element within his performance is his relationship with alcohol. Floyd's hedonism is in diametric opposition to Delia Smith's sobriety. In one introduction to a cookery sketch he says, after arriving at his hotel, 'Normally I'd head straight for the bar, but it was nearly morning and I was ravenous, so I made a beeline for the kitchen to cook a classic Vietnamese dish for early breakfast.' In programme six, he appears to subvert his own discourse of excess by declaring that the viewer will see a 'new him', who will be 'so fit and bright-eyed and bushy-tailed because this month not a drop of alcohol is going to pass my lips'. As the viewer would expect, he is shown guzzling red wine later on in the same programme.

These examples illustrate Floyd's role as active consumer – he performs a cookery sketch because *he's* hungry. In a wider sense his role, as adventurer, within the journey is to consume the people he meets and places he visits. It is via his impressions that the viewer learns something: as much of his uniquely personal experience of the place as the place itself. Thus, as with the Cook-Ed., a personality register may shape the mode of the Tour-Ed. within a series.

Tour-Educative: *Rhodes Around Britain* and *Madhur Jaffrey's Flavours of India*

In *Floyd*, the Cook-Ed., Personality and Tour-Ed. came together via Keith Floyd's *education* in and recreation of local cuisine drawn from his peripatetic location. By contrast, the presenters of *Rhodes Around Britain* (*Rhodes*) and *Madhur Jaffrey's Flavours of India* (*Madhur*) are constructed, via an alternative configuration, as knowledgeable tourists in their own countries. Unlike *Delia* and *Floyd*, *Rhodes* (BBC Education Department) and *Madhur* (BBC Multicultural Programmes Unit) were produced by departments within the corporation working to educational, racial and cultural remits. As I shall demonstrate, the particular configurations of the Cook-Ed., Per., Tour-Ed. and Raw-Ed. within the two series may be explained within the context of their wider educational projects.

One important way in which both presenters' knowledge is expressed is within the Cook-Ed. Gary Rhodes takes up recipes characteristic of a popular and traditional British menu. In programme five, Rhodes returns to Thanet College, where he took a basic training course in 1976, and asks the students, 'So what's cooking today, gents?'. On hearing that traditional British faggots and 'good old' rhubarb are on the menu, he comments, 'I knew I'd leave an impression; back to tradition.' Yet, at the same time, Rhodes's typically intricate methods of presentation belie the simplicity of the dishes themselves. As he states in programme five, when introducing a cookery demonstration of a leek pie: 'I'm going to take a simple dish and make it special' articulating his investment in the presentation as a site of fantasy, before going on to pipe mashed potatoes onto a bed of peppered leeks. This juxtapositional celebration of the classic (recipe) and the modern (trendy notions of culinary aesthetics) resonates within Rhodes's Personality construct and the series' Tour-Ed. discourse.

Rhodes's journey features a tour of the iconography of British heritage, from a Punch and Judy show to a number of fish and chip shops and public houses. Epitomising the British 'have-a-go' spirit of amateurism, he joins in with a group of Morris dancers, drinks Guinness and argues with the locals in a bar in Belfast, and celebrates Burns night with a party of Glaswegians (Wales is conspicuous by its absence). At one end of the axis is his gaining experience of a region through being indigenized by local communities, and at the other is knowledge, which involves Rhodes imparting cookery methods in live demonstration to groups of spectators. Via Rhodes's tour, the series constructs a British community that is regionally differentiated and paradoxically unified by a shared heritage. This celebration of 'the past' and of its traditions and cuisine may be set against the modern modes of transport that Rhodes uses to 'travel back in time' to these communities: he returns to Thanet College in a blue Lotus, flies to Glasgow in a helicopter and travels by speed-boat to the oyster beds off Whitstable. He is constructed as a working-class boy (or the equivalent of a classic British recipe) made good, as expressed by his presentation/packaging. Moreover, just as his tour serves as the adhesive which binds the disparate elements of the British 'community' construct, so it paradoxically renders him as a perpetual outsider, a transient drifter.

It is possible to identify a number of bi-polar oppositions within this text:

The authenticity of classic British cuisine	Presentation of the cuisine as site of fantasy
Experience	Knowledge
Tradition	Change
Classicism	Modernity
The Raw	The Cooked ⎫ which will be explored
Nature	Culture ⎬ further in the
	⎭ following section

These oppositions are reminiscent of structuralist definitions of the Western as: 'a series of antinomic elements defined in opposition as the axis around which the drama and its [the Western genre] conflicts are structured' (Neale, 1980: 58.) Indeed, Stephen Neale's discussion of the male hero of the Western provides a useful perspective from which to view *Rhodes*'s Tour-Ed. and Gary Rhodes's position within it. The Western, Neale suggests,

> is marked by a spatial economy whose polar instances are natural landscape on the one hand and the township/homestead on the other. Here the body of the hero is located dynamically at their intersection, oscillating between them ... the Western offers maximum scope for variations and permutations on the relation of the male figure ... as well as variations and permutations on the speed and mode of its movements.

Like the Western hero, Rhodes stands between Nature and Civilisation, Tradition and Change. He offers both a sense of adventure and the reassurance of culinary knowledge and skill; it is thus appropriate that his recipes consistently offer adventurous 'variations and permutations' on traditional national themes. As a cook, though, Rhodes perhaps has to work harder than the conventional male hero to assert his masculinity; not only is there an emphasis on the physical hunting for food – which will be discussed in the next section – but Rhodes, like a lad on a package holiday, flirts outrageously with the women he meets on his travels.

In the first programme of the *Madhur* series, Jaffrey states that 'Every part of India has a dish, a vegetable or fruit that in some way characterises the place or cuisine.' This articulates the central premise of the series: that the spirit of a region may be uncovered by looking at its use of a particular food, its methods of production and preparation, and for whom it is prepared. Whilst this mode of Tour-Ed. would appear to target an unfamiliar viewer, this is complicated by the particular formation of the Cook-Ed.

Jaffrey's recipes tend to be complex, involving many stages of preparation. In programme one she demonstrates a recipe for lamb encrusted with spices, which involves some 14 preparatory stages and takes over one and a half hours to prepare and cook. This sequence, like many of her other demonstrations, is edited elliptically, using dissolves to mark time-shifts, and a number of preparatory stages such as the boning of the lamb are passed over. The omission of stages which require a somewhat advanced culinary knowledge renders her recipes less easily reproducible by the inexperienced viewer/cook. Moreover, Jaffrey rarely makes any concession to the viewer/cook who may be unfamiliar with the ingredients that she uses. On the one hand, then, the demonstrations address a viewer/cook who is relatively familiar with Indian cuisine. On the other, the series' premise – to demystify culture through an exploration of its cuisine – suggests that it is the unfamiliar viewer who is the object of the series' address. Though apparent in the mode of Cook-Ed., the primary site of the negotiation of the dual address is the Tour-Ed.

As with the Tour-Ed. in *Floyd* and *Rhodes*, the formal characteristics in *Madhur* consist of long-shots, to allow maximum exposure of landscapes; rapidly cut montage sequences, in a style reminiscent of a tourist's snap-shots; narration relaying historical, geographical and cultural information, as well as personal impression; and the use of local people's kitchens as locations for the cookery demonstrations to invoke an 'authenticity' in the representation of culture and cuisine.

In *Madhur*, this picturesque register involves a spectacularization of the exotic other which serves to complicate the project of demystification articulated by Jaffrey's commentaries. Ironically, one of the only visual references to Western influence upon India is found in programme four, where *tourists* are shown arriving on a beach in Goa. This sequence is particularly interesting in that Jaffrey's accompanying voice-over states:

> Welcome to Goa . . . over the seas the Arabs have come and ruled, the Portuguese came and stayed for four hundred and fifty years. And the latest invasion is that of tourists . . . the hippies were the forerunners of the tourist invasion. Now its coastline hotels increasingly draw middle-class Europeans.

Her analogy between the 'tourist invasion' and past colonisation of the region suggests that both are ideologically unsound. Yet the stunning beauty of the region, as rendered by the Tour-Ed.'s particular visual repertoire, will undoubtedly tempt some viewers from arm-chair to sun-chair. In addition, Jaffrey is herself constructed as a tourist elsewhere in the text. In programme three, there is a sequence of eight shots of the Golden Temple in the Punjab, lit up by fireworks against the night sky. Jaffrey's voice-over informs the viewer that 'Many tourists come just to stand and marvel at the beautiful spectacle'. As she finishes speaking, there is a cut from a long-shot of the Temple to a medium-shot of Jaffrey standing and marvelling at the temple in the background. On the one hand, then, Jaffrey is constructed as a tourist, in a way similar to Keith Floyd. On the other, she has pre-existing local knowledge, which she imparts to the viewer, in a way similar to that of Gary Rhodes.

However, the processes by which she demonstrates her knowledgeability differ from that of Rhodes. Whereas he pitches in, catching fish with local fish-farmers that he later cooks, for example, Jaffrey maintains her distance, so much so that she is often only involved in the action via her voice-over. The contrast may be understood in terms of gender. Jaffrey, by virtue of her femininity, is freed from the necessity of having to legitimize her interest in cookery by being presented as a hunter-gatherer. Furthermore, unlike Rhodes, who learns something of the community by the experience of joining them, Jaffrey 'already knows', and is thus constructed as part of the community by virtue of her pre-existing knowledge of its customs and cuisine.

To a British audience, particularly within the context of white-dominated television presentation, Jaffrey is marked by her ethnicity. In the series she is shown to be returning to her homeland, as exemplified in programme four, where she visits an old friend. This is despite the fact that she is an actress who comes from a wealthy family who has lived in the West for much of her life. Whilst all televisual cooks (and, one may argue, presenters in general) are mediators, it is particularly evident that both Jaffrey's personality construction and her role within the text are sites for the mediation of discourses of ethnicity. This mediation is articulated by her dress, which oscillates between saris and baseball caps; her use of two languages, situating her as (cultural) translator; and by her knowledge and experience of both cultures. Her status is thus akin to a cultural ambassador, occupying an informed yet distanced vantage point across two landscapes. Thus whilst Rhodes and Jaffrey function similarly as agents of the Tour-Ed., they operate in strikingly different ways. Rhodes swings between the antinomic groupings, his *movement* serving as the site of the interplay of Cook-Ed., Personality and Tour-Ed. Jaffrey is herself the primary site upon which such elements are mapped.

Raw-Educative: *Rhodes Around Britain* and *Madhur Jaffrey's Flavours of India*

The Raw-Ed. pertains to the contextualization of ingredients in their original state/habitat, the methods by which produce may be harvested/hunted and, relating to this, the labour involved in such processes. As with the Tour-Ed., the Raw-Ed. may serve as the cipher for educational projects of a series that go beyond the Cook-Ed.

Each programme in the *Rhodes* series contains at least one item focusing on Rhodes travelling to the 'source' of a (potential) raw ingredient, motivated by a range of reasons. In the case of programme one, he visits an Ostrich farm, and during an interview with a farmer discovers that the meat is high in fibre and low in cholesterol and thus 'good' for anyone with a heart condition. Here, the motivation is largely Cook-Ed. in that it informs the viewer, who is assumed to be unfamiliar with the newly available meat product. In contrast to this is an item featured in programme five, which shows Rhodes joining in with some workers harvesting oysters, and getting waterlogged boots as a result. This contributes to Rhodes's Personality construct and the Tour-Ed. as previously discussed. In both cases, though, the emphasis on origins also serves to introduce the Raw-Ed. discourse into the text.

The foregrounding of the origin of a raw ingredient, as well as the labour involved in the production of a commodity, invokes an 'authenticity' that contributes to the educational project of the series. Rhodes preaches that one must embrace the raw in order to transform it. However, to convince the viewer Rhodes has to counter the pervading cultural distaste for lumps of raw meat uneffacedly connected to their animal origin by providing constant reassurance. For example, during the demonstration of the recipe for salmon, he says: 'Well, look at this, it really is wonderful. Clean both sides. The texture, the muscle, look at the lovely lines . . . it really is beautiful . . . it's going to be succulent and juicy.'

The sensuality of his verbal and gestural registers (he often kisses his fingers and caresses the produce) serves to eroticize the recipes. This is interesting when seen in the light of Lisa M. Heldke's (Curtin and Heldke, 1992: 222) assertion that:

> Growing and preparing food are activities which often require and generate emotional energy – and which see emotion and eroticism as vital to the activity. In contrast to the received view of theory and practice, which tends to divorce reason from emotion and eroticism, a transformed conception of food-making practice views them as thoughtful practices in which these forms of interaction are inter-related and mutually constitutive.

Recalling the Personality construction of Delia Smith, I would argue that the predominantly normative cookery instruction and efficient mode of presentation are related to the received view of theory and practice – cooking is contextualized as a practical and social skill. By contrast, *Rhodes*'s eroticization of food, in part to sanction the discourse of the Raw-Ed., allows a reading of a transformed conception of food-making practice which repositions even British food as sensual and pleasurable. As such, Rhodes's mode of presentation of the Cook-Ed. and Raw-Ed. is framed by a wider 'Food-Educative' project.

This Raw-Ed. project can be found in *Madhur* also. As in *Rhodes*, the cookery demonstrations often follow a linked item focusing on a particular raw ingredient, method of harvest or social custom. For example, in programme four, a sequence of ten shots of fishermen and trawlers is accompanied by Jaffrey's voice-over commentary, which states:

> Behind the tourism and hotels is the real economy. It employs thousands and still uses traditional nets. They've just been fishing on this trawler and caught a whole load of fish. And amongst the things they have are prawns . . . I'm going to make a delicious fish dish.

Another example is found in programme three, where Jaffrey traces the 'narrative' of a coconut from a tree, through various ways in which the by-products are used – as she informs us, we probably have a doormat made from a coconut by-product – to a cookery demonstration using coconut milk. However, Jaffrey's mode of Raw-Ed. discourse differs from that of Rhodes in a number of ways, going beyond simply embracing the raw in order to transform it.

Her contextualization of the ingredients that she prepares, via commentaries on processes of production, labour and export, often hints at a critique. In programme one there is a sequence featuring women sorting black peppercorns, accompanied by Jaffrey's voice-over, which states 'The work is very labour intensive', highlighting the labour element of the production-consumption equation. This is further emphasised during a later sequence, which depicts women harvesting tea, bent double by the weight of the bundles they are carrying. Jaffrey comments 'and of course all these spices are as fundamental to an Indian meal as tea is in Britain'. Her statement works with the visual images to expose the intensive manual labour involved in the production of a commodity so avidly consumed in a country that seemingly eschews consideration of the product's origins. In programmes two and three one finds examples, in Jaffrey's commentary, of a shift in this focus on manual labour to issues of exportation of products to the West. In a sequence featuring nomads, Jaffrey informs the viewer of their continual battle for survival against the elements, before going on to discuss how they are famous for their embroidery, which fetches hundreds of pounds in the West. In programme three her voice over, which accompanies images of fishermen returning to shore states: 'Whatever they bring back, be it squid or shrimp, it is auctioned off as soon as the boat touches land. The big fish, like these huge rays, or the best of the prawns, crabs and lobsters are sold off for export. Local villagers can only afford the little fish.'

As these examples suggest, Jaffrey's mode of Raw-Ed. contains oblique references to a potential, or actual, exploitation in every stage of the production–consumption process that points to the existence of a progressive educational dynamic. However, drawing on my previous discussion of the picturesque register of the Tour-Ed., one sees that the critical charge of the Raw-Ed. may often be short-circuited by other elements within the text.

Conclusion

I started by questioning the notion of the transparency of cookery programmes. Certainly, food and the instruction of cookery methods feature in each of the case-study series. However, the Cook-Ed. is not immutable and isolated; its formation varies according to the nature of its inflection by the other identifiable elements such as the Per., Tour-Ed. and Raw-Ed. To deny the impact of these aspects is to overlook a fundamental part of the internal mechanics of the genre, and of its making of meaning.

My concern has been with these internal mechanics. However, the elements that I have identified extend beyond the immediate texts. In order to reproduce a recipe one often needs to refer to the (lucrative) series spin-off book to locate precise measurements and methods: illustrative of the ongoing Cook-Ed. discourse. Presenter/cooks move outside of their programmes into a range of other texts, from cookery books, advertising and product endorsements, to web-sites and to chat-shows, their personality constructions continually being affirmed or transformed by these contexts. Bennett and Woollacott (1987: 44) discuss the similarly expansive 'Bond phenomenon', saying: 'the figure of Bond has been constructed and been operative in the relations between a considerable and accompanying set of texts, different in its total size and composition as well as in its internal configuration at different moments'. They go on to list some of the various textual sites of 'Bond', from novels and films to photo-features of the 'Bond Girls', before stating:

> Added to these have been the sedimentations of Bond in the world of objects. Through its uses in advertising and commodity design, the figure of Bond has become tangled up in the world of things . . . functioning like textual meteorites.

One may similarly view the various manifestations of the cookery programmes as 'textual meteorites': sites for the extension, disruption or transformation of the discourses within the original text. A study of the processes of extension and circulation upon the elements identified here would, I believe, offer up considerable currency. Perhaps my research will serve as an *apéritif*, to whet the critical appetite sufficiently for such a project to be undertaken.

References

BARTHES, R., 1973: *Mythologies*. London: Paladin.

BENNETT, T. and WOOLLACOTT, J., 1987: *Bond and Beyond: The Political Career of a Popular Hero*. London: Macmillan.

BOURDIEU, P., 1984: *Distinction*. London: Routledge and Kegan Paul.

CURTIN, D. W. and HELDKE, L. M. (eds), 1992: *Cooking, Eating, Thinking: Transformative Philosophies of Food*. Indianapolis: Indianapolis University.

FORT, M., 1995: 'The TV dinners: chefs on the box – a recipe for culinary success?'. *Guardian*, 3 March.

NEALE, S., 1980: *Genre*. London: British Film Institute.

PHILLIPS, P., 1991: 'Floyd on the tucker trail'. *Radio Times*, 6–12 April.

Television has always relied on cinema for its more routine programming as well as its special event features. With the advent of VCRs, the possibility of recording, renting or buying videos made the process of watching film on television more amenable to the viewers' control. Dinsmore uses interviews with keen viewers of films on video to examine the phenomenon of domestic viewing of cinematic texts, and her detailed account of two interviews is significant in a number of respects. Dinsmore's essay offers an example of the qualitative audience work discussed by Geraghty in Section II. She describes the arrangements for her interviews and the way in which her gender and student status set up a particular relationship with her interviewees. A vivid insight into the experience of this kind of audience work is offered by her description of the way interviews were taken over by the interviewee when favourite (and carefully chosen) clips were shown.

But Dinsmore contributes in other ways to debates about how television should be studied. Firstly, she reminds us that 'television' may now actually cover a number of previously rather different experiences which come together via the television screen. Like Hirsch in Section II, she suggests that our understanding of television viewing needs to take into account these closely related technologies. Secondly, Dinsmore draws on traditions in Television and Cultural Studies which have placed television viewing in a broader social situation by looking at the circumstances of television viewing. Dinsmore does not concentrate on the more usual contexts of gender relations, age or the family. Instead she draws on a rather different set of references to place video viewing in the context of collecting and leisure activities. In this sense, Dinsmore takes head on her interviewees' own feeling that their viewing situation is not normal and asks what that may mean. Thirdly, Dinsmore's work reminds us that while videos provide ephemeral pictures they also have a material presence. Far from being virtual, videotapes sprawl over shelves, pile up round the set and resist being labelled and controlled. Just as work on cinema spectatorship rested on a physical relationship between screen, projector and solitary viewer, so Dinsmore seeks to explore the consequences for viewing of the physical nature of video as a format.

Dinsmore's essay inevitably highlights the experience of those who might be called 'exceptional' viewers as she reflects on their attitudes to technology and to collecting and viewing. But because she is talking to cinephiles, she is able to challenge assumptions about the differences between cinema and television. She suggests that knowledge and cognition are underestimated elements of pleasure, and while she emphasises the importance, in some circumstances, of technology (Matthew's 'surround-sound' speakers), she also comments on her male interviewees' pleasures and absorption in the text, an interesting outcome in the light of the gender differences which underpin much work on television viewing.

What is also interesting about Dinsmore's piece is that while it is based on interviews with what might be considered exceptional viewers, it leads to reflections which are pertinent to those who use and watch videos more generally. Her comments speak to anyone who has hunted for a particular video in the pile on the floor or watched children rearrange the living room into a cinema for a video viewing. In addition, her emphasis on the way in which Max and Matthew handle technology, text and viewing time are a useful antidote to accounts which relate modes of viewing over-prescriptively to the different technological arrangements of cinema, video and television.

20

Chaos, Order and Plastic Boxes: The Significance of Videotapes for the People who Collect Them

Uma Dinsmore

As a screen for watching videotaped feature films that were originally produced for cinematic exhibition, the combination of television set with VCR can turn a viewer's home into a species of domestic cinema. My research[1] into the different ways that film can be 'domesticated' in such home viewing situations is based on interviews with viewers whose passion for film has led them to build collections of videotapes. Drawing upon interviews with two such viewers,[2] this chapter reflects practically and theoretically upon the process of conducting audience research of this type.

Research into the viewing of films on videotape in the domestic context bridges the gap between television and film studies. Whereas film studies is frequently focused upon exclusively textual interpretations, television studies has tended to be concerned with the dynamics of watching television programmes in groups (e.g. Morley, 1986; Lull, 1988). The theoretical and practical ramifications of this position are significant, forming the basis of a continuing academic debate, whose central opposition has been elegantly summarised by Ann Gray in her essay 'Behind closed doors: video recorders in the home' (Gray, 1987). Gray characterises media (TV) studies as focused upon a social audience positioned by context, and film studies as concerned with a psychological audience positioned by text. The problem with this division is, as Gray explains, that '*neither* of these two perspectives is sufficient *in themselves* to gain a full understanding of what happens when men and women watch films' (Gray, 1987: 44, my italics). Research that exclusively addresses the 'social audience' privileges context over text, whilst research that is only concerned with the 'psychological audience' privileges text over context.

Exploring the experiences of people who view films at home provides a valuable opportunity not only to bring the study of film *text* and film viewing *context* together, but also to think through an aspect of film culture that has been much neglected, namely the *materiality* of the film text on videotape: the significance of the cassette itself, in its plastic box or cardboard sleeve, as a prized collectable item, or as a dust-covered object on a shelf. Asking questions about how viewers collect and watch their tapes can help us to develop a more integrated understanding of these three elements of the film viewing experience. Methods of audience research which seem most effectively to facilitate such an integrated understanding have been developed in recent feminist audience studies which explore the social, material and historical context of film reception (see Bobo, 1988; Gray, 1992; and Stacey 1994).

Interviews, letters and questionnaire responses have been used by such researchers as a way to find out about viewers' opinions of the films they watch and how they watch them. This does not mean that audience research, by virtue of its supposed direct line to viewer response, presents unquestionable truths, nor that it offers a more 'real' approach to the study of media than do other methods, but it can provide a way to address some of the questions that cannot be answered adequately by theoretical, textual or historical enquiry.

The questions about video viewing which I have asked have been directed at a very narrowly circumscribed group of viewers: those who take, or have taken, a joint pleasure in cinema and home cinema (video viewing). I interview people in their homes, almost always in the room where they watch and store their tapes, and the interview usually takes about an hour and a half. I use a semi-structured format, in that the initial questions refer to the questionnaire, and the later part of the interviews are more general, covering issues of taste, more detailed accounts of specific viewing experiences, or any topics which the interviewee wants to talk about but which have not been addressed in the earlier part of the interview. This combination of formality and informality is intended to synthesise the advantages of an open-ended interview, where the interviewee determines the topics of discussion, with the more structured format in which the interviewer has a standard set of questions for each respondent (see van Zoonen, 1994: 137; Werner and Schoepfle, 1987: 294; Bernard, 1994).

In her valuable overview of qualitative techniques for feminist media research, Liesbet van Zoonen stresses the importance of 'rapport' in interviews, and points out that inequalities of status may be an obstacle to achieving what she defines as 'a relation of trust and respect that stimulates and facilitates the participant's articulation of her experience' (1994: 137). One of my concerns about conducting interviews was that people would regard my presence in their home as an intrusion. In practice, many respondents expressed their relief at having someone to talk to about films, and all the interviewees appeared to be delighted to have a researcher visit them and listen to them talk about a subject they love passionately. Ellen Seiter, in her revealingly frank account of a 'troubling' interview (Seiter, 1990), recognised that her respondents regarded an interview with a pair of academics as a special experience. Her observations rightly draw attention to issues of power and status in the interview situation, issues which I believe to have been at work in my own interviews in a slightly different way than that described by Seiter. As a research student, rather than a 'real' academic, I was rarely perceived to be a person of authority and standing. The combination of my student status, my size, my appearance, and my manner of interacting with interviewees invariably meant that interviewees mis-read my age, so that (even in cases where I was several years older than the respondents) interviewees would behave towards me with generous/tolerant indulgence and concern: 'are you really going to be safe on your own?' they would ask, offering to feed me cake, drive me to stations, or call up reputable cab companies. Because the presence of a more youthful researcher seemed less threatening to respondents, I tended to collude in this mis-reading of my age, treating it as a positive interview strategy.

Ann Gray's account of her experiences interviewing for *Video Playtime* reveal how good rapport can turn a research interview into 'fun' (Gray, 1992: 33), and both of the two interviews I have selected for presentation here conform to Gray's description. The first was with Matthew,[3] a 34-year-old single suburban male, who found- out about the research project through my letter in *Home Entertainment* magazine, to which he subscribes. He lives alone, describes himself as working-class, and is employed full-time as a service engineer. British-born of Indian parents, Matthew is the only questionnaire respondent and interviewee who is not white. He has vocational qualifications and a 32-inch widescreen television with a sophisticated surround-sound system. The second interviewee, Max, is a 39-year-old married suburban male. He lives with his wife, describes himself as middle-class, and is employed full-time as a personnel manager. He is white, has postgraduate qualifications and a medium-sized television with a basic VCR.[4]

I interviewed Matthew on a weekday evening after he had finished work. He lives alone in a bungalow on the outskirts of Chelmsford, and our meeting took place in his living/viewing room, where the television was positioned some eight feet away from the centre of a large and comfortable settee. A low, square, glass-topped coffee table, cleared of all objects, was placed between the settee and the screen; some gym equipment was in the left-hand corner of the room, and an ironing board was set up near the door which led off into the hall and the kitchen. Six speakers (for surround-sound viewing) were positioned around the room (behind the settee, on top of the set, and to the side).

I interviewed Max on a Saturday afternoon in the viewing room of the new, spacious, detached and colour-coordinated home which he shares with his wife. Prior to the interview, Max took great pleasure in showing me around the whole house, pointing out the collection of framed cigarette card series, and *Photoplay* covers that decorated the walls of most rooms. The tour ended in what Max described as 'my room': an upstairs study lined with bookshelves containing many biographies of stars and books about the film industry. A large built-in cupboard at one end of the room was crammed with piles of old movie magazines. Max had recently sorted through his collection, preparing in advance for my visit by getting down albums containing letters and autographed photographs of (mostly female) movie stars, which he had started to collect when he was a schoolboy. He had lots of reference books both in the viewing room for consultation during viewing, and in the upstairs study.

In his discussion of the 'mental climate of collecting' (Benjamin, 1992: 68), Walter Benjamin reflects on his feelings as he unpacks the books in his library; surveying the mess of half-empty packing cases and higgledy piggledy piles, he observes that 'Every passion borders on the chaotic', and asks 'For what else is this collection but a disorder to which habit has accommodated itself to such an extent that it can appear as order?' (62). As I began to analyse Matthew and Max's comments about the way that they organised their collections of video-tapes, Benjamin's observations offered a strikingly accurate description of how interviewees dealt with their tapes. His perception of the way in which a habitually accommodated *dis*order can eventually come to function as a species of order is particularly apposite, and I utilise this concept in my analysis of Matthew and Max's organisational strategies.

Matthew's videos were on public display, with the pre-recorded tapes gathered together on a shelf unit at one side of the room. Max's collection, although larger, was less visible; in contrast to the visual images of film stars which proclaimed his cinephilia from the walls of his home, Max's tapes were stored behind closed doors, in low black cabinets and anonymous cupboards. The different ways of storing their tapes and the very different attitudes and levels of interest which the two men expressed about their tapes as collected *objects* prompted me to explore the boundaries of the dual material/textual nature of videotapes, and to reflect upon how tensions caused by this simultaneous duality are manifested in the relationship between the collector and his collection.

In response to my questions about the way they ordered their collections, both Matthew and Max identified the organic development of an indexing system, describing how the collections were born in chaos and gradually evolved into a more ordered state. Both collectors had accommodated themselves to the disorder of their collections to the extent that, as Benjamin observed, the disorderliness functioned for a period as if it were an organised system. In neither case had there been a single point at which initial disordered chaos transformed into indexed order; rather, it became apparent to the collectors that although their 'habitual accommodation' to the disorder made it possible to locate individual tapes, this intuitive understanding was likely to be overwhelmed by the increasing size of the collections: the expanding collections required more attention and demanded more complex management strategies. The transition from the accommodated disorder to a consciously organised storage and retrieval system is delicate: 'any order is a balancing act of extreme precariousness . . . Thus there is in the life of a collector a dialectical tension between the poles of order and disorder' (Benjamin, 1992: 62).

When he first began to collect tapes five years ago, Matthew kept them all together in a pile on the floor in no special order. He collects what he described as 'action adventure type' films and sci-fi movies, both of which he defines as 'mostly mainstream'. He now has about 100 films on 50 tapes, and is self-deprecating about the apparent lack of order in the collection; he laughed as he told me 'They're still not organised'. Seeking more information about his informal/intuitive indexing system, I asked how he would find a particular movie:

> MATT: Umm. Well, I'll just sort of flick through them. *I've got the pre-recorded ones all stacked over there.* But there's no real arrangement at all.
> UD: But that's all right?
> MATT: *At the moment it is* - if it gets a lot bigger than I'm going to have to start sort of, alphabetical order, but I'm not quite there. (my emphasis)

Matthew's answer revealed that the state of there being 'no real arrangement at all' in fact involved a division based on purely physical criteria: the pre-recorded tapes, in bigger and more substantial packaging, were grouped together on a shelf unit at one side of the viewing room, whereas all the 'ordinary' tapes that contained movies recorded from the TV, and were protected only by cardboard sleeves, were stacked by the fireplace. But this division, as Matthew's final comment shows, was perceived to be only temporarily adequate: it was all right, *at the moment*. The physical criteria for his tape-grouping is transitional, sustainable only for as long as the collection does not get 'a lot bigger'; when the collection outgrows this informal/intuitive 'non-arrangement' then it will be, or at least Matthew claims that he has plans for it to be, alphabetised.

The point at which an informal/intuitive ordering strategy becomes unsustainable varies both according to the collector's capacity for remembering the details of his or her collection, and according to their willingness to live with a disordered collection: although Matthew sensed that a more rational/formal indexing scheme was becoming necessary as his collection reached 50 tapes (100 films), another interviewee, Luke, was content for his collection of 350 tapes to remain in random piles on the floor.

After 15 years of taping, Max had recently admitted to himself that his collection of 341 tapes (about 900 films) was beginning to outgrow the intuitive 'non-arrangement' system. He mostly collected films made between 1930 and 1965 which featured his favourite stars, and also kept movies produced by the Warner Brothers studio. When I asked him to tell me about how the tapes were catalogued and indexed, Max apologised that it was only a 'crude' system, and produced a large and unruly sheaf of A4 paper, explaining that his secretary had volunteered to type out a list on her word processor, but that so far he had only produced a hand-written version of all the titles. In response to my query about whether the numbers of the tapes on the written list corresponded to the chronology of recording, Max was both amused and adamant:

MAX: No. No, no, no, no, no. I didn't catalogue them . . . for months if not years, and suddenly I decided, right, I better do something about this. So I did.

UD: So are you going to take up this offer then, of having them all put on a word processor?

MAX: Yeah. She's going to do it for me . . . We'll get there in the end. *It was beginning to irritate me. . . . there were literally scores of videos everywhere and I didn't know what was on them* (. . .)

UD: So all the details are there, but in no especial order, so . . . if you have an inkling to watch one of these films, how do you manage to find it?

MAX: *I just have to go through the whole thing – I've got some sort of instinct that I think I know where it is,* and then I just get to the place, and I just dig it out from somewhere. *It's not terribly scientific, is it?* [Laughter]

(My emphasis)

Max's account of the slow imposition of order on the tapes reveals that his sense of having to 'do something about' the lack of order in his collection was not prompted by any anticipated pleasure in the process of classification itself, but rather grew from a direct conflict between two different aspects of collecting videotapes: Max was irritated by the way that the *material* presence of those tapes dumped in the corner compromised his ability to watch their textual content; he could not access the films because 'there were literally scores of videos everywhere and I didn't know what was on them . . .'. His interest in the tapes is almost exclusively textual, and he regards their physical presence, as objects that need to be sorted, tidied and listed, as a source of tiresome tasks. Max's instinctive disinclination to impose order on his collection echoes Walter Benjamin's recognition that the temporarily chaotic state of his recently unpacked books has a vibrant appeal that cannot be matched by what he describes as 'the mild boredom of order' (Benjamin, 1992: 61). Max tolerates the material presence of the tapes because he prizes their textual content as a means to move beyond the limitations of the mundane, everyday world of irritating domestic objects and instead to live in the imaginary, ideal and perfect world of the classical Hollywood movies that he has enjoyed watching since he was an adolescent: 'And I just thought when I was fourteen, this is what I want to be about, this is the world I want to inhabit – you know?'

The tension between the material and textual attributes of Max's videotapes is partially resolved by his decision to embark on a process of cataloguing and indexing the tapes: he recognises that the management of the material objects is necessary to gain the access he desires to the textual worlds whose images they contain, but he takes no pleasure in organising the collection in this way. He is amused by the way he has been navigating through the collection until this point (*It's not terribly scientific, is it?*) and although he recognises the inadequacy of the intuitive/informal approach to such a large collection (*I just have to go through the whole thing),* he takes a degree of pride in the fact that his knowledge of the collection is so intimate that he has effectively managed for years to avoid having to engage with the material and bureaucratic demands of collecting – *I've got some sort of instinct that I think I know where it is.*

The most intense pleasure which Max took in collecting films was *mental* rather than material, the collection of the tapes reflecting his mental collection of information and details about movies. The relationship between the mental and physical aspects of collecting are usefully outlined by James Clifford, who identifies some of the obligations of the collector in his essay on collecting exotic or tribal art and artefacts for display in museums, but as observations on the domestic practice of collecting more everyday objects, such as videotapes, his remarks have resonance: 'If the passion is for Egyptian figurines, the collector will be expected to label them, to know their dynasty ... to tell "interesting" things about them, to distinguish copies from originals ... ' (Clifford, 1985: 238–9). Max both conforms to and counters Clifford's characterisation: his knowledge about his favoured period of film history was formidable, and he certainly, to borrow Clifford's terms, 'knew the dynasty' of the films and the stars he loved, and delighted in telling interesting things about them. At this textual level, Max's pleasure in his collection corresponds to Benjamin's account of the way in which, 'for a true collector the whole background of an item adds up to a magic encyclopaedia whose quintessence is the fate of his object' (Benjamin, 1992: 63). But for Max, the 'background' of the tapes which interests him is purely discursive; he is not charmed by the appeal which Benjamin ascribes to questions of period, region, craftsmanship or former ownership, and neither the physical form of his favoured texts as tapes, nor the taxonomic structure of the collection hold any value or interest for him. Perhaps, it might be argued, this lack of interest in the physical collection itself is determined by the very nature of videotapes themselves: they are standard, black plastic boxes containing reels of brown magnetic tape, and Max's indifference to the videos could be simply because he regards them as rather dull or ugly objects that can only be distinguished from each other by the writing on their labels. This, perhaps, is why he has them stored out of sight, behind the closed doors of cabinets and cupboards.

But Max's indifference to the tapes as objects is by no means shared by all the interviewees. Many took pleasure in the fact that they had developed elaborate referencing systems for their tapes; most kept their tapes on display, lined up like books, with the 'spine' labels visible,[5] and some, like Matthew, kept the pre-recorded tapes, with their bigger, more robust and more colourful covers, in a separate place from the less attractive ordinary tapes in their plain cardboard sleeves. Matthew had purchased some tapes in boxed sets, and his comments about them provide a fascinating insight into the relationship between the material and film-textual reasons for buying these items. At one level, Matthew's reasons for buying pre-recorded tapes was simply to avoid the interruptions or cuts that might spoil a TV broadcast version of the film:

MATT: I've actually got a copy of *Predator* – which is [recorded] off of ITV, and that's one that I may like to replace with a bought copy.
UD: Why's that?
MATT: Because it's got ads in it.

Other, film-textual reasons for investing in an additional pre-recorded version of a movie were linked to the perceived inadequacy of the image and/or sound quality on the existing copy:

MATT: I originally had a normal panned and scanned version [of *Star Wars*] . . . And they brought out the re-mastered and edited, letter boxed format, and *since I'd bought the [widescreen] TV since I'd bought the original – I went and bought that*.

Matthew's reference to the purchase of his widescreen TV as an incentive to buy an additional copy of the re-mastered *Star Wars* tape indicates the close connection that exists between the nature of the viewing hardware owned by interviewees and the types of software which they prefer: early in the interview Matthew explained that one of the chief criteria for inclusion in his collection was that the films be in widescreen format,[6] and his purchase of a pre-recorded version of *The Abyss* was motivated by this:

MATT: I went out and bought the widescreen collector's edition . . . it hasn't got any add ons, like interviews or extracts. But it's got all the, what the director cut out of the original cinema version.
UD: And does that make it worth paying the extra money do you think?
MATT: Err. Yeah, I think so, yeah. It wasn't more than the normal film, I think, or it might have been a pound more or something. Yeah. Yeah.

In this case, Matthew got a good deal: the cost of widescreen, collector's special edition versions is frequently, and disproportionately, much higher than that of the ordinary tape.[7] Distributors often include extra footage or trailers and interviews as a means to justify the higher price, and Matthew regards this as one of the attractions of the 'special' tapes: in a discussion of the different aspect ratios of the films in the *Alien* trilogy, he commented:

MATT: . . . that's another reason for buying [boxed] sets as well, because it's got the few extra bits on it – especially on this one [*Aliens*].
UD: Were there extra trailers?
MATT: It's got the trailers, but also on the *Alien* the first one, it's got bits that were cut out of the original – stuck on the end, showing you bits that they thought about putting into the film that they never actually used.

But although the content and/or image/sound quality of any particular pre-recorded tape mattered to Matthew, for him (and a number of other interviewees) the film/textual nature of the tape was not the only justification for its purchase. Towards the end of the interview, Matthew took his tapes of the *Alien* trilogy down from the shelves to show me.

> MATT: I bought the boxed set – three – I've got the plastic box [gets off the shelf. The box is a sturdy plastic carrying case, with a moulded, and fairly detailed, coloured semi 3D reproduction of the queen Alien figure bursting out of the side of the case] . . . It's got the making of *Alien Three* and it's got the three movies in widescreen – plus some little bits of collectors' pieces.
> UD: So was one of the reasons for buying it like this the fact that you got all this extra stuff with it?
> MATT: Yeah, yeah, because it's collectable I suppose. It's got one of those limited edition things – 4951.[8]

Here, Matthew's tone was that of the satisfied consumer; he is aware of the discrepancy in price between ordinary and specially packaged tapes, but feels that the money is well spent. His satisfaction is achieved at both material and textual levels, not only does he have an appealing and unusual means of storing his tapes as a set, but the extra footage and trailers provide him with a privileged 'insider's' knowledge of the films he enjoys watching repeatedly. However, although the marketing tactics of the video distributors offer him a source of pleasure, they also cause him considerable irritation:

> MATT : *I was really annoyed* when I bought that *Star Wars* trilogy, because apparently they did a box as well . . . so I've just got the three tapes – in their little cardboard box – Apparently they've done it in a similar package to this, in a box, with a sort of book I think – yeah – *But had I known that was coming out I would have waited and bought that.* [My emphasis]

Matthew's annoyance is expressive of a consumer-oriented suspicion of the videotape companies that is characteristic of the editorial tone of *Home Entertainment,* a magazine which he read regularly, and by whose reports he had been guided in the purchase of his video equipment, so it is not surprising to note that the systems of values which the publication propagates are similar to those Matthew employed in his selection and classification of pre-recorded tapes.

Matthew's use of the terms and values expressed in *Home Entertainment* provide him with an effective filtering system; the critical framework of the magazine's reviews, and Matthew's developing preferences for widescreen, stereo sound and special collector's editions, function as a net with which he is able to extract individual tapes from the sometimes overwhelming and certainly 'relentless tide of availability' (Cummings, 1993: 27). Matthew's comments about the importance of owning certain types of pre-recorded tapes show how the value of the *Aliens* trilogy, for example, can be measured in a number of different ways, some connected to the material presence of the tapes as collectable objects, and some related to the film recorded on the tape. Matthew justifies the purchase of the tapes in this particular format by referring to the rarity of the boxed set (special collector's edition), its packaging, and the extra information contained on the packaging; he also spoke about the aspect ratio of the versions of the films recorded on these tapes, about the inclusion of scenes not recorded on other taped version of the movies and about the importance of getting the 'director's version' and the 'widescreen version'. Matthew's rules about inclusion were loose in relation to the generic content of the tapes ('action-adventure type/mostly mainstream'), but strict in relation to the format of the recording (widescreen, preferably uncut, with stereo sound). In contrast, Max's criteria for inclusion reversed these priorities: he enforced more rigorous rules in relation to period and genre (Warner Brothers', black and white dramas, for example, featuring particular stars), but was tolerant to the point of indifference in relation to the physical form of the recordings (making no judgements about tape quality, ad breaks, or poor quality sound).

The complicated dynamics of the collectors' attitudes towards both the material presence and the textual content of their tapes is illuminated not only by the criteria for inclusion which Max and Matthew employed, but also by the very different ways in which they showed me clips from their favourite movies. The distinctions between their criteria for selecting the extracts, and their comments' during the screening of the clips give some indication of how watching films in a domestic context is a source of many different types of pleasure.

Both men showed me clips from films that they had watched repeatedly. Max selected a clip from *Humoresque* (Negulesco, 1946, USA), a black and white Warner Brothers drama starring Joan Crawford. Max explained why he loved the film, telling me that watching this particular scene would help me to understand what he prized about star quality. Whilst he showed me the clip, Max spoke about the memories he had of viewing the film at different points in his life, and he also told me stories about the different actors who appeared on screen. His pleasure in the film was enhanced by the connections which he could make between the film text and his knowledge about it, about its star, and about how it linked into a whole social and professional Hollywood world, with whose details he was intimately familiar.

Matthew picked a scene from the beginning of *Aliens* (Cameron, 1986, USA) to show me. The film is the second part of a popular sci-fi adventure trilogy starring Sigourney Weaver as Ripley. Matthew showed me a clip in which a laser beam is being swung round the inside of a dark metal capsule; as the scene played, Matthew switched the ratio settings on the screen in order to demonstrate the optimum viewing ratio for this particular film. He expressed sadness at the fact that his amplifier had 'gone smack', and apologised for the sound quality ('just ordinary stereo'), explaining that the effect of the surround-sound speakers would be to make it seem as if you are inside the capsule. Unlike Max, who explained that he would often watch only those bits of *Humoresque* in which his favourite stars appeared, Matthew identified his particular pleasure in repeat viewings of *Aliens* as being tied to the flow of the narrative: no matter how many times he watched the film, Matthew explained that he would always watch it through continuously and completely, because its major appeal was excitement, and without narrative continuity that excitement palled.

This strong commitment to narrative continuity, even with repeatedly viewed films, was also expressed by many other interviewees, including Simon, who had lost count of the number of times that he had watched *Aliens* all the way through. 'It is just so exciting', he explained:

> . . . it's the kind of movie that I think, oh, well I'll watch a bit of it, and then I put it on and I've got to watch the whole thing all the way through. Yeah, I've got to watch it all, I can't stop. And when it was on TV recently, I flipped over the channel, and I thought 'Oh, *Aliens* is on, well I'll watch ten minutes and then go to bed' – no, I sat up and watched it until the very end.

The high value which he placed on the uninterrupted unfolding of a film-story meant that Matthew preferred to edit out any adverts as he taped a film. This recording strategy was also adopted by other interviewees: many of whom told me that they did not use remote control techniques when watching movies that were broadcast with adverts because they either refuse to record films from commercial channels altogether, or they edit out the adverts at the time of recording. In these cases the issue of viewer control is not about control at the time of watching but rather about control at the time of recording. The pause or stop button is used not as a means to arrest the progress of the film as it is viewed, but instead to eliminate commercial breaks as the movie is being recorded. If we term the recording of a movie onto a blank cassette as a species of domestic cultural production (or at least re-production), then viewer control can be seen to be exercised at the point of production as well as, or instead of, at the point of reception.

As an enthusiastic technophile, who took pleasure in the capacity of his video equipment to ensure optimum visual and auditory experience of the films in his collection, Matthew's choice of clip and manner of displaying it to me indicated that his investment in his collection was as much material as it was textual. As a self-confessed technophobe, who took no interest in the physical properties of his tapes or viewing equipment, Max's choice of clip and his techniques for showing it to me demonstrated very clearly that his investment in his collection was almost exclusively textual. The two interviewees' very different responses and modes of displaying their favourite clips provide a vivid sense of the tensions and overlaps between videotape as a simultaneously textual and material phenomenon.

As a source of information and reflection on video viewing and collecting, interviews can offer access to aspects of video culture that are invisible or inconceivable to the researcher working with purely textual, theoretical or historical material. Gaining access to the viewing environment can give the researcher the opportunity to bring another 'layer' of data (their own observations) into consideration. In analysis, the combination of a transcript of the words spoken in an interview, with notes taken by the interviewer (not just about the interview, but about the environment in which it was conducted), can open up surprising aspects of the research. For instance, at the outset of my investigations into home cinema, I had not expected to find that viewers would have a great deal to say about the material status of the videocassettes which they collected, but evidence from 18 interviews seems to indicate that the physical state of the collection, the way it is organised, and the viewer's comments about this, can be as illuminating an indication of the range of pleasures offered by video culture as are direct observations on film texts.

An interview, when conducted as part of an audience research project that also makes use of questionnaires, group viewing sessions and written responses from interviewees, functions as one stage of a research plan that can produce different types of data. Working with a variety of different forms of information in this way to explore one phenomenon is described by methodologists as 'triangulation': 'the act of bringing more than one source of data to bear upon a single point' (Marshall and Rossman, 1989: 146), and it is a strategy whose methodological eclecticism has been recognised as appropriate to the field of ethnographic media research: 'Ethnography is a multifaceted process in which the requirements of detail and richness, rigour and systematicity, have to be carefully balanced, and where there is *no single adequate methodological procedure*' (Morley and Silverstone, 1991: 160). Multifaceted research methods are necessary to explore an activity such as watching movies at home on a television screen because they bring together such a variety of different viewing and collecting strategies: there are aspects of video-viewing that can only be understood in terms of cinema spectatorship, but equally, there are elements of the experience that make sense only with reference to behaviours associated with TV watching; and the collecting and purchasing patterns described by interviewees need to be set in the wider context of consumer attitudes to the proliferation of audio-visual hardware and software. In so far as it brings together previously distinct areas of media study, video audience research has the capacity not just to expand the scope of television studies, by recognising the multiple uses which viewers make of their sets, but also to develop a broader awareness of the connections between domestic and public viewing strategies; to acquire a nuanced understanding of these aspects of video culture ideally requires an integrated analysis of film text, viewing context and the materiality of the film text.

Notes

1.   PhD thesis in progress: 'The domestication of film: video, cinephilia and the collection and viewing of videotapes in the home', Department of Media and Communications, Goldsmiths' College, University of London.

2.   Selected from a set of 18 interviews conducted beween December 1995 and March 1996. All interviewees were contacted via a letter published in *Home Entertainment Magazine*, and displayed in the National and Regional Film Theatres.

3.   An alias, as are all interviewee names used in this piece.

4.   On the questionnaire, Max was the only person to answer the question about the size of his TV by writing a question mark. He is a self-confessed technophobe who never learnt how to use Video-Plus, cannot programme his video-recorder and takes little interest in his audio-visual equipment.

5.   Often these labels were deliberately and beautifully uniform: typed, numbered, and colour or brand-coded, so that the collection as a whole acquired a distinct visual identity.

6.   The relationship is not just one-way: another interviewee, Paul, bought an unusual and expensive all-format VCR specifically so that he would be able to play videotapes recorded in different international formats.

7.   A fact recognised by *Home Entertainment Magazine:* 'It is our understanding that video distributors charge a higher price for widescreen movies because they are touted as special or collector's editions, and they know that this market will sustain a higher price.' (Clerkson, 1996:5)

8.   On the constructed appeal of the 'collector's edition', see Appadurai and Spooner on the relationship between exclusivity and authenticity (Appadurai, 1988: 44; Spooner, 1988: 226).

References and Further Reading

APPADURAI, A., 1988: 'Introduction: commodities and the politics of value'. In Arjun Appadurai (ed.), *The Social Life of Things: Commodities in Cultural Perspective.* New York: Cambridge University Press.

BENJAMIN, W., 1992, originally published 1931: 'Unpacking my library: a talk about book collecting'. In Walter Benjamin, *Illuminations.* trans. Harry Zohn, ed. Hannah Arendt. London: Collins.

BERNARD, H. R., 1994: *Research Methods in Anthropology: Qualitative and Quantitative Approaches,* (2nd edn). Newbury Park, CA: Sage.

BOBO, J., 1988: 'Black women as cultural producers'. In Deirdre Pribram, (ed.), *Female Spectators: Looking at Film and Television*. London: Verso.

CLERKSON, A., 1996: 'Are we being exploited?' [response to reader's letter], in *Home Entertainment*, 34, April: 5.

CLIFFORD, J., 1985: 'Objects and selves – an afterword'. In *Objects and Others: Essays on Museums and Material Culture*, ed. George W. Stocking, Madison: University of Wisconsin Press, 236–40.

CUMMINGS, N., 1993: 'Reading things: the alibi of use'. In Neil Cummings (ed.), *Reading Things (Sight Works, Volume Three)*. London: Chance Books, 12–29.

GRAY, A., 1987: 'Behind closed doors: video recorders in the home'. In Helen Baehr and Gillian Dyer (eds), *Boxed In: Women and Television*. London: Pandora.

———, 1992: *Video Playtime: the Gendering of a Leisure Technology*. London: Routledge.

LULL, J., 1988: *World Families Watch Television*. Newbury Part, CA: Sage.

MARSHALL, C. and ROSSMAN, G., 1989: *Designing Qualitative Research*. Newbury Park, CA: Sage.

MORLEY, D. 1986: *Family Television*. London: Comedia/Routledge.

MORLEY, D. and SILVERSTONE, R., 1991: 'Communication and context: ethnographic perspectives on the media audience'. In Klaus Bruhn Jensen and Nicholas J. Jankowski, (eds), *A Handbook of Qualitative Methodologies for Mass Communication Research*. London: Routledge, 149–62.

SEITER, E., 1990: 'Making distinctions in TV audience research: case study of a troubling interview'. *Cultural Studies*, 4, 1, January: 61–71.

SPOONER, B. 1988: 'Weavers and dealers: the authenticity of an oriental carpet'. In A. Apadurai (ed.), *The Social Life of Things: Commodities in Cultural Perspective*. New York: Cambridge University Press.

STACEY, J., 1994: *Star Gazing*. London: Routledge.

TASHIRO, C. 1997: 'The contradictions of video collecting'. *Film Quarterly*, 50, 2, Winter: 11–18.

VAN ZOONEN, L., 1994: *Feminist Media Studies*. London: Sage.

WERNER, O. and SCHOEPFLE, G. M., 1987: *Systematic Fieldwork, Vol. 1 Foundations of Ethnography and Interviewing*. Newbury Park, CA: Sage.

Index